# The International Library of Ethics, Law and Technology

Volume 21

Technologies are developing faster and their impact is bigger than ever before. Synergies emerge between formerly independent technologies that trigger accelerated and unpredicted effects. Alongside these technological advances new ethical ideas and powerful moral ideologies have appeared which force us to consider the application of these emerging technologies. In attempting to navigate utopian and dystopian visions of the future, it becomes clear that technological progress and its moral quandaries call for new policies and legislative responses. Against this backdrop this new book series from Springer provides a forum for interdisciplinary discussion and normative analysis of emerging technologies that are likely to have a significant impact on the environment, society and/or humanity. These will include, but be no means limited to nanotechnology, neurotechnology, information technology, biotechnology, weapons and security technology, energy technology, and space-based technologies.

More information about this series at http://www.springer.com/series/7761

Markus Christen • Bert Gordijn • Michele Loi
Editors

# The Ethics of Cybersecurity

Springer Open

*Editors*
Markus Christen
UZH Digital Society Initiative
Zürich, Switzerland

Bert Gordijn
Dublin City University
Dublin, Ireland

Michele Loi
Digital Society Initiative
University of Zurich
Zürich, Switzerland

ISSN 1875-0044 ISSN 1875-0036 (electronic)
The International Library of Ethics, Law and Technology
ISBN 978-3-030-29052-8 ISBN 978-3-030-29053-5 (eBook)
https://doi.org/10.1007/978-3-030-29053-5



This Springer imprint is published by the registered company Springer Nature Switzerland AG.
The registered company address is: Gewerbestrasse 11, 6330 Cham, Switzerland

# Contents

# About the Contributors

**Alberto Blanco-Justicia** is a Postdoctoral Researcher at Universitat Rovira i Virgili. He obtained his MSc in Computer Security in 2013 from Universitat Rovira i Virgili, and his PhD in Computer Engineering and Mathematics of Security from the same university in 2017, with a thesis focused on the reconciliation of privacy, security and functionality in e-commerce applications. His research interests include data privacy, data security and cryptographic protocols. He has been involved in several European and national Spanish research projects, as well as technology transfer contracts.

**Markus Christen** is a Research Group Leader at the Institute of Biomedical Ethics and History of Medicine and Managing Director of the UZH Digital Society Initiative. He received his MSc in Philosophy, Physics, Mathematics and Biology from the University of Berne, his PhD in Neuroinformatics from the Federal Institute of Technology in Zurich and his Habilitation in Bioethics from the University of Zurich. His research interests include empirical ethics, neuroethics, ICT ethics and data analysis methodologies.

**Josep Domingo-Ferrer** is the Distinguished Professor of Computer Science and an ICREA-Acadèmia Researcher at Universitat Rovira i Virgili, Tarragona, Catalonia, where he holds the UNESCO Chair in Data Privacy and is the founding director of CYBERCAT-Center for Cybersecurity Research of Catalonia. He received his MSc and PhD degrees in Computer Science from the Autonomous University of Barcelona. He also holds an MSc in Mathematics. His research interests include data privacy, data security, statistical disclosure control and cryptographic protocols, with a focus on the conciliation of privacy, security and functionality. He is an IEEE Fellow, an ACM Distinguished Scientist and an elected member of Academia Europaea.

**Gloria González Fuster** is a Research Professor in the Faculty of Law and Criminology at the Vrije Universiteit Brussel (VUB). She is Co-Director of the Law, Science, Technology and Society (LSTS) Research Group, and a member of the Brussels Privacy Hub (BPH); she investigates legal issues related to privacy, personal data protection and security, and teaches 'Data Policies in the European Union' at the Data Law option of the Master of Laws in International and European Law (PILC) of VUB's Institute for European Studies (IES). She studied law at the Universidad Nacional de Educación a Distancia (UNED), journalism in the Faculty of Communication Sciences of the Universidad Autónoma de Barcelona (UAB) (including a stay at the Université Paris VIII) and modern languages and literature at the Université Libre de Bruxelles (ULB).

**Bert Gordijn** has been a Full Professor and Director of the Institute of Ethics at Dublin City University (Ireland) since 2008. He is a Visiting Professor at Lancaster University (UK), Georgetown University (USA), the National University of Singapore, the Fondation Brocher (Switzerland), Yenepoya University (India) and the University of Otago (New Zealand). He has served on advisory panels and expert committees of the European Chemical Industry Council, the European Patent Organisation, the Irish Department of Health and UNESCO. He is currently the Secretary of the European Society for Philosophy of Medicine and Healthcare and President of the International Association of Education in Ethics.

**Florian Grunow** is a Security Analyst and currently CEO of ERNW GmbH, Heidelberg, Germany. He holds a Master of Science degree in computer science with a focus on software engineering and a Bachelor of Science degree in medical computer sciences. He is committed to practical security education, both internally at ERNW and by giving public talks.

**Dominik Herrmann** is a Full Professor of Privacy and Security in Information Systems at University of Bamberg (Germany). Prior to this, he was a Temporary Professor at the University of Siegen between October 2015 and March 2017. He holds a PhD in Computer Science (University of Hamburg, 2014) and a Diploma with Honors in Management Information Systems (University of Regensburg, 2008). He has received a series of awards, including the GI-Dissertationspreis 2014 for the best computer science dissertation in Germany. He was also named a Junior Fellow of the German Computer Science Society for his services to the profession.

**Reto Inversini** studied Geography at the University of Berne and Information Technology at the University of Applied Sciences in Berne. He worked for Amnesty International as a network and systems engineer and for the Swiss Federal Administration as a security architect. He currently works as a malware analyst and security officer for the Swiss Governmental CERT (GovCERT.ch). He is a part-time lecturer at the University of Applied Sciences in Bern in the domains of network engineering and information security. His focus lies on network intrusion detection and malware analysis. It is important to him that core values of our society such as individual responsibility, democracy, freedom of speech and privacy are preserved while increasing the security of the Internet.

**David-Olivier Jaquet-Chiffelle** is a Full Professor at the School of Criminal Justice, University of Lausanne, Switzerland. He is the head of the Master programme in forensic science, orientation digital investigation and identification. He accomplished his PhD in Mathematics at the University of Neuchâtel, Switzerland. He spent a post-doc at Harvard University (Boston, USA). He then strengthened his experience in cryptology while working for the Swiss government at the Swiss Federal Section of Cryptology. He has a long experience in projects related to identity, security and privacy. His current research includes cybercrime, security and privacy, and new forms of identities in the information society, as well as authentication, anonymisation and identification processes, especially in the digital world.

**Lina Jasmontaite** is a PhD candidate at the Vrije Universiteit Brussel. She joined the Law, Science, Technology and Society (LSTS) Research Group in September 2016. Currently, she works on the awareness raising project under the Rights, Equality and Citizenship Programme 2014–2020 titled 'Support Small and Medium Enterprises on the Data Protection Reform II' (STARII). Under the supervision of Professor Gloria González Fuster, she contributed to the Horizon 2020 project titled 'Constructing an Alliance for Value-driven Cybersecurity' (CANVAS). She is also a Contributing Fellow at the Brussels Privacy Hub, where she explores the legal implications of new technologies that are being operationalised in humanitarian practice. Her PhD research concerns primarily the interaction between data breach notification obligations foreseen in the General Data Protection Regulation and the Network and Information Security Directive.

**Alexey Kirichenko** received his MSc in Mathematics from Leningrad (St. Petersburg) State University, Russia, and completed his PhD in Theoretical Computer Science at Aalto University, Finland. He joined F-Secure in 1997 and was for a long time leading the development of the company's cryptographic modules and authorisation infrastructure. Since 2007, he has been working as Research Collaboration Manager, coordinating F-Secure's participation in European and Finnish national research collaboration projects. He represents F-Secure in WG6 of European Cyber Security Organisation (ECSO) and significantly contributed in the ECSO SRIA preparation. Prior to joining F-Secure, he worked in the Computer Graphics area at Altsys Corp., and prior to this he lectured in mathematical courses at St. Petersburg Electro-Technical University. He is actively involved in training the Finnish national team for the International Mathematical Olympiad.

**Nadine Kleine** studied sociology and political science at the University of Potsdam, Germany, as well as cultural sciences with a focus on technology at the BTU Cottbus-Senftenberg, Germany. She was a Research Associate at the Institute for Social Research and Technology Assessment (IST), Regensburg University of Applied Studies, where she worked on the H2020 project "Constructing an Alliance for Value-driven Cybersecurity" (CANVAS) concerning issues of cyber security and ethics in healthcare. Currently, she researches worker's autonomy and acceptance of digital technologies in the work environment as a member of the doctoral research group "Trust and Acceptance in Augmented and Virtual Working Environments" (va-eva) and is involved in the project "Teamwork 4.0" at the Department of Economic and Industrial Sociology, both at the University of Osnabrueck.

**David Koeppe** studied economics at the Free University of Berlin (Diplom-Kaufmann) and has worked in various positions in hospitals since 1995. As Privacy Officer of the Vivantes Group (Netzwerk für Gesundheit GmbH), he is intensively involved with all facets of data protection in the health care sector. Within the framework of the society 'Gesellschaft für Datenschutz und Datensicherheit e.V.' (Society for Data Protection and Data Security), he is leading the working group 'Data Protection and Data Security in Health and Social Services' and the regional experience exchange group in Berlin. He is the co-editor of the *Handbuch Datenschutz und Datensicherheit im Gesundheits und Sozialwesen* (Datakontext, 2016) and co-author of a number of published data protection tools.

**Michele Loi** (PhD, Luiss Guido Carli) is an applied philosopher working at the intersection between digital ethics and bioethics. Besides researching the ethics of cybersecurity, he is also interested in fairness and transparency in machine learning and in the regulation access and use to big data in health. Currently, he is affiliated as Postdoctoral Researcher with the Digital Ethics Lab, Digital Society Initiative and with the Institute of Biomedical Ethics and the History of Medicine (both University of Zurich). His research on the ethics of cybersecurity has been funded by the CANVAS project, the same H2020 project funding the project of this book.

**George Lucas** is retired as Distinguished Chair of Ethics at the US Naval Academy (Annapolis, Maryland). He is a Senior Fellow at the Stockdale Center for Leadership and Ethics at US Naval Academy. His most recent book is *Ethics and Military Strategy in the 21st-Century: Moving Beyond Clausewitz* (Routledge, 2019).

**Paul Meyer** is Fellow in International Security and Adjunct Professor of International Studies at Simon Fraser University and a Senior Fellow with The Simons Foundation in Vancouver, Canada. He is also a Senior Advisor with ICT4Peace, an NGO devoted to preserving a peaceful cyberspace. Previously, he had a 35-year career with the Canadian Foreign Service, including serving as Canada's Ambassador to the United Nations and to the Conference on Disarmament in Geneva (2003–2007). He writes on issues of nuclear non-proliferation and disarmament, space security and the diplomacy of international cyber security.

**Seumas Miller** holds research positions at Charles Sturt University, Technical University Delft and the University of Oxford. He is the author or co-author of 20 books, including *Social Action* (CUP, 2001), *Moral Foundations of Social Institutions* (CUP, 2010), *Terrorism and Counter-terrorism* (Blackwell, 2009), *Shooting to Kill: The Ethics of Police and Military Use of Lethal Force* (OUP, 2016) and *Institutional Corruption* (CUP, 2017), and of over 200 academic articles. He is currently working on a co-authored book on the ethics of cybersecurity with a computer scientist, Terry Bossomaier.

**Gwenyth Morgan** is a PhD candidate at the ADAPT Centre for Digital Content Technologies and at the Institute of Ethics in All Hallows Drumcondra. She is conducting her research on the topic of ethically appropriate business responses to ransomware attacks and data breaches. Her work encompasses ethics and cybersecurity, ranging from ethical issues in cybersecurity relating to dataveillance, hacking back and the use of AI, to the dynamic and ambiguous relationship between businesses and security researchers, i.e., white hats, grey hats and black hats. She aims to open up the field of ethics and cybersecurity research in such a way that business ethics theories such as stakeholder theory can be used to practically establish how businesses can ethically manage and respond to issues that arise in cybersecurity. She teaches bachelor's and master's students at the Dublin City University on the topics of applied ethics, ethics of technology and health care ethics.

**Henning Pridöhl** is a Research and Teaching Assistant in the Privacy and Security in Information Systems Group at University of Bamberg. Prior to this, he was a Research Assistant in the Security in Distributed Systems Group at University of Hamburg. He holds an MSc in Computer Science from the University of Hamburg, where he graduated in 2016. He enjoys playing Capture The Flag security competitions and mentors young hackers in programming and IT security.

**Eva Schlehahn** is a Senior Legal Researcher and Consultant employed at Unabhängiges Landeszentrum für Datenschutz (ULD) in the German federal state of Schleswig-Holstein. Her work focuses on the requirements of the European General Data Protection Regulation (GDPR) and Privacy Enhancing Technologies (PETs). Since 2010, she has been working in various EC-funded FP7 and H2020 R&D projects focused on a multitude of data protection relevant topics. In her work, she has obtained a variety of know-how and experience related to topics such as cloud computing, identity and consent management, accessibility, UI design and usability, IT security, data privacy vocabularies and ontologies, data policy enforcement, surveillance technologies, requirements analysis and conceptualisation. Her research interests include interdisciplinary requirements analysis, balancing and evaluation, specifically considering Privacy by Design solutions.

**Salome Stevens** is a Teaching and Research Fellow at the Department of Criminal Law of the University of Zurich. She is pursuing her PhD on the subject of cybersecurity. Before joining the university, she worked as a Legal and Political Advisor for the Federal Department of Foreign Affairs and the Police Force, as well as for the private sector and the United Nations. She also supported several NGOs in their mandate to prevent international crime and fight impunity. Throughout her professional development, she has lived in Switzerland, Italy, Israel and the United Arab Emirates.

**Ibo van de Poel** is Anthoni van Leeuwenhoek Professor in Ethics and Technology and head of the Department of Values, Technology and Innovation at the Faculty of Technology, Policy and Management at the Technical University Delft in the Netherlands. He has published on engineering ethics, the moral acceptability of technological risks, design for values, responsible innovation, moral responsibility in research networks, ethics of newly emerging technologies and the idea of new technology as a social experiment. He has recently received an ERC Advanced grant for 'Design for changing values: a theory of value change in sociotechnical systems'.

**Eleonora Viganò** is a Postdoctoral Researcher at the Institute of Biomedical Ethics and History of Medicine and at the Digital Society Initiative of the University of Zurich. Her research is funded by the Cogito Foundation and the CANVAS project. She is a Moral Philosopher with a strong interest in the neuroscience of ethics. Her research interests include intrapersonal conflicts of values, the morality of prudence, and the implications for ethics of the neuroscientific discoveries on decision making. She has recently started working on ethical trade-offs in cybersecurity and on trust and transparency in machine learning algorithms.

**Karsten Weber** studied philosophy, informatics and sociology at University Karlsruhe (TH), Germany, and from 1996 to 1999 worked there as a Junior Researcher. After his doctorate in 1999, from 1999 to 2008 he was a Senior Researcher at European University Viadrina in Frankfurt (Oder), Germany. From 2006 to 2012, he worked as a Professor of Philosophy at University Opole, Poland. Since 2007, he has held an honorary professorship for Culture and Technology at BTU Cottbus-Senftenberg, Germany. At TU Berlin from 2008 to 2009, he was a Professor for Information Ethics and Data Protection and from 2009 to 2011 Professor for Computer Science and Society. From 2011 to 2016, he was Chair for General Science of Technology at BTU Cottbus-Senftenberg. Since 2013, Prof. Weber has taught technology assessment at OTH Regensburg, Germany and is co-head of the Institute for Social Research and Technology Assessment (IST) and one of the three directors of the Regensburg Center of Health Sciences and Technology (RCHST).

**Emad Yaghmaei** is a Senior Researcher at the Faculty of Technology, Policy and Management at the Technical University Delft. His research interests include the innovation management issues arising from the intersections of science, technology and society. The emphasis of his research and consulting is on innovation and technology management of emerging technologies such as ICT, the Internet of Things, nanotechnology and so on to identify and work on the social impacts of these technologies. He has been working on monitoring industry business innovation across non-financial values. He is currently focusing on Responsible Research and Innovation (RRI) principles in an industrial context to demonstrate how industry can work productively together with societal actors and integrate methodologies of RRI into research and innovation processes.

# Acronyms and Abbreviations

| | |
|---|---|
| ACM | Association for Computing Machinery |
| AI | Artificial Intelligence |
| APT | Advanced Persistent Threat |
| ASLR | Address Space Layout Randomization |
| AV | Anti Virus |
| C&C | Command and Control |
| CA | Certification Authority |
| CANVAS | Constructing an Alliance for Value-driven Cybersecurity |
| CCC | Convention on Cyber Crime |
| CENELEC | European Committee for Electrotechnical Standardization |
| CERT | Computer Emergency Response Team |
| CFI | Control-Flow Integrity |
| CFSP | Common Foreign and Security Policy |
| CJEU | Court of Justice of the European Union |
| CNIL | Commission Nationale de l'Informatique et des Libertés |
| CoE | Council of Europe |
| DDoS | Distributed Denial of Service |
| DEP | Data Execution Prevention |
| DNS | Domain Name System |
| DPI | Deep Packet Inspection |
| DPIA | Data Protection Impact Assessment |
| EC | European Commission |
| ECHR | European Convention of Human Rights |
| ECSO | European Cyber Security Organisation |
| ECHR | European Court of Human Rights |
| EDPS | European Data Protection Supervisor |
| EFF | Electronic Frontier Foundation |
| eHC | electronic Health Card |
| ENISA | European Network and Information Security Agency |
| EU | European Union |
| FRS | Face Recognition System |

| | |
|---|---|
| GAFAM | Google, Apple, Facebook, Amazon and Microsoft |
| GDPR | General Data Protection Regulation |
| GGE | Group of Governmental Experts |
| HTTP | Hypertext Transfer Protocol |
| ICRC | International Committee of the Red Cross |
| ICT | Information and Communication Technology |
| IMD | Implantable Medical Device |
| IoT | Internet of Things |
| ISACA | Information Systems Audit and Control Association |
| ISO | International Organization for Standardization |
| ISP | Internet Service Providers |
| ITU | International Telecommunication Union |
| LEA | Law Enforcement Agency |
| MAC | Message Authentication Code |
| MDR | Medical Device Regulation |
| MitM | Man in the Middle |
| NATO | North Atlantic Treaty Organization |
| NER | Named Entity Recognition |
| NIDS | Network Intrusion Detection Systems |
| NIS | Network and Information Security |
| NSA | National Security Agency (USA) |
| OJ | Official Journal of the European Communities |
| OSCE | Organization for Security and Cooperation in Europe |
| PGP | Pretty Good Privacy |
| PPDM | Privacy-Preserving Data Mining |
| QC | Quantum Computing |
| ROP | Return-Oriented Programming |
| SDC | Statistical Disclosure Control |
| SDM | Standard Data Protection Model |
| SME | Small and Medium Enterprises |
| SOST | Surveillance-Oriented Security Technology |
| SQL | Structured Query Language |
| TAO | Tailored Access Operations |
| T-CY | Cybercrime Convention Committee |
| TEU | Treaty on European Union |
| TFEU | Treaty on the Functioning of the European Union |
| TLS | Transport Layer Security |

# List of Figures

# List of Tables

# Chapter 1
# Introduction

**Markus Christen, Bert Gordijn, and Michele Loi**

**Abstract** This introduction provides a short overview on the book "The Ethics of Cybersecurity". The volume explains the foundations of cybersecurity, ethics and law, outlines various problems of the domain such as ethical hacking and cyberwar, and it lists recommendations and best practices for cybersecurity professionals working in various application areas. Furthermore, the introduction outlines the background of the European CANVAS project, from which this volume emerged.

**Keywords** Cybersecurity · Ethics · Law · Trust · Values

The increasing use of information and communication technology (ICT) in all spheres of modern life makes the world a richer, more efficient and interactive place. However, it also increases its fragility, as it reinforces our dependence on ICT systems that can never be completely safe or secure. Therefore, cybersecurity has become a matter of global interest and importance. Accordingly, we can observe in today's cybersecurity discourse an almost constant emphasis on an ever-increasing and diverse set of threats, ranging from basic computer viruses to sophisticated kinds of cybercrime and cyberespionage activities, as well as cyber-terror and cyberwar. This growing complexity of the digital ecosystem in combination with increasing glo bal risks has created the following dilemma. Overemphasising cybersecurity may violate fundamental values such as equality, fairness, freedom or

M. Christen (✉)
UZH Digital Society Initiative, Zürich, Switzerland
e-mail: christen@ethik.uzh.ch

B. Gordijn
Dublin City University, Dublin, Ireland
e-mail: bert.gordijn@dcu.ie

M. Loi
Digital Society Initiative, University of Zurich, Zurich, Switzerland

Institute of Biomedical Ethics and History of Medicine, Zurich, Switzerland
e-mail: michele.loi@uzh.ch



M. Christen et al. (eds.), *The Ethics of Cybersecurity*, The International Library of Ethics, Law and Technology 21,
https://doi.org/10.1007/978-3-030-29053-5_1

privacy. However, neglecting cybersecurity could undermine citizens' trust and confidence in the digital infrastructure, in policy makers and in state authorities. Thus, cybersecurity supports the protection of values such as nonmaleficence, privacy and trust, and therefore imposes a complex relationship among values: some may be supportive and others conflicting, depending on context. For example, whereas cybersecurity is in most cases a precondition to protect data and thus the privacy of people, it may also make private information more accessible to cybersecurity experts, in order to detect malicious activities.

Understanding this and other value dilemmas has become imperative, yet cybersecurity is still an under-developed topic in technology ethics. Although there are numerous papers discussing issues such as 'big data' and privacy, cybersecurity is—if at all—only discussed as a tool to protect (or undermine) privacy. Nevertheless, cybersecurity raises a plethora of ethical issues such as 'ethical hacking', dilemmas of holding back 'zero day' exploits, weighting data access and data privacy in sensitive health data, or value conflicts in law enforcement raised by encryption algorithms. For example, a governmental computer emergency response team (CERT) may fight a ransomware attack by turning off the payment servers and destroying the business model of the attackers to prevent future attacks—but this means that people whose data already has been encrypted would never retrieve it. A medical implants producer may want to protect the data transfer between implant and receiver server by means of suitable cryptology—but this significantly increases the energy consumption of the implant and frequently requires more surgeries for battery exchange. Finally, a white hat hacker may discover a dangerous vulnerability in an IoT device and inform the manufacturer—but the company does not attempt to correct the error and the hacker considers how to generate public attention for the case. Such issues are usually discussed in an isolated manner, whereas a coherent and integrative view on the ethics of cybersecurity is missing. Only a few authors such as Kenneth Einar Himma (2005, 2008) have worked systematically on the ethical issues of cybersecurity for a longer time, and recent authors on this topic have focused on more specific issues such as cyberwar (Lucas 2017; Taddeo and Glorioso 2017). A rare example of broader coverage of the topic is Manjikian (2017).

This book aims to provide the first systematic collection of the full plethora of ethical aspects of cybersecurity. It results from the research activities of the CANVAS Consortium—Constructing an Alliance for Value-driven Cybersecurity—that unified technology developers with legal and ethical scholar and social scientists to approach the challenge of how cybersecurity can be aligned with European values and fundamental rights. The project was funded by the European Commission and aimed to bring together stakeholders from key areas of the European Digital Agenda—business/finance, the health system and law enforcement/national security—in order to discuss challenges and solutions when aligning cybersecurity with ethics. A special focus of CANVAS was on raising the awareness of the ethics of cybersecurity through teaching in academia and industry.

In a series of four White Papers, the CANVAS consortium provides an extensive overview of the discourse of ethical, legal and social aspects of cybersecurity. The first White Paper 'Cybersecurity and Ethics' outlines how the ethical discourse on cybersecurity has developed in the scientific literature, which ethical issues have gained interest, which value conflicts are being discussed, and where the 'blind spots' are in the current ethical discourse on cybersecurity (Yaghmaei et al. 2017). Here, an important observation is that the ethics of cybersecurity is not yet an established subject. In all domains, cybersecurity is recognised as being an instrumental value, not an end in itself, which opens up the possibility of trade-offs with different values in different spheres. The most prominent common theme is the existence of trade-offs and even conflicts between reasonable goals, for example between usability and security, accessibility and security, and privacy and convenience. Other prominent common themes are the importance of cybersecurity to sustain trust (in institutions) and the harmful effect of any loss of control over data.

The second White Paper 'Cybersecurity and Law' explores the legal dimensions of the European Union's value-driven cybersecurity policy (Jasmontaite et al. 2017). It identifies the main critical challenges in this area and discusses specific controversies concerning cybersecurity regulation. The White Paper recognises that legislative and policy measures within the cybersecurity domain challenge EU fundamental rights and principles, stemming from EU values. Annexes provide a review of EU soft-law measures, EU legislative measures, cybersecurity and criminal justice affairs, the relationship of cybersecurity to privacy and data protection, cybersecurity definitions in national cybersecurity strategies, and brief descriptions of EU values.

The third White Paper 'Attitudes and Opinions regarding Cybersecurity' summarises the currently available empirical data regarding the attitudes and opinions of citizens and state actors regarding cybersecurity (Wenger et al. 2017). The data emerges from the reports of EU projects, Eurobarometer surveys, policy documents of state actors and additional scientific papers. It describes what these stakeholders generally think, what they feel and what they do about cyber threats and security (counter)measures.

Finally, the fourth White Paper 'Technological Challenges in Cybersecurity' summarises the current state of discussion regarding the main technological challenges in cybersecurity and their impact, including ways and approaches to address them, on key fundamental values (Domingo-Ferrer et al. 2017).

These White Papers serve as a baseline for this volume, which involves the contributions of CANVAS researchers as well as those of external experts. The first part of the volume outlines the general problems associated with the ethics of cybersecurity. This involves defining the basic technical concepts of cybersecurity, the values affected by cybersecurity, and the ethical and legislative framework, with a particular focus on Europe. The second part of the volume introduces a variety of ethical questions raised in the context of cybersecurity. The contributions are mostly structured along the major domains of interest that were investigated in the CANVAS project: business/finance, the health system, and law enforcement/national security. The last part of the volume is dedicated to recommendations in order to tackle some of the ethical challenges of cybersecurity. Overall, given the broad scope of the topics addressed in this book, it will not only be relevant for scholars focusing on philosophy and the ethics of technology. Many practitioners in cybersecurity—providers of security software, CERTs or Chief Security Officers in companies—are increasingly aware of the ethical dimensions of their work. We therefore hope that the practical focus of this book will also help those experts to not only gain awareness of the ethics of cybersecurity but also provide them with the concepts and tools to tackle them.[1]

As cybersecurity is a quickly evolving domain, this book will not provide a complete overview of all relevant topics. Emerging issues concern, for example, cybercurrencies or the role of artificial intelligence (AI) in cybersecurity. The latter will become important both as a tool to complement the toolset for defending against attacks (e.g., for supervising large networks) as well as for more efficient attacks. AI may also become a dangerous tool for very new kinds of attacks (e.g. for learning instabilities in electronic stock markets and providing buy/sell 'signals' that destabilise the stock market). Furthermore, 'hacking' AI systems—which in the future may play important roles such as in autonomous driving—through compromised data may also become an increasingly relevant issue for cybersecurity. In addition, as processes and interactions in many social spheres increasingly rely on ICT systems, traditional security issues interfere with cybersecurity issues in domains such as food-security or migration and security. In this book, we only cover a few of these emerging issues, such as the danger of 'hacking democracy' through ICT-mediated means such as deep fakes and botnets (see Chaps. 11 and 12) and partly AI threads related to critical infrastructure (Chap. 8). Others should become topics of a new book, perhaps with more emphasis on autonomous decision-making systems and machine learning.

## 1.1 Explaining the Foundations

In the first chapter, *Dominik Herrmann* and *Henning Pridöhl* provide a technical introduction to the topic of this book. In this chapter, they review the fundamental concepts of cybersecurity by explaining common threats to information and systems to illustrate how matters of security can be addressed with methods from risk management. They also describe typical attack strategies and principles for defence. They review cryptographic techniques, malware and two common weaknesses in software: buffer overflows and SQL injections. This is followed by selected topics from network security, namely reconnaissance, firewalls, Denial of Service attacks and Network Intrusion Detection Systems. Finally, they review techniques for continuous testing, stressing the need for a free distribution of dual-use tools.

*Ibo van de Poel* then provides an introduction into the core values and value conflicts in cybersecurity. He does so by distinguishing four important value clusters that should be considered by deciding about cybersecurity measures: security, privacy, fairness and accountability. Each cluster consists of a range of further values that may be seen as articulating specific moral reasons relevant in devising cybersecurity measures. Following this introduction, potential value conflicts and value tensions are discussed as well as possible methods for dealing with these conflicts.

The next chapter by *Michele Loi* and *Markus Christen* provides an in-depth discussion of ethical frameworks for cybersecurity. These include the principlist frame-

[1] For doing this, the CANVAS project has also created a whole spectrum of practical tools such as briefing material, a reference curriculum on the ethics of cybersecurity including teaching material, and a Massive Open Online Course. This material is available on the CANVAS website www.canvas-project.eu.

work employed in the Menlo Report on cybersecurity research and the rights-based principle that is influential in the law, in particular EU law. The authors show that since the harms and benefits caused by cybersecurity operations and policies are of a probabilistic nature, both approaches cannot avoid dealing with risk and probability. Therefore, the ethics of risk is introduced in several variants as a necessary complement to such approaches. They propose a revised version of this framework for identifying and ethically assessing changes brought about by cybersecurity measures and policies, not only in relation to privacy but more generally to the key expectations concerning human interactions within the practice.

Finally, *Gloria González Fuster* and *Lina Jasmontaite* introduce the legislative framework for cybersecurity. The authors provide an overview of the current and changing legal framework for regulating cybersecurity with a particular focus on the new EU Data Protection Regulation. By invoking a historical perspective, the chapter analyses the policy developments that have shaped the cybersecurity domain in the EU. It reviews the mobilisation of multiple domains (such as the regulation of electronic communications, critical infrastructures and cybercrime) in the name of cybersecurity imperatives, and explores how their operationalisation surfaced in the EU cybersecurity strategy. It highlights how the perception of cybersecurity's relation with (national) security play a determinant role in EU legislative and policy debates, whereas fundamental rights considerations are only considered to a limited extent.

## 1.2 Outlining the Problems

The chapter by *Gwenyth Morgan* and *Bert Gordijn* provides a care-based stakeholder approach to the ethics of cybersecurity in business. After sketching the main ethical issues discussed in the academic literature, the chapter aims to identify some important topics that have not yet received the attention they deserve. The chapter then focuses on one of those topics, namely ransomware attacks one of the most prevalent cybersecurity threats to businesses today. Using Daniel Engster's care-based stakeholder approach, the responsibilities that businesses have to their stakeholders are analysed—in particular with respect to patching identified vulnerabilities and paying the ransom.

*Karsten Weber* and *Nadine Kleine* investigate in their chapter the specific ethical issues of cybersecurity in health care. Using the approach of principlism, enhanced with additional values, they demonstrate how value conflicts can emerge in that domain and they provide possible solutions. With the help of implantable medical devices and the electronic Health Card as case studies, they show that these conflicts cannot be eliminated but must be reconsidered on a case-by-case basis.

The cybersecurity of critical infrastructures is analysed in the chapter of *Eleonora Viganò, Michele Loi* and *Emad Yaghmaei*. They provide a political and philosophical analysis of the values at stake in ensuring cybersecurity for national infrastructure. Based on a review on the boundaries of national security and cybersecurity with a focus on the ethics of surveillance for protecting critical infrastructure and the use of AI, they apply a bibliographic analysis of the literature until 2016 to identify and discuss the cybersecurity value conflicts and ethical issues in national security. This is integrated with an analysis of the most recent literature on cyber-threats to national infrastructure and the role of AI. They show that the increased connectedness of digital and non-digital infrastructure enhances the trade-offs between values identified in the literature of the past years.

In the next chapter *David-Olivier Jaquet-Chiffelle* and *Michele Loi* discuss an inherent ethical issue of cybersecurity: ethical and unethical hacking. They provide a conceptual analysis of ethical hacking, including its history, in order to provide a systematic classification of hacking. They conclude by suggesting a pragmatic best-practice approach for characterising ethical hacking, which reaches beyond business-friendly values and helps with taking decisions respectful of the hackers' individual ethics in morally debatable, grey zones.

The interrelation of cybersecurity and the state is then investigated in the chapter by *Eva Schlehahn*. The author provides an overview of state actor's opinions and strategies relating to cybersecurity matters, with a particular focus on the EU. Furthermore, the role of the new European data protection framework is addressed, while it is explained why data protection also has a close relationship to cybersecurity matters. The main tensions and conflicts in relation to IT and cybersecurity are depicted, which evolve primarily around the frequently negative effect on the rights of data subjects that IT and cybersecurity measures have. In particular, the issue of governmental surveillance is addressed, with its implications for the fundamental rights of European citizens.

*Seumas Miller* then approaches this political dimension by analysing the tricky balance between freedom of communication and security in the cyber domain. The author provides definitions of fake news, hate speech and propaganda, and shows how these phenomena are corruptive for epistemic norms. He elaborates on the right to freedom of communication and its relation both to censoring propaganda and to the role of epistemic institutions, such as a free and independent press and universities. Finally, he discusses the general problem of countering political propaganda in cyberspace.

The contribution of *George Lucas* goes in a similar direction, but he particularly discusses the case that increasingly, state actors undermine cybersecurity, broadly construed by both propaganda and other types of cyber operations. He presents the current cyber domain as a Hobbesian state of nature, a domain of unrestricted conflict constituting a "war of all against all". The fundamental ethical dilemma in Hobbes's original account of this 'original situation' was how to establish a more stable political arrangement, comprising a rule of law under which the interests of the various inhabitants in life, property and security would be more readily guaranteed. The author discusses how to achieve an acceptance of general norms of responsible individual and state behaviour within the cyber domain, arising from experience and consequent enlightened self-interest.

Finally, *Reto Inversini* proposes focusing on 'cyberpeace' as a guiding principle in cybersecurity. He analyses elements of cyber conflicts and attacks, defines the term cyber peace and identifies the components that make such a state possible. The chapter closes with an assessment of the different roles and responsibilities of stakeholders to reach and preserve a state of peace in the digital sphere.

## 1.3 Presenting Recommendations

The first chapter of the final part is dedicated to technological means. *Josep Domingo-Ferrer* and *Alberto Blanco-Justicia* review the entire spectrum of privacy-enhancing techniques (PET). They first enumerate design strategies and then move to privacy-enhancing techniques that directly address the *hide* strategy but also aid in implementing the *separate*, *control* and *enforce* strategies. Specifically, they consider PETs for: (1) identification, authentication and anonymity; (2) private communications; (3) privacy-preserving computations; (4) privacy in databases; and (5) discrimination prevention in data mining.

The next chapter outlines some concrete best practices and recommendations for cybersecurity service providers. Based on a brief outline of dilemma that cybersecurity service providers may experience in their daily operations, *Alexey Kirichenko*, *Markus Christen*, *Florian Grunow* and *Dominik Herrmann* discuss data handling policies and practices of cybersecurity vendors along the following five topics: customer data handling, information about breaches, threat intelligence, vulnerability-related information and data involved when collaborating with peers, CERTs, cybersecurity research groups, etc. They also include a discussion of specific issues of penetration testing such as customer recruitment and execution as well as the supervision and governance of penetration testing. The chapter closes with some general recommendations regarding improving the ethical decision-making procedures of private cybersecurity service providers.

*Salome Stevens* then analyses a highly debated strategy of businesses to counteract cyber threats: hacking back. Several security experts call for a more active cyber-defence of companies, including offensive actions in cyberspace taken with defensive purposes in mind. The lack of legal regulations, however, raises insecurities over the legal scope of action of private companies. The authors investigate questions such as: When is a private company allowed to act? When by such an act could it itself be implicated into committing illegal actions? The chapter concludes by giving recommendations for companies on how to define ethical cyber-defence within their security strategy.

How the awareness for cybersecurity can be enhanced in health care is then discussed by *David Koeppe*. Given that the medical domain is characterised by special processing situations and, in particular, by the very high protection requirements of data and processes, cybersecurity is a must and requires the setup of proper information security management systems. The authors discuss the key requirements of such management systems—also given the requirements of the new EU data protection regulation.

Finally, *Paul Meyer* discusses norms of responsible state behaviour in cyberspace. The chapter sketches the increasing 'militarisation' of cyberspace as well as the diplomatic efforts undertaken to provide this unique environment with some 'rules of the road'. The primary mechanism for discussing possible norms of responsible state behaviour has been a series of UN Groups of Governmental Experts which have produced three consensus reports over the last decade. The author calls for renewed efforts to promote responsible state behaviour that will require greater engagement on the part of the private sector and civil society, both of which have a huge stake in sustaining cyber peace.

In conclusion, it is our sincere hope that this book enables the reader to gain a broad understanding of the various ethical issues associated with cybersecurity. We close by expressing our gratitude to the two anonymous reviewers of this manuscript, who provided helpful comments, and to Edward Crocker, proof reader of Cambridge Proofreading & Editing LLC. This book has been supported by the European Union's Horizon 2020 research and innovation programme under grant agreement No 700540 and the Swiss State Secretariat for Education, Research and Innovation (SERI) under contract number 16.0052-1. We are thankful to our funding institutions.

## References

Domingo-Ferrer J, Blanco A, Arnau P et al (2017) Canvas White Paper 4 – Technological Challenges in Cybersecurity SSRN. https://ssrn.com/abstract=3091942 or https://doi.org/10.2139/ssrn.3091942. Last access 7 July 2019

Himma KE (2005) Internet security: hacking, counterhacking, and society. Jones and Bartlett Publishers, Inc., Missisauga

Himma KE, Tavani HT (eds) (2008) The handbook of information and computer ethics. Wiley, Hoboken

Jasmontaite L, González FG, Gutwirth S et al (2017) Canvas White Paper 2 – Cybersecurity and Law. SSRN. https://ssrn.com/abstract=3091939 or https://doi.org/10.2139/ssrn.3091939. Last access 7 July 2019

Lucas G (2017) Ethics and cyber warfare: the quest for responsible security in the age of digital warfare. Oxford University Press, New York, p 187

Manjikian M (2017) Cybersecurity ethics: an introduction. Routledge, London/New York

Taddeo M, Glorioso L (eds) (2017) Ethics and policies for cyber operations. Springer, Cham

Wenger F, Jaquet-Chiffelle DO, Kleine N et al (2017) Canvas, White Paper 3 – Attitudes and Opinions Regarding Cybersecurity. SSRN. https://ssrn.com/abstract=3091920 or https://doi.org/10.2139/ssrn.3091920. Last access 7 July 2019

Yaghmaei E, van de Poel I, Christen M et al (2017) Canvas White Paper 1 – Cybersecurity and Ethics. SSRN. https://doi.org/10.2139/ssrn.3091909. Last access 7 July 2019

# Part I
# Foundations

# Chapter 2
# Basic Concepts and Models of Cybersecurity

**Dominik Herrmann and Henning Pridöhl**

**Abstract** This introductory chapter reviews the fundamental concepts of cybersecurity. It begins with common threats to information and systems to illustrate how matters of security can be addressed with methods from risk management. In the following, typical attack strategies and principles for defence are reviewed, followed by cryptographic techniques, malware and two common weaknesses in software: buffer overflows and SQL injections. Subsequently, selected topics from network security, namely reconnaissance, firewalls, Denial of Service attacks, and Network Intrusion Detection Systems, are analysed. Finally, the chapter reviews techniques for continuous testing, stressing the need for a free distribution of dual-use tools. Although introductory in nature, this chapter already addresses a number of ethical issues. For instance, well-intended security mechanisms may have undesired side effects such as leaking sensitive information to attackers. As asymmetries and externalities are at the core of many security problems, devising effective security solutions that are adopted in practice is a challenge.

**Keywords** Advanced persistent threat · Availability · Black hats · Certificates · Confidentiality · Cryptography · Integrity · Malware · Supply-chain attack · Vulnerabilities · White hats

## 2.1 Introduction

Honesty was never a given in human history. In the physical world, we can rely on decades of experience to defend against malicious actors. We have devised sophisticated laws that govern what is acceptable and what is illegal. In addition, we have a number of technical means at our disposal to secure our property and our secrets.

D. Herrmann (✉) · H. Pridöhl
Privacy and Security in Information Systems Group (PSI), University of Bamberg, Bamberg, Germany
e-mail: dominik.herrmann@uni-bamberg.de; henning.pridoehl@uni-bamberg.de

 
M. Christen et al. (eds.), *The Ethics of Cybersecurity*, The International Library of Ethics, Law and Technology 21,
https://doi.org/10.1007/978-3-030-29053-5_2

However, we are still in the process of learning how to secure cyberspace. Cyberspace has become the handle of choice to refer to the virtual world created by networked computer systems that affect large parts of our lives; securing it is challenging. According to Bruce Schneier "complexity is the enemy of security" (Chan 2012). There are not only more devices hooked up to the Internet, but also more manufacturers building them, which increases both the size and diversity of the systems forming the cyberspace and thus the probability of failures.

Moreover, cybersecurity is subject to significant asymmetries. Attackers can choose from a large variety of approaches, while defenders have to pay attention to every detail and be prepared for anything at any time. Therefore, successful attacks are not necessarily the result of negligence. Sometimes security controls are in place but are not used properly, for instance, because they conflict with the needs of users. Given these difficulties, there is now much interest in reactive security, which embraces the insight that we cannot prevent all attacks.

In this chapter, we introduce the basic concepts of cybersecurity. We start by defining common threats in Sect. 2.2 and reviewing typical attack and defence techniques in Sect. 2.3. Subsequently, we present security fundamentals in various domains, namely cryptography for data security in Sect. 2.4, malware in Sect. 2.5, software security in Sect. 2.6 and network security in Sect. 2.7. Finally, we stress the importance of continuous testing in Sect. 2.8 before we conclude the chapter in Sect. 2.9.

## 2.2 Threats

Before we can discuss attacks and defences in cyberspace, we must clarify what is at stake. In the following, we review the fundamental protection goals that help us gain a comprehensive picture of all aspects of security.

Before the term 'cybersecurity' became fashionable, discussions focused on computer security. The goal of computer security is to protect assets. Valuable assets can be hardware (e.g. computers and smartphones), software and data. These assets are subject to threats that may result in loss or harm.

Computer security consists of information security and systems security. It is instructive to consider the foundations of these two fields, which laid the ground for cybersecurity. Information security is concerned with the protection of data (potentially processed by computers) and any information derived from its interpretation. In systems security, we aim to ensure that (computer) systems operate as designed; i.e. attackers cannot tamper with them.

### 2.2.1 *Information Security*

We begin our discussion of threats with information security. There are three protection goals in information security: confidentiality, integrity and availability (Anderson 1972; Voydock and Kent 1983), commonly referred to as the 'CIA triad' (the origin of this abbreviation is unknown). Security measures have the purpose of addressing one or more of these objectives, as follows:

- Confidentiality: prevent unauthorised information gain.
- Integrity: prevent or detect unauthorised modification of data.
- Availability: prevent unauthorised deletion or disruption.

These protection goals apply both to data at rest, i.e. stored on a computer or on paper, and to data in transit, i.e. when data is sent over a network. The definitions refer to 'unauthorised' activities, which implies that there is an understanding about which actors are supposed to be allowed to interact with the data.

In some scenarios, there is only one authorised actor. An example in the context of the protection goal confidentiality is a smartphone or a computer with encrypted storage (sometimes called 'full-disk encryption'). In this case, only the owner of the device is authorised. An example for the goal availability is to backup data so that it remains accessible when a machine fails.

Most of the time, there are several authorised actors; often there are precisely two. For instance, the protection goal confidentiality may be relevant when a sender sends an e-mail to a particular recipient. Confidentiality is also essential during online banking. Here, we also want integrity protection for the exchanged messages to avoid transactions being modified.

The three fundamental protection goals of confidentiality, integrity and availability refer to the content. Besides content, we may also be concerned with the identity of other actors. For instance, we would like to know when the sender of an e-mail message has been forged. The protection goal *authenticity* prevents actors from impersonating someone else, usually by providing others with a means to verify a claimed identity. A related and even stronger protection goal is *non-repudiation*, which prevents actors from denying that they carried out a particular act, for instance, sending a message. Authenticity and non-repudiation are necessary to hold actors accountable (Gollmann 2011: 38).

### 2.2.2 *Systems Security*

How should we design systems so that they provide security for data stored on them? This question is at the centre of systems security. Consequently, the protection goals that are pursued in systems security are the same ones as in information security.

Often there are multiple ways to achieve the desired goal. For instance, confidentiality can be achieved by encrypting data or by a combination of authentication (e.g. by requiring users to enter a password) and access control (rules that govern which user is allowed to access which particular files). Designing systems that use a suitable combination of security measures is a non-trivial task.

However, systems security is not limited to achieving information security. Some systems hold no particularly interesting data at all. However, we rely on them and their functionality, i.e. the proper flow of a process. For instance, if an authentication system component of an operating system contains a bug, attackers may be able to shut it down (preventing authorised users from controlling the server) or bypass it (allowing unauthorised users to control the server). Integrity and availability are common protection goals in systems security. Keeping a particular procedure confidential may be a goal to secure intellectual property. However, it is considered bad practice to hide how a system works for reasons of security (cf. Sect. 2.3.2).

Of particular interest in systems security are so-called *cyber-physical systems* that affect the real world, such as traffic lights, autopilots, industrial robots, and control systems for chemical processes or power plants. Some of these systems are considered critical infrastructures; i.e. failures may have a significant impact on society. Policy makers are concerned that future wars might be fought by attacking critical infrastructures to cause chaos—without having to use physical force (Wheeler 2018). Well-known attacks on cyber-physical systems include the Stuxnet malware, which was used to sabotage an Iranian uranium enrichment facility at Natanz in 2010 (Langner 2013) and an attack on a Ukrainian power plant in 2015 (Zetter 2016).

### 2.2.3 Security Versus Safety

The cybersecurity community differentiates between security and safety (cf. Fig. 2.1). Harm can be caused by humans or by nonhuman events (Pfleeger et al. 2015). Examples of nonhuman events are natural disasters such as earthquakes, fires, floods, loss of electrical power, faults of hard disks and so on. Human threats are either benign or malicious. Benign threats are the result of accidents and inadvertent human errors such as mistyping a command, whereas malicious acts result from bad intentions.

Ensuring that a system remains operational during natural disasters and when faced with human errors (i.e. benign threats) is a matter of *safety*. Safety is crucial in cyber-physical systems, where the failure of a system may harm humans. Safety has a long tradition in engineering, for instance, in cars and airplanes that contain many critical systems designed for maximum dependability.

In contrast, matters of *security* focus on malicious acts of humans, which are called attacks. There are random attacks and directed attacks. In random attacks, attackers do not care who they attack as long as there is something to gain from the victim (cf. pickpockets in the physical world). In the electronic domain, phishing

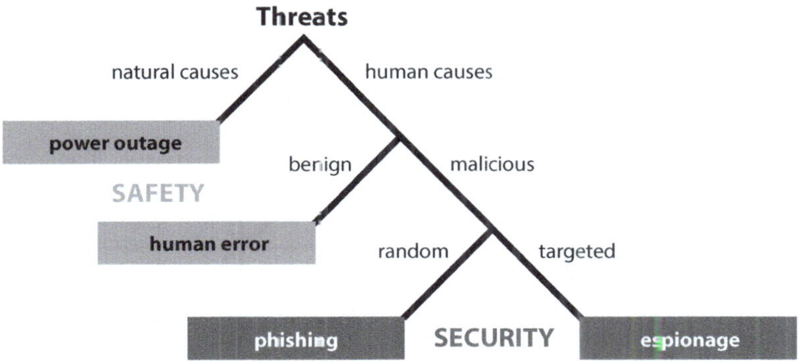


**Fig. 2.1** Safety versus security

scams are a well-known example. In contrast, targeted attacks are directed at a particular victim. Targeted attacks are more difficult to defend against than random attacks because attackers act strategically, i.e. they may dynamically change their course of actions in response to security measures.

### *2.2.4 Security as Risk Management*

Building software and hardware are complex and error-prone tasks. On average, every 1000 lines of code contain three to 20 bugs, and even a thorough code review reduces this number only by one order of magnitude (McConnell 2004). There are various ways in which these bugs can affect the security of a system. The 'Common Weakness Enumeration' (https://cwe.mitre.org) is a community-developed list of weaknesses. *Weaknesses* are generic types of mistakes that occur frequently. We discuss two common weaknesses in more detail later on, namely buffer overflows (see Sect. 2.6.1) and SQL injections (see Sect. 2.6.2).

A concrete realisation of a weakness in a particular product is called a *vulnerability*. A vulnerability is "a flaw or weakness in a system's design, implementation, or operation and management that could be exploited to violate the system's security policy" (Shirey 2007). Vulnerabilities in widely deployed products are assigned a unique identifier and archived in the 'Common Vulnerabilities and Exposures' (https://cve.mitre.org), which contained more than 115,000 entries in June 2019.

An attack on a system is possible if a system is exposed to an attacker and if it contains weaknesses that can be exploited. Unreachable systems cannot be attacked, and the mere presence of, e.g. a buffer overflow in a program, does not necessarily mean that it is exploitable. Furthermore, the fact that a system exposes an exploitable vulnerability does not mean that an attack is inevitable. The notion of *risk* captures this uncertainty. The severity of a risk is the product of the impact of an attack on an asset (typically concerning monetary loss) and the likelihood that the attack takes place. The likelihood of an attack depends on exposure and exploitability but also on

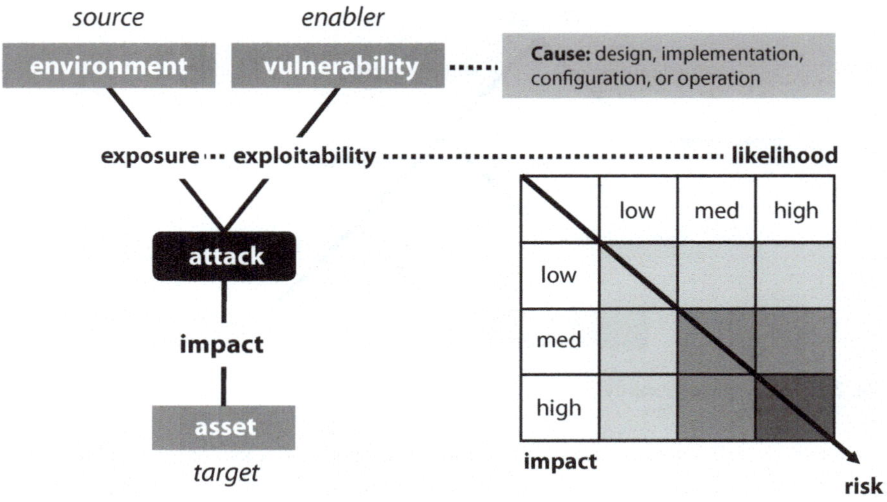


**Fig. 2.2** Relationship between vulnerability and risk

the question of whether the attack has the desired impact to reach the goal of an adversary. In practice, it is difficult to predict impact and likelihood accurately. Figure 2.2 illustrates the relationship between risk and vulnerabilities.

There are various ways to handle risks (Shostack 2014). Firstly, risks can be avoided, e.g. by refraining from implementing a feature. Secondly, risks can also be mitigated, e.g. by implementing security controls (also called countermeasures) that decrease the likelihood and impact of a risk. Thirdly, risks can be transferred, e.g. by buying insurance that covers potential losses. Fourthly, risks can be accepted, i.e. by deciding to cover the costs of an attack. Acceptance may make sense for risks that are very unlikely.

In practice, system designers often try to transfer risks to the users of a system, creating a so-called *negative externality*. Transferring risks is feasible because of an asymmetric power ratio between system designers and users. This situation is problematic because operators of a system may have less incentive to take security seriously when the impact of attacks does not affect them but someone else.

## 2.3 Approaches for Attack and Defence

For an attack to succeed, an attacker needs a working method, an opportunity to attack and a motive (Pfleeger et al. 2015). It is therefore instructive to survey different types of attackers and attack techniques.

### 2.3.1 *Attackers and Their Motives*

What kind of attackers exist and what are their motives? In most cases, the same as in the physical world. For instance, corporate spies carry out cyber-attacks on organisations to obtain trade secrets. There are also cyber criminals, individuals or groups that seek financial gain. One of their methods of operation is holding their victims to ransom, either by installing ransomware on their machines, by threatening to release sensitive information, or by threatening to carry out a Denial of Service attack (cf. Sect. 2.7.3). The most advanced attackers are nation states that, for example, aim to influence politics in a counterpart or extend their power. Nation states can conduct very sophisticated attacks that require many financial resources. Many attacks by nation states reach the level of an *advanced persistent threat (APT)*, i.e. an attack that involves advanced techniques that allow an attacker to covertly compromise and potentially even control the systems of a victim for long periods of time.

Besides these 'professional' attackers, there are also hobbyists. The term 'script kiddies' refers to unskilled attackers that are only able to use ready-to-run tools for their attacks (see also Chap. 9). Moreover, there are hacktivists that perform attacks to further a cause and create publicity, e.g. free speech and anti-surveillance. Finally, there are rogue hackers that mostly attack systems out of curiosity. There are also hackers that attack for personal gain. They make fun of their victims by defacing their websites, brag about their abilities in their community and may even sell off sensitive data on the black market.

The term 'black hats' is used for attackers with malicious motives. In contrast, 'white-hat hackers' are interested in improving overall security. They report all discovered vulnerabilities to the respective system operators.

Many efforts aim to keep attackers 'out'. This practice neglects insiders that have much better opportunities to attack than outsiders do. Insiders may be disloyal employees (users or operators) in a particular organisation. A comprehensive view of insiders should also include all employees that work at vendors, i.e. suppliers that provide tools used within an organisation. There have been several attempts to attack high-profile targets by infecting their vendors with malware. This approach, which is called a *supply-chain attack*, is quite powerful and difficult to detect (Korolov 2018).

### 2.3.2 *Defences*

Most defences focus on proactive security. However, this is not sufficient because it is impossible to prevent all attacks with absolute certainty. Proactive techniques are therefore combined with reactive techniques to handle the residual risk. In total, there are six approaches to secure a system (Pfleeger et al. 2015: Section 2.1.5). We begin by describing the three proactive approaches.

- *Preventive controls* ensure that an attack against a target is not possible or not successful, e.g. by controlling exposure (e.g. by a firewall) or exploitability (e.g. by fixing a buffer overflow vulnerability).
- *Deterrence* merely increases the effort for an adversary, aiming to make the target unattractive. An example of a deterrence control is two-factor authentication, which requires additional proofs of identity (e.g. possession of a particular smartphone) besides knowing the correct password. Determined adversaries may still succeed if they can get access to the second authentication factor.
- In *deflection*, the goal of the defender is to redirect the efforts of an adversary to another target. Deflection can be achieved, for instance, by deploying *honeypots* within an organisation (Spitzner 2002). A honeypot is a non-production system that is intentionally set up to fool attackers. Adversaries cannot easily distinguish honeypots from production systems, and they are configured to look like attractive targets.

The next three approaches provide reactive security:

- *Detection controls* can focus either on real-time notifications or on documentation. Intrusion Detection Systems such as Snort (https://www.snort.org) can alert operators about suspicious network traffic in real time so that system administrators can thwart an ongoing attack. In contrast, logging solutions collect evidence that may become useful during a so-called 'post-mortem analysis' of a security incident. Logs may contain network traffic (often stored in the so-called NetFlow format that includes metadata but not the content of communication), user interactions, executed programs, modified files, and any other pieces of information that may be useful to track down the perpetrators ('attribution'). Post-mortem analysis may also be capable of figuring out the extent of the attack, i.e. what files and systems have been compromised.
- *Mitigation controls* reduce the impact of an attack. A frequently deployed mitigation control is network segmentation, which prevents machines located in different parts of a corporate network from communicating with each other. Thus, an adversary who has compromised the workstation of an employee in the human resources department cannot steal blueprints that are only accessible by members of the research department.
- *Recovery controls* help to revert the effects of an attack as fast as possible and to resume normal operation. Recovery measures include off-site backups as well as emergency playbooks that offer guidance during a crisis.

Typically, organisations will combine various techniques from the six categories. Ideally, they prevent the majority of the attempted attacks. The remaining attacks will then hopefully be detected and handled with reactive security techniques.

Saltzer and Schroeder (1975) have devised generic *Security Design Principles* for building secure systems. Over time, the principles have been refined (Smith 2012). We summarise them in the following:

- *Continuous improvement.* Security is a process and operators have to make changes to keep it secure on a continuous basis.

- *Least privilege.* Users and components should not have more access rights than necessary to carry out their tasks.
- *Defence in depth.* A single security mechanism should not be relied upon. Instead, multiple mechanisms should be used simultaneously, increasing the effort for adversaries.
- *Open design.* Mechanisms should not rely on the fact that adversaries do not know their design (no 'security by obscurity').
- *Chain of control.* Only trustworthy software should be executed whenever possible and non-trustworthy components should be restricted.
- *Deny by default.* Unless explicitly specified, no access should be granted.
- *Transitive trust.* If A trusts B and B trusts C, then A may also trust C.
- *Trust but verify.* Even if a component is trustworthy, its identity must be verified.
- *Separation of duty.* Critical tasks should be split up and delegated to separate components or individuals.
- *The principle of least astonishment.* Good usability of security mechanisms is essential; mechanisms should be comprehensible and consequences should be intuitive.

### 2.3.3 Stages of an Intrusion

We now consider a typical workflow during an attack by discussing the *Cyber Kill Chain*, a popular framework proposed by Lockheed Martin (Hutchins et al. 2011). It separates the actions of attackers that attempt to 'hack' into a secured network:

1. *Reconnaissance*: Research, identification and selection of targets, e.g. by crawling websites for e-mail addresses, social relationships, or information on specific technologies in use by the target.
2. *Weaponisation*: Coupling a remote access Trojan with an exploit into a deliverable payload. Typically, client application data files such as the Portable Document Format (PDF) or Microsoft Office documents serve as the weaponised deliverable.
3. *Delivery*: Transmission of the weapon to the targeted environment. Prevalent delivery vectors for weaponised payloads are e-mail attachments, websites and removable media such as USB sticks.
4. *Exploitation*: After the weapon is delivered to the target host, the malicious code of the attacker is triggered, either by exploiting an application or operating system vulnerability (such as a buffer overflow), by convincing users to click on an e-mail attachment or by leveraging operating system features that execute code automatically (e.g. 'autorun.inf' in Windows).
5. *Installation*: Installation of a remote access tool on the target system, which allows the adversary to maintain persistence inside the environment.

6. *Command and Control (C&C)*: Typically, compromised hosts connect outbound to a controller server on the Internet. Once the C&C channel is established, intruders have 'hands on the keyboard' access inside the target environment.
7. *Actions*: After progressing through the first six phases, intruders can take actions to achieve their original objectives, e.g. data exfiltration, which involves collecting and extracting information from the victim environment.

The Cyber Kill Chain has been adopted by many practitioners to reason about security architectures. However, this framework is also subject to criticism (Engel 2014; Sheridan 2018). The Cyber Kill Chain has been proposed at a time when security focused on prevention. Reactive security measures were mostly non-existent at that time. Once attackers had breached the firewall, they could often move around the network without much restriction. Nowadays, many networks implement the principles of least privilege, separation of duties, and defence in depth. As a result, lateral movement becomes noisier, which gives defenders more chances to detect attackers.

Moreover, the Cyber Kill Chain focuses on attacks that involve running malware (cf. Sect. 2.5) on the machines of users that work inside the infrastructure of a victim. Not all attacks require all the steps mentioned above. For instance, sensitive data stored on an improperly secured web server may be exfiltrated with a single request exploiting an SQL injection vulnerability (cf. Sect. 2.6.2).

## 2.4 Threats and Solutions in Data Security

Storing and transmitting data is at the core of many computing tasks. Adversaries may interfere either with 'data at rest' (stored on a system) or 'data in transit'. In this section, we review common attacks on data and introduce the concepts of cryptographic countermeasures. Our discussion focuses on data in transit, using a simplistic model that consists of a sender and a recipient of messages.

### *2.4.1 Unauthorised Disclosure of Information*

We begin with attacks on confidentiality, which means we consider adversaries that are interested in learning secrets. Obtaining data at rest, e.g. on the system of the sender or the receiver, will generally require attackers to intrude into a system (cf. Sect. 2.3.3). In contrast, data in transit can be obtained more stealthily by eavesdropping on the transmission. Eavesdropping is possible in many distributed systems that consist of multiple components, which communicate over public networks. Attackers that control intermediary systems (such as routers or Wi-Fi access points) that are used to forward traffic between sender and receiver have access to all exchanged messages. Eavesdropping is also possible in case of wireless communication if the attacker is close enough to the communicating parties. Eavesdroppers are said to be passive attackers because they do not interfere with transmissions.

The standard countermeasure to prevent attacks on confidentiality is to encrypt data. A prerequisite for encrypted communication is for the sender and recipient to establish a *cryptographic key*, often just a sufficiently large number of random bits. In the case of *symmetric* cryptography, sender and receiver use the same key. The key has to be exchanged 'out of band', i.e. over a channel that is not under the control of the considered adversaries.

The sender feeds a message together with the key to an encryption function, obtaining the encrypted text (ciphertext) of the message. The recipient decrypts the ciphertext by supplying it along with the same key to the decryption function. An eavesdropper would have to guess the key by attempting all possible combinations. For a popular key size such as 256 bits, this would require $2^{256} \approx 10^{77}$ trials. Equipped with one million computers, each of which being capable of trying out one billion keys per second, an adversary would still need more than 1054 years on average to complete such a task.

Note that encryption is typically only applied to the content of messages, i.e. the identities of sender and recipient are transmitted in the clear. Routers need these addresses to forward a message towards its destination. This fact allows eavesdroppers to perform traffic analysis attacks: Adversaries still learn who communicates with whom, at what time, and how often. Traffic analysis attempts can be made more difficult by using multiple layers of encryption and forwarding messages over additional nodes to obfuscate their route. The Tor network (http://torproject.org) is a practical system that uses these techniques.

### 2.4.2 *Unauthorised Modification and Fabrication*

In the following, we discuss attacks on integrity by active attackers. Common objectives include modifying messages exchanged between the sender and recipient or sending faked messages to the recipient.

For technical reasons not elaborated here, merely using encryption is not sufficient to prevent modification of the underlying plaintext. Therefore, even encrypted messages need additional integrity protection. A basic integrity protection technique works as follows: the sender supplies the message (its content and possibly also the sender and receiver addresses) along with a cryptographic key (which has to be exchanged out of band, like before) into a function that generates a *message authentication code (MAC)*. The MAC is sent to the recipient together with the message. The recipient feeds the message, the key, and the MAC to a verification function that checks whether the MAC fits the message. As adversaries do not have access to the key, they cannot generate a correct MAC after they have modified a message. This technique cannot prevent modifications; however, it allows the recipient to detect whether any tampering has taken place.

If there is an agreement between sender and recipient that all messages are going to contain a MAC, attackers cannot create fake messages on their own. However, attackers can intercept a message of another user and send them to the designated recipient once again. Such a *replay attack* is useful for messages that instruct the recipient to perform a particular action, for instance, to unlock a door or to reset the password of an account. Replay attacks can be detected by the recipient as follows: sender and receiver agree that the sender adds a counter value to each message, which is supposed to be incremented with every message. Replays can then be detected because their counter value is smaller than a previously seen value or equal to the last seen one. The attacker cannot manipulate the counter value as it is also protected by the MAC.

Nevertheless, even replay detection is not sufficient in all cases. Consider the example of modern cars with a 'smart' entry system. Whenever the key is close to the car, the doors will automatically unlock if you attempt to open them. Car thieves have found a cheap technique to exploit this comfortable feature by working in teams (Greenberg 2017). The first perpetrator either gets close to the victim (in a coffee shop queue) or to the key (which may sit on a cupboard right behind the front door at home), carrying an antenna working on the same frequency as the smart key. The antenna is connected to a wireless transmitter with an extended range. The second perpetrator walks up to the car with the same equipment. This setup allows the thieves to carry out a *relay attack*, which makes the car believe that its key is close. Many modern cars have been shown to be vulnerable to relay attacks (Francillon et al. 2011). In principle, cars could be programmed to detect relay attacks, for instance, by measuring the delays between messages. Until manufacturers have upgraded security, consumers have to take care of themselves, e.g. by shielding the key or removing its battery.

### 2.4.3 The Benefits of Asymmetric Cryptography

Up to now, we have discussed what is called symmetric encryption and symmetric authentication—an approach that has several weaknesses. Firstly, these approaches require that each pair of senders and receivers that wants to communicate with each other have exchanged a secret key out of band. For $n$ participants $0.5 \cdot n\ (n-1)$ keys have to be exchanged, i.e. in a system comprised of 20 components there would be 190 different keys. Thus, the symmetric approach scales poorly.

Secondly, sender and receiver have to store identical keys on their devices. This design increases the risk of key compromise because the adversary can obtain the keys either from the sender's or the receiver's device.

Thirdly, there are applications where symmetric message authentication is not sufficient. Consider a message containing the statement "I, Bob Miller, owe 100 Euros to Laura Fisher." Assume that Laura receives a letter with this statement in her mailbox, however without any further indication of the sender. If the letter also contains a MAC and Laura can verify the MAC with the key she has exchanged with Bob, then Laura can be confident that it was indeed Bob who sent the letter. She has confirmed the authenticity of Bob's identity. However, let us assume that Bob later denies that he wrote the message. In that case Laura will not be able to convince a court that the MAC proves that Bob Miller wrote this message—after all, the key used for the MAC is not only known to Bob but also to her, i.e. she could have forged that message herself.

Asymmetric cryptography (also called public-key cryptography) allows us to overcome these limitations. In contrast to the symmetric approach, every entity (user or component) creates a *key pair*, which consists of a public key and a private key. The public key is shared with everyone else, and the private key is kept a secret.

Senders have to obtain the public key of the recipients with whom they want to communicate. As with symmetric cryptography, the key exchange is a sensitive matter. In particular, integrity protection is required, i.e. all parties must be certain that they obtained the authentic public keys. Without integrity protection, an adversary could interfere with the initial transmission of the public key. This would allow the adversary to forward the public key of a self-generated key pair to other parties. As a result, the adversary would become a so-called *man in the middle (MitM)*. MitM attackers can impersonate communication parties and decrypt messages designated for them. After decryption with the adversarial key, a MitM can encrypt the message with the public key of the designated recipient and forward the message towards the recipient, which makes it impossible for the recipient to detect that any kind of eavesdropping or manipulation has taken place. Although the concept of MitM attacks is considered basic knowledge, MitM attacks keep taking place in practice (cf., e.g. Cimpanu 2018; Seals 2018; Walker 2018).

Once senders have obtained a public key of their communication partner, they can create an encrypted message by feeding the message and the public key into an encryption function to obtain the ciphertext. The recipient can then retrieve the plaintext of the message by feeding the ciphertext and the corresponding private key to a decryption function.

Message authentication works similarly. A sender signs a message by feeding it together with the sender's private key into a signing function. Everyone who is in possession of the public key of the sender can then verify the message. The verification function consumes a message, the public key of the purported sender, and the signature. If verification succeeds, this means that the message has not been tampered with (integrity) and that the signature was genuinely generated by the private key that belongs to the public key used during verification (non-repudiation).

Asymmetric cryptography is in widespread use today. Most prominently, it is used to secure e-mails with the S/MIME and OpenPGP message formats. It also plays a vital role in securing the World Wide Web, which we discuss in the next section.

### *2.4.4 Case Study: Secure HTTP*

Browsers typically communicate with web servers via HTTP (Hypertext Transfer Protocol), which is specified (among others) in RFC 7230 (Fielding and Reschke 2014). Today, many web servers respond by redirecting the browser to an HTTPS URL, which ensures that the connection between browser and server is protected against eavesdropping and tampering. Furthermore, HTTPS prevents adversaries on the network from impersonating a web server (which would allow adversaries, among others, to steal log-in credentials that are entered on web sites hosted there).

The security mechanisms of HTTPS are implemented with the Transport Layer Security (TLS) protocol. The most recent version, TLS 1.3, is specified in RFC 8446 (Rescorla 2018). This means that web servers are equipped with key pairs, which are associated with one or more domain names (e.g. www.uni-bamberg.de). The asymmetric key pair of a web server is *not* used to encrypt the actual data. The reason for this design is to provide a property known as *forward secrecy*: Even attackers that obtain the private key of a web server in the future shall not be able to learn the contents of a communication that has been observed (and stored) in the past. Therefore, the asymmetric key pair is only used to establish ephemeral symmetric session keys, which are then used to encrypt and authenticate the requests of the browser and the responses of the server.

In principle, this key establishment takes place for every new connection. This design, however, opens up a possibility for MitM attacks that aim to impersonate the destination web server. To prevent any tampering with the messages in the key establishment phase, the web server signs some of the messages with its private key. The browser can verify their integrity and authenticity with the public key of the web server. However, typically the client will not know the public key of the web server. This problem is tackled by making web servers send their public key to the client during the key establishment. However, without additional safeguards, this approach would allow MitM attackers to impersonate a web server by injecting their own key into the communication. This problem is overcome by introducing so-called *certificates*. Instead of sending the raw public key, a web server sends a certificate, which contains its public key, the domain names for which this certificate is valid, and a digital signature of a so-called Certification Authority (CA). CAs are organisations that issue certificates. A certificate is only issued to web server operators that can prove ownership of the domains to be included in the certificate. This approach prevents MitM attackers from forging certificates on the fly.

To verify the certificate presented by a web server, the browser needs the public key of the CA that issued that certificate. Browsers are equipped with the public keys of a number of large CAs by default (root certificates). If a web site uses a certificate from a different CA, the web server will include the certified public key of one or more intermediate CAs so that the browser can follow the chain of trust until one of the trusted root certificates is reached.

It is insightful to review different attacks against HTTPS. The objective of the adversary is either to eavesdrop on data in transit or to impersonate a particular web server while users attempt to connect to it, with the ultimate goal of learning sensitive pieces of information such as the passwords of users. We review two well-known attacks in the following.

The first attack, *sslstrip*, was presented by Marlinspike (2011). This attack can be conducted by adversaries that control routers, for instance, a Wi-Fi access point that is being used by a victim to connect to the Internet. Whenever the victim visits a website via HTTP, sslstrip watches the (unencrypted) HTTP response for attempts by the web server to redirect the user's browser to the secure HTTPS version. In this case, sslstrip removes the redirection from the HTTP response. As a result, the user's browser will never learn that the web server intended to serve a secure version. Many users will not notice the mishap and enter sensitive data. The adversary can trivially eavesdrop on all communication before sslstrip forwards the traffic to the web server (of course, encrypted with HTTPS, as requested by the server).

Universally preventing sslstrip attacks is not trivial because of the conservative architecture of the World Wide Web: It relies on HTTP for initial contact. As a first step, the Electronic Frontier Foundation (EFF) has released the browser extension HTTPS Everywhere that replaces all HTTP connection attempts with HTTPS for a list of websites known to support HTTPS (Electronic Frontier Foundation 2018). A more generic approach envisions that web servers indicate that they support HTTPS by adding a 'Strict Transport Security' header to their responses (Hodges et al. 2012). The information that a web server supports HTTPS is then cached by browsers for a defined amount of time, which prevents sslstrip attempts after the initial connection. The initial connection remains vulnerable as it still relies on HTTP.

The second attack on HTTPS connections exploits the fact that every CA in the root certificate store can be used to issue a certificate for any domain name and that all major browsers will trust those certificates. Given that browsers trust several hundreds of CAs, there is a substantial risk that one of them will be compromised. Several CAs have been hacked in the past, resulting in the issuance of rogue certificates. Well-known cases are the CAs TürkTrust, Comodo, and DigiNotar (Laurie 2014).

In the past, users could not make out rogue certificates and there was no affordable way for most site owners to detect that another CA has issued a certificate for their domain.

A promising approach to detect rogue certificates is the *Certificate Transparency* initiative, which requires all CAs to add every issued certificate into one of several publicly verifiable append-only log files (Laurie et al. 2013). These log files are implemented in a tamper-proof fashion so that CAs cannot retroactively lie about a certificate they have issued. Browsers will only accept certificates from CAs that participate in this programme, which serves as a strong incentive for CAs to participate. Site owners can run monitors that continuously check whether certificates for their domains have been issued by rogue CAs, which minimises the amount of time such certificates can be used for malicious purposes. However, the deployment of Certificate Transparency comes with a catch, as we discuss in Sect. 2.7.1.

## 2.5 Malware Threats and Solutions

Malicious software, malware for short, is a significant threat to information and systems security. Malware is "a program that is inserted into a system, usually covertly, with the intent of compromising the confidentiality, integrity, or availability of a victim's data, applications, or operating system or otherwise annoying or disrupting the victim" (Souppaya and Scarfone 2013). Following the approach of Stallings and Brown (2014), we discuss propagation methods and payloads. After that, we consider countermeasures.

### *2.5.1 Propagation and Delivery*

Some malware is designed to spread on its own. A well-known example is the SQL Slammer worm that infected more than 75,000 hosts over the Internet in 2003 (Moore et al. 2003). SQL Slammer exploited a buffer overflow vulnerability (cf. Sect. 2.6.1) in Microsoft's SQL Server. The vulnerable systems were reachable because the servers were not protected by a firewall (cf. Sect. 2.7.2).

Since then, the prevalence of firewalls has increased significantly. Therefore, malware authors have to rely on the help of humans for delivery. There are still some viruses around that infect files or file systems in the hope that users will exchange these with others, e.g. via USB sticks. However, most malware is now delivered via the Internet.

In the absence of vulnerabilities, the only way to infect a system consists in convincing a user to execute the malware. A typical approach consists in attaching malware to e-mails and tricking victims to execute it, exploiting their curiosity and insufficient technical expertise. Such attacks employ the same techniques that are also used for phishing. Sophisticated attackers use social engineering techniques to improve their chances, in quite the same way as so-called *spear-phishing* attacks target a particular person.

Another technique is called *drive-by download*. Here, users are tricked into visiting a website that is controlled by an attacker. The website is crafted to exploit a vulnerability (e.g. a buffer overflow, cf. Sect. 2.6.1) in the browser, ultimately forcing the browser to execute the malicious payload of the attacker. A more sophisticated variant of drive-by downloads are *malvertising* attacks (Nichols 2015). Here, attackers insert their malicious code into ads that they place on popular websites, which results in the infection of all visitors that have not patched their browser.

Adversaries that have researched their targets very well may be able to carry out a *waterholing* attack. A waterholing attack is possible if an adversary finds a way to either compromise a website that is typically visited by a victim or a server that hosts updates for software that is used by the victim. The attacker can then place the malware on this website, waiting for the victim to download it. In 2017, a state-sponsored waterholing attack was conducted by releasing a maliciously infected update for the CCcleaner tool (Amir 2017).

### 2.5.2 Payloads

Once a piece of malware is run on a target, it will execute its payload. The malware will typically deceive the user about its purpose, for instance, by exposing some benign functionality or an error. This kind of malware is called a *Trojan horse*.

In the past, the primary objective of malware was system corruption, by either deleting all files on a machine or preventing it from booting its operating system. Later on, malware authors discovered that they could exploit the fact that many users do not have backups: so-called *ransomware* encrypts the files on a system and demands the payment of a ransom in exchange for the decryption key and a tool that recovers the data.

Other payloads include key loggers to exfiltrate account credentials as well as remote control tools. Attackers that control a large number of systems can build up botnets that perform orchestrated activities such as sending out large amounts of spam e-mails or Distributed Denial of Service attacks (cf. Sect. 2.7.3).

### 2.5.3 Countermeasures

Baseline countermeasures against malware are the timely installation of security patches and user awareness training. These countermeasures try to avoid automated exploitation of known vulnerabilities and unintended execution of malware by naïve users. A typical—and if consequently followed also sensible—recommendation is to scrutinise e-mails with attachments, refraining from opening suspicious ones. However, it is difficult to spot a professionally executed spear-phishing attack.

Automated prevention of malware infections is the purpose of the so-called 'anti-virus' (AV) solutions. AV solutions monitor a system for suspicious activities that are indicative of malware. In principle, there are two approaches to decide whether a particular executable is malicious or not. The traditional method relies on malware signatures that are continually updated by the vendor. The effectiveness of signature-based AV tools is limited because they fail to detect slightly modified malware samples. In addition, AV tools increasingly rely on static and dynamic code analysis (heuristics). However, even this behaviour-based approach is not able to detect malware with 100% accuracy. Moreover, it may result in many false alerts (cf. Sect. 2.7.4).

Although widely deployed in organisations, some security practitioners are sceptical of AV tools. Firstly, professional attackers test their malware with a large number of AV tools, tweaking until it is not detected anymore. Secondly, some AV tools have been shown to introduce additional vulnerabilities (Anthony 2017a). A particularly interesting case is Windows Defender, the default AV engine of Windows, which scans all incoming e-mails for malware. Due to a vulnerability in Windows Defender, attackers could send specially crafted e-mails to victims that contained code that was automatically executed upon reception—even if the user never opened the e-mail (Anthony 2017b).

An alternative approach to AV solutions consists in executing suspicious files within a *sandbox*. Sandboxes are isolated machines instrumented with extensive monitoring capabilities. In contrast to behaviour-based AV tools, sandboxes do not have to make a real-time decision. While promising, sandboxes are no silver bullet. Malware authors have adapted to this new countermeasure; for instance, by delaying the execution of the payload until the timeout of the sandbox analysis has expired.

In some cases, it may be tempting to use active defence in order to defeat malware, for instance, by attempting to shut down its command and control infrastructure (cf. Sect. 2.3.3). Whether 'hacking back' is legal and ethically justifiable is an ongoing debate (Dittrich 2012; Schmidle 2018; see also Chap. 16). There have been incidents where interference with good intentions has caused harm. A noteworthy example is the case of the German e-mail provider Posteo that has deleted a mailbox used by the authors of the Petya ransomware (Cimpanu 2017). As a result, users who were willing to pay (or had already paid) the ransom could not get in touch with the authors any more to obtain the decryption key for their data. Initially, Posteo's decision was received critically. However, later on it was discovered that the particular variant of Petya used in the attack had been programmed to *delete* files (rather than encrypting them). Therefore, Posteo's act could be justified in the end, because no one would have gotten back their files anyway (Spring 2017).

## 2.6 Threats and Solutions in Software Security

Software security is concerned with weaknesses that result from programming errors. In the following, we present two common weaknesses, namely, buffer overflows and SQL injections. Subsequently, we discuss how vulnerabilities are found and reported to the vendors.

### *2.6.1 Case Study: Buffer Overflows*

The most dominant security weakness in applications written in C and C++ are buffer overflows (Erickson 2008). To understand how buffer overflows work and what risks they impose, we have to introduce the basic ideas of memory management in C/C++ applications. Computations usually require some storage space in the computer's main memory, namely a buffer. A buffer has a specific location in the main memory and a given size. In C/C++, software developers are responsible for ensuring that buffers are large enough for the input they should hold. Programming languages that put this burden on the software developer are said to miss a security feature called 'memory safety'.

```
1 #include <stdio.h>
2 void main(void) {
3     int privilege_level = 1;
4     char buf[124];
5     fgets(buf, 1024, stdin);
6     if(privilege_level > 10) {
7         printf("You have admin rights. Level: %d \n",
8                privilege_level);
9     }
10    printf("Your input was: %s \n", buf);
11 }
```

**Fig. 2.3** Example of a C program with a buffer overflow vulnerability

If software developers fail to allocate enough space for a buffer, they introduce a weakness into the code, a buffer overflow. An adversary can turn this weakness into a vulnerability by writing or reading outside the buffer, affecting other buffers located in the main memory, either before or after the original buffer. Modifying the content of this other buffer can influence the behaviour of the application; in particular, it may allow the adversary to execute arbitrary commands. Thus, a buffer overflow can result in the loss of confidentiality, integrity and availability.

To get the picture, consider the source code in Fig. 2.3, which reads input from the user and outputs it again. It contains an administration function that can only be activated by exploiting a buffer overflow.

Line 1 includes a common software library that makes it easier for the developer to read in user input and generate output shown to the user. In line 2, we define the main function of the program. Everything from line 3 to line 10 is part of this function and is executed in sequential order when the main function is executed; this happens at the start of the application. Line 3 defines a variable called 'privilege_level', which can store integer values. Initially, the privilege_level variable has a value of '1'. Variables allocate space in the main memory, in this case 4 bytes. Line 4 allocates 124 bytes for a buffer called 'buf', also in the main memory, next to the privilege_level variable. In line 5, the program reads a user's input from the keyboard by invoking the function 'fgets' (which is defined in the file 'stdio.h'). fgets is instructed to read up to 1024 bytes and write them into the buffer buf. However, buf can only store 124 bytes, thus introducing a buffer overflow. Line 6 checks for a condition: lines 7 and 8 only get executed if privilege_level is above 10. These lines print the user's current privilege level.

An adversary can exploit the buffer overflow to gain administrative privileges and execute lines 7 and 8. He starts the application and provides a specially crafted input. This input consists of arbitrary 124 bytes to fill buf, followed by 4 bytes with the value he wants privilege_level to have. So if he enters 'AAA...AAABBBB' (124 times 'A' followed by four 'B's), the application will print: 'You have admin rights. Level: 1111638594'. Internally, the application calls fgets on the adversary's input.

Consequently, fgets writes 128 bytes to buf. Since buf has only a size of 124 bytes, fgets continues writing to the memory location 'behind' buf, which in our example holds the value for privilege_level (the concrete locations of variables in memory depend on various factors; in our example we assume them to be as explained). Thus, privilege_level gets overwritten with four 'B's, which are consecutively interpreted as 1111638594.

We have discussed a simple example where we can spot the buffer overflow in the source code easily. However, in the source code of real-world applications, buffer overflows are more subtle, often hidden in calculations of buffer sizes. In addition, user input is not restricted to direct input on the keyboard, as in our example above. In real-world applications, buffer overflows may show up when reading image, audio, and video files, during the execution of JavaScript on web pages, and while processing network communication data.

Buffer overflows result from human mistakes. Thus, they cannot be prevented in all circumstances. Several techniques have been developed to make the exploitation of buffer overflows more difficult (e.g. Larsen and Sadeghi 2018). These techniques include data execution prevention (DEP), address space layout randomization (ASLR), stack canaries, and control-flow integrity (CFI). The diversity of defenses is the result of a cat-and-mouse game between defenders and attackers. Attackers consistently discover new ways to circumvent protections, for instance, return-oriented programming (ROP) against DEP (Buchanan et al. 2008).

### *2.6.2 Case Study: SQL Injections*

Web applications commonly store their data in SQL (Structured Query Language) databases. However, this requires careful handling of users' input to avoid so-called SQL injections (Stuttard and Pinto 2011). To understand SQL injections, we first introduce the basics of SQL-based database systems.

SQL databases store data in tables. Each table has a name and several columns. Every row holds an individual record; just as we would expect it for a table. We will consider a table named 'users' with the columns 'id', 'email', 'password' and 'last_active' (cf. Table 2.1). To query the database, we use a domain-specific language, the SQL. An SQL statement describes which data to fetch from the database.

The idea behind an SQL injection is to maliciously modify the statement, either to extract additional information from the database or to modify the behaviour of an application, e.g. to bypass a login screen. We elaborate on the latter.

**Table 2.1** A table in an SQL database that is used by an application vulnerable to SQL injections

| id | email | password | last_active |
|---|---|---|---|
| 1 | john@example.com | 3858f62230ac3c915f300c664312c63f | 2018-09-01 |
| 2 | jane@example.com | 96948aad3fcae80c08a35c9b5958cd89 | 2018-10-14 |

```
1 <?php
2 $email = $_POST['email'];
3 $pw = hash_password($_POST['password']);
4 $query = "SELECT id, last_active
5           FROM users
6           WHERE email = '$email' AND password = '$pw'";
7 $resource = $db->query($query);
8 if($resource->numRows() == 1) {
9     $user = $resource->fetchRow();
10    echo "User logged in. ID: ", $user['id'];
11 }
12 ?>
```

**Fig. 2.4** Login source code fragment of a PHP program that is vulnerable to SQL injections

We consider the program shown in Fig. 2.4, which implements a login form in PHP, a programming language often used for web applications.

Line 2 reads the e-mail address from the user input in the browser, while line 3 reads the user's password. Additionally, line 3 applies a hash function to the entered password to compare it against the value stored in the database later on. This avoids storing the password in clear text, which is considered bad practice. Lines 4–7 construct an SQL statement. There are different types of SQL statements; the most common ones are SELECT, UPDATE, INSERT and DELETE. Our statement selects certain data from the database; hence it starts with a SELECT followed by the columns we are interested in, namely 'id' and 'last_active'. However, the database system still needs to know which table we want to query, since multiple tables might use the same column names, e.g. 'id' to store a unique identifier for every record. Therefore, we use the FROM keyword to specify the table we are interested; in our case: 'users'. Now that the database system is aware of the table and its columns we wish to receive, we can apply a filter to fetch only a subset of all rows in the table. The WHERE condition on line 6 performs filtering: we state that we are only interested in rows which match the entered e-mail address and the provided password. Since e-mail addresses are unique, a correct input on the login form (consisting of e-mail address and password) will fetch exactly one row from the database, e.g. issuing the following SQL statement: SELECT id, last_active FROM users WHERE email = 'john@example.com' AND password = '38...3f'. The SQL statement is sent to the database system on line 7, while line 8 checks if exactly one row is returned. If that is the case, we execute lines 9 and 10 to read the result from the database and display the value stored in the id column of the row that matches the user's e-mail and password.

While this implementation of the login form works well for non-malicious inputs, it is prone to SQL injections and allows an adversary to bypass the login. In line 6, the application passes user input to an SQL statement without sanitising it first. We assume an adversary would enter some arbitrary password 'abc' into the password field and write the following into the e-mail address field in the login form:

'OR 1 = 1 LIMIT 1 --

```
1 <?php
2 $stmt = $db->prepare(
3     "SELECT id, last_active FROM users
4      WHERE email = ? AND password = ?")
5 $stmt->bind_param("ss", $email, $password);
6 $result = $stmt->execute();
7 ?>
```

**Fig. 2.5** PHP code with a prepared statement to protect against SQL injection attacks

This will result in a valid SQL statement, which the application sends to the database system: SELECT id, last_active FROM users WHERE email = '' OR 1 = 1 LIMIT 1 -- ' AND password = 'abc'. We briefly discuss why this SQL statement results in a successful login without knowing a password. Compared to the benign SQL statement, the adversary alters the WHERE condition and adds an additional LIMIT keyword. In SQL, two dashes followed by a space (-- ) start a comment which will be ignored by the database system. Hence, our condition only reads WHERE email ='' OR 1 = 1 and is followed by LIMIT 1. The condition is true if the e-mail is empty (which is never the case) or if 1 is equal to 1 (which is always the case). Consequently, the condition matches all rows. However, the code checks in line 8 whether the database has returned exactly one row. Hence, the adversary adds a LIMIT 1 clause to ask the database system to return only the first row matching the condition. Thus, the check on line 8 passes and line 9 receives a valid row from the 'users' table. The adversary has successfully bypassed the login without knowing a password or e-mail address. More critically, an adversary could use the same SQL injection vulnerability to steal the whole database content, using a UNION SELECT statement.

SQL injections can be prevented by using prepared statements, which address the underlying problem of SQL injections: confusion of data and code. In our example above, the e-mail address field should have been treated as data. Prepared statements explicitly separate data from code, making SQL injections impossible. To this end, the SQL statements contain placeholders rather than the actual data. The pieces of data that are inserted instead of the placeholders are sent separately to the database. The source code in Fig. 2.5 illustrates prepared statements.

Line 2–4 create a prepared statement 'stmt' using questions marks ('?') as placeholders for data. On line 5, actual values are assigned to the question marks (declaring them as two strings). After that the query is executed on line 6. The data will be used by the database system in the places marked with the placeholders.

In real-world applications, SQL injections appear especially when SQL statements are constructed dynamically, e.g. when conditions are added and removed based on the users' input. Since SQL injections are easily avoidable, their occurrence is an indicator for the lacking security education of developers.

### 2.6.3 *Finding and Handling Vulnerabilities*

Vulnerabilities can be found in applications using different methods; they may be kept secret or reported to vendors, either publicly or privately. Vendors respond in different ways to those reports and differ in their approaches to addressing the issue. Besides fixing known vulnerabilities, vendors can take preventive measures to avoid vulnerabilities in the first place or apply defence-in-depth techniques for mitigation. We elaborate on these aspects, beginning with how to find vulnerabilities and concluding on techniques for prevention and mitigation.

As seen in the previous case studies, vulnerabilities can be found by carefully reading the source code. This method is called a code audit and is typically performed by trained security auditors. Security auditors may use tools for assistance. Those tools highlight source code locations that potentially contain a vulnerability. However, false positives are quite common. These locations are reported to contain a vulnerability, although they are fine.

Furthermore, there are plenty of false negatives because it is not possible to detect all vulnerabilities automatically. Firstly, code audit tools apply heuristics, i.e. approximations of how the source code may behave; they are only as good as their heuristics are. Secondly, complete reasoning about the source code would be equivalent to deciding the halting problem,[1] which is known to be impossible (Chess and McGraw 2004). Therefore, complete reasoning is not possible. Thirdly, identifying security-related logic bugs—i.e. bugs that are highly specific to the concrete behaviour of an application—require a machine-readable specification of the application's behaviour, which in most cases does not exist. Moreover, a specification does not necessarily cover the human intent, thus being erroneous itself. Consequently, tools can never replace a security auditor in a code audit.

Performing a code audit requires access to the source code of an application. Unless an application is open source software, the source code is typically not available to external auditors, who analyse an application without being instructed by the vendor. In this case, auditors have to perform reverse engineering, i.e. understand the application's machine code, which is intended to be run by a computer and not easily understandable for humans. Even with tool support, it is impossible to recover the source code completely. Despite these hurdles, many vulnerabilities are found with reverse-engineering techniques.

[1] The halting problem asks an abstract machine model, the Turing machine, to decide whether a computer program terminates (halts) on a given input or runs forever. It is undecidable, i.e. it cannot be answered for all computer programs and inputs, despite the fact that there is a 'yes' or 'no' answer for every program and input. The Church-Turing thesis states that what humans and Turing machines can compute is equivalent. Given this thesis, humankind cannot answer all questions for which there are answers; even with unlimited computational resources (Sipser 2012).

A third technique is fuzzing. Fuzzing feeds millions of different random inputs to an application and checks for unintended behaviour such as crashes. A crash is a good indicator of the existence of a vulnerability. Inputs that lead to crashes are then stored for later analysis. To generate those inputs, a fuzzer modifies existing inputs and observes which parts of an application are executed given the modified input. To increase the likelihood of a crash, the fuzzer tries to execute all parts of an application. The motivation behind this method is to find parts that are usually not executed on expected user inputs and are therefore untested for (security) bugs. Fuzzing has proven surprisingly effective: for instance, a fuzzer found several vulnerabilities in the popular OpenVPN software even after two code audits had already been performed (Vranken 2017).

After a vulnerability is found, the security auditor may decide to keep it secret or to report it. Motivations for keeping a vulnerability secret include planned criminal actions, espionage by secret services, and accessing a suspect's device by law enforcement. In all those cases, it is likely that an exploit is developed to make use of the vulnerability. A vendor cannot fix a vulnerability as long as he is not aware of it. Thus, unreported vulnerabilities often stay unfixed for a long time. Vulnerabilities without a fix are called 'zero days' or '0-days'.

There are two approaches to the publication of vulnerabilities: full disclosure and responsible disclosure. In full disclosure, the vulnerability is disclosed in public, without notifying the vendor in advance. Advocates of full disclosure argue that all users of a vulnerable software should have the same information regarding the vulnerability to be able to assess their risks and take appropriate countermeasures until a fix is released. They accept the risk that adversaries may use the information to develop an exploit and target the users of the vulnerable software. Furthermore, proponents of full disclosure argue that full disclosure puts more pressure on the vendor to faster create and ship a fix and to care more about security in the first place.

In contrast to full disclosure, responsible disclosure (sometimes also called coordinated disclosure) mandates informing the vendor first, usually granting it a specific timeframe to release a fix before going public. The length of this embargo is a trade-off between putting pressure on the vendor and giving the vendor the opportunity to investigate the issue thoroughly, including extensive testing of the fix. A typical value is 90 days. Vendors may ask for an extension of the embargo. However, it is at the discretion of the finder to grant it. For instance, there has been a high-profile case in which security researchers working at Google have not granted Microsoft an extension (Tung 2018).

Responsible disclosure is not without flaws. Some software is distributed by different organisations that may release a fix at different times. This is the case for Linux distributions that contain thousands of different software packages. A fix released by one Linux distribution can provide information about the vulnerability, which can then be used by adversaries to attack users of other Linux distributions that have not released a fix yet. Furthermore, the more people are involved with developing and distributing a fix, the more likely it is that information about the vulnerability leaks before a fix is shipped.

Vendors should follow established best practices for adequate handling of vulnerabilities (see also Chap. 15). Firstly, they should provide a dedicated security contact on their website to ensure that vulnerability reports reach the right group within an organisation. Otherwise, support staff who are not educated in reading technical security reports might ignore those reports due to misunderstandings. In addition, it is recommended to provide a public key (cf. Sect. 2.4.3) for exchanging encrypted mails with the security contact, e.g. using OpenPGP. Secondly, the vendor should acknowledge the receipt of a vulnerability report and after investigating the issue, confirm the problem (if it is valid). Thirdly, the vendor is expected to suggest a schedule for a coordinated release of a fix and the report. Guidelines and detailed recommendations have been published by Householder et al. (2017).

Vulnerability finders invest their time to make users of the vendor's software more secure. Legal threats as a response to a report are considered immoral and may result in a Streisand effect, i.e. trying to hide or censor some information has the effect of unintentionally distributing the information more widely. Today, this often occurs through social media and results in negative publicity for the software vendor.

Instead of legal threats, the security community encourages vendors to be transparent about security problems in their products. Moreover, vendors should provide as much information as possible to allow their users to accurately assess any risks they may be exposed to. Quickly providing a fix is considered best practice. Besides, some vendors offer a bug bounty program, which provides vulnerability reporters with monetary compensation.

## 2.7 Threats and Solutions in Network Security

Many systems are interconnected over networks. This increases their exposure. In the following, we consider selected threats to networked systems.

### *2.7.1 Case Study: Reconnaissance*

Reconnaissance of the target is an essential part of sophisticated attacks. Networked systems provide a significant amount of information that can be used to launch attacks that are tailored to the environment of the victim and thus more likely to succeed.

Attackers benefit from the fact that the Internet has been designed to be an open network. For instance, information about network operators is publicly available so that system administrators of different parts of the world can communicate with each other in case of problems. This kind of information can be looked up with the so-called 'whois service', a distributed database that holds contact information about anyone who has leased IP addresses or domain names. Given some seed information such as an IP address (e.g. 141.13.240.24) or a domain name (e.g. www.uni-bamberg.de) of a target, the whois service helps attackers finding other and related systems run by the same organisation. Moreover, whois 'leaks' names and contact information of employees, which can be useful for social engineering.

Some of the information shared via whois is considered personal data and therefore protected under the General Data Protection Regulation of the European Union. As a result, the German registrar DENIC stopped unrestricted access to contact information for all '.de' domains in 2018 (DENIC eG 2018). This move considerably increases the effort for system administrators that want to contact domain owners to resolve problems (Winterfeldt 2018).

Whois is not the only system that leaks information. For instance, attackers can use the Domain Name System, which is a distributed database that maps domain names such as example.com to IP addresses. Many administrators assign telling names to their servers that help attackers understand the purpose of a system. Reverse DNS lookups allow attackers to look up these hostnames (e.g. webmail05.example.net) given the IP address of a system of interest.

Moreover, attackers can exploit two relatively new systems that aim to increase transparency, but come with an inherent security trade-off, namely Certificate Transparency (cf. Sect. 2.4.4) and Passive DNS. These systems have been created to mitigate particular security problems. However, they have the side effect of leaking sensitive information to attackers. Certificate Transparency creates transparency about all TLS certificates that are registered. Passive DNS services make available all domain names that are looked up by a group of DNS clients. Both services leak the hostnames of internal systems, helping attackers find potential targets.

Finally, attackers use port scanners to enumerate all publicly reachable hosts and services. With tools such as nmap, attackers can obtain a list of open ports and additional information such as the software that might be offering the ports as well as the operating system. If system administrators of a target have been careless or negligent, they might have forgotten to set up strict firewall rules (cf. Sect. 2.7.2) that prohibit unauthorised connection attempts to sensitive services from the outside. Although port scans are not harmful on their own, they certainly help to increase the effectiveness and efficiency of attacks.

A relatively new development is that attackers do not necessarily have to use a port scanner themselves. For an initial sweep of a target, attackers can also rely on the information provided by services such as shodan.io and censys.io. These two services continuously scan (a large part of) the Internet and make the results available on their website via a convenient full-text search engine. Their actual purpose is to help system administrators secure their networks by simplifying continuous monitoring. However, they also help attackers find improperly secured systems without having to send a single packet to a target. This dilemma makes shodan.io an interesting tool for creating awareness about vulnerable industrial control systems that are insufficiently protected (cf., e.g. Gallagher 2018).

### 2.7.2 *Case Study: Perimeter Security Via Firewalls*

Firewalls are systems that are deployed to restrict the access to services on the network layer. These services are either internal services that should not be available from outside an organisation's network or services on the Internet that should not be accessed by the employees of an organisation.

On the network, information is sent in packets. Each packet consists of a header and a payload. The payload contains the data that is being sent. The header contains information about the sender, the receiver, and the so-called ports being used. Services listen on particular ports (identified by a number between 1 and 65535). A packet is delivered to a service, if the port number stated in the packet corresponds to the port number of the service.

Most firewalls filter packets solely based on their header. To allow only access to specific services, a system administrator can configure a firewall to drop all packets that do not match a list of specific port numbers. The underlying assumption behind such firewall rules is that particular services listen on specific ports, e.g. web servers listen on port 443 (the default port for HTTPS, cf. Sect. 2.4.4) for encrypted communication. However, this assumption does not hold necessarily, since services can be reconfigured to listen on arbitrary ports.

Thus, firewalls can be bypassed using ports that are commonly allowed in the firewall's configuration, such as port 443. If users inside a corporate network want to access the Internet without any restrictions, they can run a tunnel service on a publicly reachable Internet server on port 443 and send their communication through this tunnel, which forwards it to the Internet, bypassing the firewall.

As a response to tunnel services, some firewalls check if the packets contain data for a specific service, e.g. they check if packets for port 443 actually contain HTTPS data. This technique is called Deep Packet Inspection (DPI). It is an open debate whether DPI is an acceptable practice. Opponents of DPI argue by comparing packets to postal mail: the packet's header is like the address data on the envelope and must be read by the postal service for delivery, while the packet's payload is like the letter inside the envelope. DPI looks at the payload; therefore, it is like opening the envelope of every letter, thus violating postal privacy. It is noteworthy that even DPI cannot entirely prevent users bypassing a firewall. Thus, data exfiltration prevention is another cat-and-mouse game between attackers and defenders. For example, there are sophisticated tunnelling techniques, e.g. DNS tunnels such as *iodine* (Nussbaum et al. 2009), that trick DPI solutions by hiding the exchanged data within DNS messages (which are typically not restricted by firewalls).

### 2.7.3 Case Study: Denial of Service Attacks

In a Denial of Service (DoS) attack, an adversary tries to occupy a massive amount of the victim's resources. The goal is to deny these resources to legitimate users. Typical DoS attacks either create large amounts of traffic to fill up the victim's communication lines or exhaust the victim's computational resources.

Adversaries can also instruct many machines to participate in an attack. This results in a Distributed Denial of Service (DDoS) attack. To perform a DDoS attack, an adversary compromises thousands of machines. These machines then form a so-called botnet. One of the largest botnets for DDoS attacks, called Mirai, was built using insecure Internet of Things (IoT) devices, such as routers and IP cameras. Users often employ these devices without knowing their security ramifications. Once deployed, IoT devices are often poorly maintained and seldomly receive any security updates. The Mirai botnet attacked KrebsOnSecurity, a blog maintained by the security journalist Brian Krebs, with a bandwidth of 620 GBit/s (Krebs 2016). For comparison, many commercial websites are only connected to the Internet with a bandwidth of 1 GBit/s.

One particularly intriguing type of DoS attacks are amplification attacks. In an amplification attack, an adversary uses a third party, e.g. a DNS server, to perform the attack. The DNS server responds to a small request sent by the adversary with a large answer. To attack a victim, the adversary spoofs his sender address, setting it to the address of the victim. Consequently, the DNS server receives the small request from the adversary and sends a large response to the victim. Thus, the adversary's DoS traffic is amplified by the DNS server. Spoofing the sender address is possible because Internet Service Providers do not filter the traffic of their customers properly.

DoS attacks are made possible because of externality effects. Firstly, vendors of cheap IoT devices have no incentive to provide security updates for the whole lifetime of a product. Secondly, there is virtually no reason for Internet service providers to check for address spoofing. In both cases, there is a party that is passively responsible but does not bear the costs of attacks. To improve the state of affairs, vendors and service providers have to be externally incentivised, for instance, through legal regimes.

Often, attackers use DoS attacks to force victims into paying ransoms. Online shops lose money when they are not reachable for their customers. Therefore, they will do almost anything to stop an ongoing DoS as quickly as possible. Defending against DoS attacks is difficult for server operators in practice. After all, the defender must provision more resources than the attacker can consume, which is quite costly. Therefore, there is now a market for DoS protection. Companies in this market provide large amounts of resources and filter their customer's traffic for DoS attacks. Legitimate traffic is forwarded to the customer, while DoS traffic is discarded.

### 2.7.4 Case Study: Network Intrusion Detection Systems

Network Intrusion Detection Systems (NIDS) such as Snort try to detect attacks on the network layer. They look into the packets that arrive over the network and decide whether the communication associated with the packets might be an attack. There are two different types of NIDS: signature-based and anomaly-based.

*Signature-based NIDS* can only detect attacks that are already known. They rely on a database of signatures to identify attacks. A signature describes the content of network packets that can be observed during a specific attack; for instance, there is one signature for the Heartbleed attack (http://heartbleed.com) as well as one signature for the Shellshock attack (Seltzer 2014). Thus, to detect current threats, the database of a NIDS must be updated on a regular basis.

In contrast, an *anomaly-based NIDS* analyses network communication patterns within a network. After the NIDS has learned what 'normal' communication patterns look like, the NIDS tries to detect deviations. Those anomalies are then considered to be attacks or at least unwanted behaviour. Whereas anomaly-based NIDS have the advantage that there is no database to maintain, they rely on the questionable assumption that there was no malicious activity during training. Moreover, whenever the communication patterns on the network change, e.g. because new software is introduced, the NIDS has to be retrained.

Neither signature-based nor anomaly-based NIDS can detect all threats. Their information is limited to network communication. They have no information about the inner workings of the software used on the network. For instance, communication exploiting logic bugs can be difficult or impossible to distinguish from benign communication.

Furthermore, network communication is increasingly encrypted. Encrypted traffic cannot be analysed by NIDS. This limitation can be overcome by allowing the NIDS to intercept all encrypted traffic by adding its certificate to the root certificate store on all clients. This approach, which is called TLS interception, is a very intrusive form of Deep Packet Inspection (cf. Sect. 2.7.2). TLS interception has been called into question, because it allows the administrators of the NIDS to eavesdrop on all encrypted communication. Moreover, TLS interception often decreases the actual security of encrypted communications (Waked et al. 2018).

The evaluation of the accuracy of a NIDS is not straightforward. We have to consider four metrics: the true positive rate (attacks that are detected), the false negative rate (attacks that are not detected), the false positive rate (benign communication wrongly flagged as an attack) and the true negative rate (benign communication not flagged as attack).

Even very accurate NIDS generate many false positives (false alarms) because malicious traffic is much more seldom than 'normal' traffic. This is known as the *base rate fallacy* (Axelsson 1999). Assume that 1 out of every 100,000 packets has a malicious payload (this is the base rate). Further assume that a hypothetical NIDS has an accuracy of 99.9%, which refers to the true positive rate and to the true negative rate, which are equal here. Most of the very few malicious packets will be classified correctly. However, during the reception of the 99,999 benign packets, the NIDS will generate about 100 false alarms. In other words: the operators of this hypothetical NIDS have to handle 100 times more false alarms than malicious payloads. The imbalance between false alarms and real alarms is not a theoretical problem, it is one of the most pressing issues in practical NIDS.

## 2.8 Continuous Testing

Properly securing a system means that defenders have to perform regular checks. After all, every change to the infrastructure, every update for a software package and every change in operational procedures may introduce vulnerabilities.

As described in Sect. 2.6.3, code audits can be used to detect vulnerabilities in software. Finding vulnerabilities in distributed systems is more involving. Common practices consist in running security scanners and performing penetration tests.

Security scanners such as Nessus and OpenVAS allow system operators to check their infrastructure for a wide array of known vulnerabilities by probing all devices within a defined address range. The specifics that determine how a scanner checks for a particular vulnerability are provided by the vendors of such scanners.

Whereas security scanners are typically set up by the operators of a system, penetration tests are usually conducted by specialised firms. Penetration tests are useful because they simulate a real attack. Among other things, they allow organisations to understand whether previously launched awareness campaigns on social engineering were effective and whether operators react sensibly when under pressure.

Many penetration testers use a toolkit called Metasploit (metasploit.com), which makes it possible to validate whether a particular vulnerability can be exploited—by actually exploiting it and launching a selectable payload. From an ethical perspective, Metasploit is interesting because it encapsulates exploits in ready-to-run packages, which eases the job of security analysts. Sharing exploit code is considered essential to improve security. However, in former times when exploits were shared on mailing lists, it was regarded as good practice to intentionally modify the code so that script kiddies would not be able to execute it. Metasploit has broken with this tradition, lowering the bar considerably.

Given its potential for damage, it is not surprising that there have been attempts to regulate the distribution of dual-use tools such as Metasploit (Schneier 2007; Hulme 2012). However, such a policy is mostly ineffective. Attackers will always find ways to get access to such tools. Moreover, restrictions make it difficult to use offensive tools for educational purposes, which would decrease the competence of the defenders in the long run.

## 2.9 Conclusion

In this chapter, we introduced the basic concepts and models of cybersecurity. Given the complexity of this field, there are many directions for further exploration. Nonetheless, even the basics presented in this chapter raise several ethical questions.

First, ethical issues are relevant for cybersecurity professionals, i.e. on the level of individuals. Security analysts may have to decide how they should deal with a newly discovered vulnerability. Should they only disclose it to the responsible vendor or also inform the public? If they decide to publish it, which details should be made available before the vulnerability is fixed? On the one hand, publishing too much or too early might cause significant harm. On the other hand, keeping the vulnerability secret prevents users of the vulnerable product from taking action on their own, and it decreases the vendor's incentive to actually ship a fix in a timely manner. This is only one example where the actual outcomes of various alternatives are difficult to predict, which is why there is no consensus about vulnerability disclosure in the community (more in Chaps. 3 and 4).

Ethical issues are also encountered on an organisational level. Most organisations struggle with finding a justifiable balance between investing in security and accepting the remaining risks. Security cannot be bought from the shelf because organisations have different needs. Moreover, effective security relies on humans—and humans tend to act (or fail) in surprising ways. Organisations may also be inclined to exploit power asymmetries that allow them to externalise their costs by transferring risks to users or other unrelated parties.

Finally, ethical issues also arise on an architectural level. It is challenging to predict how a new system or security mechanism will be used. This is particularly an issue for dual-use tools whose impact on security depends on the intentions of the actor. Another example is Certificate Transparency, which has been designed to solve a particular security issue. However, it can also be misused for reconnaissance. Of course, this kind of exploitation was foreseeable for experts, but it still startles system administrators whose internal hosts are now exposed in a public database. Building useful systems with limited misuse potential is a challenging problem for which we do not yet have readily available solutions.

Tackling ethical questions in the field of cybersecurity is difficult due to its very nature: We usually have to make decisions based on insufficient information. We often do not fully understand the consequences of turning a particular lever and systems exhibit surprising (emergent) behaviour once users (and creative adversaries) lay their hands on them. In rare cases, we may be able to collect some facts (e.g. by studying past events); however, it is questionable whether these are still applicable. After all, cybersecurity is an endless cat-and-mouse game with constantly changing rules.

**Acknowledgements** The chapter was created with funding from the European Commission (H2020-700540 CANVAS). The authors are grateful to Stephanie Loreck and Oleg Geier for comments on a draft of this chapter.

## References

Amir W (2017) CCleaner backdoor attack: a state-sponsored espionage campaign. https://www.hackread.com/ccleaner-backdoor-attack-a-state-sponsored-espionage-campaign/. Last access 7 July 2019

Anderson JP (1972) Information security in a multi-user computer environment. Adv Comput 12:1–36

Anthony S (2017a) It might be time to stop using antivirus. https://arstechnica.com/information-technology/2017/01/antivirus-is-bad/. Last access 7 July 2019

Anthony S (2017b) Massive vulnerability in Windows Defender leaves most Windows PCs vulnerable. https://arstechnica.com/information-technology/2017/05/windows-defender-nscript-remote-vulnerability/. Last access 7 July 2019

Axelsson S (1999) The base-rate fallacy and its implications for the difficulty of intrusion detection. In: Proceedings of the 6th ACM conference on computer and communications security, CCS '99. ACM, New York, pp 1–7

Buchanan E, Roemer R, Shacham H et al (2008) When good instructions go bad: generalizing return-oriented programming to RISC. In: Ning P, Syverson PF, Jha S (eds) Proceedings of the 2008 ACM conference on computer and communications security, CCS 2008, Alexandria, Virginia, USA, October 27–31, 2008, ACM New York, pp 27–38

Chan CS (2012) Complexity the worst enemy of security. https://www.schneier.com/news/archives/2012/12/complexity_the_worst.html. Last access 7 July 2019

Chess B, McGraw G (2004) Static analysis for security. Secur Priv 2(6):76–79

Cimpanu C (2017) E-mail provider shuts down Petya Inbox Preventing Victims from re-covering files. https://www.bleepingcomputer.com/news/security/email-provider-shuts-down-petya-inbox-preventing-victims-from-recovering-files/. Last access 7 July 2019

Cimpanu C (2018) Popular Android Apps vulnerable to man-in-the-disk attacks. https://www.bleepingcomputer.com/news/security/popular-android-apps-vulnerable-to-man-in-the-disk-attacks/. Last access 7 July 2019

DENIC eG (2018) Extensive changes planned for DENIC Whois domain query: proactive approach for data economy and data protection. https://www.denic.de/en/whats-new/press-releases/article/extensive-innovations-planned-for-denic-whois-domain-query-proactive-approach-for-data-economy-and/. Last access 7 July 2019

Dittrich D (2012) So You Want to Take Over a Botnet… In: Kirda E (ed) 5th USENIX workshop on large-scale exploits and emergent threats, LEET '12, San Jose, CA, USA, April 24, 2012 Berkeley USENIX Association. https://www.usenix.org/conference/leet12. Last access 7 July 2019

Electronic Frontier Foundation (2018) HTTPS everywhere. https://www.eff.org/https-everywhere. Last access 7 July 2019

Engel G (2014) Deconstructing The Cyber Kill Chain. https://www.darkreading.com/attacks-breaches/deconstructing-the-cyber-kill-chain/a/d-id/1317542. Last access 7 July 2019

Erickson J (2008) Hacking: the art of exploitation, 2nd edn. No Starch Press, San Francisco

Fielding R, Reschke J (2014) Hypertext Transfer Protocol (HTTP/1.1): message syntax and routing. Request for comments, RFC 7230. https://tools.ietf.org/html/rfc7230. Last access 7 July 2019

Francillon A, Danev B, Capkun S (2011) Relay attacks on passive keyless entry and start systems in modern cars. In: Network distributed system security. The Internet Society, NDSS, Reston

Gallagher S (2018) Vulnerable industrial controls directly connected to Internet? Why not?. https://arstechnica.com/information-technology/2018/01/the-internet-of-omg-vulnerable-factory-and-power-grid-controls-on-internet/. Last access 7 July 2019

Gollmann D (2011) Computer security, 3rd edn. Wiley, Chichester

Greenberg A (2017) Just a pair of these $11 radio gadgets can steal a car. https://www.wired.com/2017/04/just-pair-11-radio-gadgets-can-steal-car/. Last access 7 July 2019

Hodges J, Jackson C, Barth A (2012) HTTP Strict Transport Security (HSTS). Request for comments, RFC 6797. https://tools.ietf.org/html/rfc6797. Last access 7 July 2019

Householder AD, Wassermann G, Manion A et al (2017) The CERT® guide to coordinated vulnerability disclosure. Special report CMU/SEI-2017-SR-022, Carnegie Mellon University, CERT Division

Hulme GV (2012) Metasploit review: ten years later, are we any more secure? https://searchsecurity.techtarget.com/feature/Metasploit-Review-Ten-Years-Later-Are-We-Any-More-Secure. Last access 7 July 2019

Hutchins EM, Cloppert MJ, Amin RM (2011) Intelligence-driven computer network defence informed by analysis of adversary campaigns and intrusion kill chains. Lead Issue Inf Warf Secur Res 1:80

Korolov M (2018) What is a supply chain attack? Why you should be wary of third-party providers. https://www.csoonline.com/article/3191947/data-breach/what-is-a-supply-chain-attack-why-you-should-be-wary-of-third-party-providers.html. Last access 7 July 2019

Krebs B (2016) KrebsOnSecurity hit with record DDoS. https://krebsonsecurity.com/2016/09/krebsonsecurity-hit-with-record-ddos/. Last access 7 July 2019

Langner R (2013) To kill a centrifuge: a technical analysis of what Stuxnet's creators tried to achieve. https://www.langner.com/wp-content/uploads/2017/03/to-kill-a-centrifuge.pdf. Last access 7 July 2019

Larsen P, Sadeghi AR (eds) (2018) The continuing arms race: code-reuse attacks and defences. Association for Computing Machinery and Morgan & Claypool, New York

Laurie B (2014) Certificate transparency. Queue 12(8):10:10–10:19

Laurie B, Langley A, Kasper E (2013) Certificate transparency. Request for comments, RFC 6962. https://tools.ietf.org/html/rfc6962. Last access 7 July 7 2019

Marlinspike M (2011) sslstrip. https://moxie.org/software/sslstrip/. Last access 7 July 2019

McConnell S (2004) Code complete: a practical handbook of software construction, 2nd edn. Microsoft Press, Redmond

Moore D, Paxson V, Savage S et al (2003) Inside the Slammer Worm. IEEE Secur Priv 1(4):33–39

Nichols S (2015) You've been Drudged! Malware-squirting ads appear on websites with 100+ million visitors. https://www.theregister.co.uk/2015/08/14/malvertising_expands_drudge/. Last access 7 July 2019

Nussbaum L, Neyron P, Richard O (2009) On robust covert channels inside DNS. In: Gritzalis D, López J (eds) Emerging challenges for security, privacy and trust, 24th IFIP TC 11 international information security conference, SEC 2009, Pafos, Cyprus, May 18–20, 2009. Proceedings, IFIP Advances in Information and Communication Technology, vol 297. Springer, Berlin/New York, pp 51–62

Pfleeger CP, Pfleeger SL, Margulies J (2015) Security in computing, 5th edn. Prentice Hall Press, Upper Saddle River

Rescorla E (2018) The Transport Layer Security (TLS) Protocol Version 1.3. Request for comments, RFC 8446. https://tools.ietf.org/html/rfc8446. Last access 7 July 2019

Saltzer JH, Schroeder MD (1975) The protection of information in computer systems. Proc IEEE 63(9):1278–1308

Schmidle N (2018) The digital vigilantes who hack back. https://www.newyorker.com/magazine/2018/05/07/the-digital-vigilantes-who-hack-back. Last access 7 July 2019

Schneier B (2007) New German hacking law. https://www.schneier.com/blog/archives/2007/08/new_german_hack.html. Last access 7 July 2019

Seals T (2018) Bluetooth bug allows man-in-the-middle attacks on phones, laptops. https://threatpost.com/bluetooth-bug-allows-man-in-the-middle-attacks-on-phones-laptops/134332/. Last access 7 July 2019

Seltzer L (2014) Shellshock makes Heartbleed look insignificant. https://www.zdnet.com/article/shellshock-makes-heartbleed-look-insignificant/. Last access 7 July 2019

Sheridan K (2018) The cyber kill chain gets a makeover. https://www.darkreading.com/threat-intelligence/the-cyber-kill-chain-gets-a-makeover/d/d-id/1332892. Last access 7 July 2019

Shirey R (2007) Internet security glossary, Version 2. Request for comments, RFC 4949. https://tools.ietf.org/html/rfc4949. Last access 7 July 2019

Shostack A (2014) Threat modeling: designing for security, 1st edn. Wiley, Indianapolis

Sipser M (2012) Introduction to the theory of computation, 3rd. Cengage Learning, Boston

Smith R (2012) A contemporary look at Saltzer and Schroeder's 1975 design principles. IEEE Secur Priv 10(6):20–25
Souppaya M, Scarfone K (2013) Guide to malware incident prevention and handling for desktops and laptops. NIST Special Publication SP Gaithersburg 800–883
Spitzner L (2002) Honeypots: tracking hackers. Addison-Wesley Longman Publishing Co., Inc., Boston
Spring T (2017) ExPetr called a Wiper Attack, not Ransomware. https://threatpost.com/expetr-called-a-wiper-attack-not-ransomware/126614/. Last access 7 July 2019
Stallings W, Brown L (2014) Computer security: principles and practice, 3rd edn. Prentice Hall Press, Upper Saddle River
Stuttard D, Pinto M (2011) The web application Hacker's handbook: finding and exploiting security flaws, 2nd edn. Wiley, New York
Tung L (2018) Google's Project Zero exposes unpatched Windows 10 lockdown bypass. https://www.zdnet.com/article/googles-project-zero-reveals-windows-10-lockdown-bypass/. Last access 7 July 2019
Voydock VL, Kent ST (1983) Security mechanisms in high-level network protocols. ACM Comput Surv 15(2):135–171
Vranken G (2017) The OpenVPN post-audit bug bonanza. https://guidovranken.com/2017/06/21/the-openvpn-post-audit-bug-bonanza/. Last access 7 July 2019
Waked L, Mannan M, Youssef A (2018) To intercept or not to intercept: analyzing TLS interception in network appliances. In: Proceedings of the 2018 on Asia conference on computer and communications security, ASIACCS, vol 18. ACM, New York, pp 399–412
Walker J (2018) Cybersecurity company hit by man-in-the-middle attack. http://www.digitaljournal.com/tech-and-science/technology/cybersecurity-company-hit-by-man-in-the-middle-attack/article/510402. Last access 7 July 2019
Wheeler T (2018) In cyberwar, there are no rules. https://foreignpolicy.com/2018/09/12/in-cyber-war-there-are-no-rules-cybersecurity-war-defence/. Last access 7 July 2019
Winterfeldt B (2018) The fight is on to save access to WHOIS: a call to action for brand owners. http://www.circleid.com/posts/20180419_fight_is_on_to_save_access_to_whois_call_to_action_brand_owners/. Last access 7 July 2019
Zetter K (2016) Inside the cunning, unprecedented hack of Ukraine's power grid. https://www.wired.com/2016/03/inside-cunning-unprecedented-hack-ukraines-power-grid/. Last access 7 July 2019

# Chapter 3
# Core Values and Value Conflicts in Cybersecurity: Beyond Privacy Versus Security

**Ibo van de Poel**

**Abstract** This chapter analyses some of the main values, and values conflicts, in relation to cybersecurity by distinguishing four important value clusters that should be considered when deciding on cybersecurity measures. These clusters are security, privacy, fairness and accountability. Each cluster consists of a range of further values, which can be viewed as articulating specific moral reasons relevant when devising cybersecurity measures. In addition to the four value clusters, domain-specific values that are served by computer systems, such as health, are important. Following a detailed discussion of the four relevant value clusters, potential value conflicts and value tensions are considered. The relationships of five pairs of values (privacy-security, privacy-fairness, privacy-accountability, security-accountability and security-fairness) are analysed in terms of whether they are largely supportive or conflicting. In addition, possible methods for addressing these potential value conflicts are discussed. It is concluded that values, and value conflicts, in cybersecurity should be considered in context, also taking into account the specific computer systems at play, to enable the use of nuanced and fine-grained methods for addressing the relevant value conflicts.

**Keywords** Accountability · Fairness · Privacy · Security · Value conflict · Values

## 3.1 Introduction

Moral dilemmas in cybersecurity are often framed in terms of privacy versus security. If we want to avoid illegal access to ICT (Information and Communication Technology) systems through hacks, cybercrime or cyberwarfare, we need to be willing to accept the monitoring of Internet traffic and hence give up (some) privacy, so the suggestion goes. Although we may indeed sometimes be confronted with

I. van de Poel (✉)
Department Values, Technology and Innovation, School of Technology, Policy and Management, TU Delft, Delft, The Netherlands
e-mail: i.r.vandepoel@tudelft.nl



M. Christen et al. (eds.), *The Ethics of Cybersecurity*, The International Library of Ethics, Law and Technology 21,
https://doi.org/10.1007/978-3-030-29053-5_3

such dilemmas, the privacy versus security tension, as a general framing of moral issues in cybersecurity, is too simplistic. Privacy and security are not always in conflict but are sometimes mutually reinforcing. Whether privacy and security are conflicting or supportive depends on the specific context or application being considered. Moreover, it depends on technical and design choices that can also be made differently so that the conflict can sometimes be designed out. The privacy versus security framing is also too simplistic in that it ignores the fact that a range of other values are at stake in cybersecurity.

The aim of the chapter is twofold. First, it sets out to develop a coherent and comprehensive account of the main values relevant to cybersecurity. This concerns both the values at stake when cybersecurity is somehow compromised as well as those values that should be considered when devising (technical or institutional) measures to maintain or increase cybersecurity. Second, the chapter aims to shed more light on value conflicts in cybersecurity and the possible methods for addressing such conflicts.

The chapter begins with a philosophical clarification of the notion of value. Values are understood as evaluative dimensions that can be used to evaluate the goodness of certain state-of-affairs. Different values thus correspond to different varieties of goodness. In addition, values are conceived as arising in response to certain morally problematic situations, or certain moral concerns. Therefore, they correspond to certain moral reasons (for or against certain actions). This understanding of values allows several value clusters to be discerned in relation to cybersecurity. A value cluster is here understood as a number of values which are a response to similar types of moral concerns and express similar moral reasons. It is argued that, in relation to cybersecurity, four values cluster can be discerned: security, privacy, fairness and accountability.

After addressing these value clusters in more detail, the chapter discusses value conflicts. A value conflict is understood as a situation in which it is not possible to fully realise or respect a range of relevant values simultaneously. Value conflicts are thus practical conflicts, as opposed to values contradicting each other at a general or abstract level. Identifying value conflicts requires a consideration of the specific application or context. Moreover, whether values conflict depends on what is technically possible and what design choices have been made. I discuss some of the main value conflicts in cybersecurity and possible methods to address them.

## 3.2 Values and Value Clusters

### *3.2.1 What Are Values?*

Although the notion of 'value' is generally used in philosophy and the social sciences, there does not seem to be a generally accepted definition of what values are. In general, values are associated with what is *good* and *desirable,* and they are often believed to provide people with a certain orientation for how to behave. Within this general characterisation, additional conceptions of values are possible.

In the social sciences, values are often associated with attitudes, preferences and interests, and are usually seen as subjective (Williams Jr. 1968; Rokeach 1973; Schwartz and Bilsky 1987). Here, I employ a more philosophical understanding of values, in which values are associated with what is *good*. So conceived, the notion of value can refer to what is good (ontology), or what we belief (epistemology) or express (semantics) to be good (Hirose and Olson 2015). Values help to evaluate certain state-of-affairs in terms of goodness, and different values can therefore be understood as varieties of goodness (von Wright 1963). For example, computer systems may be evaluated in terms of the values of privacy and cybersecurity, by which each constitute a different variety of the goodness of such systems.

Values belong to the evaluative domain of the normative, whereas norms and reasons belong to the deontic domain of the normative (Stocker 1990; Dancy 1993; Raz 1999). The evaluative refers to the normative evaluations we make of state-of-affairs or persons (in terms of goodness). Conversely, the deontic refers to the reasons we have for doing certain things (or refraining from doing them) or to what we should do. The deontic is concerned with rightness (of actions) whereas the evaluative is concerned with goodness (of state-of-affairs).

Since values are evaluative, they are not directly action guiding. Nevertheless, it is often believed that there is a correspondence between values and reasons (for action) of the following kind (cf. Scanlon 1998; Raz 1999):

> *V: If x is a value (or a valuable object) then one has reasons (of a certain kind) for a positive response (a pro-attitude or a pro-behaviour) towards x*

For example, if cybersecurity is a value, we might have reason to increase it through technical and institutional measures; and if privacy is also a value, we might have reason to respect the privacy of computer users in devising such cybersecurity measures. Increasing and respecting are both positive responses.

Statement V is intended to be neutral with respect to the question of whether values ground reasons (as consequentialists typically believe) or reasons ground values (as deontologists typically hold) or that neither can be reduced to the other. As Dancy (2005) notes, whatever position one takes in this debate, something like statement V seems to be true.

It should be stressed that the above account of values does not assume consequentialist ethics. Deontologists may also employ the notion of value, although values may have a different epistemological and ontological status for them than for consequentialists; for the former, values typically follow from reasons (and other deontic concepts such as norms) rather than the other way around (cf. Anderson 1993).

In this respect, it is also important to stress that the positive response mentioned in statement V can take another form than just increasing or maximising the value x. Consequentialists often believe not only that the goodness of the outcomes (consequences) of actions determine the rightness of actions but also that right actions increase or even maximise the 'amount' of value or goodness. Although increasing or maximising a value can be termed a positive response (or a pro-behaviour), it is certainly not the only possible positive response. Values can, for example, also be *respected;* and a valuable object can be *admired.* Respect and admiration are also positive responses, but they do not have the consequentialist overtone that increasing or maximising value has.

What the appropriate positive response to a value (or a valuable object) is depends both on the value at stake as well on the specific context. For example, in some contexts, we might have reason to maximise privacy, whereas in other contexts it may be sufficient to respect a certain minimal amount of privacy. The proper response to a value in a specific context is often not prima facie obvious; it may require judgment and deliberation.

### 3.2.2 Value Clusters

If values are varieties of goodness, it seems natural to assume that there exists a plurality of values. Some philosophers have, nevertheless, maintained that there is one overarching value, such as human happiness or human dignity, to which all other values can be related or even reduced; a doctrine known as value monism. Here, I assume that the opposite thesis of value pluralism is true; i.e. there exists a variety of values which cannot be reduced to each other (Mason 2018).

A next question that arises is whether there is a limit to the number of values we can discern or whether it is in principle always possible to discern additional values. One reason to think that there is no limit to the number of values we can discern is that we can almost always make values more specific. For example, starting from the very general and abstract value of security, we can distinguish between individual and collective security. Next, individual security can be further divided between, for example, physical and psychological individual security. This process can go on for quite a while. We might even want to argue that the value of security of person X is not exactly the same value as the security of person Y. In other words, if we zoom in on specific values, and on the specific contexts in which we use value terms, it seems we could almost endlessly discern more specific values.

My aim in this contribution is to discern and analyse the core values in cybersecurity. This is, by its nature, an exercise on a rather general and abstract level. The goal is to come to a set of general values that may require further specification when applying them in specific contexts but that nevertheless provide some insight into the moral concerns and problems that might arise in relation to cybersecurity. However, even at this general level, we might distinguish a large number of different values. For example, in the literature study we conducted for the CANVAS project[1] we found a large number of value terms in the domains of health, business and national security in relation to cybersecurity (Yaghmaei et al. 2017).

---

[1] See https://canvas-project.eu/canvas/

To create more order in this multiplicity of relevant values, I propose introducing the notion of 'value cluster'. A value cluster is a range of values that express somewhat similar moral concerns. In line with the above-proposed characterisation of values, values in a value cluster correspond to similar moral reasons for action, or to similar norms. Moreover, the values that are part of one value cluster are typically articulated in response to somewhat similar morally problematic situations. It should be stressed that I use the notion of value cluster here relative to a particular domain or societal activity. In this case, the domain is cybersecurity and the value clusters I distinguish are defined in relation to cybersecurity.

## 3.3 Value Clusters in Cybersecurity

A first value cluster in relation to cybersecurity is that of *security*. Security can be understood in a number of more specific ways, pinpointing different more specific values that are part of this cluster, such as individual security or national security. In this cluster, I also locate the value of cybersecurity and a range of values closely related, or instrumental, to cybersecurity such as information security, and the confidentiality, integrity and availability of (computer) data. The main reasons to which this value cluster corresponds are the protection of humans and other valuable entities against all kinds of harm. The values in this cluster may be seen as a response to morally problematic situations in which harm is (potentially) done, ranging from data breaches and loss of data integrity to cybercrime and cyberwarfare.

A second relevant value cluster is *privacy*. This cluster contains, in addition to privacy, such values as moral autonomy, human dignity, identity, personhood, liberty, anonymity and confidentiality. Values in this cluster correspond to reasons (and norms), for example we should treat others with dignity, we should respect people's moral autonomy, we should not store or share personal data without people's informed consent, and we should not use people (or data about them) as a means to an end. Typically morally problematic situations to which these values are a response include the secret collection of large amounts of personal data for cybersecurity purposes or the unauthorised transfer of personal data to a third party.

A third cluster is *fairness*. This consists of values such as justice, fairness, equality, accessibility, freedom from bias, non-discrimination, democracy and the protection of civil liberties. This cluster of values is a response to the fact that cybersecurity threats, or measures to avoid such threats, do not affect everyone equally, which may sometimes be morally unfair. Another type of moral problem is: These values are a response to the fact that cybersecurity threats, or measures to increase cybersecurity, may sometimes undermine democracy, or civil rights and liberties. Important moral reasons that correspond to this value cluster are that people should be treated fairly and equally, and that democratic and civil rights should be upheld.

The fourth and final value cluster I distinguish is that of *accountability*. Values in this cluster include transparency, openness and explainability. This value cluster is relevant because cybersecurity measures taken by, for example, governments can potentially harm others, such as citizens, which requires accountability. Accountability, as a more procedural value, is particularly relevant because cybersecurity measures often require the weighing of a range of conflicting substantive values (such as security, privacy and fairness). Typical reasons to which the value of accountability is related include the obligation to account for one's actions but also being blamed for unjustified behaviour or paying damages, or a fine, for the harm that arises from unjustified behaviour.

In addition to the four value clusters, there are values connected to specific applications for which cybersecurity is an issue. These values are *domain-specific*. Examples are values such as health (in the medical domain) or national security. Although these values are different from domain to domain, and sometimes even from application to application, they are connected to a range of more instrumental or technical values related to the proper functioning of applications. I include here more specific values such as efficiency, ease of use, understandability, data availability, reliability, compatibility and connectivity. These technical values are nevertheless often morally relevant as they are frequently instrumental, if not essential, for achieving specific moral values.

### *3.3.1 Security*

The first value cluster is that of security. Below, I propose a general conceptualisation of the value of security that indicates how cybersecurity can be seen as a specific kind of security, roughly understood as the state of computer systems being free from cyber threats. There are, however, many varieties of security, some of which are also directly relevant for the discussion about cybersecurity. These include, for example, personal or individual security but also national security, or the security of certain businesses (cf. Kleinig et al. 2011). It is important to realise that these different, more specific types of security often correspond to distinct values that may conflict with each other on occasion. Nevertheless, the various security values may be said to belong to one value cluster. This is the case not only because they all fit the same general conceptualisation of security, but also because they are all responses to similar morally problematic situations, i.e. situations in which something valuable is threatened by an external danger. Moreover, they also all correspond to similar moral reasons, i.e. moral reasons for protecting what is of value against an external threat or danger.

In very general terms, security may be understood as follows:

> *Security is the state of being free from danger or threat*

Often we speak about the security of a certain entity X from a specific type or kind of danger Y. In such cases, the following general characterisation seems to apply:

> *The security of X from Y is the state of an entity X being free from danger or threat of kind Y*

Here, X can refer to an individual agent, a person, but also to collective social entities such as an organization, a business or a state. X may also refer to a technical system, such as a computer system. Depending on X, we can thus distinguish more specific types of security such as personal security, national security and computer security.

Y can refer to specific types of danger or threat. For example, when we talk about personal physical security, Y refers to physical dangers or threats (to individuals). In the case of national security, Y may refer to, for example, terrorist attacks or an invasion by a foreign country, but nowadays also to (foreign) cyberattacks.

Two further remarks are necessary regarding this general characterisation. First, sometimes a distinction is made between the values of safety and security along the following lines: safety is protection against accidental or unintentional danger (e.g. a collapsing bridge or an earthquake), whereas security is protection against intended harm (e.g. theft or a terrorist attack) (Hansson 2009). The above characterisation does not follow this distinction but rather subsumes it under one general concept of security. This follows the conventional manner of discussing cybersecurity. For example, according to the 2016 EU scoping paper, "Cybersecurity refers to the protection of networks and information systems against human mistakes, natural disasters, technical failures or malicious attacks" (Scientific Advice Mechanism High Level Group 2016: 2). This includes, obviously, unintentional as well as intentional harm.

Second, this characterisation stresses the absence of danger or threat. We might argue that this is only part of the story as security—in particular personal or individual security—may also be understood as a certain peace of mind and the presence of preconditions in which people can live a meaningful and happy life (cf. Kleinig et al. 2011; Waldron 2011). Following the well-known distinction between negative and positive freedom (Berlin 1958), a similar distinction could perhaps be made between negative and positive security here.[2] For the current purpose, I adhere to the negative ("absence of") characterisation of security, as that seems most important when it comes to cybersecurity. Nevertheless, the positive aspect seems important for understanding the moral importance of the value of security in certain contexts, as we will see.

Now that we have a general characterisation of the value of security, we may inquire into the moral importance of this value. Philosophers often make a distinction between instrumental and intrinsic values (e.g. Frankena 1973). Instrumental values are merely valuable because they contribute to something that is valuable, whereas intrinsic values are believed to be good in themselves.[3] In the literature

[2] The positive connotation is, for example, also present in a notion such as food security, which does not primarily refer to the absence of danger or threat (famine) but rather to the availability of (enough) food. Similarly, we might understand cybersecurity as the presence of reliable computer and network infrastructure, although most current definitions stress the absence of, or protection against, certain dangers and threats.

[3] Intrinsic values are also sometimes called final or terminal values, while instrumental values are also sometimes called extrinsic. The different terminologies may not always trace the same distinction (cf. Korsgaard 1983).

review conducted for the CANVAS project, cybersecurity was in most cases described as an instrumental value (Yaghmaei et al. 2017). The reason for this seems quite obvious. Computer systems are not valuable in themselves but because of the functions they fulfil in society, or for individuals and groups, and because of the economic value they represent. Computer systems may also be used for bad purposes, and, in such cases, cybersecurity may even be deemed undesirable.

A value that is closely related to cybersecurity is information security. This value is often understood in terms of the confidentiality, integrity and availability of information. For example, according to the Information Systems Audit and Control Association (ISACA), information security "[e]nsures that … information is protected against disclosure to unauthorised users (confidentiality), improper modification (integrity), and non-access when required (availability)" (ISACA 2016). Confidentiality can be understood as being instrumental to privacy, as it prevents unauthorised access to information, which is often essential in maintaining privacy. The integrity and availability of information are instrumental for the (original) purpose of the information system by ensuring that required information is reliably available and accurate. This seems to suggest that information security is merely an instrumental value. Whereas cybersecurity may be more encompassing than information security—it may, for example, also relate to security from unauthorised access to cyberphysical systems (such as the energy grid or a water barrier)—the above seems to support the thesis that cybersecurity is mainly an instrumental value.

However, even if cybersecurity is an instrumental value, we should be careful in drawing too strong conclusions about its moral importance. If we consider, for example, cybersecurity threats to heart monitoring devices in hospitals or aviation systems then in both cases, a lack of cybersecurity may lead to a loss of human lives. In similar ways, cybersecurity is important for the protection of a large number of human and moral values. What these values are depends on the specific technical application and context. However, for some contexts, it would be a misunderstanding to think that cybersecurity is devoid of moral importance just because it is an instrumental value, as in those contexts cybersecurity may be a *sine qua non* for upholding other values with great moral importance, including values of personal security and health. As Dewey (1922) already highlighted in his criticism of the distinction between instrumental and intrinsic values, such distinctions tend to uncritically reify the gap between means and ends; what is a means in one context may well be an end in another (and vice versa).

Whereas cybersecurity is usually seen as instrumental value, several authors have argued that personal (or individual) security is an intrinsic value (e.g. Himma 2016). The main argument for this seems to be that without some degree of personal security, individual people do not have a life at all, let alone a meaningful and happy one. This appears to show that some degree of security is required for individuals to live a good life. However, it is not obvious that this is enough to make security an intrinsic value. We might also argue that it is merely an enabling value (Raz 2003); i.e. a value that is necessary for people to have a meaningful life and to acquire other values. The reason why security understood as the mere absence of threat may not be an intrinsic value is that a life that merely consists of the absence of threat seems hardly worth living; it is only when people start to do other valuable things that such a life becomes worthwhile.

Whereas there are good reasons to think of personal security as an intrinsic or at least an enabling value, this is less clear from more collectivist notions of security such as national security or business and organisational security. These would seem to be instrumental values, as their moral importance is derived from how they help support other values such as personal security.[4] Moreover, discussions of national security may create a slippery slope, as it allows certain political groups the possibility to claim the moral importance of certain restrictive measures that in practice restrict individual values, including personal security, rather than support them. At the same time, it is clear that some degree of national security is required to ensure personal security. Nevertheless, collectivist notions of security such as national security seem to derive their moral importance from how they eventually impact the security, but also other values such as privacy or liberty, of individuals rather than being intrinsically valuable (cf. Waldron 2011).

### *3.3.2 Privacy*

Privacy is generally seen as an important value in relation to cybersecurity. There is, however, no agreement on how exactly to understand and conceptualise the value of privacy (Moore 2003). Proposed understandings include such notions as "the right to be let alone" (Warren and Brandeis 1890), "informational control" (Westin 1967), an extension of personality and personhood (Pound 1915) and an act of self-care (Allen 2016). Privacy also has several dimensions. Koops et al. (2017) distinguish between bodily, intellectual, spatial, decisional, communicational, associational, proprietary and behavioural privacy and view informational privacy as crosscutting through these categories.

Where cybersecurity is concerned, privacy is usually understood in informational terms. Such informational privacy is about what information about a person is (not) known to, or shared with, others. A further distinction is between notions of privacy stressing the *confidentiality* or *secrecy* of data (and information) and those stressing *control* over what data (or information) is shared with whom. If the first understanding is adhered to, it might be best not to collect and store personal data in the first place to enhance privacy (Warnier et al. 2015). Obviously, that will often be neither possible nor desirable (for other reasons). According to the control conception of privacy, the collecting, storing and sharing of data is not always problematic, rather privacy is about giving people control over the collection, storage and sharing of their own personal data. Here, the notion of 'informed consent' is important. Informed consent means that the collecting, storing and sharing of personal data

[4] A similar stance has been taken by the approach to national and international security known as 'human security'; see e.g. Gregoratti (2013).

require the deliberate and informed consent of the data subject. People may thus also deliberately decide to share information about themselves with others. For both the confidentiality and the control notion, privacy breaches may result from unauthorised access to data and, in this sense, cybersecurity is instrumental, if not crucial, to protecting privacy.

What information is appropriate to share with whom may not only be dependent on the autonomous choices of individuals (as the control notion of privacy stresses) but also be different for various social spheres. The question of what is appropriate to share with an employer is different from what information can appropriately be shared with a physician or spouse. This idea is captured in the notion of privacy as contextual integrity (Nissenbaum 2004).

Some authors have argued that privacy is an intrinsic value, whereas others see it primarily as an instrumental one (e.g. Kleinig et al. 2011; Himma 2016). Those who tend to see it as an intrinsic value may point out that some degree of privacy is indispensable for (moral) autonomy. If one's thoughts and actions are continuously known to others, it will undermine one's capacity to decide and act in a morally autonomous way. Since moral autonomy is crucial for human agency and human dignity, some minimal degree of privacy is required to live a good life. Those who conceive of privacy as an instrumental value may object that what is valued here is not so much privacy in itself but rather what it allows or enables. The relationship between privacy and the ability to live a morally worthwhile life may in this respect not be so different from that between personal security and a good life, as discussed before. We might therefore conceive of privacy as an enabling value, i.e. as a value that is necessary as a precondition for a good life, but one that is not necessarily itself intrinsically valuable; however it is also not a mere instrumental value in the sense that it cannot be replaced by others means and is indispensable for living a worthwhile life.

A somewhat related debate is the one between authors who adhere to reductionist accounts of privacy and those who provide non-reductionist accounts (Katell and Moore 2016). According to reductionist accounts, the moral importance of privacy is based on other values such as autonomy, human dignity and liberty. In the final analysis, there is nothing that the value of privacy adds to the relevant moral considerations and reasons that cannot already be derived from those others values. Privacy, in other words, is merely a placeholder for moral concerns that can already be derived from other values. Van den Hoven, for example, has argued that privacy derives its moral importance from four types of moral considerations: (1) prevention of information-based harm, (2) prevention of informational inequality, (3) prevention of informational injustice, and (4) respect for moral autonomy (Van den Hoven 1998; Van den Hoven and Vermaas 2007). Conversely, non-reductionists do not need to deny that privacy is related to a range of other values and part of a broader value cluster as I have called it, but they at least maintain that the value of privacy articulates moral considerations and corresponds to moral reasons that cannot, or at least cannot fully, be expressed by other values.

As Katell and Moore (2016) stress, even if reductionism about privacy were true, in many practical contexts it would still be useful to use the notion of privacy. After all, many of the social and political debates about ICT technologies, including those on cybersecurity, are framed in terms of privacy. Nevertheless, it is often helpful to unpack the other values and reasons that are implied when the value of privacy is articulated in concrete situations and debates. This is so because it is frequently the case that what is at stake in such situations is not just the threat of unauthorised access to personal data but rather a range of broader moral concerns related to such values as autonomy, identity and liberty. This is one of the reasons why it is useful to think in terms of value clusters rather than individual values. As indicated before, the value cluster of privacy also contains such values as moral autonomy, human dignity, identity, personhood, liberty, anonymity and confidentiality. Some of the values have a more justificatory relationship to privacy, i.e. they articulate why privacy is morally important (such as moral autonomy, human dignity, identity, personhood and liberty), whereas others (such as anonymity, confidentiality and control) seem more instrumental for preserving privacy.

There is a mutual relationship between how privacy is exactly understood and conceptualised and what other values are (more closely) related to it. For example, Whitman (2004) argues that in the US context, privacy is merely understood (and laid down in laws) in relation to liberty and in particular to moral concerns about government infringements in the personal life sphere of citizens. Such conceptions of privacy tend to stress liberty and the protection of citizens against state actors. He contrasts this with the European, primarily French and German, tradition in which privacy is more closely linked to human dignity and that stresses the relationship between people, so that privacy is also a concern between individuals, or between individuals and companies, rather than between citizens and the state. Arguably, in the current age of information systems and big data, both conceptions are important when it comes to privacy concerns.

### 3.3.3 Fairness

The third value cluster relevant to cybersecurity is that of fairness. This is a relevant value because both cybersecurity threats and measures to increase cybersecurity impact people differently, which may raise fairness issues. This is connected to a range of other values such as equality, justice, non-discrimination and freedom from bias. In addition, democracy is a relevant value because some cybersecurity measures may be so consequential and invasive that they require democratic legitimation rather than being the authority of private actors such as companies.

In political and moral philosophy, many different notions and theories of both democracy and fairness have been developed. I refrain from delving here into all the subtleties but rather restrict myself to highlighting how these values are affected by cybersecurity concerns and how they are relevant for the institutional and technical design of cybersecurity measures.

Justice and fairness are important values because cybersecurity measures typically come with costs and benefits that may be unequally distributed across the various actors involved. Parts of these costs and benefits are financial and economic in nature, and a first question that will therefore arise is whether a certain proposed cybersecurity measure is worth the cost. Strictly speaking, this is more a question about efficiency (i.e. the ratio between benefits and costs) than a question of justice and fairness (i.e. the distribution of costs and benefits). It should be noted, however, that if certain cybersecurity measures are not taken for efficiency reasons (i.e. because the benefits are not considered worth the costs), there will likely be distributional effects. This is the case because, if and when cybersecurity breaches materialise, the costs and harms caused by such breaches will likely not be equally distributed. Indeed, if people are victim to cybersecurity breaches, questions may arise about a right to compensation or the need for insurance.

The fact that costs and benefits are usually not equally distributed implies that even if from a societal point of view it is efficient or cost-effective to take certain cybersecurity measures, it is possible that for none of the actors involved are such measures also individually cost-effective. This may be particularly problematic if the distribution of costs and benefits is somehow unfair. An example is a company that offers services that are sensitive to cyber-attacks. As long as the costs (and other harm) due to the cyberattacks can be externalised (for example to the users of their services), it may not be cost-effective for the company to take certain cybersecurity measures. However, such externalisation of costs may be considered unfair, which in turn may lead to the introduction of a legal obligation (by the government) for the company to compensate its customers for damages due to avoidable cybersecurity breaches. This new distribution of costs and benefits may make certain cybersecurity measures cost-effective that were not so before. In this sense, questions about the cost-effectiveness of cybersecurity measures cannot be completely separated from questions about the fair or just distribution of costs and benefits.

Fairness and justice considerations do not only accrue to distributional effects but may also imply that people have a right to some minimal level of information access (Van den Hoven and Rooksby 2008) or even access to ICT services.[5] Given the crucial importance of information, and also of certain ICT services, in today's society, we may question whether access to such goods and services should not become a basic right. Perhaps, now or in the future, we should grant everybody the right to affordable, secure and accessible ICT services. If such rights were introduced, it would also have implications for the minimal level of cybersecurity that should be guaranteed for everybody. Of course, many questions can be asked regarding whether it is desirable to introduce such rights and about who bears the duties that correspond to such rights. Nevertheless, what these deliberations reveal is that questions about what constitutes a desirable level of cybersecurity do not just

[5] A report by special rapporteur Frank La Rue to the UN in 2011 stated: "Given that the Internet has become an indispensable tool for realizing a range of human rights, combating inequality, and accelerating development and human progress, ensuring universal access to the Internet should be a priority for all States. Each State should thus develop a concrete and effective policy (…) to make the Internet widely available, accessible and affordable to all segments of population" (Rue 2011: 22). This was interpreted by some as a plea for Internet access as a human right.

concern efficiency and cost-effectiveness but also fairness, justice and perhaps even human rights.

Fairness and justice may require impartiality but they would not seem to require that people are always or necessarily treated equally (Miller 2017). In most theories of fairness or justice, it is allowed, and sometimes even required, to treat people differently if they somehow deserve different treatment. What factors are relevant in justifying (or requiring) different treatments may be different for different theories and accounts. Nevertheless, some factors are almost universally seen as constituting improper ground for different treatments. This includes such factors as race, gender and sexual preferences. Here, the value of non-discrimination is relevant.[6]

Non-discrimination may be a particularly important value for cybersecurity because it is known that ICT technologies may be vulnerable to bias, i.e. they may unjustifiably treat people differently on the basis of, for example, gender, race or marital status. Such bias may be intentional, but it is often the unintended result of how such systems are designed and used. Friedman and Nissenbaum (1996) discuss three sources of such bias, namely pre-existing bias in human practices, institutions, and attitudes that is reified in computer systems; technical bias (resulting from technical requirements and constraints); and emergent bias that emerges from the use of the system (e.g. use in another context than originally foreseen). The increased use of big data and of self-learning algorithms has further increased the problem of bias (Barocas and Selbst 2016; O'Neil 2016; Ferguson 2017). Algorithmic bias may, in particular, result when algorithms are trained with biased data sets, or on a limited group of people or cases. Large-scale data collection for cybersecurity, therefore, is likely to also be vulnerable to bias if non-discrimination is not from the start considered in the design, training and use of relevant algorithms.

The value of democracy is relevant to cybersecurity in a number of ways. Cyberattacks may undermine the democratic process, as suggested by the 2016 US president elections, which witnessed the hacking of the Democratic Party, trolling and the spread of fake news (see also Chap. 11). It has also been suggested that cybersecurity measures, such as end-to-end-encryption, may protect democratic liberties such as freedom of speech (cf. Christen et al. 2017). However, cybersecurity measures may occasionally also undermine democracy. A particular concern is the strategic use of cybersecurity by national governments for national security aims (see also Chap. 12). Although such use may be justified, it raises a number of concerns (Kleinig et al. 2011; Newell 2016; Rubel 2016; Strossen 2016). One is that it may undermine the civil liberties of citizens. Second, because such use is by its nature often secretive, there may be a lack of democratic legitimacy. A further concern is that government agencies that find cybersecurity weaknesses may strategically keep these secret in order to use them against other countries (or even against their own population). This is not only problematic because such use usually lacks democratic legitimation but also because it increases cybersecurity risks for citizens

[6] However, positive discrimination would seem warranted in some cases, as justice may require advantaging underprivileged groups in specific circumstances.

and companies. It thus leads to fairness concerns because these societal actors have to bear the burden of the costs of cybersecurity threats that have not been revealed by government agencies.

### 3.3.4 Accountability

The value of accountability (and related values such as transparency, openness and explainability) is particularly relevant to cybersecurity in two types of situations. One are situations in which someone (allegedly) harms someone else, or infringes on the rights of that person. In such situations, we typically hold the (alleged) perpetrator accountable. The other are situations in which there is a power imbalance between two agents and in which the more powerful is in the position to introduce rules or measures that may harm the less powerful ones. For example, governments and companies may be accountable to citizens and consumers for what cybersecurity measures they take even if there is not (yet) a suspicion of undue harm.

In the first type of situation, accountability is closely related to responsibility and its different meanings, such as blameworthiness, liability and obligation-responsibility (Van de Poel et al. 2015). An agent may be said to be accountable if there is a reasonable suspicion that that agent did something wrong or caused undue harm. Accountability here implies an obligation to account for one's actions and their consequences. Such an account may show that the agent is not blameworthy (despite the reasonable suspicion), but if the account is unsatisfactory, the agent may be blameworthy or liable to correct his or her wrong or to pay damages. Accountability is also related to responsibility-as-obligation; in particular, an agent may be accountable if there is a reasonable suspicion that it did not fill its obligation-responsibilities.

What sets the second type of situation apart from the first is that there is not (yet) a reasonable suspicion of wrongdoing. Rather, the need for accountability is based on power imbalances. Although such power imbalances exist in any society, they seem to be aggravated in today's information society by the unequal access to large amounts of data and information. Moreover, citizens and consumers seem increasingly dependent on government and large commercial organisations for the secure storage of (personal) data. This would seem to imply that such powerful organisations are accountable for what cybersecurity measures they take. Such accountability would imply some degree of transparency about what cybersecurity measures are taken. In addition to such transparency, it would also imply a willingness and ability to account for the decisions on which such measures are based. This is particularly important because cybersecurity involves a range of values that are potentially conflicting. There might not be one best way to reconcile these values or to strike a balance between them, which makes it even more important that powerful actors account for how they make such decisions. Accountability here implies a certain traceability of how decisions are made but also the articulation of the reasons and motivations underlying such decisions.

## 3.4 Value Conflicts in Cybersecurity

It is often said that some of the values relevant to cybersecurity are in conflict with each other. The most frequently mentioned conflict is that between security and privacy, but this is certainly not the only possible value conflict in the domain of cybersecurity. Moreover, as already indicated in the introduction, it is not the case that (cyber)security and privacy are always in conflict.

### *3.4.1 What Are Value Conflicts?*

What does it mean to say that two values are conflicting? If values are varieties of goodness and are used for (moral) evaluation, then one interpretation of a value conflict is that two (or more) values are conflicting if (and only if) they provide opposite or contradictory evaluations of the same state-of-affairs (or object or policy). Therefore, if something is evaluated as good on the basis of one of the values it should, by definition, be bad on the basis of the other value. In cybersecurity, the values of transparency (or openness) versus confidentiality may provide an example. What is transparent is not confidential, and vice versa.

Such value conflicts that seem to derive from oppositions at the semantic level of values are, however, relatively rare. More often, value conflicts seem to derive from the practical implications of values. Under this interpretation, values conflict if they express or correspond to contradictory norms or reasons for actions. For example, if a value such as privacy would require that a certain piece of information is kept confidential, whereas transparency would require that same piece of information to be made public, then the values of privacy and transparency are conflicting.

It should be noted that the question of to which reasons a value corresponds is one of interpretation and judgment, and depends both on the value at stake and the specific context (see Sect. 3.2.1). More specifically, it depends on how the values at stake are conceptualised and specified. Conceptualisation is "the providing of a definition, analysis or description of a value that clarifies its meaning and often its applicability" (Van de Poel 2013: 261). For example, privacy may be conceptualised in terms of *confidentiality* as well as in terms of *control* over information. On the second conceptualisation, it would seem less likely that privacy conflicts with transparency, although it is certainly not impossible.

Moreover, whether values conflict will also depend on their specification. Specification may be understood as the translation of values into more specific norms and requirements (Van de Poel 2013). If privacy is conceptualised in terms of confidentiality, a specification would further specify what (personal) information should exactly stay confidential, and to whom. This means that on some specifications of privacy as confidentiality, privacy and transparency would conflict whereas on other specifications, the values would not conflict. Of course, there are limits to how a value can be specified. In general, a specification may be considered adequate if meeting the more specific norms and requirements would count as a proper response to the value at stake (cf. the earlier discussion about values in Sect. 3.2.1).

With the above in mind, we can now more precisely define value conflicts. One possible definition is the following:

> *Values are conflicting for a particular X, in context C, if it is practically impossible to respond properly to all values that are relevant to X in context C simultaneously*

Here X can be a state-of-affairs but also (and more relevant to the current discussion) a certain (technical or institutional) cybersecurity measure. This definition would also allow value conflicts if there is only one value, because it may also be practically impossible to respond properly to that one value for that particular X. For example, for a particular cybersecurity policy it may turn out to be impossible to respect (which is a proper response) the value of privacy.

If X is a cybersecurity policy (or measure), the natural response to such value conflicts may be to look for another policy, or measure, that does properly respond to all relevant values. Van den Hoven, Lokhorst, and Van de Poel (2012) argue that in such situations of value conflict (or a moral dilemma), there is a second-order obligation to look for options that help to avoid the value conflict, now or in the future. This may be done through technical or institutional innovation or design, as such innovation or design may extend what is feasible and so allow options that overcome the initial value conflict (Van den Hoven 2013; Van de Poel 2017).

Nevertheless, sometimes it may turn out to be impossible to find options that allow all relevant values to be responded to in an appropriate way. This bring us to the final definition of value conflicts. This definition takes as a starting point the situation in which we need to choose between different options (such as different cybersecurity measures or policies) and in which none of the options seem best in light of all the values at stake. This results in the following definition of value conflict (Van de Poel and Royakkers 2011):

1. *A choice has to be made between at least two options for which at least two values are relevant as choice criteria.*
2. *At least two different values select at least two different options as best.*
3. *There is no single value that trumps all others as choice criterion. If one value trumps another, any (small) amount of the first value is worth more than any (large) amount of the second value.*

It is this type of value conflict that I focus on in the remainder.

### 3.4.2 Value Conflicts in Cybersecurity

I now examine a number of more specific value conflicts in cybersecurity. Since value conflicts are usually practical conflicts, whether two values are conflicting will depend on the specific context. Nevertheless, it is possible to distinguish a num-

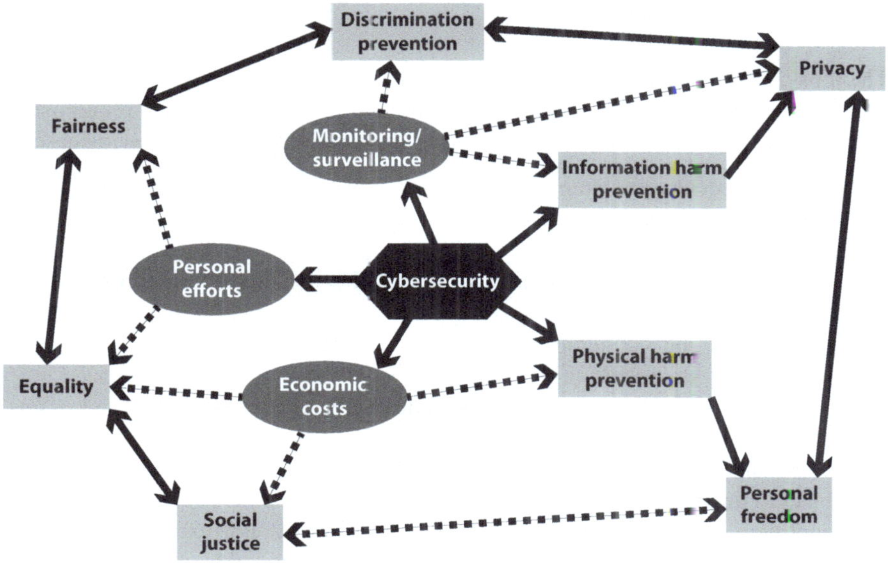


**Fig. 3.1** Value tensions in cybersecurity. (Reproduced from Christen et al. 2017)

ber of more general value tensions in cybersecurity. Christen et al. (2017) present the following figure as a graphical representation of potential value conflicts in cybersecurity.

The grey rectangles in Fig. 3.1 represent values. The values of 'information harm prevention' and 'physical harm prevention' belong to the cluster of security I previously discussed; privacy and personal freedom belong do the privacy cluster; and discrimination prevention, fairness, equality and social justice belong to the fairness cluster. Accountability is not mentioned in the figure, which may be explained by the fact that this is more of a procedural value.

Full arrows represent a supporting or reinforcing relation, while dotted arrows represent potential tensions. As shown, cybersecurity is directly instrumental for harm prevention (and so for personal security). It may, however, also involve monitoring and surveillance, which may in turn negatively affect a number of values. Similarly, it involves personal efforts as well as economic costs that may also negatively affect a number of values.

Below, I discuss relations between value clusters, taking the four earlier distinguished value clusters as a starting point. For each relation between value clusters, I discuss whether it is largely supportive or conflicting (or can be both), and if there are conflicts, I discuss ways in which these conflicts may be approached.

#### 3.4.2.1 Privacy Versus Security

The most frequently mentioned conflict in cybersecurity is most likely that between privacy and security. However, closer examination shows that the relationship between security and privacy is much more complex. Consider the following cases[7]:

1. Sometimes security is attained at the cost of privacy. An example is full cable monitoring which contributes to (cyber)security but would seem (in most cases) an unjustified privacy intrusion.
2. Sometimes security helps to achieve privacy. For example, limited or targeted monitoring may help to detect security incidents, which in turn may prevent data leaks, so that the confidentiality of personal information is maintained and, hence, privacy is served.
3. In computer systems, privacy requires some degree of cybersecurity. Privacy sets limits on who has access to what (personal) information. Without some degree of cybersecurity, these limits cannot be maintained, and personal information is subject to unauthorised access.
4. Sometimes, privacy is attained at the cost of security. For example, complete anonymity and secrecy of communications can be exploited by malicious agents.
5. Sometimes, privacy contributes to security. For example, if certain information about users of a system is kept confidential, spear phishing attacks can no longer leverage excessive available user information to choose attack targets.

As these examples demonstrate, security and privacy are not necessarily conflicting but also can support each other. Some degree of cybersecurity is, moreover, required to guarantee privacy. Nevertheless, the question can be asked how we are to deal with those situations in which privacy and security are conflicting.

In the philosophical literature, some authors have argued that security trumps privacy, while others have held that privacy trumps security. Himma (2016), for example, argues the former. His argument is based on the assumption that (personal) security is much more indispensable for a worthwhile life (including values such as autonomy and freedom) than privacy, because without some degree of security, we may not have a life at all. He admits, however, that this does not mean that any amount of security increase (however small) can justify any amount of privacy loss (however large).[8]

Conversely, Moore (2016) argues that privacy and accountability trump privacy. He does so by debunking four often-used arguments for sacrificing some privacy (or accountability) for security. These (fallacious) arguments are (1) "just trust us", i.e. give the benefit of the doubt to those in power and assume that officials will not override individual rights without just cause, (2) the nothing to hide argument, (3)

---

[7] These examples are based on a presentation by Josep Domingo-Ferrer on the 26th of April 2018 in Brussels concerning the CANVAS white paper on Technological challenges to cybersecurity (Domingo-Ferrer et al. 2017). See also Chap. 13.

[8] On this basis, one might wonder whether the point he makes is really about trumping values, or more about the centrality of certain values for a good or worthwhile life.

The "security trumps" view, and (4) the consent argument, i.e. people voluntarily offer (private) information all the time. While his debunking of the four arguments is convincing, it is questionable whether it follows that privacy (and accountability) trump security, in the sense that no amount of privacy or accountability should be given up to achieve more security.

The problem with trumping arguments is that they discuss value conflicts at a too general level. What values require in a specific situation, and whether values are conflicting, always requires judgement in the specific context (see also Chap. 7). Moreover, it seems very unlikely that either security trumps privacy or privacy trumps security in all possible situations one can imagine (or cannot yet imagine for that matter). Trumping accounts, then, are not able to do justice to how the value of privacy and security play out in specific situations and, therefore, offer an inadequate response to cases of value conflict.

The question, then, remains: how are we to deal with those situations in which the conflict between privacy and security is real? Although this may always require context-specific judgments, the earlier presented examples suggest a somewhat more general approach to the conflict between privacy and security. What we see from these examples is that conflicts in particular arise in two types of situations:

1. All data are gathered or monitored (as in the case of full cable monitoring) so that security is achieved at the cost of privacy
2. No data is gathered or monitored (as in the case of complete anonymity or secrecy) so that privacy is achieved at the cost of security

This suggests that, at least in a practical sense, the conflict boils down to conflicting requirements that follow from the values of security and privacy regarding what data should be collected, stored and shared, and for what purpose. This means that in looking for potential solutions to the value conflict, we should put centre stage questions such as:

- How much data and what data need to be gathered?
- What data should be accessible to whom?
- For how long should these data be stored?

It should also be noted that on a control account of privacy, it is entirely conceivable that individuals consent to the monitoring (and temporary storage) of their data for cybersecurity ends. After all, individuals will value their personal security and this will require some degree of cybersecurity. Therefore, if privacy is understood in control terms rather than confidentiality terms, it may be easier to solve the conflict between privacy and cybersecurity. Another notion that may be important in answering the mentioned questions is contextual integrity. The information that can be properly monitored and gathered in the light of privacy concerns will be different for different spheres in society such as business, health care, insurance, personal life and politics.

One of the implications of this is that to properly deal with the potential conflict between privacy and (cyber)security, we need fine-grained technical and institutional infrastructure that enables the fine-tuning of the data that are monitored, gathered, stored, and shared to the different public spheres and the informed consent of individuals. This allows a sophisticated attuning of privacy and security concerns to the specific context, considering all the relevant value considerations.

#### 3.4.2.2 Privacy Versus Fairness

The relationship between privacy and fairness is often seen as supportive. There are at least two general arguments for why privacy supports fairness. One is that privacy limits what data can be collected about individuals, which can prevent unfair treatment. If, for example, no data about race are collected, it limits the possibilities for discrimination or algorithmic bias based on race.[9] Secondly, it may be argued that some degree of privacy for office holders and political representatives is required in a well-functioning democracy (cf. Lever 2016; Mokrosinska 2016). One reason for this is that otherwise, some private circumstances may be held against political representatives or office holders that endanger their proper and independent functioning, which is required in a democracy. They may, for example, be blackmailed, which may introduce conflicts of interest and forms of secrecy that undermine the democratic process.

Conversely, democracy is supportive of privacy because privacy is often considered a civil liberty or basic right in democratic societies (see also Chaps. 4 and 5). Most democratic countries have laws that protect the privacy of their citizens.

Nevertheless, on occasion, fairness and democracy may also conflict with privacy. Fairness, for example, may require the sharing of some information with the government, in particular in those cases where fairness requires that people are not treated exactly the same. For example, fair taxation may require information about people's income, information that some people may consider private. Conflicts may also occur in cases where democracy seems to require a certain transparency or openness regarding how governmental decisions are made and what the government does (e.g. in terms of surveillance) (cf. Mathiesen 2016). Such transparency or openness may be in conflict (at least at first sight) with the confidentiality requirements that follow from privacy concerns. Since the call for transparency and openness of government operations is often based on considerations of accountability, I first discuss the relationship between privacy and accountability before discussing potential methods for addressing this value conflict.

---

[9] It does not make it entirely impossible, however. The reason is that discrimination or bias may also be based on proxies. For example, discrimination based on postal codes may in effect be a form of discrimination based on race or income (due to geographical segregation).

#### 3.4.2.3 Privacy Versus Accountability

Privacy and accountability, at first sight, seem to be at tension with each other. Accountability requires the ability and willingness to account for one's actions, in particular for how and why certain decisions were made. This require a certain transparency, and the revelation of information that may be privacy-sensitive.

It should be noted that this tension does not just occur if privacy is understood in terms of confidentiality. In addition, regarding the control notion of privacy, an agent may prefer not to share certain information that is required for proper accountability. An agent may even strategically choose not to reveal certain information to evade accountability under the guise of privacy concerns. Under such circumstances, privacy may even become a means for offenders or criminals (including cyber criminals or cyber attackers) to avoid accountability and responsibility (and hence punishment).

This suggests that control conceptualisations of privacy that give full and unlimited control to individuals regarding what data and information they share with whom are problematic in terms of accountability. One way to address this may be to build in restrictions on what information individuals can reasonably decide not to share with others. It could be argued that a control notion of privacy should be grounded not in absolute liberty but in moral autonomy (and human dignity). Moral autonomy not only implies a certain freedom in shaping one's life but also the willingness to take responsibility for one's actions, and to account to others where that is warranted. If privacy as control is understood in such a way the conflict with accountability is softened (although, perhaps, not completely avoided).

More generally, dealing with the potential conflict between privacy and accountability would require focusing on what information should be shared (or not be shared) with whom. Accountability does not require the disclosure of all information but rather those pieces of information that are crucial in the light of accountability. Moreover, accountability may require the disclosure of some information to some people but not to others. These requirements need not be in conflict with privacy, as privacy also typically does not require that all (personal) information remains confidential.

For example, political accountability may require that it becomes known who made what decision based on what information and which considerations went into a decision, but it does typically not require disclosure of other personal information. In some situations, it may even be irrelevant who exactly decided what for political accountability, and it may be enough to disclose how a decision was made in terms that are more general. Moreover, as we have seen before, political accountability may be served by some degree of privacy, because this avoids office holders or political representatives being held accountable for things that are private and not politically relevant.

The above does not rule out the fact that privacy and accountability may, on occasion, correspond to conflicting requirements about what information to disclose (or keep confidential) to whom. Such conflicts can, of course, occur. Nevertheless, it brings the discussion to where it should be, namely regarding what information should be shared and what should be kept confidential to whom in the light of privacy and accountability concerns, and indeed other values such as democracy, fairness and security.

#### 3.4.2.4 Security Versus Accountability

I have argued before that (cyber)security measures, or the lack thereof, require some form of accountability. This is the case because a lack of appropriate cybersecurity measures may create undue harm. However, in as far as accountability requires a revelation of what cybersecurity measures are exactly taken, it may be in conflict with cybersecurity itself. The reason for this is that cybersecurity threats often arise not just from unintentional harm but from the actions of malicious agents or adversaries. These agents will typically strategically adapt their adversary strategies to what cybersecurity measures are taken (or the lack thereof). In this sense, cybersecurity is akin to an arms race, meaning that too much public accountability may undermine the effectiveness of cybersecurity measures.

A similar conflict may occur in those cases where cybersecurity weaknesses are exploited for national security ends. Here again, the revelation of these security strategies, or even of the cybersecurity weaknesses on which they are based, may undermine the effectiveness of those strategies and hence decrease security. Therefore, there seems to be a very real tension between accountability and security.

While this tension may require some form of balancing or trade-off, there are also institutional mechanisms that may help to alleviate the tension. One such institutional mechanism is to create fora for accountability that do not require the full public disclosure of (cyber)security measures, for example, parliamentary committees, cybersecurity committees or councils to which governments, or companies, are accountable for the cybersecurity measures they take (or fail to take). Such institutions may work under certain confidentiality requirements in the sense that they cannot disclose certain cybersecurity measures (or the lack thereof) if that is likely to help cyber attackers or criminals.

These types of institutional mechanisms may still imply a trade-off between accountability and security as they are likely to neither attain full accountability nor full security. The main point, nevertheless, is that the tension between accountability and security should be an incentive to look for new institutional arrangements that allow both values to be better served simultaneously than current institutions. In as far as trade-offs are still inevitable, they should not only be considered in terms of security versus accountability but also in terms of the other values at stake, including the values of privacy and fairness and the values served by the computer systems that are the possible target of cyberattacks.

#### 3.4.2.5 Security Versus Fairness (and Democracy)

Security may conflict with fairness and democracy, in particular when cybersecurity is used for national security aims, for example large state surveillance programmes or cyberattacks on other countries by government agencies. Such activities may put at risk civil liberties and the privacy of citizens (e.g. Rubel 2015; Strossen 2016). This may sometimes be justified but would then require at least some form of democratic legitimacy and accountability. However, the fact that these activities are often secretive makes democratic legitimation and accountability frequently more difficult to achieve.

It is important here to distinguish between different kinds of security, in particular national versus personal security (Kleinig et al. 2011; Waldron 2011). National security should not be seen as an intrinsic value but rather as a value that derives its moral importance from other values such as personal security. It is important to be aware that some measures to increase national security, such as the secretive large-scale surveillance of citizens, may not only serve personal security (through increasing national security) but also endanger it. In particular, if such programmes, in effect, diminish civil liberties without clear democratic legitimacy and a lack of accountability, the loss in personal security may occasionally be bigger than the net gain through increased national security.

This is not to deny that national security is a legitimate concern; arguably, it may require more attention than in the past in the light of an increase in the number of terrorist attacks (at least in Western countries) and an increase in foreign cyberattacks by state agencies (and others). The point is that in addressing conflicts of security versus fairness and democracy, we should not just examine national security but primarily examine the effect on personal security (of citizens).

One particular issue here is that national security measures, and also other types of cybersecurity measures, may well increase the personal security of some while diminishing the personal security (and civil liberties and privacy) of others (Waldron 2011). In other words, such measures have distributive effects that raise questions of fairness. As argued before, it can often be difficult to neatly separate such fairness questions from questions about the right level of (cyber)security that is still worth the costs involved (financial and otherwise).

It might be thought that fairness requires equal treatment and therefore translates into an equal distribution of the costs and benefits of cybersecurity. However, this is far less obvious than may appear. People are not to the same degree vulnerable to cyber threats so that benefits of cybersecurity measures are likely to be unequally distributed. Moreover, it seems just (or fair) that people or organisations that (deliberately) exploit weaknesses in cybersecurity at the cost of others should also bear a larger burden of the costs, if only to compensate for the harm they have done. Another consideration is that in order to increase the total level of (cyber)security we should sometimes be willing to accept some inequalities.

Therefore, although unequal distributions of the costs and benefits of cybersecurity, or national security, are not necessarily or always unfair (or unacceptable), fairness requires that some minimal level of basic rights, including a certain right to personal security, civil liberties and privacy protection, is guaranteed for all (Rawls 1999 [1971]). This again underlines the fact that in considering value tensions between security and other values (privacy, accountability, democracy), we should always and primarily keep in mind the effect of different choices on personal security rather than simply focusing on national security and cybersecurity (which are largely instrumental values). Moreover, to guarantee some minimal degree of personal security for all, we must also pay attention to privacy, civil liberties and democratic rights.

## 3.5 Conclusions: Beyond Security Versus Privacy

I began this chapter by stating that the framing of ethical and value issues in cybersecurity in terms of security versus privacy is unsatisfactory. In concluding, I wish to highlight three ways in which we should go beyond this framing if the approach in this chapter is on the right track.

First, we should consider a broader range of values. In particular, I have pointed out that in addition to the value clusters of security and privacy, there are two other values clusters particularly important for cybersecurity, namely fairness and accountability. Moreover, there are those values that are related to cybersecurity in more specific domains (or applications), such as the business domain (Chap. 6), the health domain (Chap. 7) or the national security domain (Chap. 8). These values are also indispensable in understanding value issues and value tensions in relation to cybersecurity. By considering all these values, we gain a much richer picture of both the value issues and conflicts in cybersecurity.

Second, I have argued for a contextual approach when it comes to identifying and addressing value conflicts. This is in line with my general understanding of values as varieties of goodness that require an appropriate response and correspond to certain types of moral considerations and reasons. The question of what constitutes a proper response to a certain value is context-specific and always requires judgement. A value analysis of cybersecurity, therefore, requires contextual judgements. Moreover, values are usually not conflicting in the abstract, but in a specific context. Privacy and security, for example, conflict in some contexts and applications but not in others. Without a proper analysis of context, we are in danger of understanding value conflicts in cybersecurity in too general terms, for example as a conflict between privacy and security, which may hinder rather than help in better addressing such value conflicts.

To better address value conflicts in cybersecurity, then, requires a superior understanding of what is at stake in those conflicts. This not only requires an understanding of what specific values require in a specific situation but also an understanding of why and how values may conflict or support each other. I have discussed this in more general terms for a number of potential value conflicts in cybersecurity. It became apparent that a crucial issue in several of these potential conflicts is what data or information should be monitored, collected, stored and shared for what purposes, and who is entitled to access such data. Attaining more precision about this type of question would be, at the very least, a step towards alleviating conflicts between, in particular, security, privacy and accountability. In other words, we should zoom in on what the various relevant values require in a specific situation and how these requirements can be reconciled, for example through technical and institutional solutions rather than very general philosophical arguments about why security trumps privacy or vice versa.

**Acknowledgements** This chapter was written as part of the CANVAS project, which received funding from the European Union's Horizon 2020 research and innovation programme under Grant Agreement No 700540. Part of the research for this chapter was also done for the project ValueChange, which has received funding from the European Research Council (ERC) under the European Union's Horizon 2020 research and innovation programme under Grant Agreement No 788321.

## References

Allen AL (2016) The duty to protect your own privacy. In: Moore AD (ed) Privacy, security, and accountability: ethics, law and, policy. Rowman & Littlefield International, London/New York, pp 19–18

Anderson E (1993) Value in ethics and economics. Harvard University Press, Cambridge, MA

Barocas S, Selbst AD (2016) Big data's disparate impact. Calif Law Rev 104:671–732

Berlin I (1958) Two concepts of liberty. Clarendon Press, Oxford

Christen M, Gordijn B, Weber K et al (2017) A review of value-conflicts in cybersecurity. ORBIT J 1. https://doi.org/10.29297/orbit.v1i1.28

Dancy J (1993) Moral reasons. Blackwell Publishers, Oxford

Dancy J (2005) Should we pass the buck? In: Rønnow-Rasmussen T, Zimmerman MJ (eds) Recent work on intrinsic value. Springer, Dordrecht, pp 33–44

Dewey J (1922) Human nature and conduct; an introduction to social psychology. Holt, New York

Ferguson AG (2017) The rise of big data policing: surveillance, race, and the future of law enforcement. New York University Press, New York

Frankena WK (1973) Ethics, 2nd edn. Prentice Hall, Englewood Cliffs

Friedman B, Nissenbaum H (1996) Bias in computer systems. ACM Trans Inf Syst 14:330–347

Gregoratti C (2013) Human security. In: Encyclopædia Britannica. https://www.britannica.com/topic/human-security. Last access 7 July 2019

Hansson SO (2009) Risk and safety in technology. In: Meijers A (ed) Handbook of the philosophy of science. Volume 9: Philosophy of technology and engineering sciences. Elsevier, Oxford, pp 1069–1102

Himma KE (2016) Why security trumps privacy. In: Moore AD (ed) Privacy, security, and accountability: ethics, law and, policy. Rowman & Littlefield International, London/New York, pp 145–170

Hirose I, Olson J (2015) The Oxford handbook of value theory. Oxford University Press, New York

ISACA (2016) Cybersecurity fundamentals glossary 2016. https://www.isaca.org/Knowledge-Center/Documents/Glossary/Cybersecurity_Fundamentals_glossary.pdf. Last access 7 July 2019

Domingo-Ferrer D-F, Blanco A, Arnau JP et al (2017) Canvas White Paper 4 – technological challenges in cybersecurity. SSRN. https://doi.org/10.2139/ssrn.3091942

Katell M, Moore AD (2016) Introduction: the value of privacy, security and accountability. In: Moore AD (ed) Privacy, security, and accountability: ethics, law and, policy. Rowman & Littlefield International, London/New York, pp 1–17
Kleinig J, Mameli P, Miller S et al (2011) Security and privacy: global standards for ethical identity management in contemporary liberal democratic states. ANU Press, Canberra
Koops B-J, Newell BC, Timan T et al (2017) A typology of privacy. Univ Penn J Nat Law 38:483–575
Korsgaard CM (1983) Two distinctions in goodness. Philos Rev 92:169–195
Lever A (2016) Democracy, privacy and security. In: Moore AD (ed) Privacy, security, and accountability: ethics, law and, policy. Rowman & Littlefield International, London/New York, pp 105–124
Mason E (2018) Value pluralism. In: Zalta EN (ed) The Stanford encyclopedia of philosophy, Spring 2018 edn. https://plato.stanford.edu/archives/spr2018/entries/value-pluralism/. Last access 7 July 2019
Mathiesen K (2016) Transparancy for democracy: the case of open governmnet data. In: Moore AD (ed) Privacy, security, and accountability: ethics, law and, policy. Rowman & Littlefield International, London/New York, pp 125–144
Miller D (2017) Justice. In: Zalta EN (ed) The Stanford encyclopedia of philosophy, Fall 2017 edn. https://plato.stanford.edu/archives/fall2017/entries/justice/. Last access 7 July 2019
Mokrosinska D (2016) Privacy, freedom of speech and the sexual lives of office holders. In: Moore AD (ed) Privacy, security, and accountability: ethics, law and, policy. Rowman & Littlefield International, London/New York, pp 89–104
Moore AD (2003) Privacy: its meaning and value. Am Philos Q 40:215–227
Moore AD (2016) Why privacy and acountability trump security. In: Moore AD (ed) Privacy, security, and accountability: ethics, law and, policy. Rowman & Littlefield International, London/New York, pp 171–182
Newell BC (2016) Mass surveillance, privacy and freedom: a case for public access to government surveillance information. In: Moore AD (ed) Privacy, security, and accountability: ethics, law and, policy. Rowman & Littlefield International, London/New York, pp 203–222
Nissenbaum H (2004) Privacy as contextual integrity. Wash Law Rev 79:119–157
O'Neil C (2016) Weapons of math destruction: how big data increases inequality and threatens democracy, 1st edn. Crown, New York
Pound R (1915) Interests of personality. Harv Law Rev 28:343–365
Rawls J (1971) A theory of justice, Rev edn. (1999) The Belknap Press of Harvard University Press, Cambridge, MA
Raz J (1999) Engaging reason. On the theory of value and action. Oxford University Press, Oxford
Raz J (2003) The practice of value (with commentaries by Christine Korsgaard, Robert Pippin, & Bernard Williams; edited and introduced by R. Jay Wallace). Oxford University Press, Oxford
Rokeach M (1973) The nature of human values. The Free Press, New York
Rubel A (2016) Privacy, transpararency and accountablity in the NSA's bulk metadata program. In: Moore AD (ed) Privacy, security, and accountability: ethics, law and, policy. Rowman & Littlefield International, London, pp 183–202
Rue FL (2011) VI. Conclusions and recommendations. Report of the special rapporteur on the promotion and protection of the right to freedom of opinion and expression. https://www2.ohchr.org/english/bodies/hrcouncil/docs/17session/A.HRC.17.27_en.pdf. Last access 7 July 2019
Scanlon TM (1998) What we owe to each other. Harvard University Press, Cambridge, MA
Schwartz SH, Bilsky W (1987) Toward a universal psychological structure of human values. J Pers Soc Pyschol 53:550–562
Scientific Advice Mechanism High Level Group (2016) Scientific advice mechanism scoping paper. European Commission, Cybersecurity
Stocker M (1990) Plural and conflicting values. Clarendon Press, Oxford
Strossen N (2016) Post-9/11 government surveillance, supression and secrecy. In: Moore AD (ed) Privacy, security, and accountability: ethics, law and, policy. Rowman & Littlefield International, London/New York, pp 223–246

Van de Poel I (2013) Translating values into design requirements. In: Michelfelder D, McCarty N, Goldberg DE (eds) Philosophy and engineering: Reflections on practice, principles and process. Dordrecht: Springer, 253–266.
Van de Poel I (2017) Dealing with moral dilemmas through design. In: van den Hoven J, Miller S, Pogge T (eds) Designing in ethics. Cambridge University Press, Cambridge, pp 57–77
Van de Poel I, Royakkers L (2011) Ethics, technology and engineering. Wiley-Blackwell, Oxford
Van de Poel I, Royakkers L, Zwart SD (2015) Moral responsibility and the problem of many hands. Routledge, New York
Van den Hoven J (1998) Privacy and the varieties of informational wrongdoing. Aus J Prof App Ethics 1:30–43
Van den Hoven J (2013) Value sensitive design and responsible innovation. In: Owen R, Bessant J, Heintz M (eds) Responsible innovation. Wiley, Chichester, pp 75–84
Van den Hoven J, Rooksby E (2008) Distributive justice and the value of information: a (broadly) Rawlsian approach. In: van den Joven MJ, Weckert J (eds) Information technology and moral philosophy. Cambridge University Press, Cambridge
Van den Hoven J, Vermaas PE (2007) Nano-technology and privacy: on continuous surveillance outside the panopticon. J Med Philos 32:283–297
Van den Hoven J, Lokhorst G-J, Van de Poel I (2012) Engineering and the problem of moral overload. Sci Eng Ethics 18:143–155
Von Wright GH (1963) The varieties of goodness. Routledge & Kegan Paul, London
Waldron JJ (2011) Safety and security. Neb Law Rev 85:454–507
Warnier M, Dechesne F, Brazier F (2015) Design for the value of privacy. In: van den Hoven J, Vermaas EP, van de Poel I (eds) Handbook of ethics, values, and technological design: sources, theory, values and application domains. Springer, Dordrecht, pp 431–445
Warren SD, Brandeis LD (1890) The right to privacy. Harv Law Rev 4:193–220
Westin AF (1967) Privacy and freedom. Atheneum, New York
Whitman JK (2004) The two western cultures of privacy: dignity versus liberty. Yale Law J 113:1151–1221
Williams RM Jr (1968) The concept of values. In: Sills DS (ed) The concept of values. Macmillan Free Press, New York
Yaghmaei E, van de Poel I, Christen M et al (2017) Canvas White Paper 1 – cybersecurity and ethics. SSRN. https://doi.org/10.2139/ssrn.3091909

# Chapter 4
# Ethical Frameworks for Cybersecurity

**Michele Loi and Markus Christen**

**Abstract** This chapter presents several ethical frameworks that are useful for analysing ethical questions of cybersecurity. It begins with two frameworks that are important in practice: the principlist framework employed in the Menlo Report on cybersecurity research and the rights-based principle that is influential in the law, in particular EU law. It is argued that since the harms and benefits caused by cybersecurity operations and policies are of a probabilistic nature, both approaches cannot avoid dealing with risk and probability. Therefore, the chapter turns to the ethics of risk, showing that it is a necessary complement to such approaches. The ethics of risk are discussed in more detail by considering two consequentialist approaches (utilitarianism and maximin consequentialism), deontological approaches and contractualist approaches to risk at length, highlighting the difficulties raised by special cases. Finally, Nissenbaum's 'contextual integrity' approach is introduced, which has become an important framework for understanding privacy, both descriptively and normatively. A revised version of this framework is proposed for identifying and ethically assessing changes brought about by cybersecurity measures and policies, not only in relation to privacy but more generally to the key expectations concerning human interactions within the practice.

**Keywords** Consequentialism · Contextual integrity · Cybersecurity · Ethics of risk · Human rights · Principlism

---

M. Loi (✉)
Digital Society Initiative, University of Zurich, Zurich, Switzerland

Institute of Biomedical Ethics and History of Medicine, Zurich, Switzerland
e-mail: michele.loi@uzh.ch

M. Christen
UZH Digital Society Initiative, Zürich, Switzerland
e-mail: christen@ethik.uzh.ch



M. Christen et al. (eds.), *The Ethics of Cybersecurity*, The International Library of Ethics, Law and Technology 21,
https://doi.org/10.1007/978-3-030-29053-5_4

## 4.1 Introduction

The term cyber*security* explicitly conveys its main ethical goal, namely to create a state of being free from danger or threat in cyberspace, if we follow the general definition of the English term 'security' (Oxford Dictionary). However, in ethics, the concept of security rarely plays a central role in theory building. For example, if we search the *Stanford Encyclopedia of Philosophy* for 'security', the term only appears in the entry under information ethics (which is the context that interests us here) and in political philosophy, referring to the security of nation states. This is remarkable, as from a purely biological perspective, organisms (and groups of social animals) invest considerable resources in protecting themselves against threats. Certainly, conditions resulting from insecurity such as harm or injustice are central topics in ethical theorising. Nevertheless, the positive orientation aimed to overcome those conditions refer to values like justice or benevolence, not security (probably with the exception of social security).

Why is this? One reason could be that the term 'security' used in a more general sense has certain negative connotations, particularly within ethics. These may refer to the problems that result when security is enforced by states through coercive capacities, to the observation that authoritarian regimes often rely on security when actually promoting injustice, or to the more general impression that a state of security involves a static and closed setting of societies. In that sense, within moral theory security is usually not an ethical value of its own, but rather an *instrumental value* to protect *ethical values* (but see also the considerations in Chap. 3) Thus, as an instrumental value, security can also be unethical, when either the protected goals or the means used to establish security are unethical. The same holds for cybersecurity.

Cybersecurity, understood broadly, is usually considered as a whole bundle of technologies and policies to protect the cyber-infrastructure. Following Hildebrandt (2013), we can distinguish three main classes of technology for cybersecurity: technologies that ensure confidentiality of information (including authentication of the intended recipients of communication); technologies that detect and counter online threats and vulnerabilities; and technologies that detect and counter cybercrime such as forgery, fraud, child pornography and copyright violations committed in cyberspace. In each of those application domains, different ethical problems emerge.

Given that cybersecurity is by itself not a genuine ethical value, we may pose a follow-up question of how to analyse the ethical questions raised by enforcing cybersecurity. In this chapter, we present several ethical frameworks useful for analysing ethical questions that arise in the context of cybersecurity. We start with two frameworks that are important in practice: the principlist framework employed in the Menlo Report on cybersecurity research (Sect. 4.2) and the rights-based principle that is influential in the law, in particular EU law (Sect. 4.3). We show that since the harms and benefits caused by cybersecurity operations and policies are often probable, rather than certain, both approaches cannot avoid dealing with risk and probability. Therefore, we turn to the ethics of risk, demonstrating that it is a necessary complement to such approaches (Sect. 4.4). Section 4.5 considers the ethics of risk in more detail by considering at length two consequentialist approaches (utilitarianism and maximin consequentialism), deontological approaches and contractualist approaches to risk, highlighting the difficulties raised by special cases. Finally, in Sect. 4.6, we introduce Nissenbaum's 'contextual integrity' approach and extend it to address all the human interactions (and not only informational exchanges) affected by new cybersecurity applications.

## 4.2 Principlism

The Menlo report was intended to guide research in cybersecurity, understood traditionally as a form of investigation aimed at generalisable knowledge for the benefit of society, and *in so far as it deals with human subjects*. However, it can also be applied more broadly to cybersecurity operations that involve a research component, e.g. acts of inspections and the collection of intelligence, such as those carried out by computer emergency response teams, if there is direct interaction with a human or if there are human data (Johnson, Bellovin, and Keromytis 2011). Cybersecurity—"the subdiscipline of computer science concerned with ensuring simultaneously the confidentiality, integrity, and availability of IT systems against the attacks of some set of adversaries" (Spring and Illari 2018, para. 1) can arguably produce general knowledge (Spring and Illari 2018) of a particular form. The general knowledge produced does not take the form of scientific theories, rather the discovery and modelling of peculiar *mechanisms* (e.g. mechanisms that disrupt the intended working of an information system). This knowledge of mechanisms provides, in the long run and in a patchwork way, cybersecurity experts with general knowledge on how to detect and respond to information security challenges, and how to improve cybersecurity defences (Spring and Illari 2018).

Principlism is a system of ethics based on a limited number of principles (usually 3 or 4) with a grounding in common-sense morality and professional ethical practice (see also Chap. 7). An instance of principlism is the Belmont Report for the protection of human research subjects, which includes three principles: Respect for Persons, Beneficence, and Justice. The Menlo Report (US Department of Homeland Security Science and Technology Directorate) adapted this approach to the context of Information and Communication Technology Research (Kenneally et al. 2010; Kenneally and Bailey 2013), using the same principles and highlighting ways of applying them to the cybersecurity domain.

Principlism is a form of deontology (deontology = the study of duty). The main principles of the theory can be regarded as the sources of prima facie duties in the sense of W.D. Ross (2002). According to Ross, an action's moral rightness cannot be explained in terms of its being productive of the good; rather, it should be analysed by considering prima facie duties. For example, if I fulfil my promise to you, what makes it *right* that I do so is not the consequences of fulfilling my promise but rather the fact that I promised. Of course, this is not to imply that I should respect my promise even when this would produce disastrous consequences. The way Ross explains this is by claiming that the duty to 'respect one's promises' is not *the only* duty and it is only a prima facie duty. A person also has a duty to *relieve distress,* which (in certain situations) may override the duty to keep one's promise. The prima facie duty to keep one's promise makes it *right* to keep one's promise if it is a stronger prima facie duty than conflicting prima facie duties, or if there are no other prima facie duties. The theory of prima facie duties is an alternative to the consequentialist theory that all conflicts of duties should be resolved by asking which action produces the most good. Instead, with prima facie duties there is no higher-order theory to determine how conflicts of duties are to be resolved.

It is not difficult to see that the logic of Ross's prima facie duties can be applied to principlism. The three (or four) principles in principlism can be regarded as prima facie duties: from the moral point of view, we *always* have good reasons to respect persons, to pursue the good of others, to avoid harming them, and to act justly in the absence of countervailing considerations. However, in practice, the duties implied by those principles may conflict and, when this happens, the principles must be balanced against each other. In the tradition of principlism, the balance of different duties occurs according to intersubjective agreements that, as in prima facie duties theories, are not theoretically predetermined in advance.

The principlist approach is a modest, minimalist framework that affords significant flexibility. It leaves to the researchers, or cybersecurity operatives, the difficult task of identifying the specific factors and circumstances that should carry weight in deliberations concerning a concrete case and the even more difficult task of weighing these considerations against each other when trade-offs occur.

Let us now briefly introduce the three principles of the Menlo Report. Respect for persons concerns all those cases in which data may be linked with identifiable persons, e.g. data concerning communication between individuals or IP addresses which may be linked to individuals. Respect also involves all research in which consent *can* be asked and in which it is realistically considered a necessary condition of research, for example some forms of experimental (psychological) research on human factors in cybersecurity, performed in the lab with research subjects recruited for that purpose (e.g. Hadlington 2017). One area of cybersecurity research that involves such methods is research on human factors of cybersecurity, which includes the experimental study of user acceptance, confusion, frustration, cognitive workload, error/risk reduction and the optimisation of error-tolerant systems (Boyce et al. 2011). Realistically, however, consent is often impracticable; in such contexts, the principle of beneficence may be the basis of a duty to do research when the cost-benefit ratio clearly favours it (Kenneally et al. 2010). The benefit principle applies in all generality to cybersecurity research; it should be understood as the principle of maximising probable benefit and minimising probable harm. Minimising harm also requires considering the full spectrum of risks to persons, including reputational, emotional, financial and physical harm (Kenneally et al. 2010). Justice involves a distributive aspect, concerning the fair distribution of the benefits and possible burdens of research. So for example, research should not be designed in such a way that one group benefits from the research while another group bears the burdens (e.g. re-identification).

## 4.3 Human Rights

The idea of a balance, familiar in the context of prima facie duties, is often used to discuss a trade-off between the extent to which human rights can be respected and security be achieved. The existence of a trade-off implies the weighing of different duties: e.g. which duty—protecting the security of personal information (e.g. by favouring the diffusion of encryption technology) or preventing criminal attacks (e.g. by limiting the diffusion of encryption technology or requiring device makers to build back doors)—should take priority in a given context?

Note that the duty of protecting the security of personal information is here both a duty of cybersecurity *and* a duty in relation to human rights (the human right to privacy). This should not be a surprise. Indeed, cybersecurity technology that aims to protect privacy and confidentiality, such as encryption, is in general aligned with human rights; the threat to human rights is typically not cybersecurity, but *inadequate* cybersecurity or the lack thereof. However, there might be cases in which cybersecurity technology for the protection of privacy and confidentiality is *both* a means to privacy *and* a threat. Cybersecurity technologies such as encryption are naturally accompanied by *authentication* (which distinguishes those who have the right to obtain the non-encrypted information from the rest); authentication involves certification and the management of credentials. This requires the collection of information about individuals, which may expose users to privacy infringement.

Other kinds of cybersecurity technologies—those involved in monitoring web trafficking and fighting cybercrime—are in more direct conflict with human rights. Monitoring is associated with surveillance and surveillance involves threats of censorship (which can be a violation of the human right to free speech) and eavesdropping (which can be violation of the human right to due process). Moreover, monitoring is associated with profiling. Profiling "may be used by the police or security agencies to find criminals or terrorists; by airports to decide who to check more carefully" (Yaghmaei et al. 2017: 29–30). Hence, profiling is associated with potential violations of the human right against *discrimination*, because in profiling "people are approached, judged or treated in a certain way because these have characteristics that fit a certain profile and that are associated with certain other traits (i.e. traits other than by which they are identified as belonging to the profile)" (Yaghmaei et al. 2017: 29). The main ethical issue in profiling is not privacy, although personal information may be used to build profiles. It is the fact that "profiling may inflict all kinds of undeserved harm on people, from nuisance to false accusations to even, in extreme cases, imprisonment of innocent people" (Yaghmaei et al. 2017: 29–30). This happens because in profiling "a generalisation is made based on limited information about a person" (Yaghmaei et al. 2017: 30). The statistical discrimination involved in *any* form of profiling is only in conflict with the *human right* to non-discrimination when profiling involves specific (typically legally protected) categories:

> The fundamental right of non-discrimination concerns the prohibition of discrimination in the context of occupation or employment, the provision of goods and services or other important domains of everyday life such as housing, social security or healthcare. Such prohibitions, which vary across jurisdictions, are limited to a set of grounds and do not touch price discrimination based on economic calculation or actuarial approaches to insurance. (Hildebrandt 2013, 368)

Protecting the human right to non-discrimination is one of the goals of (most) data protection regulation and is enshrined in Chapter III of the EU Charter, which

> includes [...] gender equality (Article 23) [and] also prohibits '[a]ny discrimination based on any ground such as sex, race, colour, ethnic or social origin, genetic features, language, religion or belief, political or any other opinion, membership of a national minority, property, birth, disability, age or sexual orientation' (Article 21). The underlying objectives of equality and non-discrimination principles have been further pursued in the EU secondary law such as the Equal Treatment Directive in the context of employment (Directive 2006/54/EC) and the Directive implementing the principle of equal treatment between persons irrespective of racial or ethnic origin (Directive 2000/43). (Jasmontaite et al. 2017, 81; see also Chapter 5)

The cybersecurity technologies protecting individuals from cybercrime may conflict with human rights. Cybercrime may be defined to include four different broad categories of crime: *cybertrespass, cybervandalism, cyberpiracy* and *computer fraud* (Brey 2007). The first concerns gaining unauthorised access to data and information systems, the second disrupting processes and corrupting data, the third reproducing and distributing software or content which violates intellectual property and the fourth the misrepresentation of identity or information for the sake of deception for personal gain (Brey 2007).

The tension between the third type of cybersecurity and human rights should be clear from the outset, for the fight against cybercrime often involves "technologies to gain secret access to computing systems, to capture, observe and/or intercept data and content" (Hildebrandt 2013: 371). However, gaining access to and capturing data involves exactly the kind of cyber-threats to the privacy of information and confidentiality of communication that the first kind of cybersecurity technologies is designed to protect people from.

Hildebrandt (2013) observes that the expression 'to balance' can be used in this context to indicate two very different concepts. In the sense of a trade-off, the concept of a balance implies that it is necessary to curtail, imperfectly realise or narrowly specify a right's content in order to achieve a high enough level of security. But the core of the human right in question should not be compromised to achieve a marginal gain in cybersecurity and other ways of enhancing cybersecurity without undermining rights have to be explored, even if they are significantly less efficient, easy to realise or comprehensive. The idea of a 'balance' may also refer to something different from a trade-off. Balance, as in the expression of 'checks and balances', indicates quite a different concept. This is the idea that any increase in security measures needs to be accompanied by a proportional increase in alternative safeguards of the human rights, which cybersecurity risks undermining. Importantly, balancing cybersecurity and human right, in this sense, means creating checks and balances to protect human rights that may be threatened by heightened cybersecurity measures.

What are the rights that need to be balanced with cybersecurity? According to Hildebrandt, those rights are privacy, data protection, non-discrimination, due process and free speech. We have already mentioned examples involving some of these above. With the emergence of the Internet of Things (IoT), the right to physical integrity becomes also paramount, due to the capacity of attacks to undermine the physical integrity of individuals whose life-sustaining functions depend on the proper functioning of ICT mechanisms, for example in the health domain (Weber 2010; Mittelstadt 2017; Weber et al. 2018). For example, it is the physical integrity of a person that is a stake, if a 'black hat' hacker—a hacker moved by malicious intent—aims to access the software in a pacemaker in order to disrupt it and kill or harm the person who has it (Newman 2017).

Interestingly, Hildebrandt argues that if privacy is understood as "the freedom from unreasonable constraints on the construction of one's identity" (Agre and Rotenberg 1998: 7) then the other four rights are actually implied by the right to privacy in the era of smart environments (but arguably this extension does not include the fifth right we added to Hildebrand's list, of physical integrity). Hildebrandt explains the connection as follows: data collection and the profiling of the data subject define our identity for others and make us vulnerable to be defined by other people in ways that we would not choose to endorse profiling enables discrimination practices against specific individuals or types or categories or groups of individuals—it bypasses conscious, reflective attitudes and plans that are key to being able to use due process. Free speech is also affected by the inability to control processes that steer our thinking (and expression) in ways that are unreflective, sometimes even unconscious. This includes "freedom from monitoring, filtering, and blocking of Internet traffic" (Hildebrandt 2013: 369). Of course, not all forms of monitoring, filtering and blocking of traffic have a negative impact on the human interests that the human right to free speech is meant to protect. The problem is, however, that essentially the same technologies that allow an Internet service provider, for example, to inspect traffic to identify and block malware, or other illegal content (including pirated media) may also be used to monitor and filter the contents of speech in a politically non-neutral way, which counts as a violation to the core interest that the human right to free speech is meant to protect. Thus, all cybersecurity technologies involving the monitoring and filtering are potential threats to this right. Interestingly, European law allows Internet service providers to inspect packages against malware and other security threats if this results from their own initiatives, but prohibit courts to oblige them to do so, to protect copyright (Hildebrandt 2013: 369). This example demonstrates that courts themselves (in this case the European Court of Justice) engage in balancing (in both senses of the expression) when interpreting the scope of fundamental human rights. In this case, the courts may have reasoned that citizens' interest in avoiding cybertrespass and cybervandalism has sufficient weight to justify the use of monitoring and filtering technology in spite of the risks involved, whereas citizens' (and companies') interests in avoiding *cyberpiracy* do not. Alternatively, they may have reasoned that the monitoring and filtering of malware, given its nature, is less likely to imply censorship consequences than the monitoring and filtering of content related to intellectual property.

The following example, inspired by a real-world case study (Dittrich et al. 2011), illustrates the principlist and rights-based approach applied to the deployment of cybersecurity technology for *monitoring* computer systems in a response to a cybersecurity attack.

> *An information warfare monitor:* You are investigating a malicious botnet, the victims of which included the foreign embassies of dozens of countries, the Tibetan government-in-exile and multinational consulting firms. You begin your research by reviewing data collected by passive monitoring of suspected victim networks, which confirms the intrusions and identifies the malware. You collect more data from compromised computers with the owners' consent, monitor the command and control (C&C) infrastructure enough to understand the attackers' activities and to enable notification of infected parties at the appropriate time, work with government authorities in multiple jurisdictions to take down the attacker's C&C infrastructure, and store and handle data securely. (Adapted from Dittrich et al. 2011)

An information warfare monitor poses threats to right to privacy and of free speech of the suspected and actual victims (which may be particularly relevant for an exiled government). These threats are posed by the passive monitoring of suspected victim monitors (without consent) and subsequent data collection from the affected computers (with consent). In terms of the principlist approach, informed consent and notification fulfil the duty of *respect of persons*. In terms of the rights-based approach, they can be regarded as a way to balance (in the sense of checks and balances) the risk to the privacy of the victims caused from monitoring. Informed consent, it may be claimed, reduces the vulnerability to which a privacy breach and surveillance expose the subject of the right. Moreover, from a principlist point of view, security measures taken in the storing and handling of data from the computers of the victim (e.g. encryption, anonymisation, etc.) fulfil the duty of *beneficence* (which includes nonmaleficence as risk reduction). From the perspective of a human rights approach, they can be seen as a way to balance (in the sense of 'checks and balances') the heightened risk to privacy and informational self-determination of all other persons that the data in the infected computers may identify.

## 4.4 From Principlism and Human Rights to the Ethics of Risk

Hildebrandt advocates a legal approach (the 'triple test'; explained below) which involves both balancing as a trade-off and balancing as in 'checks and balances'. Some kind of trade-off is unavoidable when considering a rich and diversified set of human rights, because the duty implied by respect for one right may contradict the duty implied by respect for a different right. However, the idea of accepting a trade-off involving a human right may appear to contradict the very idea of a right, if a right is a side-constraint; that is, a rigid constraint defining the permissible scope of all other moral actions (Nozick 1974), or a 'trump card' (Dworkin 1977); that, is a consideration defeating all other utility considerations. According to those views, rights are different from other interests because they are the kind of things that societies cannot violate *even when* the violation clearly leads to a maximisation of aggregate interests (Rawls 1999: 3).

However, unless rights are very few and limited in the kind of duties they entail,[1] they are very likely to logically contradict each other in practical contexts. This is especially true of human rights as they are quite numerous and tend to have significant implications in terms of the resources and duties required by society to satisfy them.

The way Hildebrandt and John Rawls[2] address the problem of trade-offs involving rights is by acknowledging the necessity of limiting rights "without losing their substance" (Hildebrandt 2013: 375). What that means, in practice, is that one has to draw a distinction between the core elements of a right, which ought never be sacrificed (what Rawls calls "the central range of applications" [Rawls 1982: 11]) and those elements that are peripheral and should be satisfied, when possible, and sacrificed when they conflict with the core elements of another right. The hope is to be able to achieve, in a rationally defensible way, what Rawls calls a fully adequate scheme of rights and liberties. In doing so, pragmatic elements (what historical experience teaches us about the co-possibility of satisfying different rights within a coherent institutional arrangement) also play a role. However, deciding what applications of a human right are central to its meaning requires some kind of theory about the social function of the right in question.[3]

Hildebrand's triple test, which derives from an interpretation of the second paragraph of Art. 8 of the European Convention of Human Rights (binding for the 52 states of the Council of Europe), requires that a right's infringement "must be in accordance with the law, necessary in a democratic society and have a legitimate aim" (Hildebrandt 2013: 375). The necessity requirement "is understood as a requirement of proportionality between infringing measure and legitimate aim" (Hildebrandt 2013: 376). Proportionality is, philosophically, a difficult notion, but in the context of Hildbrandt's reasoning it may be interpreted, again, as a weighing

[1]This is arguably the case of a framework that only includes Nozickian libertarian ownership rights. These are strict negative rights prohibiting aggression and other forms of non-consensual interference aimed at dispossessing individuals of the fruits of their labor and of voluntary exchanges with other individuals.

[2]See for instance (Rawls 1982, 1996 Lecture VII: §8–11).

[3]This, of course, leaves open the question of how to address a conflict of rights when the clash involves the peripheral area of both rights, or the core area of both rights. There is no time here to dwell on the analysis of this problem. Perhaps it is acceptable to claim that it is compatible with respect for human rights to decide democratically which of two rights to sacrifice when both are involved only peripherally; the real tragic case is the one of a conflict between the cores of two rights, and perhaps a viable approach here is compensation (not necessarily only monetary). One potential solution that appears problematic here is a *maximising* one (i.e. to choose the combination of rights that maximises a given parameter). Any sufficiently *pluralist* conception of the fundamental interests and values behind such rights entails that there is no single metric to be maximised. That element of pluralism is perhaps what distinguishes, most fundamentally, a rights approach from a utilitarian one.

of the likelihood that, should a given privacy infringement not be allowed, an interest in the central range of application of some other right will be at risk, combined with a weighing of the likelihood that the cybersecurity measure adopted will not undermine the overall protection of the core human interests protected by the right in the core range of application of the right. An illustration of this could be the interpretation offered above of a high court decision to allow ISP to monitor and filter Internet traffic against malware and other cyberthreats, but to prohibit lower courts to oblige ISP to monitor and filter Internet traffic against violations of copyright laws.

Note, however, that even in a human rights approach, it is impossible to escape some probabilistic assessment of the risks of violating a right. Thus a right-based theory, no less than principlism, involves the assessment of risk and probabilities at some level of analysis. The evaluation of probabilities is explicit in the idea of risk-benefit analysis that is also explicitly invoked by the Menlo report in the application of the benevolence principle in practice.

It seems legitimate to conclude that the ethical assessment of cybersecurity always depends on risk assessment of a probabilistic form. Risk-assessment is normally understood as an aspect of the consequentialist approaches that justify the line of action that produces the biggest net benefit. When the outcomes are uncertain, actions and policies can only be assessed in terms of their *expected* net benefit. However, beyond utilitarianism (that is *only* concerned with outcomes) risk-benefit assessments are an integral aspect of any ethical framework that assesses the morality actions *also* in relation to their outcomes; for example, it is invoked by most interpretations of the duty of *beneficence* in principlist approaches in research ethics. Note that the Menlo Report states very clearly that the risk-benefit assessment under the heading of beneficence is not meant to be restricted in scope to research subjects. Instead, "[…] researchers should systematically assess risks and benefits across all stakeholders. In so doing, researchers should be mindful that risks to individual subjects are weighed against the benefits to society, not to the benefit of individual researchers or research subjects themselves" (Dittrich and Kenneally 2012 L 9).

Balancing a cybersecurity measure that poses a threat to privacy with heightened privacy guarantees requires an assessment of proportionality between the risk that a cybersecurity measure is meant to protect society against and the threat (free speech, due process, non-discrimination or data protection) that it constitutes against a human right. This presupposes a consideration of the *probability* of the violation of a right in the core area of application of such right.

## 4.5 Cybersecurity and the Ethics of Risk

In what follows, we shall consider a single cybersecurity case as a way of illustrating different approaches to the ethics of risk.

*Responding to ransomware:* You are the leader of a CERT team and you have identified ransomware (a software virus that encrypts the data in the computers infected and directs the victims to a payment service where, after paying 1000€, the victims can obtain the decryption key). You know that a partner software company has already begun to code an algorithm to decrypt the data; you estimate that the company has a 65% chance of success within one month (and a 0% chance of succeeding later). At the moment, 1000 computers are affected, all belonging to the network of an important hospital. Unfortunately, it is impossible to reconstruct what data was saved in each computer and the date of the latest backup. The probability that an alteration or deletion of data in a single computer will cause the death of a patient is 1/1000 for each device.

You can choose one of two response strategies:

- *Policy A*: you quarantine all the affected computers and shoot down the payment servers. These measures, with foreseen 100% efficacy, will prevent the spread of the infection and reduce the incentives for attackers to involve other computers in similar attacks in the near future. However, the malware is designed to detect your response and retaliate to it. It will irreversibly introduce random changes in the data in ways that are extremely hard to detect, or simply delete it. It is not possible to identify the data causally linked to the lives of patients in a reasonable amount of time.
- *Policy B:* you do not isolate the affected system and do not bring down the payment server; after one month, either you have obtained the decrypting tool with no losses; or you have not, in which case the infection will have spread to other 1,000,000 computers, with an expected aggregate economic loss for your society of €400,000,000, mostly consisting of donations of €500 to the hackers.

### 4.5.1 Expected Utility Maximisation

According to the moral theory of utilitarianism, the moral appraisal of any action is solely a function of the utility consequences of that action, i.e. of the sum total of well-being (or happiness) produced. (The net amount of aggregate well-being due to an action may also be negative if well-being losses are greater than gains.) Three features of utilitarianism are worth noticing: it is consequentialist welfarist (the ethical appraisal of consequences only considers the well-being of sentient beings involved) and aggregative (individual losses of well-being to one individual may be compensated by greater gains to others). Utilitarianism is also a strictly *maximising* theory: the *right* action is the one that maximises well-being in the aggregate. Even an action that produces a net gain of well-being relative to a previous state of the world is *wrong*, if a different action leading to a *greater* increase of utility is feasible.

Since the consequences of virtually every action are to some degree uncertain, any action-guiding version of utilitarianism must *not* assess actions based on the outcome that actually materialises. The action-guiding version of utilitarianism prescribes the maximisation of *aggregate expected utility*, by which one means the probability-weighted average of utility in all possible states of the world that an action could cause.

The ethical dilemma for our case is to compare an expected disutility of €260,000,000€ (65% chance of a possible €400,000,000 damage if the decryption tool is not developed) with the probability of causing one or more deaths. The probability that no single computer is essential to the life of a patient is $(999/1000)^{1000}$, which entails a $1-(999/1000)^{1000}$ —roughly a 63%—chance that one person will die because of the first policy. Thus, policy A imposes a significant risk to a single individual. As a guide to cases like this, the guidance by utilitarian risk-benefit assessment strikes some as counterintuitive. It requires the decision-maker to compare a high expected likelihood of death, for a single person, with aggregate disutility for a large group, formed by individuals each of whom suffers a very small loss compared to death. It may seem plausible that, no matter how large in the aggregate, the sum of many small individuals losses cannot justify imposing a high risk of death for a single person. Utilitarianism, however, implies that the opposite must be the case: no matter how valuable a personal life (assuming a finite value), the aggregate of small damages inflicted to a group will count for more, if the group is large enough.

### 4.5.2 The Maximin Rule

A close relative of utilitarianism (or better, expected utility consequentialism) is what one may call *maximin* consequentialism. According to the maximin rule, in Hansson's formulation:

> the utility of a mixture of potential outcomes is equal to the lowest utility associated with any of these outcomes. (Hansson 2003: 296)

The 'mixture' of the potential outcomes of an action is the set of all outcomes whose probability of occurring is more than zero. The maximin rule orders the desirability of actions according to the desirability of their worst possible outcomes. The algorithm for the cybersecurity professional in the case at hand is:

1. assess the total utility of the worst outcome ($O_A$) associated with A, considered as if it were certain;
2. assess the total utility of worst outcome ($O_B$) associated with B, considered as if it were certain;
3. if $U(O_A) > U(O_B)$, choose A; if $U(O_A) < U(O_B)$, choose B, if $U(O_A) = U(O_B)$ draw a lottery with a 50% chance of A and B.

The worst outcome for action A is the certain death of one person; the worst outcome for action B is a certain damage of €400,000,000. The maximin approach requires that we compare the two outcomes and choose the lesser of the two. Note that this approach suffers from an objection analogous to utilitarianism, namely that, unless an individual life has an infinite moral value, it may justify the sacrifice of a human life to avoid a large sum of individually limited economic damages.

Maximin is also subject to another objection. Suppose that $O_A$ is an outcome with a very small probability, e.g. a 1/1,000,000,000 chance of causing non-permanent health damage to all patients, amounting to a loss of 1,000,000,000€ in medical expenses and compensation. Utilitarianism entails that $O_A$ should be chosen, because the expected *dis*utility of $O_B$, being certain, is much higher, than the disutility of $O_A$, which is discounted by its low probability. Maximim requires choosing $O_B$, because it does not discount the disvalue of $O_A$ because of its low probability. Many would find utilitarianism more plausible than Maximin, given that in everyday life we consider it rational to engage in activities, such as crossing the street, which have a very small probability of leading to very bad outcomes (death after being hit by a car), even for the sake of a very small utility gains (e.g. purchasing ice cream).

Arguably, a significant proportion of those who believe that an individual life should be considered more important than a loss of €400,000,000 (distributed in small €500 losses for each individual), may nonetheless agree that strategy A is justifiable, given that the risk of causing death is so small. For example, we allow people to drive cars, in spite of the fact that allowing car driving increases the risk of death for innocent pedestrians, which may in fact be higher. Maximin consequentialism, however, obliges you to base your decision on what the worst possible outcome is for each scenario, in a method that is totally insensitive to its probability.

Therefore, the problem with this approach is that it would prohibit all cybersecurity measures that have some probability, no matter how low, of causing very significant harm as a side-effect (no matter how unlikely the causal chain that would lead to such outcome). Another problem is the difficulty of enumerating the low-probability events that may be associated with a given policy. As Hansson points out, we have to stop considering low-probability events that may follow from our actions at a certain point, and there may be no non-arbitrary cut-off point. This would introduce a degree of moral arbitrariness in the moral evaluation of such risks that counts against adopting the Maximin rule (Hansson 2003: 296).

### 4.5.3 Deontological and Rights-Based Theories

Deontological approaches are typically built around a list of morally prohibited acts, that is, acts that are prohibited no matter what, i.e. irrespective of the consequences. Suppose, for example, that it is not permissible to expose the private health condition of an individual to the public against his consent. A strict deontological moral system entails that it is always wrong to do so, even if, let us suppose, knowing this information would allow millions of shareholders of a company led by the sick man to reduce their exposure to financial risk. Let us refer to the acts that are prohibited—even when they would maximise utility—as 'violations of deontological constraints'. Deontological approaches to *risk* claim that moral agents act wrongly if acting involves a non-null risk of violating a deontological constraint.

(Absolutist) rights-based theories are similar to deontological theories, but they are framed in a manner that shifts our attention to the person obligations are owed to, rather than to the agent who is obligated. If persons have rights, certain things cannot be done to them no matter how good the general consequences, while other things are owed to them, no matter what the costs are. By extension, rights-based theories *of risk* claim that moral agents ought not to perform actions that have a more than a null risk of violating the rights of other people. For example, every innocent person may be believed to have a negative right to life, entailing a duty of other people not to act in ways that would cause that person to die.

Let us move to a more rigorous formulation of such views. Following Hansson, let us define:

> *Probabilistic absolutism:*
> [for deontological theories]: If it is morally prohibited to perform a certain action, then this prohibition extends to all mixtures in which this action has non- zero probability.
> [for rights-based theories]: If someone has a moral right that a certain action not be performed, then this right extends to all mixtures in which this action has non-zero probability. (Hansson 2003: 298)

In Hansson's terminology, *mixtures* are value carriers (actions, outcomes). For example, in the CERT case, the CERT manager is addressing the following two mixtures:

> A: shutting down the payment server, limiting the range of computers affected by ransomware and indirectly causing a person's death;
> B: not shutting down the payment server, allowing ransomware attacks to continue and allowing economic damage to occur.

According to probabilistic absolutism, if 'indirectly causing an (innocent) person's death' is impermissible, then every act that has a small probability of causing a person death is impermissible too. Thus, probabilistic absolutism prohibits A even when the probability of harming a patient is very low (e.g. equal to or less than 0.001% in the variation of the ransomware scenario discussed in Sect. 4.5.2).

The problem with this theory is that it is, in general, too demanding for the moral subject who, by virtue of some apparently innocent act, associated with some terrible outcome by virtue of a very unlikely chain of events, risks violating his duties. It also prevents the execution of many acts of beneficence (often attempts to do the good have a very small probability of doing some evil). Often, agents will face a dilemma in which they will violate duties whichever option they choose.

Some of the implausible consequences of probabilistic absolutism are avoided by risk-deontological and risk-rights-based theories acknowledging a *probability limit*.

> *Probability limit for risk-deontological theories:* Each prohibition of an action is associated with a probability limit. The prohibition extends to a mixture that contains the action if and

> only if the action has, in that mixture, a probability that is above the probability limit. (Hansson 2003: 298)[4]

In the threshold approach, risk-deontological (or risk-rights-based) constraints generate moral duties *only if* the risk of violating a deontological constraint (or another person's rights) is higher than a given *threshold value*. Therefore, it is legitimate to ignore risk-deontological (or risk-rights-based) prohibitions when we do actions that only have a very low chance of causing violations of these constraints.

This approach may seem to deliver a reasonable method to assess the scenario described above. With a probability threshold set to 5%, policy A would be impermissible in the first case discussed (where the risk of death of a patient was >60%) but not in the second one (where the probability of health damage was extremely low).

The main problem with the theory is that it appears difficult to justify such thresholds (e.g. how low should the probability of killing an innocent be to allow it to occur?). Not only it is difficult to justify a single threshold, but it seems even harder to justify different thresholds for different types of harm (e.g. how high should the threshold for allowing economic damage be set, in comparison to the threshold for causing death?) a priori.

Justice theories may explain some intuitions concerning the imposition of risk. Some of these theories imply that it is *ceteris paribus* ethically wrong to impose risk on individuals who are already vulnerable to risk instead of targeting less vulnerable people (Wolff and De-Shalit 2007; Ferretti 2009, 2016). For example, if a threat exists that could lead to the irremediable loss of equally sensitive data, it is *ceteris paribus* wrong to let the risk be imposed on poor instead of wealthier people. This is because, for the former, losing €500 due to the ransom may involve a significant sacrifice of economic security, which may increase their exposure to other kinds of risk (e.g. tackling disease or unemployment). Ferretti's (2016) theory focuses on total risk, suggesting that the threshold level should be different when duties affect persons in circumstances that already add to/reduce their total risk level. Similar implications can be drawn from capability-based theories of disadvantage and risk (Wolff and De-Shalit 2007; Murphy and Gardoni 2012).[5]

These *non-deontological* theories explain intuitions, which may be quite widespread, that what counts as an "acceptable level of risk" depends on both the kind of risk in question and the situation of the person affected by this risk. In contrast to the latter, risk-deontological (or risk-rights based) theories of risk assume an equal risk-threshold for all. The risk-deontological approach as such does not provide

---

[4] The probability limit for rights-based theories can be defined along similar lines.

[5] These theories measure the impact of risk in terms of their impact on capabilities, defined as genuine opportunities to achieve *valuable* functionings (Sen 2009; Nussbaum 2006). The approach by Wolff and De Shalit (2007) focuses in particular on the fact that certain categories of risks tend to affect more than one capability. It attributes more harmful effects to 'cross-category risks' and 'inverse cross-category risks'.

any principled guidance to assign different levels of risks in different cases.[6] In order to justify a *different* risk threshold, one needs to appeal to some independent conception of *fairness* in risk distribution. One last approach we will consider is the one provided by *contractualism.*

### 4.5.4 Contractualism and Risk

Aggregative views in general (not just aggregative views on risk) are exposed to peculiar counterexamples; the cybersecurity response to ransomware in Sect. 4.5.1 may be taken as one such example. The cybersecurity response A, which imposes a 65% risk that a person will die, seems morally objectionable because the sum of individual small losses, no matter how large, cannot justify imposing a significant risk of death to a single person.

The philosopher Thomas Scanlon has proposed *contractualism* as an alternative to utilitarianism. Contractualism compares the strength of the individual claims without aggregating them (Scanlon 1998: 235). Scanlon's way of comparing individual complaints has later been labelled the MiniMax Complaint principle, which states that "when we would not be violating any moral constraints, we are morally required to act in the way that minimises the strongest individual complaint" (Horton 2017, 55). In our example, the relevant complaints concern (a) the life of one individual person whose medical treatment depends on the integrity of the encrypted data and (b) the individual loss of €500 of one individual, not yet affected, who will end up paying a ransom for his encrypted data if further attacks are not prevented by shooting down the payment server. Since the complaint against death is greater than the complaint against a ransom, one ought not to quarantine the computers and to shoot down the payment servers.

There is a lively philosophical debate on how to interpret the MiniMax Complaint principle in cases involving risk. Consider the choice between two vaccines, assuming that choosing either one is necessary to avoid the spread in the population of an epidemic that will unavoidably kill everyone on Earth. Vaccine A has a one in a million chance of killing the user as a side effect; vaccine B leads to the certain paralysis of one limb for all users. The *ex post* version of the MiniMax Complaint (Scanlon 1998; Reibetanz 1998; Otsuka 2015), requires choosing B, since it adopts the perspective of a person who is certainly going to die as a result of A. Here it is assumed that in a population of several billion people it is almost certain that someone will die, but the identity of this person cannot be known in advance. In the *ex post* approach, the claim of the *statistical individual who will unavoidably die* is stronger (for *ex post* contractualism) than the claims of every person who, if the

[6] However, they can be used to represent all the appropriate beliefs. For example, a deontological theory can be a simple list of many different duties and rights, associated with specific probabilities specified at the level of concrete situations.

other vaccine is chosen, will only end up paralysed. Many find this counterintuitive.

An alternative theory is *ex ante* contractualism (Lenman 2008; James 2012; Frick 2015). A simple *ex ante* version compares complaints in terms of *expected* harm, that is to say, the outcome is weighted by the probability of its occurrence. Thus, the risk of 1 in a billion chance of losing life may be considered weaker than having a paralysed limb with full certainty. Thus the *ex ante* view justifies using vaccine A. This is considered more plausible by those who think, for example, that compulsory vaccination for non-lethal diseases is not necessarily morally wrong, even it is known in advance that some people will die because of lethal complications.

*Ex ante* contractualism may appear to have plausible implications in the case of a CERT's response to ransomware. When the risk of a patient's death (for each patient) is very low, it entails that it is permissible to quarantine the system and put the server used for the payments of the ransom offline. When the risk is significant, it prohibits sacrificing the patients.

But even *ex ante* contractualism has detractors. The objections against it can be explained more easily by focusing on a different case:

> *A choice of anti-malware:* You are dealing with malware that turns the affected computers into nodes in a botnet performing a distributed denial-of-service attack against servers in an important hospital, which risks placing the lives of its patients at risk. You have three anti-malware tools in your arsenal, all of which are effective against the malware. However, the malware is designed to retaliate by wiping out the entire hard disk, as soon as it is disconnected from the malicious server. A preliminary study of the malware shows that it could be fought with three different software approaches. Each of them fails in specific ways to limit the damage. Due to time and resource constraints, you can develop only one of these before the malware spreads, causing morally intolerable human damage. Which one do you develop?

– Anti-malware 1: it protects all computers but deletes all Excel and Word files during installation.
– Anti-malware 2: it only works on non-Apple operating systems, which entails that Apple systems will have to be quarantined (and will lose all data). Ten percent of the computers in the botnet are Apple ones.
– Anti-malware 3: it works perfectly on all computers, except on those with some specific UUIDs, Universal Unique Identifiers, assigned by the malware itself. It is impossible to determine the UUID generated by the malware without triggering a malware response that would erase all data. Hence, for every practical purpose, the UUID of each infected computer can be considered unknown and unknowable. It is known, however, that the malware will wipe out all the data if the last numerical digit of the UUID it assigned to device is 0. Since every Arabic numeral has the same chance of being the last numerical digit in these UUIDs, every computer has an *ex ante* 10% probability of being wiped out completely and a 90% probability of being rescued completely.

Let us begin by comparing Anti-malware 1 vs. 2. *Ex ante* contractualism here entails weighing the *ex ante* complaint of Mac users (having the hard-disc completely wiped out) vs. the *ex ante* complaint of other users (having only text and spreadsheet files deleted), considered individually. Since Mac users have the strongest *ex ante* complaint (they are 100% sure of having all their files deleted), contractualism requires that you choose anti-malware 1. In the imaged scenario, Apple software runs on 10% of the affected computers; note, however, that contractualism would have implied the same response if there had been a single Mac user in the botnet.

Let us now consider anti-malware 1 vs. anti-malware 3. Suppose that you have established empirically that each computer owner strongly prefers a lottery with a 90% chance of rescuing the data and a 10% probability of losing all data in the computer, compared to the certain loss of all their text and spreadsheet files. *Ex ante* utilitarianism entails, in this case, that you ought to choose anti-malware 3.

Is the choice of malware 3 morally unobjectionable? Similar cases in moral philosophy have been criticised for two reasons. First, it treats identified individuals, such as owners of Mac computers, differently from *statistical* individuals, e.g. owners of computers with a UUID whose last numeral digit is 0, whose identity can be determined only *after* they suffered from the harm. However, the difference between statistical individuals and identified individuals seems entirely morally arbitrary—in no way are statistical individuals less worthy of respect. Second, it uses statistical individuals as means: their interests are sacrificed to promote the aggregate good (Rüger 2018).[7]

In summary, it seems reasonable to expect that some situations faced in cybersecurity analysis and operation deal with outcomes that are not certain, but to which probabilities (often, mere subjective probabilities) can be assigned. Unfortunately, utilitarianism suffers from known objections (sacrificing the individual for the greater good) and there are hard cases in which the most intuitively plausible version of contractualism is no different from utilitarianism in this respect.

## 4.6 Contextual Integrity

Contextual integrity is a framework for understanding privacy, both descriptively (i.e. why do people find some technologies upsetting?) and normatively (should society favour the introduction of certain technologies?) (Nissenbaum 2004, 2009). The main insight of this theory is that privacy violations consist of violations of social norms concerning the transmission of information between persons. The relevant social norms are specific for the social contexts/practices and the social roles that individuals have within those practices. For example, the transmission of information between patient and physician in a hospital, spouses within a family, priest

[7] Philosophers have tried to avoid these types of problems by providing more sophisticated formulations of both *ex ante* and *ex post* versions of contractualism. All appear to be vulnerable to counterexamples and, for this reasons, it has been argued that the Minimax Complaint view should be abandoned altogether when dealing with risk (Horton 2017).

and confessor within the church, employer and employee within a company, policemen and citizen within the state, need not be (and usually are not) governed by the same informational norms. Individuals have privacy when established expectations concerning the way information should be transmitted are respected—this is compatible with people expecting different people in different contexts to handle their information in very different ways. However, not all changes of social norms and expectations concerning information should be considered violations of privacy since, as we shall see, some changes in informational norms may be justified, all things considered.

Contextual integrity is a mildly conservative theory. The violation of a contextual integrity norm provides a prima facie case for considering a new practice (e.g. the introduction of a new cybersecurity technology) as a sensitive privacy issue. However, the overall evaluation of the innovation may turn out to be justified in the end. Thus, the theory has a conservative bias, but it does not support conservative prescriptions in every case. Violating established expectations can be significantly harmful,[8] but it may not be wrong overall. The conservative bias of the theory can be overcome by pointing out, following the work of Michael Walzer (1983), that a transformation even in an established social norm can provide a more sensible method to achieve the goals that actors in a practice are set to achieve, without altering the most general relevant principles applying to the domain, and without violating the fundamental rights and interests of all those affected (Nissenbaum 2009: Chap. 8).

In recent work (2009), Nissenbaum explains how to use the theory as a basis for the empirical analysis of technologies that are perceived as raising a privacy problem; the feeling of a technology being problematic is explained as a consequence of its violation of expectations concerning information, given the existing context-relevant social norms. The moral assessment is driven by the assessment of the goal of the practice and the framework of more general principles and values applying across domains. Nissenbaum's privacy as contextual integrity is directly relevant to assessing cybersecurity technologies whose goal is to ensure the confidentiality of information. It is also pertinent to assessing technologies for detecting online threats and counter cybercrime, since such technologies are likely to effect the way information is accessed and used as a side effect.

[8] Nissenbaum (2004, Chap. 8) justifies the conservative inclination of the theory by considering arguments for conservativism provided by the radical utilitarian philosopher Jeremy Bentham (1747–1832) and the conservative philosopher Edmund Burke (1729–1797). Bentham argues that laws contradicting established ones tend to undermine the sense of security that derives from established expectations about the law. Thus, radical legal innovations could bring about—at least during the transition to a new legal regime—a utility loss, making it more difficult for agents to plan rationally in the pursuit of their own goals. Burke, on the other hand, considers established customs as the product of accumulated wisdom, which normally exceeds the ability of the individual minds to build models of social interactions and solutions for social problems that work in practice. Arguably, both arguments apply also to abrupt changes in conventional norms concerning information.

Moreover, some aspects of Nissenbaum's framework can be expanded and applied beyond its original scope, i.e. privacy. In particular, let us assume that the moral importance of contextual integrity derives from the value (in terms of security, peace of mind and the ability to rationally plan one's life) of fulfilling expectations. If so, there is no reason to consider only expectations connected with *informational* norm, as Nissenbaum's approach does. Her theory can be generalised into a more overarching theory that requires cybersecurity agents to consider established social norms and expectations concerning the actions (e.g. 'investigating a crime', 'assessing the trustworthiness of an employee', 'responding to an emergency in a patient') and not only those associated with the way information is accessed, transacted and used.

We thus conclude this essay by sketching a methodology for the ethical assessment of cybersecurity technology, which is essentially a version of Nissenbaum's contextual integrity privacy framework (2009: Chap. 9), extended to include social norms and expectations affecting all human interactions that are constitutive of an established social practice. The approach applies to all cases in which the adoption of a cybersecurity policy, or technology, affects the way information is exchanged. It also applies to all cases in which it affects the relations between people with established roles (roles linked to stable expectations) within the institution (e.g. hospital, company) or practice (e.g. diagnosis, marketing) that is affected by them. Following Nissenbaum, the framework consists of the following steps:

1. Establish the prevailing context of the cybersecurity measures in question (e.g. finance, law-enforcement, administration, business, medicine or some combination of more than one context);
2. Ascertain the information attributes (e.g. citizen's name, age, amount and entity of commercial transactions, purchase type) affected by the cybersecurity measures proposed; ascertain what aspects of human interactions (which are not defined by informational exchanges) are affected
3. Determine what changes in the principles/social norms governing the transmission of information are foreseeably due to the cybersecurity measures; determine other foreseeable changes in human interactions and modalities of operation in practice;
4. Red flags: if the new cybersecurity measures generate changes in the actors (e.g. client, financial institution employee, police investigator, nurse, physician), attributes (e.g. the kind of information/interaction affected) or relevant social norms, flag the measure as a prima facie violation of the contextual integrity of the domain in question. This counts as a prima facie violation and counts against the measure unless it can be justified in steps 5 and 6 below.
5. For a technology that has raised a red flag, determine what are the socially valuable goals and the core EU values and rights affected by the change in informational norms and expectations concerning the social interactions that have been detected;

6. For a technology that has raised a red flag, determine if the changes caused in this way improve the prospects of the actors to achieve the valuable goals of the practice; determine also whether they conflict with core EU values and rights.

## 4.7 Conclusions

This chapter presented several ethical frameworks for evaluating cybersecurity threats, countermeasures and policies. The chapter began with an examination of two influential approaches, the principlist approach (especially influential for the ethics of cybersecurity *research*) and the human rights approach (especially important for the law, in particular EU law). Both approaches are non-utilitarian, in that they do not define as morally right, or morally required, those cybersecurity acts (or policies) that maximise the good, defined as a single value (e.g. utility, or happiness). We then demonstrated that both these non-utilitarian approaches raise questions about the ethics of risks and present different ethical approaches to evaluating risk. Finally, we presented Helen Nissenbaum's contextual integrity theory both as a framework to understand why some technological changes are perceived as problematic and as a normative approach to assess whether they count as privacy violations all things considered. We proposed a revised version of Nissenbaum's contextual integrity framework for identifying and ethically assessing changes brought about by cybersecurity measures and policies, not only in relation to privacy but more generally to the key expectations concerning human interactions within the practice.

**Acknowledgements** The chapter was created with funding from the European Union's Horizon 2020 research and innovation programme under grant agreement No 700540 and the Swiss State Secretariat for Education, Research and Innovation (SERI) under contract number 16.0052-1.

## References

Agre PE (1998) Introduction. In: Agre PE , Rotenberg M (eds) Technology and privacy: the new landscape. The MIT Press, Cambridge, MA/London, pp 1–28, at 7

Boyce MW, Duma KM, Hettinger LJ (2011) Human performance in cybersecurity: a research agenda. Proc Hum Factors Ergon Soc Annu Meet 55(1):1115–1119. https://doi.org/10.1177/1071181311551233

Brey P (2007) Ethical aspects of information security and privacy. In: Security, privacy, and trust in modern data management, data-centric systems and applications. Springer, Berlin/Heidelberg, pp 21–36. http://link.springer.com/content/pdf/10.1007/978-3-540-69861-6.pdf#page=36

Dittrich D, Kenneally E (2012) The Menlo report: ethical principles guiding information and communication technology research. US Department of Homeland Security

Dittrich D, Bailey M, Dietrich S (2011) Building an active computer security ethics community. IEEE Secur Priv 9(4):32–40
Dworkin R (1977) Taking rights seriously. Harvard University Press, Cambridge, MA
Ferretti MP (2009) Risk and distributive justice: the case of regulating new technologies. Sci Eng Ethics 16(3):501–515. https://doi.org/10.1007/s11948-009-9172-z
Ferretti MP (2016) Risk imposition and freedom. Pol Philos Econ 15(3):261–279. https://doi.org/10.1177/1470594X15605437
Frick J (2015) Contractualism and social risk. Philos Pub Affairs 43(3):175–223. https://doi.org/10.1111/papa.12058
Hadlington L (2017) Human factors in cybersecurity; examining the link between internet addiction, impulsivity, attitudes towards cybersecurity, and risky cybersecurity behaviours. Heliyon 3(7):e00346. https://doi.org/10.1016/j.heliyon.2017.e00346
Hansson SO (2003) Ethical criteria of risk acceptance. Erkenntnis 59(3):291–309
Hildebrandt M (2013) Balance or trade-off? Online security technologies and fundamental rights. Philos Tech 26(4):357–379. https://doi.org/10.1007/s13347-013-0104-0
Horton J (2017) Aggregation, complaints, and risk. Philos Pub Affairs 45(1):54–81. https://doi.org/10.1111/papa.12084
James A (2012) Contractualism's (not so) slippery slope. Leg Theory 18(3):263–292. https://doi.org/10.1017/S135232521200002X
Jasmontaite L, Fuster GG, Gutwirth S et al (2017) Canvas White Paper 2 – cybersecurity and law. SSRN scholarly paper ID 3091939. Rochester: Social Science Research Network. https://papers.ssrn.com/abstract=3091939. Last access 7 July 2019
Johnson ML, Bellovin SM, Keromytis AD (2011) Computer security research with human subjects: risks, benefits and informed consent. In: International conference on financial cryptography and data security. Springer, Berlin, pp 131–137
Kenneally E, Bailey M (2013) Cyber-security research ethics dialogue & strategy workshop
Kenneally E, Michael Bailey M, Maughan D (2010) A framework for understanding and applying ethical principles in network and security research. In: International conference on financial cryptography and data security. Springer, Berlin, pp 240–246
Lenman J (2008) Contractualism and risk imposition. Pol Philos Econ 7(1):99–122. https://doi.org/10.1177/1470594X07085153
Mittelstadt B (2017) Designing the health-related internet of things: ethical principles and guidelines. Information 8(3). http://www.mdpi.com/2078-2489/8/3/77htm. Last access 7 July 2019
Murphy C, Gardoni P (2012) The capability approach in risk analysis. In: Handbook of risk theory. Springer, Dordrecht, pp 979–997
Newman LH (2017) Medical devices are the next security nightmare. Wired. https://www.wired.com/2017/03/medical-devices-next-security-nightmare/. Last access 7 July 2019
Nissenbaum H (2004) Privacy as contextual integrity. Wash Law Rev 79(1):119
Nissenbaum H (2009) Privacy in context: technology, policy, and the integrity of social life. Stanford University Press, Stanford
Nozick R (1974) Anarchy, state, and utopia. Basic Books, New York
Nussbaum MC (2006) Frontiers of justice: disability, nationality, species membership. The Belknap Press, Cambridge, MA
Otsuka M (2015) Risking life and limb: how to discount harms by their improbability. In: Cohen GI, Daniels N, Eyal N (eds) Identified versus statistical lives: an interdisciplinary perspective. Oxford University Press, Oxford
Rawls J (1982) The basic liberties and their priority. The Tanner Lectures on Human Values 3:3–87
Rawls J (1996) Political liberalism, expanded edn. Columbia University Press, New York
Rawls J (1999) A theory of justice, 2nd edn. Harvard University Press, Cambridge, MA
Reibetanz S (1998) Contractualism and aggregation. Ethics 108(2):296–311. https://doi.org/10.1086/233806
Ross WD (2002) The right and the good. Stratton-Lake P (ed) Oxford University Press, Oxford

Rüger K (2018) On ex ante contractualism. J Ethics Soc Philos 13(3). https://doi.org/10.26556/jesp.v13i3.323
Scanlon T (1998) What we owe to each other. Belknap Press of Harvard University Press, Cambridge, MA
Sen AK (2009) The idea of justice. Harvard University Press, Cambridge, MA
Spring JM, Illari P (2018) Building general knowledge of mechanisms in information security. Philos Tech. https://doi.org/10.1007/s13347-018-0329-z
Walzer M (1983) Spheres of justice: a defense of pluralism and equality. Basic Books, New York
Weber RH (2010) Internet of things–new security and privacy challenges. Comput Law Secur Rev 26(1):23–30
Weber K, Loi M, Christen M (2018) Digital medicine, cybersecurity and ethics: an uneasy relationship. Am J Bioeth 18(9):52–53
Wolff J, De-Shalit A (2007) Disadvantage. Oxford political theory. Oxford University Press, Oxford
Yaghmaei E, van de Poel I, Christen M et al (2017) Canvas White Paper 1 – cybersecurity and ethics. SSRN scholarly paper ID 3091909. Social Science Research Network, Rochester. https://papers.ssrn.com/abstract=3091909. Last access 7 July 2019

# Chapter 5
# Cybersecurity Regulation in the European Union: The Digital, the Critical and Fundamental Rights

**Gloria González Fuster and Lina Jasmontaite**

**Abstract** This chapter provides an overview of the European Union (EU) policies and legislative measures developed in an attempt to regulate cybersecurity. By invoking a historical perspective, policy developments that have shaped the cybersecurity landscape of the EU are highlighted. More concretely, this contribution investigates how the EU has been delimiting and constructing its cybersecurity policies in relation to different and sometimes opposing objectives, and questions what such choices reveal about (and how they determine) the evolution of the EU's cybersecurity policy and its legal contours. For this purpose, the major steps in the evolution of the EU's agenda on cybersecurity are analysed, ranging from the adoption of the 2013 Cybersecurity Strategy to other numerous norms, initiatives and sectorial frameworks that tackle issues arising from the active use of information systems and networks. The chapter reviews the mobilisation of multiple areas (such as the regulation of electronic communications, critical infrastructures and cybercrime) in the name of cybersecurity imperatives, and explores how the operationalisation of such imperatives surfaced in the EU cybersecurity strategy published in September 2017. The chapter suggests that one of the key challenges of cybersecurity regulation is to impose the right obligations on the right actors, through the right instrument. Reflecting on issues surrounding the current liability framework dating from the 80s, it considers how principles such as data protection by design and default as well as the 'duty of care' have emerged. Finally, the chapter considers how the perception of cybersecurity's relationship with (national) security plays a determinant role in the current EU legislative and policy debates, where fundamental rights considerations, despite being acknowledged in numerous policy documents, are only considered in a limited manner.

**Keywords** Cybercrime · Cyberdefence · Cybersecurity · EU law

G. G. Fuster · L. Jasmontaite (✉)
Vrije Universiteit Brussel (VUB), Research Group on Law, Science, Technology and Society (LSTS), Brussels, Belgium
e-mail: gloria.gonzalez.fuster@vub.be; lina.jasmontaite@vub.be



M. Christen et al. (eds.), *The Ethics of Cybersecurity*, The International Library of Ethics, Law and Technology 21,
https://doi.org/10.1007/978-3-030-29053-5_5

## 5.1 Formulating Cybersecurity as a Policy Area and Its Objectives

The publication of the First European Union (EU) Cybersecurity Strategy in 2013 marked the formal establishment of 'cybersecurity' as a new policy area in the EU (European Commission and High Representative 2013). This recognition was a long awaited development acknowledging the blurring of lines in three initially distinct but converging policy areas of (1) network and information security measures that target operators of essential services, and providers of critical and digital infrastructures; (2) electronic communications, including privacy and data protection issues; and (3) cybercrime (van der Meulen et al. 2015; Christou 2016). It took over 20 years for a gradually growing number of scattered initiatives addressing issues concerning the digital environment—ranging from digital signatures and ecommerce to cybercrime and critical infrastructure—to be recognised under an overarching umbrella term of cybersecurity. In addition, the area has, most recently included measures concerning cyberdefence (Christou 2016).

This chapter aims to capture the current state of the art of the cybersecurity landscape in the EU. It does so by analysing EU policies and legislative measures in an attempt to regulate cybersecurity; identifying the challenges of conceptualising this policy area; reflecting on the limitations imposed on cybersecurity regulation by the principle of conferral and the way this affects the choice of regulatory measures and addressees of regulation; and, finally, discussing the triggers shaping cybersecurity regulation, in particular political developments and the perception of EU values and interests.

It is now established that a highly fragmented legal framework constitutes the European cybersecurity policy area and that this area is bound to develop further given the EU's digital dependency. As suggested by Ramses Wessel, cybersecurity forms "an excellent example of an area in which the different policy fields need to be combined (a requirement for horizontal consistency), and where measures need to be taken at the level of both the EU and Member States (calling for vertical consistency)" (Wessel 2015: 405). Therefore, it is proposed that the five strategic EU cybersecurity priorities listed below capture the complexity of the policy area and provide insights into how both horizontal and vertical consistency could be attained. The five strategic EU cybersecurity priorities are (European Commission and High Representative 2013: 4–16):

- *Achieving 'cyber resilience'* by establishing minimum requirements for the functioning, cooperation and coordination of national competent authorities for network information systems.
- *Reducing cybercrime* by (a) ensuring a swift transposition of the cybercrime related EU Directives, (b) encouraging ratification of the Council of Europe's Budapest Convention on Cybercrime (Council of Europe 2001), and (c) funding programmes for the deployment of operational tools.

- *Developing cyberdefence policy and capabilities related to the Common Security and Defence Policy (CSDP)* by (a) assessing operational EU cyberdefence requirements, (b) developing the EU cyberdefence policy framework, (c) promoting dialogue and coordination between civilian and military actors in the EU, and (d) facilitating a dialogue with international partners.
- *Developing the industrial and technological resources for cybersecurity* by (a) establishing a public-private platform on Network and Information Security (NIS) solutions, (b) providing technical guidelines and recommendations for the adoption of NIS standards and good practices, and (c) encouraging the development of security standards for technology 'with stronger, embedded and user-friendly security features'.
- *Establishing a coherent international cyberspace policy for the EU and promoting core EU values* by mainstreaming cyberspace issues into EU external relations and Common Foreign and Security Policy (CFSP), and by supporting capacity building on cybersecurity and resilient information infrastructures in third countries. More specifically, the EU should ensure that its consultations with international partners on cyber issues are designed to complement the existing bilateral dialogues between the Member States and third countries. These consultations shall be driven by the EU core values of human dignity, freedom, democracy, equality, the rule of law and the respect for fundamental rights. Following the objectives of this priority, the EU aims to attain a high level of data protection, including the protection of personal data transferred to third countries.

In summary, the term 'cybersecurity', from an EU perspective, entails a combination of cyber resilience, cybercrime, cyberdefence, (strictly) cybersecurity and global cyberspace issues.

By identifying these five distinct priority areas, the 2013 Strategy aimed "*to make the EU's online environment the safest in the world*" (European Commission and High Representative 2013) —somehow challenging the cliché that no technical environment is 100% secure. It is hard to measure the current cybersecurity capacity at the EU level and whether it effectively results in *the safest* possible online environment. Two ransomware attacks known under the names of WannaCry and Petya (malware) that broke out in 2017 indicated that many improvements, in particular in terms of the response and cooperation among different actors concerned with cybersecurity at EU and national level, could still be made.

The two mentioned attacks are also interesting to consider from another perspective. They constitute a particularly good demonstration of a series of characteristics of cybersecurity as a policy area. First, this policy area recognises that cyber-attacks are the new reality and that such attacks not only can have cascading effects that are hard to predict and but that they may also cripple many more organisations in Europe than anticipated. At the same time, the recognition of the seriousness of cyber-attacks increases in the aftermath of cyber-incidents that inflict damage on EU-based businesses. Secondly, tackling cyber-attacks requires close cooperation between well-established networks composed of both public and private entities.

Thirdly, ineffective cybersecurity policies may obstruct the smooth functioning of the Digital Single Market, which in turn may have detrimental monetary implications for individuals, businesses and the public sector.

In autumn 2017, preceding the mentioned two cyber-attacks, the European Commission (EC) and the High Representative of the Union for Foreign Affairs and Security Policy published a Joint Communication to the European Parliament and the Council of the European Union titled *Resilience, Deterrence and Defence: Building strong cybersecurity for the EU* (the Second EU Cybersecurity Strategy or 2017 Joint Communication) which built on previous initiatives and sectorial frameworks, such as the legal frameworks for telecommunications, electronic commerce and electronic signatures, policy and regulatory measures, which have traditionally delineated the fragmented landscape of EU's approach to cybersecurity. The Second EU Cybersecurity Strategy emphasised the need for measures that would allow (1) building greater EU resilience to cyber-attacks, (2) facilitating detection of cyber-attacks, and (3) strengthening international cooperation on cybersecurity (European Commission and High Representative of the Union for Foreign Affairs and Security Policy 2017).

The 2017 Joint Communication illustrates well the evolution of the EU's understanding of the cybersecurity landscape. It also foresees that for the conventional idea of cybersecurity being a multi-stakeholder responsibility to be implemented in the EU, "multiple layers of government, economy and society should be involved" in order to improve cybersecurity capacity (European Commission and High Representative of the Union for Foreign Affairs and Security Policy 2017, 3). For this purpose, the Second EU Cybersecurity Strategy insists on having "more robust and effective structures to promote cybersecurity and to respond to cyber-attacks in the Member States but also in the EU's own institutions, agencies and bodies", which to some extent delineates the scope of the EU cybersecurity area (European Commission and High Representative of the Union for Foreign Affairs and Security Policy 2017: 3). Similarly important is the call for "a more comprehensive, cross-policy approach to building cyber-resilience and strategic autonomy, with a strong Single Market" which receives stronger emphasis in comparison with the First EU Cybersecurity Strategy (European Commission and High Representative of the Union for Foreign Affairs and Security Policy 2017: 3). The Second EU Cybersecurity Strategy, despite not being a legally binding instrument, also clarifies the roles of different EU agencies shaping the cybersecurity policy area.[1]

From a legal perspective, particularly relevant is the Second Cybersecurity Strategy's willingness to address liability questions in cybersecurity (European Commission and High Representative of the Union for Foreign Affairs and Security Policy 2017: 6). The Second EU Cybersecurity Strategy, following up on the Mid-Term Review on the implementation of the Digital Single Market Strategy which was published in spring 2017, highlights the need to analyse the implications of new

[1]In particular, the European Union Agency for Law Enforcement Cooperation (Europol), the European Union Agency for Law Enforcement Training (CEPOL) and the European Union Agency for Network and Information Security (ENISA) in the domain of cybersecurity.

technologies and to take steps to address the risks that they create. The Second EU Cybersecurity Strategy does not elaborate on such implications but instead relies on statements made in the Mid-Term Review—the high-level policy document representing positions of different units of the Commission working within this area. The Mid-Term Review refers to security challenges caused by Internet of Things (IoT) based applications, including "the *safety* of connected systems, products and services, as well as for businesses' liability" (EC 2017b: 11).[2] The Mid-Term Review explains that "[f]aulty sensors, vulnerable software or unstable connectivity may make it difficult to determine who is technically and legally responsible for any ensuing damage" (EC 2017b: 11). In this, the EC vows to revise the existing legal framework to address "new technological developments (including robotics, Artificial Intelligence and 3D printing), especially from the angle of civil law liability and to take into account the results of the ongoing evaluation of the Directive on liability for defective products and the Machinery Directive" (EC 2017b: 11).

The need to address liability in this context then resurfaces in the 2018 Communication on Artificial Intelligence, where it is highlighted that '[a]s with any transformative technology, some AI applications may raise new ethical and legal questions, for example related to liability' (EC 2018: 2). Liability was also referred to as a concern of cloud computing contracts (EC 2012). The frequency at which liability questions remerge in policy debates and documents suggests that it is a principled issue that requires legal consideration.

## 5.2 A Virtuous But Vicious Circle of Regulation: From Cybersecurity Law to Policy and Vice Versa

It is interesting to note that whereas the two EU Cybersecurity Strategies followed the adoption of numerous legislative measures concerning cybersecurity, they put forward policy objectives which subsequently resulted in legislation, namely the Network and Information Security Directive and the Cybersecurity Act, which further clarifies the role and mandate of the European Union Agency for Network and Information Security (ENISA). Building on this observation, we suggest that the cybersecurity area revives itself by both law and inter-area policy measures. Policy measures from various policy areas eventually led to changes and adjustments in various EU legal frameworks and *vice versa*. The following paragraphs provide two illustrative examples supporting this claim.

First, while the Second EU Cybersecurity Strategy proposes to set up an EU certification framework that would benefit both business and the users, the details over the envisioned certification framework that would "inform and reassure

[2] Whereas the word 'safety' at first glance may seem to be displaced and the term 'security' would have been a better fit, it reflects the very carefully selected language of the EC. The use of this term establishes a link with the General Product Safety Directive 2001/95/EC and The Radio Equipment Directive 2014/53/EU.

purchasers and users about the security properties of the products and services they buy and use" are provided in the proposal for a Cybersecurity Act (European Commission and High Representative of the Union for Foreign Affairs and Security Policy 2017: 5). This framework, though it would not result in "any immediate regulatory obligations", would allow certification and conformity self-assessment of ICT products and services.[3]

The mention of the 'duty of care' principle in the Second EU Cybersecurity Strategy is the second example, which reflects a vicious circle approach to cybersecurity regulation. Stakeholders are encouraged to explore this principle as it may lead to "a range of methods from design to testing and verification", which could potentially tackle and minimise software vulnerabilities (European Commission and High Representative of the Union for Foreign Affairs and Security Policy 2017: 5). The rationale of this principle was to a certain extent already pursued in the Network and Information Security Directive adopted in 2016—a year before the Second Cybersecurity Strategy was published. More specifically, the 'duty of care' principle is anchored in Article 14 of the NIS Directive, which obliges Member States to foresee security requirements and incident notification requirements for operators of essential services (e.g. providers of electricity or water). More specifically, entities that have been identified as operators of essential services by Member States have to take appropriate measures that would enable the prevention and minimisation of the "the impact of incidents affecting the security of the network and information systems used for the provision of such essential services, with a view to ensuring the continuity of those services" (European Parliament and Council of the European Union 2016: Article 14.2). The same provision also requires operators of essential services to notify as soon as reasonably possible "the competent authority or the CSIRT of incidents having a significant impact on the continuity of the essential services they provide" (European Parliament and Council of the European Union 2016: Article 14.3).

This section demonstrated that the cybersecurity area is evolving and comprised of highly fragmented measures. Cybersecurity is a horizontal problem, which is in a sense a common denominator of various new technologies connected to the World Wide Web. The following section illustrates some challenges and risks arising from the different perceptions of cybersecurity as a policy area.

## 5.3 Conceptualising Cybersecurity as a Policy Area Through Piecemeal Legislation and Policy

As mentioned, numerous policies and regulatory measures have been adopted to advance the security of citizens, businesses and public administrations in the areas of network and information security measures, electronic communications and

[3] The use of standards is generally promoted by the EC.

cybercrime. In fact, the EU has only recently started using the term 'cybersecurity' in its policy documents. We suggest that the adoption of a comprehensive EU Cybersecurity Strategy in 2013 can be considered the tipping point which triggered the increased use of the term in EU policy documents (e.g., in 2016 Communication 'Strengthening Europe's Cyber Resilience System and Fostering a Competitive and Innovative Cybersecurity Industry', and the Cybersecurity Act).

The 2013 Strategy provided in a footnote a definition according to which "[c]ybersecurity commonly refers to the safeguards and actions that can be used to protect the cyber domain, both in the civilian and military fields, from those threats that are associated with or that may harm its interdependent networks and information infrastructure" (European Commission and High Representative 2013: 3). In this context, cybersecurity's primary objectives were considered to be the preservation of "the availability and integrity of the networks and infrastructure and the confidentiality of the information contained therein" (European Commission and High Representative 2013: 3).

This definition, to a certain extent, deviated from a prior suggestion put forward by the European Network and Information Security Agency (ENISA). ENISA proposed using "a contextual definition" because cybersecurity is a broad and evolving term, arguing that whereas opting for a specific definition can allow for maintaining clarity, stakeholders and policy makers should select definitions that fit their particular needs in a specific context (ENISA 2016: 28). Consequently, various stakeholders and policy makers, including EU institutions, often opt for definitions developed by standardisation organisations, such as the European Committee for Electrotechnical Standardization (CENELEC) and the International Organization for Standardization (ISO), or international organisations, such as the International Telecommunication Union (ITU). Not surprisingly, by now numerous definitions coexist focusing on different dimensions of cybersecurity (e.g. political, military, economic, technical, legal and citizens').

Although some definitions may appear extremely broad,[4] narrow and more specific definitions, in particular related to technical requirements, might also need to be considered with caution. Whereas they may serve well during a negotiation phase, it is important to consider limitations embedded in them. For example, many definitions developed by standardisation organisations target the micro-management level. Therefore, they may carry a risk of conceptualising 'cybersecurity' in an unduly limited way. For example, cybersecurity may be seen only as a concern of risk that may arise online; it may be understood as a protection of only virtual assets; or it may only target malicious activities. Such definitions carry a risk of not considering, for instance, implications for individuals and their rights.

[4] For example, according to the ITU in Plenipotentiary Resolution 181 (Guadalajara, 2010) on definitions and terminology relating to building confidence and security in the use of information and communication technologies, consider cybersecurity to be "*the collection of tools, policies, security concepts, security safeguards, guidelines, risk management approaches, actions, training, best practices, assurance and technologies that can be used to protect the cyber environment and organization and user's assets*".

Definitions used to refer to cybersecurity by various actors, including EU Member States, bodies and institutions, typically represent different perspectives, which can potentially be at odds with each other (see for an overview Table 5.1). For example, whereas ENISA often frames cybersecurity as a mere technical issue, some Member States in their national security strategies regard cybersecurity as an issue of national security (e.g. Estonia and Slovakia).

The possibility of attaching different meanings to the term ‘cybersecurity’ has both advantages and disadvantages. It indicates the flexibility of the term that can adapt to changing circumstances. At the same time, an ever-evolving term can become overly inclusive or broad in a manner that would obstruct coherent regulation in this area and in this way hamper the development of regulatory measures. It also opens a space for friction between EU and Member States powered around the national security notion. Consequently, this shifting meaning of the term may make progress in this particular policy area hard to attain, or at least less visible.

To render the conceptualisation of cybersecurity more complicated from a legal perspective, in measures addressed to the Member States, EU institutions appear to be reluctant to even use the term. That is the case, for example, of the EU adopted Directive (EU) 2016/1148 of the European Parliament and of the Council of 6 July 2016 concerning measures for a high common level of security of network and information systems across the Union (NIS Directive). The NIS Directive lays down obligations for all Member States to adopt certain measures (e.g. national strategies on the security of network and information systems) that would enable the development of a culture of security across industries and sectors that rely on the use of information communication technologies.

Within the context of this Directive, “security of network and information systems” is regarded as “the ability of network and information systems to resist, at a given level of confidence, any action that compromises the availability, authenticity, integrity or confidentiality of stored or transmitted or processed data or the related services offered by, or accessible via, those network and information systems” (European Parliament and Council of the European Union 2016 Article 4 (2)). This definition seems to align with the conception reflected in the EU Cybersecurity Strategy, where the underlying objective of cybersecurity is considered to be the preservation of “the availability and integrity of the networks and infrastructure and the confidentiality of the information contained therein” (European Commission and High Representative 2013: 3). Nonetheless, the NIS Directive formally addresses “security of information systems and networks”, and not cybersecurity.

In short, the ambiguity embedded in and sustained by the term ‘cybersecurity’ allows for the term to be invoked across the different policy areas mentioned above. Whereas this is not problematic in itself, the fragmented approach may not be cost-efficient (ENISA 2017: 4). More importantly, it begs the question of whether EU cybersecurity shall be considered an autonomous notion, with a specific nature in EU policy as opposed to other policy levels.

**Table 5.1** Definitions of cybersecurity in national cybersecurity strategies of EU Member States

| Document title, country, year | Definition |
|---|---|
| Austrian Cyber Security Strategy, 2013 | The term 'cyber security' stands for the security of infrastructure in cyber space, of the data exchanged in cyber space and above all of the people using cyber space. |
| Croatian Cybersecurity Strategy, 2015 | Cyber security encompasses activities and measures for achieving the confidentiality, integrity and availability of information and systems in cyberspace. |
| Czech Republic Cybersecurity Strategy for the period of 2015–2020 | Cyber security comprises a sum of organisational, political, legal, technical, and educational measures and tools aiming to provide a secure, protected, and resilient cyberspace in the Czech Republic for the benefit of both public and private sectors, as well as for the general public. |
| Cybersecurity Strategy of the Republic of Cyprus: Network and Information Security and Protection of Critical Information Infrastructures, 2012 | Cybersecurity refers to the broader security of networked systems that operate in cyberspace, i.e. in most cases connected to the internet, and this term also covers the safe and secure usage of these systems by end users. |
| Dutch National Cyber Security: Strategy from awareness to capability, 2018 | Cyber security is the entirety of measures to prevent damage caused by disruption, failure or misuse of ICT and how to recover should damage occur. |
| Estonian Cyber Security Strategy, 2014–2017 | Cyber security is an integral part of national security; it supports the functioning of the state and society, the competitiveness of the economy and innovation. |
| Finland's Cyber security Strategy, 2013 | Cyber security means the desired end state in which the cyber domain is reliable and in which its functioning is ensured. |
| Italian National Strategic Framework for Cyberspace Security, 2013 | With the term cyberspace, we refer to the complex of all interconnected ICT hardware and software infrastructure, to all data stored in and transferred through the networks and all connected users, as well as to all logical connections however established among them. It therefore encompasses the internet and all communication cables, networks and connections that support information and data processing, including all mobile internet devices. |
| Cyber Security Strategy for Germany, 2011 | Cyberspace is the virtual space of all IT systems linked at data level on a global scale. The basis for cyberspace is the internet as a universal and publicly accessible connection and transport network, which can be complemented and further expanded by any number of additional data networks. IT systems in an isolated virtual space are not part of cyberspace. |
| Hungarian Government Decision No. 1139/2013 (21 March) on the National Cyber Security Strategy of Hungary, 2013 | Cyber security is the continuous and planned taking of political, legal, economic, educational, awareness-raising and technical measures to manage risks in cyberspace that transforms the cyberspace into a reliable environment for the smooth functioning and operation of societal and economic processes by ensuring an acceptable level of risks in cyberspace. |

(continued)

**Table 5.1** (continued)

| Document title, country, year | Definition |
|---|---|
| Cyber Security Strategy of Latvia, 2014–2018 | Cyber security is the collection of tools, policies, security concepts, security safeguards, guidelines, risk management approaches, actions, training, best practices, assurance and technologies that can be used to protect the cyber environment and organisation and user's assets. Organisation and user's assets include connected computing devices, personnel, infrastructure, applications, services, telecommunications systems, and the totality of transmitted and/or stored information in the cyber environment. |
| Lithuanian Cyber Security Strategy, 2011–2019 | Electronic information security equates to cyber security. |
| Luxembourg Cybersecurity Strategy, 2015 | Cybersecurity is the collection of tools, policies, security concepts, security safeguards, guidelines, risk management approaches, actions, training, best practices, assurance and technologies that can be used to protect the cyber environment and organisation and user assets. Organisation and user assets include connected computing devices, personnel, infrastructure, applications, services, telecommunications systems, and the totality of transmitted and/or stored information in the cyber environment. Cybersecurity strives to ensure the attainment and maintenance of the security properties of the organisation and user assets against relevant security risks in the cyber environment. |
| Malta, National Cyber Security Strategy, Green Paper, 2015 | Cybersecurity "is the safeguards and actions that can be used to protect cyber domain from those threats that are associated with or that may harm its interdependent networks and information infrastructure. It strives to preserve the availability and integrity of the networks and infrastructure and the confidentiality of the information contained therein." |
| Cyberspace Protection Policy of the Republic ´of Poland, 2013 | Cyberspace security—a set of organisational and legal, technical, physical and educational projects aimed at ensuring the uninterrupted functioning of cyberspace. |
| Cyber Security Concept of the Slovak Republic for 2015–2020 | Cyber security is one of the defining elements of the security environment of the Slovak Republic and a subsystem of national security. At a state level, it is a system of continuous and planned increasing of political, legal, economic, security, defence and educational awareness, also including the efficiency of adopted and applied risk control measures of a technical-organisational nature in cyber space in order to transform it into a trustworthy environment providing for the secure operation of social and economic processes at an acceptable level of risks in cyber space. |
| National Cyber Security Strategy of Spain, 2013 | Cyber security is a necessity of our society and our economic model. |
| UK National Cyber Security Strategy, 2016–2021 | 'Cyber security' refers to the protection of information systems (hardware, software and associated infrastructure), the data on them and the services they provide from unauthorised access, harm or misuse. This includes harm caused intentionally by the operator of the system or accidentally, as a result of failing to follow security procedures. |

## 5.4 Principle of Conferral Limits the Scope of Cybersecurity

Cybersecurity is nowadays typically regarded as a highly complex issue which requires the active involvement of a range of stakeholders, including the legislator. It is commonly agreed that the legislator is in particular responsible for setting up an appropriate regulatory framework within which private and public entities could carry out their tasks and duties (Bannelier and Christakis 2017; see also Chap. 10). This is a significant change from an initial understanding of cybersecurity according to which it was perceived as a purely technical matter related to measures ensuring the availability, integrity and confidentiality of information and information systems (see Chap. 2).

When discussing cybersecurity regulation in the EU, it is necessary to consider the principle of conferral. Whereas in general the EU can legislate in areas where it is more appropriate than for the Member States to act individually, introducing any regulatory measure at the EU level, including measures concerning cybersecurity, requires the legislator to provide legal justification: in other words a legal basis (Wessel 2015). In particular, the proposal for a legislative measure has to meet the criteria set out in Article 5 of the Treaty of the EU (TEU). In principle, this means that to establish competence over a policy area, a legislative measure has to fall under one of these two situations: (1) either "the proposed action cannot be sufficiently achieved by the Member States, either at central level or at regional and local level" or (2) "by reason of the scale or effects of the proposed action, be better achieved at Union level" (TEU; Article 5(3)).

Considering the principle of conferral and in particular the limited competences of the EU in security issues, the EC was obliged to provide an explanation for acquiring competence to legislate in the cybersecurity area. This occurred in the NIS Directive by establishing a link between cybersecurity and the internal market, largely resembling the reasoning used in order to introduce rules for personal data protection in 1995 (González Fuster 2014: 125). Recital 5 of the NIS Directive proclaims that the diverse Member States' practices with regards to cybersecurity measures hinder the protection awarded to consumers and business, and consequently reduce "the overall level of security of network and information systems" (European Parliament and Council of the European Union 2016). The NIS Directive was adopted to increase consistency of Member States' practices concerning cybersecurity measures.

## 5.5 Remaining Challenges to an Effective Cybersecurity Legal Framework

Different actors, including academics, policy makers and private sector representatives try to get their heads around the cybersecurity area in the EU. To ease such tasks, the European Court of Auditors, an institution that takes care of EU tax payers' interests, published a report providing an excellent overview of the EU's complicated cybersecurity policy framework. The report identifies many challenges to effective policy delivery, such as the meaningful evaluation and accountability of policy and legislative framework; addressing gaps in EU law and its uneven transposition; aligning investment levels with goals; the need for a clear overview of EU budget spending; adequately resourcing the EU's agencies; and strengthening information security governance, and threat and risk assessments (European Court of Auditors 2019).

### *5.5.1 Choice of Appropriate Regulatory Measures*

Most legal measures concerning cybersecurity are found in directives that are minimal harmonisation measures (e.g. NIS Directive and Directive on Attacks against Information Systems). In practice, this means that Member States are free to choose the form and methods to implement requirements stemming from such directives. This flexibility may be seen as a weakness of minimal harmonisation tools. However, directives are considered to be the best tool when introducing a complex legislative change, such as the introduction of a new regulatory area (Craig and de Burca 2015: 106).

In some areas that have been traditionally more strictly regulated, such as the protection of personal data and health care, there is a tendency to adopt more harmonised regulation (see also Chaps. 7 and 17). Examples include the General Data Protection Regulation (GDPR), repealing Data Protection Directive 95/46/EC and Medical Device Regulation (MDR) repealing the Directive on Medical Devices (European Union 2016: 2017).

The MDR is particularly interesting as it aims to establish a "predictable and sustainable regulatory framework for medical devices which ensures a high level of safety and health whilst supporting innovation" (European Union 2017, Recital 1). The MDR defines a 'medical device' as "any instrument, apparatus, appliance, *software*, implant, reagent, material or other article intended by the manufacturer to be used, alone or in combination, for human beings for one or more of the following specific medical purposes" (European Union 2017, Article 2.1). Such purposes may include the diagnosis, prevention, monitoring, prediction, prognosis, treatment or alleviation of disease. The term 'software' is not a new addition to this definition, and it can be found in the Directive on Medical Devices. However, the use of this term means that apps and their accessories that are developed for a medical purpose (e.g. monitoring and measuring blood pressure for diabetes management) are subject to rules as well as safety and performance requirements listed in this regulation, including a comprehensive post-market surveillance system. However, qualifying some software, such as mobile apps, as a medical device is sometimes particularly challenging. A wafer-thin line separates health and well-being apps that are considered to be medical devices from apps that are not considered to be so.

### 5.5.2 *Targeting the Right Addressees*

Cybersecurity measures at the EU level target different actors. Consequently, there are numerous addressees of legislative measures. For example, recent regulatory measures, such as the GDPR and NIS Directive, impose requirements on the ones responsible for the certain operations, namely controllers, processors, providers of essential services and providers of digital infrastructure. They all must take appropriate security measures in response to the risk that they may be subjected to.[5]

The fact that the current regulation of data protection by design focuses exclusively on data controllers (i.e., entities defining the means of the processing of personal data), however, is regrettable, as it can address only part of the problems in the area. The obligation to implement data protection by design does not extend to the actual developers of technology or service providers (Jasmontaite et al. 2018: 173). Recital 78 of the GDPR reveals some hesitations of the legislator, noting that not only controllers but also processors, producers of the products, services and applications, should be among the ones who should consider the right to data protection when developing and designing products, services and applications based on the processing of personal data. While recognising the limited legal value of this Recital (i.e. it is not legally binding but helps in the interpretation Article 25 of the GDPR), the actual software developers or producers of hardware, unless they are data controllers or processors, are de facto not subjected to the legal obligations foreseen in the EU data protection framework.

The debate within the field of data protection over who should be responsible for ensuring the rights of individuals in the online environment is, as a matter of fact, still an open matter in the EU. Discussions concerning the proposed ePrivacy Regulation also confirm that this is an unresolved issue. This being said, it may be concluded that one of the key challenges of cybersecurity regulation is to impose the right obligations on the right actors, through the right instrument—in addition to avoiding the imposition, through disparate instruments, of very similar but not exactly coincidental obligations on the same actors. For example, it is estimated that at the moment there are "at least eleven instruments of EU law having a bearing on [data and information security] breaches, five in the Area of Freedom, Security and Justice (AFSJ) and six in the internal market" (Porcedda 2018, 3).

The issue of targeting the relevant actors is also a pressing one in discussions surrounding the EU liability framework (Directive 85/374/EEC), which in many cases may inappropriately favour some software developers. Whereas software is not explicitly included under the scope of the Product Liability Directive, the academic doctrine has argued that, for the purposes of product liability, software should be perceived as a product (Alheit 2001: 194). According to Article 3 of the Product Liability Directive, which has been transposed into national laws, any person in the supply chain can be held liable and requested to compensate victims

[5] See Articles 25.1 and 32 of the GDPR and Articles 14 and 16 of the NIS Directive.

for any personal injury or damage caused to private property caused wholly or in part by a defect of a product. In such cases, the plaintiff does not have to prove negligence on the part of the producer, but only that it is was defective and the damage occurred because there was causality between the defect and damage (Alheit 2001, 197–99).

This means in practice that the EU has opted in for a strict liability regime for which no proof of fault is necessary. At the same time, it should be noted that in circumstances where a product leads to a pure economic loss or infringement of individuals' rights, the strict liability regime may not be invoked, as the damage should occur to a person or to a private property. Furthermore, the Product Liability Directive in Article 7 foresees that there are several situations in which the producer's liability can be avoided. Recognising the limitations of the current liability framework, the European Parliament noted that in the context of the IoT "tightening up liability regimes" would be desirable as it could "lead to a better quality of products and a more secure environment" (European Parliament 2017: 13).

A new approach to the liability framework could provide individuals with the comprehensive and meaningful protection of their security, including the protection of their personal data (Daley 2016). Such an approach, as proposed by Daley, would require to balance ex ante incentives to invest in security with ex post liability, incentivise software developers to publicly disclose source code, and promote trust and public confidence in embedded systems (Daley 2016). It seems that this approach, though controversial, could help to develop the "high-quality, affordable, interoperable and trustworthy cybersecurity products" that the EC called for in June 2017 (Speech by Vice-President Ansip 2017).

### 5.5.3 *The Long-Awaited Recast of Product Liability Directive, Pending*

As discussed above, it is generally assumed that clearly defined liability framework for devices, applications and services could improve the protection of individuals and consequently that of the cyberspace. However, the current liability framework dates back from the 1980s and does not address such complex issues as embedded systems, embedded software and application software. It seems that there is a common understanding and agreement that regulating software and including it into the framework of Council Directive 85/374/EEC concerning liability for defective products would represent a major milestone. This would clarify the current standing of software that is perceived differently across Member States, both as a service and as a product.

In spite of this, it seems that these questions will remain unaddressed for the time being. In this context, the EC is promoting the use of code of conducts and preparing interpretative guidance of the Liability Directive.[6] In light of the policy line taken by the EC, which does envision the recast of the Liability Directive, it comes as no surprise that the European Parliament might look for alternative legal clarification of the current legal vacuum via other legislative proposals. For example, in its amendments on the proposal for a directive of the European Parliament and of the Council on certain aspects concerning contracts for the supply of digital content, the European Parliament proposed specific rules for software that is embedded in tangible goods (smart goods). Although such 'isolationism' may be welcome, it may create fragmentation in the regulatory landscape, without necessarily improving an overall security of IT.

## 5.6 A Pressing Need to (Cyber)Secure EU Values and Interests

The observation that the "information revolution makes security an increasingly important concern in all sectors of society" has surely withstood the test of time and accurately reflects the current debates within the EU (Eriksson and Giacomello 2006). In a reflection paper on the future of cybersecurity regulation published in 2017, the EC emphasised the need to protect European values and interests against new types of threats (EC 2017c: 6). To improve the competitiveness and security of the EU, the reflection paper considered three scenarios (i.e. Security and Defence Cooperation, Shared Security and Defence, Common Defence and Security) which would allow Member States' industrial and technical resources to be pooled. Within the scope of that document, the EC questioned EU competence in the field of cybersecurity and considered ways to extend them beyond the limits of Digital Single Market. Cybersecurity becomes thus intertwined with the objectives of a Security and Defence Union and it is suggested that deeper integration, in particular the creation of a Common Defence Security, would improve cybersecurity resilience both at national and EU levels. It is also argued that a deeper integration scenario would allow for "Europe […] to deploy detection and offensive cyber-capabilities", which could be used in case of "cyber-attacks or external interference in Member States' democratic processes" (EC 2017c: 14–15).

The EC's rhetoric in recent policy documents could be regarded as favouring the consolidation of a broadened vision of cybersecurity through the specific prism of EU cybersecurity. It insists on the need for more cooperation and coordination of programmes concerning the interoperability of information systems for security, border and migration management. For example, the EC in one of its recent documents refers to 'the global cyberattack using ransomware' (known as WannaCry) as

---

[6] See, Commission publishes evaluation reports on EU rules on machinery safety and product liability, available at: https://ec.europa.eu/growth/content/commission-publishes-evaluation-reports-eu-rules-machinery-safety-and-product-liability_en, last accessed 15 November 2018.

a case demonstrating the need for expansion of EU actions, and thus acclaiming competence, within the cybersecurity domain (EC 2017a: 2). In another policy document, the EC relies on statistics about ransomware from the United States in order to strengthen its claim about the potential risks of cyberattacks for business, economy and democracy in the EU: "wider instruments for European solidarity and mutual assistance" in the field of cybersecurity could address these risks (EC 2017b: 12). This somehow far-stretched rhetoric could be in conflict with the rationale of EU better regulation policy, which should be driven by the "best available evidence" and the involvement of stakeholders (EC 2015: 5).

It is also possible to argue that the European Union could have taken a different approach in response to the increasing number of cyberattacks and cyberthreats. For example, Wojciech Wiewiórowski, Assistant EDPS, suggested that if appropriate security measures, required under data protection law, had been implemented, the mentioned attacks could have been prevented (Wiewiórowski 2017). This observation suggests that in response to cyberthreats, the European Commission may also emphasise the need for better implementation of requirements stemming from the existing EU data protection framework rather than the need for stronger cooperation mechanisms among concerned actors.

## 5.7 Concluding Remarks

The future of cybersecurity regulation appears to be at a crossroads: perceived cyber threats may shape political choices and lead to deeper integration, in particular with the ongoing discussions about the mandate of ENISA and the implementation of the Cybersecurity Act. As such, EU cybersecurity might actually have been at multiple crossroads since its inception.

This chapter aimed to reflect the particular challenges related to understanding cybersecurity regulation in the EU, based on a discussion of how such policy territory has been constructed. As outlined, numerous policy areas fall under the overarching scope of cybersecurity, and cybersecurity 'as such' is considered a horizontal issue. At the same time, the interconnected policy areas (e.g. cybercrime, IoT, autonomous vehicles, Artificial Intelligence, cloud computing) reflect and address a limited subset of cyber threats, ranging from the fight against cybercrime to the security of critical infrastructures and goods.

The EU cybersecurity landscape is continuously evolving as policy measures eventually lead to changes and adjustments in the legal framework and vice versa. The contours of this landscape have also been changing thanks to the flexibility, if not ambiguity, embedded in the very term 'cybersecurity', which entails both advantages and disadvantages. It may allow the area to integrate new technologies and policy issues as they emerge, but at the same time it can make it overly inclusive, potentially hindering the impact of regulation in this area.

When considering specific regulatory challenges, the current legal setup renders it, in a way, more difficult to impose the appropriate obligations on the right actors who could make a tangible contribution to the security of digital environments. This argument is illustrated by examples stemming from the GDPR, which does not formally address actual software developers or producers of hardware as such, unless they would qualify as data controllers or processors, and to the extent they would. The debate over who should be responsible for ensuring the rights of individuals and the security of their data as well, as well as that of any product and service connected to the online environment is, as a matter of fact, still ongoing in the EU and globally.

Emerging legal solutions for current uncertainty surrounding cybersecurity regulation might be regarded as encompassing the 'duty of care' principle, as well as the revision of the existing liability framework. However, considering the reluctance of the EC to revise the liability framework and address technical and legal riddles such as the regulation of liability of self-evolving software (i.e. Artificial Intelligence), it seems that it might be easier to introduce new principles.

Ultimately, the elastic nature of EU cybersecurity triggers questions regarding its relation to fundamental rights protection. EU cybersecurity policy seems to intermittently be *about* the protection of fundamental rights, sometimes about security *in accordance with* fundamental rights requirements, and occasionally about (almost any) cyber issues *independently from* fundamental rights considerations. A clarification of the—certainly profound—linkages between the effective regulation of cyber resilience, cybercrime, cyberdefence, (strictly) cybersecurity and global cyberspace issues would surely contribute to a more precise delineation of the necessary, albeit moving, boundaries of EU cybersecurity.

**Acknowledgements** The chapter was created with funding from the European Union's Horizon 2020 research and innovation programme under grant agreement No 700540.

## References

Alheit K (2001) The applicability of the EU product liability directive to software. Comp Int Law J South Afr 34(2):188–209

Bannelier K, Christakis T (2017) Cyber-attacks – prevention-reactions: the role of states and private actors

Christou G (2016) Cybersecurity in the European Union: resilience and adaptability in governance policy, New Security Challenges Series. Palgrave Macmillan UK, London. https://doi.org/10.1080/09662839.2016.1160892

Council of Europe (2001) Convention on cybercrime, ETS no.185, Budapest. https://www.coe.int/en/web/conventions/full-list/-/conventions/treaty/185. Last access July 7 2019

Craig P, de Burca G (2015) EU law: text, cases and materials. Oxford University Press. https://doi.org/10.1093/he/9780198714927.001.0001

Daley J (2016) Insecure software is eating the world: promoting cybersecurity in an age of ubiquitous software-embedded systems. Stanf Tech Law Rev 19(3). https://law.stanford.edu/

publications/insecure-software-is-eating-the-world-promoting-cybersecurity-in-an-age-of-ubiquitous-software-embedded-systems/. Last access 7 July 2019
ENISA (2016) Definition of cybersecurity: gaps and overlaps in standardization
ENISA (2017) Principles and opportunities for a renewed EU cyber security strategy
Eriksson J, Giacomello G (2006) The information revolution, security, and international relations: (IR) relevant theory? Int Polit Sci Rev 27(3):221–244. https://doi.org/10.1177/0192512106064462
European Commission (2012) Communication on unleashing the potential of cloud computing in Europe, COM (2012) 529
European Commission (2015) Commission staff working document, better regulation guidelines, SWD (2015) 111 Final. Strasbourg
European Commission (2017a) Communication on Seventh Progress Report towards an Effective and Genuine Security Union, COM (2017) 261 Final
European Commission (2017b) Communication on the mid-term review on the implementation of the digital single market strategy: a connected digital single market for all. COM (2017) 228 Final. COM (2017) 228 Final. http://eur-lex.europa.eu/resource.html?uri=cellar:a4215207-362b-11e7-a08e-01aa75ed71a1.0001.02/DOC_1&format=PDF. Last access 7 July 2019
European Commission (2017c) Reflection paper on the future of European Defence
European Commission (2018) Communication on Artificial Intelligence for Europe, COM (2018) 237 Final
European Commission, and High Representative (2013) Cybersecurity strategy of the European Union: an open, safe and secure cyberspace
European Commission, and High Representative of the Union for Foreign Affairs and Security Policy (2017) Resilience, deterrence and defence: building strong cybersecurity for the EU. Joint Communication to the European Parliament and the council. https://doi.org/10.1016/j.neuint.2009.06.008
European Court of Auditors (2019) Challenges to effective EU cybersecurity policy. https://www.eca.europa.eu/Lists/ECADocuments/BRP_CYBERSECURITY/BRP_CYBERSECURITY_EN.pdf. Last access 7 July 2019
European Parliament (2017) Report on the fight against cybercrime, motion for a resolution. http://www.europarl.europa.eu/sides/getDoc.do?pubRef=-//EP//TEXT+REPORT+A8-2017-0272+0+DOC+XML+V0//EN&language=en. Last access 7 July 2019
European Parliament, and Council of the European Union (2016) Directive (EU) 2016/1148 of the European Parliament and of the council of 6 July 2016 concerning measures for a high common level of security of network and information systems across the union. Off J Eur Union Vol. L 194/1. https://doi.org/10.1017/CBO9781107415324.004
European Union (2016) Regulation (EU) 2016/679 of the European Parliament and of the council of 27 April 2016 on the protection of natural persons with regard to the processing of personal data and on the free movement of such data, and repealing directive 95/46/ EC (GDPR). Off J Eur Communities https://doi.org/http://eur-lex.europa.eu/pri/en/oj/dat/2003/l_285/l_28520031101en00330037.pdf (last access July 7 2019)
European Union (2017) Regulation (EU) 2017/745 of the European Parliament and of the Council of 5 April 2017 on Medical Devices, Amending Directive 2001/83/EC, Regulation (EC) No 178/2002 and Regulation (EC) No 1223/2009 and Repealing Council Directives 90/385/EEC and 93/42/EE. Off J Eur Union https://doi.org/http://data.europa.eu/eli/reg/2017/746/oj
González Fuster G (2014) The emergence of personal data protection as a fundamental right of the EU, Law, governance and technology series. Springer, Cham. https://doi.org/10.1007/978-3-319-05023-2
Jasmontaite L, Kamara I, Zanfir-Fortuna G et al (2018) Data protection by design and by default: framing guiding principles into legal obligations in the GDPR. European data protection law review 4(2). Lexxion Publisher: 168–89. https://doi.org/10.21552/edpl/2018/2/7

Porcedda MG (2018) Patching the patchwork: appraising the EU regulatory framework on cyber security breaches. Comput Law Secur Rev 000 Elsevier Ltd:1–22. https://doi.org/10.1016/j.clsr.2018.04.009
Treaty of Lisbon Amending the Treaty on European Union (TEU) (2007) Off J Eur Union:1–272
van der Meulen N, Eun AJ, Soesanto S (2015) Cybersecurity in the European Union and beyond: exploring the threats and policy responses. http://www.europarl.europa.eu/RegData/etudes/STUD/2015/536470/IPOL_STU(2015)536470_EN.pdf. Last access 7 July 2019
Vice-President Ansip (2017) The Chatham house annual cyber conference: evolving norms, improving harmonisation and building resilience. Speech by Vice-President Ansip
Wessel RA (2015) Towards EU cybersecurity law: regulating a new policy field. In: Tsagourias N, Buchan R (eds) Research handbook on international law and cyberspace. Edward Elgar Publishing
Wiewiórowski W (2017) Privacy, security and technology: the annual privacy forum 2017

# Part II
# Problems

# Chapter 6
# A Care-Based Stakeholder Approach to Ethics of Cybersecurity in Business

**Gwenyth Morgan and Bert Gordijn**

**Abstract** This chapter focuses on ethical issues in cybersecurity in business. It first sketches the main ethical issues discussed in the academic literature thus far. Next, it identifies some important topics that have not yet received the attention they deserve. The chapter then focuses on one of those topics, ransomware attacks, one of the most prevalent cybersecurity threats to businesses today. It provides a brief overview of the main types of ransomware attacks and discusses businesses' responsibilities to their stakeholders to respond to them. Daniel Engster's care-based stakeholder approach is used to assess the responsibilities that businesses have to their stakeholders. The analysis involves establishing who counts as a stakeholder when a ransomware attack occurs and what the stakeholders' interests might be. Based on stakeholders' interests, the analysis concludes on whether businesses have an ethical responsibility to their stakeholders to (1) respond to grey hat demands by patching identified vulnerabilities within the given timeframe and (2) respond to black hat demands by paying the ransom.

**Keywords** Cybercrime · Privacy · Ransomware · Stakeholder theory

## 6.1 Introduction

Due to the uptake of information and communication technology (ICT) in the business sector, the value of information has increased. Information is now considered the new oil and as oil brought both prosperity and problems, so too does information. Prosperity emanates from the fact that businesses can utilise ICT to reduce costs and increase efficiency by providing round-the-clock availability of both information and services to customers. In providing that availability, problems arise. If information is constantly available, this means that it is constantly vulnerable to an attack. This trade-off between providing availability and securing

G. Morgan (✉) · B. Gordijn
Institute of Ethics, Dublin City University, Dublin, Ireland
e-mail: gwenyth.morgan4@mail.dcu.ie



M. Christen et al. (eds.), *The Ethics of Cybersecurity*, The International Library of Ethics, Law and Technology 21,
https://doi.org/10.1007/978-3-030-29053-5_6

information is something that businesses must grapple with in carrying out their day-to-day activities not only to protect identifiable data, i.e. individual's names, addresses, account details etc., but also to remain compliant with the General Data Protection Regulation (2018) (GDPR).

The GDPR in 2018 set the bar for businesses that collect, process, analyse and store EU citizen's identifiable information. It compels businesses who physically reside within the jurisdiction of the GDPR to be compliant, and extends to those that reside outside the EU who process EU citizens' identifiable information (European Commission 2018a, b; see also Chap. 5). The GDPR is particularly relevant when businesses are hacked, as it compels them to notify the National Data Regulator when a data leak/breach occurs. A failure to report a data leak or breach within 72 h of the breach occurring, can result in a fine up to the value of 4% of the businesses entire annual returns (European Commission 2018a, b). Additionally, if an organisation is non-compliant with the GDPR, —and it is established that non-compliance has caused material damage, such as financial loss, or non-material damage, such as reputational loss or psychological distress to individuals— those individuals can claim compensation (European Commission 2018a, b). Thus, non-compliance can result in significant legal and economic consequences for a business.

From an economic perspective, the cost of data breaches is increasing. For example, the Ponemon Institute's 2018 study suggests that the average cost of data breaches of 2500–100,000 lost or stolen records is globally US $3.86 million, which is a 6.4% increase on their 2017 report. Wenger et al. (2017) point to the reputational damage that can result from a successful cyber-attack. They state that a significantly large percentage of consumers are less likely to engage with a business that has been hacked, even if they were not directly affected by the attack. In efforts to detect and prevent cybersecurity breaches and data loss, businesses are investing large sums of money into cybersecurity. For example, a study conducted by Bromium states that large enterprise organisations are spending on average US $16.7 million annually on cybersecurity (Bromium 2016).

While individuals, businesses, acadeics and governmental organisations are trying to grapple with the legal and financial side to cybersecurity threats and responses, very few have lended their attention to the ethics of cybersecurity. Ethics and cybersecurity deserve the attention of the reader, the scholarly community and professionals for two fundamental reasons. (1) A cyber-attack is a matter of when, not if. Businesses must therefore adequately prepare themselves for the inevitable by exploring the response options available to them and making an informed decision on the most appropriate, fast and effective response that is in the interests of named stakeholders. (2) Businesses have a responsibility to ensure that the hardware and software that they use to process, store and analyse identifiable information has an adequate level of security to protect the users who have access to those systems. Businesses must also protect the confidentiality and privacy of individuals data held within those systems. For businesses to have any chance of achieving this, they must be aware of the threat landscape. In knowing the main threats, businesses can allocate sufficient resources to protect themselves, it is an efficient use of resources and it has the potential to reduce the likelihood of a successful attack.

This chapter focuses on one main threat, ransomware attacks and is structured in the following way. Firstly, we present a brief overview of the ethical issues that arise in the literature on cybersecurity in business. Next, we observe that there are important gaps in the current debate with regard to (i) education (ii) ransomware attacks and (iii) the disclosure of data breaches. We then introduce Daniel Engster's care-based stakeholder theory which we think can be used as a normative theory to analyse the under debated issues. Given the space restraints of this chapter, we do not develop a full-fledged stakeholder analysis of all three issues. Instead, we focus in on ransomware attacks, a topic that has prominently featured in the news in the past few years.

## 6.2 Ethical Issues in Cybersecurity

In a systematic literature review focused on cybersecurity and ethics, we identified the 15 most frequently discussed ethical issues in cybersecurity in the business domain. Table 6.1 ranks the frequency in which these ethical issues arise (Yaghmaei et al. 2017).

The ethical issues listed are wide ranging and are context relative. For example, privacy arises in terms of data breaches and keeping information secure from unauthorised access. It also surfaces in respect of employee privacy in the workplace. Whereas autonomy, for example, is discussed in terms of data collection, processing, analysis and storage.

**Table 6.1** Ethical issues in cybersecurity in business

| Ethical issue | Number of sources that discuss this ethical issue |
|---|---|
| Privacy | 27 |
| Protection of data | 26 |
| Trust | 23 |
| Control | 20 |
| Accessibility | 19 |
| Confidentiality | 18 |
| Responsibility on businesses to use ethical codes of conduct | 15 |
| Data integrity | 14 |
| Consent | 12 |
| Transparency | 11 |
| Availability | 9 |
| Accountability | 9 |
| Autonomy | 8 |
| Ownership | 6 |
| Usability | 1 |

See Yaghmaei et al. 2017 for details on the methodology

In addition to identifying the ethical issues in cybersecurity, we note that (1) the main threats in cybersecurity stem from attackers targeting vulnerabilities in people and technology and (2) the impacts of cybersecurity breaches can be wide ranging, from having a limited impact to having a detrimental effect on the data owner, the business and wider society (Yaghmaei et al. 2017).

## 6.3 Gaps in the Literature on Ethics and Cybersecurity

There are at least three important gaps in the ethical literature. They relate to (1) ransomware attacks, (2) education and (3) the disclosure of data breach information. More specifically, there appears to be a lack of thorough ethical analysis on (1) the ethical responsibilities that businesses have to specific stakeholders to engage with grey hats and black hats on the continuum of ransomware attacks, (2) the ethical responsibilities that businesses have to specific stakeholders to improve their employees cybersecurity awareness and expertise despite it being known that one of the main precursors of successful cyber-attacks is the inadvertent actions of employees and (3) the ethical responsibilities that businesses have to specific stakeholders to disclose data breach information.

(1) F-Secure reports that technology and people are the two main weaknesses in cybersecurity in business (F-Secure 2018). Cybercriminals exploit technology through supply chain vulnerabilities or unknown vulnerabilities (otherwise known as zero-day). The European Commission offers a certificate to ethical hackers (European Council 2018a, b). Ethical hackers, otherwise known as white hats, are security testers who try to find vulnerabilities in information systems, networks and IT infrastructures (for more details see Chap. 9). Grey hats are not traditionally known as ethical hackers as they also search for vulnerabilities but do so without the knowledge of the systems owner. Both grey hats and white hats have the intention to find the vulnerabilities before a black hat (a malicious hacker) finds them. Despite grey hats undertaking their endeavours in the absence of consent, they argue that their actions are warranted as they contribute to a safer cyber environment for all by making it more difficult for black hats to successfully attack businesses for financial, political or other malicious purposes (Leiwo and Heikkuri 1998). A discussion in the ethical literature questions whether grey hats actions are ethical (Leiwo and Heikkuri 1998; Brey 2007; McReynolds 2015). It centres on the issue of consent and concludes that grey hat actions are in fact unethical. Another popular topic relating hacking is the hacker ethic. The hacker ethic relies on the notion that all information should be free and unlimited. This is one argument used by hackers to justify exposing questionable activities or corporations or governments. Brey (2007) makes a valid point that if all information was free and unlimited, this would go against the accepted Western interpretation of intellectual property, as

it would impede individuals' ability to profit from patented information. It also would be a huge privacy infringement and, as a consequence, could not be considered ethical.

The literature fails to address businesses interactions with hackers, in particular in relation to the continuum of ransomware attacks (Yaghmaei et al. 2017). We take this opportunity to share more insights into how grey hats and black hats do "business". Consider the following. When a grey hat finds a vulnerability, he notifies the owner (in this case let us presume the owner is a business) by giving them a certain amount of time to fix the vulnerability. In failing to fix or "patch" the vulnerability, the grey hat threatens to release the vulnerability to the public. Releasing the vulnerability to the public means that the vulnerability can be accessed by anyone including malicious hackers, making the business more likely to be attacked. Conversely, a black hat might choose to install ransomware on a business's system that shuts down all business services until the business either (1) identifies and resolves the problem themselves or (2) takes the risk of paying the ransom to the hacker in the hope that the ransomware will be removed upon receipt of payment. As we can see, a ransom of sorts is involved in both activities. Instead of us hashing out whether the act of ransoming a business is unethical, we believe a more fruitful discussion can arise from juxtaposing a grey hat's ransom against a black hat's ransom from the viewpoint of specific stakeholders.

(2) People are a weakness in cybersecurity in business due to human error and due to their considerable lack of cybersecurity knowhow (Wenger et al. 2017). This weak spot is something that cybercriminals exploit to target businesses and achieve their ends. Despite businesses and international bodies acknowledging that cybersecurity awareness and education needs to improve (PECB 2017; ENISA 2018; Kaspersky Lab 2018), we note that there is little ethical research that examines the extent to which businesses are responsible for doing so (Yaghmaei et al. 2017). In this instance, we interpret ethical analysis as one that considers specific stakeholders' interests when it comes to education and assessing how those interests might conflict with one another and how such conflict could be resolved.

(3) End-users have expressed their desire to know if their data has been breached (Wenger et al. 2017). As data breaches have the potential to cause irreparable damage to a business's reputation and can incur a financial cost, it is in a business' interests to lessen the impact of a data breach. It is interesting that the ethical literature mentions businesses' responsibility to disclose data breach information when private or identifiable information has been breached. However, there is no discussion that covers the fact that non-disclosure contributes to the weakening of an already fragile cyber-environment. In addition, little is offered in respect of how underreporting cybersecurity breaches affects the authenticity of cybersecurity incident reports, which can otherwise be used as effective tools that illustrate the cyber threat landscape.

## 6.4 Care-Based Stakeholder Theory

To conduct an ethical analysis of the ethical responsibilities that businesses have to specific stakeholders to respond to grey hats and black hats ransoms, we apply a stakeholder approach. Edward Freeman is considered the founding father of stakeholder theory (ST) since the publication of his book *Strategic Management: A Stakeholder Approach* (1984). Therein, stakeholders are viewed as important but nevertheless a means through which the corporation can achieve its preordained goals (Freeman 1984). In Freeman's later work, the stakeholder assumes a more central role in the firm such that they have personal projects that the corporation should be constructed to serve (Freeman and Gilbert 1989). An even more recent paper by Freeman and Gilbert (1992) lists the shortcomings of ST, paying particular attention to the language used to describe ST. They argue that the autonomous—masculinist—individualistic mode of thinking surrounding ST reduces its applicability to business today. Two years after this publication, Freeman and Gilbert published a more elaborate paper with Wicks on the specific shortcomings of ST (Wicks et al. 1994). In their paper, they reinterpret the existing version of ST through the lens of care ethics, which they refer to as feminist ethics (Wicks et al. 1994). They note that in order for businesses to flourish in a fast-paced ever-changing business environment, there is a need to replace the masculinist language of conflict with the feminist language of communication, cooperation and collective action. One example they give is to replace notions of competition and control with cooperation and communication. They state that businesses need to share information, embrace change and improve their networks rather than try to exert control over their environment. Wicks et al. (1994) argue that ST theory considers corporations as webs of relations amongst stakeholders whose interests need to be at the core of decision-making processes and, in this way, ST is a way of interpreting the meaning of the corporation and the responsibilities that businesses have to those inside and outside the business. Burton and Dunn (1996) extend the work of Wicks et al. by claiming that care ethics has a natural affinity to ST and that Gilligan's work on care ethics is a strong lens through which to view the theory.

Burton and Dunn (1996) advocate using Wicks et al.'s (1994) application of care ethics to ST, stating that their reinterpretation offers a more practical approach to it (Burton and Dunn 1996). Daniel Engster (2011) narrows the focus on the practical application of this care-based stakeholder approach and the notion of creating a caring business. He argues that while the idea of using care ethics and ST in business seems logical, flaws still exist. He notes that businesses are left with the following three questions: (1) who exactly counts as a stakeholder? (2) how should businesses distribute care to those stakeholders? and (3) what ethical approaches should businesses adopt when conflict arises amongst stakeholders? For example, is it possible for businesses to follow a particular principle that might mitigate stakeholder conflict? Engster addresses these predicaments by combining insights taken from Freeman (1984), Freeman (2010), Freeman and Gilbert (1989, 1992), Wicks et al. (1994), and Burton and Dunn (1996).

(1) In relation to the first question, Engster argues that stakeholders should include those whose functioning and survival is directly tied to the firm's activities namely, shareholders, employees, the local community, customers, suppliers and competitors (Engster 2011). This is counter to Freeman's definition of a stakeholder, which includes all individuals who are affected by the firm. Engster states that it is impossible to include all individuals who are affected by the firm as this would exhaust businesses care, energy and resources and would not enable a business to allocate care to those who need it the most (Engster 2011).
(2) In respect of the second question, Engster offers three ethical principles that can be used as tools in the decision-making process. These principles are (a) the proximity principle, (b) the relational principle (both previously advocated by Burton and Dunn 1996) and (c) the urgency principle.

    (a) The proximity principle states that there is justification in using our limited resources to care for individuals who are in some way close to us before attempting to care for distant others. This puts limited resources to the best possible use as we can attend more directly to individuals who are close to us based on the understanding that we usually have a better idea of their circumstances, customs, and needs, and can therefore care better for them than for distant others. It can be argued that the proximity principle justifies: (a) caring for ourselves before others; (b) caring for individuals who are geographically and temporally close to us before those who are far away; and (c) caring for individuals in our own culture or state before those in foreign cultures or states.
    (b) The relational principle states that businesses should prioritise caring for individuals with whom we have a close personal relationship over others. Engster (2011) defines a close relationship as one where one party depends on the other for meeting his or her survival and developmental needs, using the analogy of the mother and baby relationship. He states that close relationships deserve priority because they are so closely tied up with the goals of caring. If we apply this interpretation of a close relationship to the business domain, the number of stakeholder relationships that ought to be considered by a business significantly reduces.
    (c) Engster (2011) advocates the use of the urgency principle wherein he encourages businesses to care for individuals who have more urgent needs over those with less urgent needs. Using the urgency principle is determined by the effect that an action/inaction could have on a person's or group's survival. Engster states that if there is a focus on the urgent needs of stakeholders over less urgent ones, this allows a business to give priority to the needs of individuals or groups who will not survive or function without acting. We note that this principle also reduces the number of stakeholders that must be considered by businesses when making decisions about the distribution of care, time and resources more feasible.

(3) When conflicts arise amongst stakeholders, care ethics dictates that the highest priority be given to shareholders and employees as their interests are "generally more important than those of other stakeholders" (Engster 2007: 107). This does not apply in all cases. For example, he sets one over-riding condition, which is that when the health and safety of employees and customers and other individuals is at stake, the interests of employees and customers should receive the highest priority. He states that prioritising the health and safety interests of employees and customers trumps even the importance of the firm's survival. Engster (2011) notes that while a strong commitment to worker health and safety and high environmental standards may result in less profit for investors and even the loss of jobs for some workers, individuals are more likely to suffer much greater and immediate threats to their survival and functioning when health, safety and environmental standards are compromised (Engster 2011). He continues his argument by stating that jobs should be favoured by businesses, at least in the short term. There are limits to this policy, as choosing jobs over profit in the long-term may result in the solvency of the firm. He notes that when job cuts are unavoidable, businesses can resort to the 'rule of consensus' which requires businesses to try and find solutions to stakeholder conflicts that are acceptable to all by communicating the proposed solutions to stakeholders and trying to solicit alternative proposals from them.

## 6.5 Ransomware Attacks

The number of malicious ransomware attacks targeting businesses tripled between 2017 and 2018 (Bromium 2016). Ransomware attacks can be divided into two categories: cryptors and blockers (see also Chap. 2). Cryptors encrypt data on the victim's device. Usually, the black hat will demand money and in receipt of same will restore the encrypted data. Blockers, otherwise known as lockers, do not interfere with the data stored on the device, instead they prevent the victim from accessing it (Ivanov et al. 2016). Ivanov et al. (2016) report that black hats are using new and more sophisticated ways to target companies that require little effort and have a large pay-off. Our research suggests that ransomware attacks are only considered as such when done through cryptos or blockers by hackers with malicious intent (i.e.) ones who hope to gain financially, politically etc. Grey hats also attack computer network systems and ransom businesses but have different intentions and foresee different outcomes. They scour networks for vulnerabilities and when a vulnerability is found, they notify the owner or business that their system contains vulnerabilities that require fixing. From the grey hat's perspective, in doing so they are helping improve the overall security of cyberspace. However, it can be argued that the virtuousness of this action is tainted as it involves gaining unauthorised access to a system without the permission of the system owner. It also involves the grey hat ransoming the business into fixing the vulnerability, as the grey hat will traditionally threaten to release the vulnerability if the business does not rectify it within a given timeframe. There is a growing body of evidence that suggests after the public release of vulnerabilities, there is a consequential increase in malicious attacks. The time between the release of a vulnerability and public release of an exploit is referred to as the vulnerability-to-exploit time period and it is decreasing steadily over time. In the past, the time between a vulnerability announcement and the release of a corresponding exploit could be measured in month or years. For example, when Microsoft announced a vulnerability on 17 October 2000, (Microsoft Security Bulletin MS00-078), the exploit followed in the form on Nimda worm on 18 September 2001. This means security teams had 336 days to patch their vulnerability. In the December 2015 Microsoft security bulletin, exploits were available for two of the eight disclosed vulnerabilities on the day that the public announcement was made (CISCO 2018). Although it could be argued that a grey hat threatening to release vulnerability information to the public acts as a catalyst for fixing the vulnerability, this, however, does not remove the threat itself. On the basis that a threat is made at all, one could counter argue that this practice is unethical as the researcher is using the business as a means to an end. Yet, when grey hats ransom businesses, not for money but for the greater good of cyberspace, they create a common ground with black hats. The common ground is ransoming and punishing businesses who do not comply with their demands. We argue that both types of hackers fall on different points on the same ransomware spectrum.

## 6.6 The Stakeholders and Their Interests

We use Engster's method to identify the main stakeholders and their interests in both grey hat and black hat ransom attacks and assess whether a conflict of interest exists amongst stakeholders. In doing so, we aim to establish what exactly are businesses' responsibilities to their stakeholders in these situations. In addition, we consult the Association for Computing Machinery (ACM) Code of Ethics & Professional Conduct ('the Code') to which all members of the ACM including all computing professionals are bound (ACM 2018a, b). As the ACM's code extends to security researchers (white hat and grey hat hackers), we include hackers as the seventh stakeholder (see also Chap. 9). We also note that the ACM rank the general public as being the first and foremost stakeholder in cybersecurity. We found this interesting, as Engster (2011) does not include the general public in his care-based stakeholder theory. In this instance, where the actions of hackers can affect the functioning and survival of members of the general public, the criteria that Engster uses to identify who counts as a stakeholder (see above), we believe that it is appropriate to name the general public as the eighth stakeholder.

### 6.6.1 Shareholders

Grey hat and black hat ransoms create more issues for shareholders than any other stakeholder. For example, it could be argued that one element of success of a firm depends on IT systems. If those systems are inadequately protected, this affects shareholders' interests. Shareholders are interested in "a fair return on his or her investment" (Engster 2011: 101). While a grey hat identifying vulnerabilities is not authorised or instigated by the shareholders, the shareholders are now in a position of reduced power as they are now subject to the terms as set by the grey hat. They have a choice to either respond to the grey hat demands or ignore them. We argue that if the shareholders choose to patch the vulnerability, the business is acting in the interests of the shareholders as it reduces their likelihood of being successfully hacked by a black hat. Without the involvement of the grey hat, the shareholders would remain in the dark, unbeknownst to the vulnerabilities in their system. If vulnerabilities exist, they are likely to be exploited. On this basis, we argue that it is imperative that businesses respond to grey hat's demands. If one weighs the decision to not patch the vulnerability within the given timeframe against ignoring the grey hat demands and the vulnerability being made public; it is in the shareholders' interests to not put the business and specific stakeholders' information and IT systems, networks and infrastructure at a higher risk of being successfully attacked by a black hat, as this can cause economic loss and reputational and psychological damage.

When a black hat ransoms a business, the situation is quite different. For the sake of argument, we assume the intention of the black hat is financial gain. Let us also assume that the black hat installs either a 'blocker' or 'locker' (Ivanov et al. 2016). In certain circumstances, responding to a black hat's demands can be in the interest of shareholders for the following reasons: (1) As the business is held to ransom, it might be in the shareholders' interests to immediately pay the ransom. This might be the case when it is not foreseeable for the business themselves to reverse engineer the attack. Assuming that both parties deliver what has been ransomed and promised, by paying the ransom the business can resume service without the potential collateral damage associated with a data leak (Brey 2007). (2) A study conducted by Datto, Inc. (2018) reveals that ransomware from 2016 to 2017 cost European SMEs £71 M in downtime, with the average ransom ranging between £350 and £1407 (Ismail 2018). If the average ransom is lower than the potential cost of a data breach or leak, and is less than the cost of service stoppage, this leads us to suggest that it is in shareholders' interests to pay the ransom. (3) Ninety-nine percent of all businesses in Europe are SMEs. SMEs may not have the means nor manpower to reverse engineer a ransomware attack. This leads us to suggest that SMEs (in particular) should attempt to negotiate a lower price with the black hat. Negotiating with ransomware families has been known to successfully reduce the cost of the ransom. Sean Sullivan, a cybersecurity specialist from F-Secure, explains that crypto ransomware works so well that it has become an industry run by families, similar to the way legitimate businesses run (Sullivan 2016). For example, the Cerber ransomware family has a user-friendly website that supports several languages and offers customers convenient support forms so the victim can ask how to get their files back. Sullivan (2016) and his colleagues investigated the customer journey more closely by examining four crypto-ransomware families and find- found that three out of the four families negotiated with the victims of the ransomware attack, offering an average discount of 29% from the original sum demanded (Sullivan 2016). Sullivan and his colleagues also found that the demanded timeline is not set in stone, as 100% of the crypto-ransomware families contacted gave extensions to the deadlines. This leads us to suggest that businesses ought to engage with hackers to negotiate not only the sum of the ransom but the timeframe within which it is expected to be paid.

### 6.6.2 *Employees*

For employees who wish to remain in long-term employment, it is in their interests for the business to remain in business. To do so, companies need to use ICT and have appropriate security defences. Grey hats are acting in the interest of the common good by trying to improve computer security defences. It is thus in employees' interests for the business to respond to grey hats' identification of vulnerabilities and patch them.

It is in the employees' interests for a business to reduce the potential collateral damage associated with a malicious black hat attack. We argue that it is in the interests of employees for businesses to firstly (a) try to find and use a decryption key and not pay the ransom and secondly (b) when decryption keys are not readily available, engage with the ransomware attacker and try to negotiate a lower fee. Both are in employees' interests, as the first avoids having to pay any financial fee at all and the second, while not ideal, can significantly lower the financial impact that an attack can have on a firm.

### 6.6.3 *The Local Community*

If it is in the interests of the employees for the business to respond and negotiate with grey hats and black hats respectively, so too is it in the interest of the local community. This is based on Engster's (2011) argument that employees tend to be part of the local community. As a result, the business impact on the local community is channelled through its relations with employees. We interpret this to mean that the interests of employees reflect the interests of the local community, but this is not always the case. For example, the local community might have invested in a business by offering them tax-cuts. This creates a business relationship somewhat similar to the relationship between shareholders and the business, based on the fact that the local community has a financial interest in the business. If the business performs well, the local community can benefit. Performing well in this context is understood as either reducing costs and/or increasing profits. If a business is successful in their endeavours to reduce costs and increase profits, they may be in a position to employ more people and/or expand its range of activities. Both endeavours can have a positive effect on the local community as it can lead to an increase in population flow to the local area, a betterment of services etc. We thus argue that it is in the local communities' interests for the business to respond and negotiate with grey and black hats respectively.

### 6.6.4 Customers

For a customer who expects fast and efficient services, responding to grey hats and black hats is in their interests. In a crypto-ransomware attack in particular, it is in customers' interests for the business to do everything it can to prevent their private information from being sold or shared with the public. Brey (2007) states that data breaches containing sensitive information can cause psychological harm. If this is true, we argue that it is in the customers' interests for the business to respond to grey hats to reduce the likelihood of a crypto-ransomware attack. Equally, we argue that it is in the customers' interests for the business to negotiate with black hats to reduce the likelihood of the customers' private and confidential information from being sold to an interested third party (Engster 2011).

### 6.6.5 Suppliers

In respect of suppliers, they have an invested interest in the targeted business. It is in their interests that companies, with whom they engage and do business with, have a secure and reliable network. We subsequently argue that it is in suppliers' interests for the targeted businesses to readily respond to grey hats' demands. In relation to a black hat attack, a stoppage of services and a data breach not only affects the business targeted, it can have a knock-on negative effect on the market. Reducing the impact, longevity and cost of black hat blockers and crypto attacks is as much in the suppliers' interests as it is in the targeted businesses' interest. This is based on the fact that the supplier is interested in continuing business as normal and does not gain by being associated with a business who has fallen victim to a ransomware attack. Furthermore, a supplier's confidential and private information stored on the targeted business' systems might be leaked, misused or altered by the malicious hackers. It is thus in the suppliers' interests for the attacked business to resolve the issue as quickly and as responsibly as possible. We argue that this can be achieved by the targeted business responding to the black hats' ransom by firstly trying to find the decryption and, if none is available, to open up a communication channel with the black hat and try to negotiate a reduced fee.

### 6.6.6 Competitors

Competitors are impacted by other businesses operations within their industry. For example, when one company in an industry operates unethically, or in a way that attracts negative attention, competitors can suffer. Additionally, in certain industries associations exist that involve members pooling resources for industry-wide promotions and lobbying efforts. If one business chooses not to abide by the associations' ethical code, this can damage not only the business themselves but the association and other members of the association. We can apply this notion to a ransomware attack. For example, if one business does not respond to a grey hat's demands, the business could be argued as passively contributing to a weaker cyber environment. In doing so, the business not only increases their likelihood of being victim to a successful black hat attack, but the business may also be in violation of their association's ethical code. A violation of ethical code depends on the code itself and the values promoted within it. In other words, the business might be in violation of the ethical code if it encourages members to engage in promoting sustainability for all members of the association through collaboration, communication, co-operation and the sharing of information.

In the case of black hat attacks, it is in all competitors' interests (especially those who are members of an association) for the business to respond ethically and responsibly. For example, if an association sets a standard that its member must follow when they find themselves victim to a black hat attack, this can create a standard within one industry. Therefore, it is not only in competitors' interests and the business's interest to choose an ethical response to black hat attacks, we argue that it is an industry-wide interest. We extend this argument further by contending that it is in competitor's interests for the business attacked to have the knowhow to not immediately pay the ransom and try to find a decryption key. Thereafter, if a decryption key is not available, the business should engage in negotiation talks with the black hat with a view to lowering the original ransom demanded.

### 6.6.7 Hackers

Falk (2014) argues that the grey hat hacker is a black hat in a morally ambiguous state and recommends that grey hacking is a morally wrong action and as such should not be encouraged nor practiced by well-meaning computer professionals". We do not agree with this line of thinking for the following reasons. Despite both grey hats and black hats ransoming businesses (Yaghmaei et al. 2017), grey hats are interested in improving the information security community by scouring for vulnerabilities. Grey hats afford businesses the opportunity to patch those vulnerabilities before they are exploited by a black hat (Brey 2007). Black hats are not interested in using their skill set for the greater benefit of wider society. They tend to use their skills for malicious and illegal purposes (Radziwill et al. 2015). Black hats also believe in the more traditional hacker ethic that all information should be free and unlimited (Leiwo and Heikkuri 1998). This notion goes against the very idea of intellectual property as it suggests that individuals could and should not be able to benefit from information considered valuable (Brey 2007).

When we consult the ACM Code, it states that all computing professionals have an obligation to minimise the "negative consequences of computing, including threats to health, safety, personal security, and privacy" in addition to minimising the possibility of indirectly and directly harming others (ACM 2018a, b). It might be argued that grey hats follow this code whereas black hats do not. One interesting point made within the ACM Code is that computer professionals should only gain unauthorised access to systems when "there is an overriding concern for the public good" (ACM 2018a, b). This statement could be interpreted as the ACM condoning grey hat behaviour going on the assumption that grey hat's actions are undertaken out of concern for the public good. Being privy to the fact that grey hats are interested in improving the security of cyberspace and are working in the interests of businesses and wider society, whereas black hats interests are malicious, self-serving and can have detrimental consequences on a business, we argue that it is in businesses' interest to know the said differences between grey hats and black hats, to respond to grey hat demands, and to explore all options available to them when they fall victim to a black hat attack.

### 6.6.8 General Public

From the general public's view, they trust businesses to keep their information safe and secure (Wenger et al. 2017). In addition, as consumers they want easy access to information without disruptions to services (Yaghmaei et al. 2017). One example of a ransomware attack causing havoc amongst the general public was the WannaCry attack on the National Health Service in 2017 (National Audit Office 2017). From the public's perspective, resuming service and access is in their interest. This leads us to suggest that it is in the public's interest for businesses to negotiate with black hats about their demands.

In relation to a grey hat's demands, it can be argued that the grey hat is extending care to the general public by identifying vulnerabilities in a system or network and forcing businesses to patch them. This argument can be made as grey hats are improving cyberspace for all by making it more secure. The more secure it becomes, the less likely it is that individuals and institutions will be successfully attacked by a malicious hacker. In this way, grey hats are working with businesses to try to reduce the prevalence of malicious attacks. This not only benefits businesses but right down to individuals who use cyberspace for personal use. Therefore, the grey hat is not only extending care to the general public and thus acting morally from a ST care perspective, but the grey hat is fulfilling the third principle of the ACM Code, which states that computing professionals must ensure that the public good is the "central concern during all professional computing work" (ACM 2018a, b). With this in mind, we argue that is in the public's interest for businesses to respond to grey hats.

## 6.7 Conflicts of Interests Between the Stakeholders

We identify two conflicts of interest: (1) between grey hats and the other named stakeholders, and (2) between black hats and the other named stakeholders.

### *6.7.1 Grey Hats' Interests Versus the Other Named Stakeholders' Interests*

(1) Grey hats gain access to systems without the consent of the system's owner. In this way, grey hats penetrate and manipulate what were otherwise believed to be private and confidential systems. Those systems can contain sensitive and valuable information relating to the other named stakeholders. As these stakeholders are obviously interested in keeping their information safe from unauthorised access, a conflict here arises between the interests of the stakeholders mentioned and the interests of grey hats. Tavani argues that the helpfulness inherent in a hacker pointing out security weaknesses may not outweigh the harm it causes, as activities in cyberspace do inflict harm in the real world. He states that the act of hacking itself undermines privacy, integrity and can compromise the accuracy of information, as all hackers cannot be trusted to freely access and modify information at will (Tavani 2013).

(2) In seeking out vulnerabilities in systems, in rare cases, grey hats can stumble upon unintentional findings that are suggestive of criminal behaviour. In such cases, the grey hat is forced to decide whether they should notify the authorities or the vendor who maintains the business' systems. If the incriminating information obtained only relates to the dubious behaviour of one individual working within a firm, rather than to the general activities of the firm, should the grey hat notify the business directly, or the authorities? Depending on the nature of the findings, the discovered data could have the potential to damage the business and its shareholders, employees, customers, suppliers and possibly even competitors. A grey hat's aim is to improve the security of cyberspace, not to incriminate unethical individuals or institutions. Therefore, it is clear that this particular, albeit rare, circumstance can create a conflict of interest between greys hats and the other named stakeholders.

(3) Grey hats want to help users protect against unpatched vulnerabilities and limit the attack surface. Publishing vulnerabilities comes with the risk of weaponis-

ing criminals and other parties who may cause harm to organisations and individuals. When a grey hat notifies a business that they have discovered a vulnerability that needs patching within a given time frame and the business fails to patch the vulnerability, it falls to the grey hat to decide how to proceed. Publishing the vulnerability increases public awareness that a particular system or device is insecure. It also provides black hats with the information they need to exploit the vulnerability. Not publishing the vulnerability can lead to a false sense of security. The conflict here arises as both publishing and unpublishing the vulnerability has the potential to benefit or cause harm to the other named stakeholders.

### 6.7.2 Black Hats Interests Versus the Other Named Stakeholders' Interests

(1) Black hats want the highest ransom fee to be paid by businesses whilst it is in shareholders, employees, customers, suppliers, competitors and the general public's interest to pay the lowest fee or no fee. The higher the ransom paid, the more likely it is that black hats can continue with their line of 'business'. If a solution could be reached without the business paying any fees at all, the interests of the stakeholders that have a financial interest in the firm (shareholders, employees, the local community, customers and suppliers) are upheld. The remaining stakeholders (competitors and the general public) have an interest in a lower or no fee due to the interconnected and interdependent nature of cyberspace. This is based on the notion that any action in cyberspace has a knock-on effect on a device, software, hardware or individual in some way shape or form.

(2) Black hats are interested in their best-case scenario. This can involve receiving the original ransom demanded, not having to share the decryption key so it can be re-used and selling the decrypted data (in a leakware or doxware ransomware attack) to the highest bidder. Businesses should be aware that paying the higher ransom does not guarantee that the black hat will share a decryption key, nor does it guarantee that the data encrypted will not be shared or sold to an interested third party. With this in mind, the worst-case scenario for the business and the other named stakeholders, is in fact the best-case scenario for the black hat, thus illustrating that a clear conflict of interest exists.

(3) It is in a black hat's interest for the business to pay the original ransom demanded without question. The other named stakeholders do not share this interest. Paying the ransom in this way sets a precedent for all other businesses. In other words, if we apply the principle of universality and all businesses began to do this, it might lead to an expectation that businesses must pay the highest ransom without question nor negotiation. It might also lead black hats to think that their ransoms are too low and encourage them to increase the cost of their demands. Assuming this to be true, businesses who pay the ransom without question nor

negotiation are not acting in the interests of the previously named stakeholders due to the potential financial impact and knock-on effect that it might have.

## 6.8 Responsibilities of Business

In today's technologically driven fragile cyber environment, it is clear that businesses have an ethical responsibility to all of their stakeholders to respond to the ransomware demands from both grey hats and black hats in one way or another. At the beginning of this analysis, it appeared that grey hat demands were questionable. However, upon conducting an ethical analysis of the main stakeholders and their interests, it seems that grey hats are acting in the interests of the business and their stakeholders by identifying vulnerabilities and forcing them to patch them, as this improves the business's computer security defences. We subsequently argue that businesses have an ethical responsibility to their stakeholders to respond to grey hat demands.

Engaging with black hats is not as straightforward. Black hats' motivations are different, and black hats cannot be trusted to stick to their end of the deal. For example, if businesses choose to pay the original ransom immediately after it becomes known that their data or services have been targeted, the business could not only be left out of pocket from paying the ransom, but their services and data might remain inaccessible despite having paid it.

An additional problem with paying the ransom demanded is that businesses could be accused of aiding or abetting cybercrime. For example, institutions such as Europol's European Cybercrime Centre, the National High-Tech Crime Unit of the Netherland's Police and security company McAfee advise companies not to pay the ransom demanded by black hats. They state on their 'No More Ransom' website (a website established to try to help victims of ransomware retrieve their encrypted data without having to pay criminals) that by sending money to cybercriminals "you'll only confirm that ransomware works and there is no guarantee you'll get the decryption key you need in return" (No More Ransom 2018).

According to Wicks et al. (1994), companies must be adaptable in a fast, ever-changing business environment if they wish to survive and thrive. With this in mind, we encourage businesses to respond readily to ransomware attacks from black hats. In an ideal situation, the faster the decryption key is to hand, the shorter the downtime period. In a situation where a decryption key is not available, and a business explicitly refuses to engage in negotiation talks with the black hat, the business is not only prolonging downtime, they are potentially worsening the financial impact of the attack. Depending on the severity of the attack, such action could affect the long-term sustainability of the firm and the ultimate goal of the firm, which is survival (Engster 2011). Going back to stakeholders' interests and the understanding that businesses have a responsibility to consider stakeholders' interests in their decision-making process, an explicit refusal to engage with black hat demands does not align with the interests of all stakeholders simply because of the financial impact of downtime, which can put the survival of the business in jeopardy.

Due to the limitations of this chapter, we assume for the sake of argument that the black hat's motivations are financial gain and they stick to their end of the ransom (i.e.) when the ransom is paid, they provide the decryption key and do not share or sell the encrypted data. Based on this assumption, we argue that companies have a responsibility to stakeholders (save for black hats) to reduce the potential collateral damage (i.e.) economic, reputational and psychological damage that a ransomware attack can cause. We suggest that businesses can do this by (1) having the knowhow to consult the decryption tools available and (2) when it becomes clear that decryption keys are unavailable, being able to open up negotiation talks with the black hat with a view to reducing the ransom demanded and, thereafter, be willing to pay the ransom at a reduced price.

Our analysis of stakeholder's interests has brought to light both the interests of the stakeholders and the conflicts of interest that arise in both grey hat and black hat ransomware attacks. After analysing the listed interests and conflicts, we argued from a care perspective that businesses have a responsibility to their stakeholders to communicate and negotiate with grey hats in respect of establishing a reasonable timeframe within which the business can patch the discovered vulnerabilities. Additionally, we argued that businesses have a responsibility to engage with black hats and negotiate a lower ransom when it becomes clear that no decryption key is available. It is noteworthy to mention that in advocating communicating and negotiating with black hats, we are not condoning black hat behaviour; we are simply offering businesses a short-term ethical solution to a much larger problem. The larger problem exists for many reasons which do not fall within the scope of this chapter.

**Acknowledgements** The chapter was created with funding from the European Union's Horizon 2020 research and innovation programme under grant agreement No 700540.

## References

ACM (2018a) 2018 ACM Code of Ethics and Professional Conduct: Draft 3. https://ethics.acm.org/2018-code-draft-3. Last access 7 July 2019

ACM (2018b) ACM Code of Ethics and Professional Conduct. https://www.acm.org/code-of-ethics. Last access 7 July 2019

Brey P (2007) Ethical aspects of information security and privacy. In: Security, privacy, and trust in modern data management data-centric systems and applications. Springer, Berlin/Heidelberg, pp 21–36

Bromium (2016) The hidden costs of detetc-to-protect security. https://learn.bromium.com/rprt-hidden-costs.html. Last access 7 July 2019

Burton B, Dunn C (1996) Feminist ethics as moral grounding for stakeholder theory. Bus Ethics Q 6:133–147

CISCO (2018) Risk triage for security vulnerability announcements. https://www.cisco.com/c/en/us/about/security-center/vulnerability-risk-triage.html. Last access 7 July 2019

Engster D (2007) The heart of justice: care ethics and political theory. Oxford University Press, Oxford

Engster D (2011) Care ethics and stakeholder theory. In: Applying care ethics to business. Springer, Dordrecht, pp 93–110

ENISA (2018) Cyber security breaches survey 2018 https://www.enisa.europa.eu/news/member-states/cyber-security-breaches-survey-2018. Last access 7 July 2019

European Commission (2018a) Data protection. https://ec.europa.eu/info/law/law-topic/data-protection_en. Last access 7 July 2019

European Commission (2018b) Can my company/my organisation be liable for damages? https://ec.europa.eu/info/law/law-topic/data-protection/reform/rules-business-and-organisations/enforcement-and-sanctions/sanctions/can-my-company-my-organisation-be-liable-damages_en. Last access 7 July 2019

European Council (2018a) Programs. Certified ethical hacker certification https://www.eccouncil.org/programs/certified-ethical-hacker-ceh/. Last access 7 July 2019

European Council (2018b) Programs. The LPT (Master) training program: advanced penetration testing course. https://www.eccouncil.org/programs/licensed-penetration-tester-lpt-master/. Last access 7 July 2019

European Parliament, (2016) General data protection regulation (EU) 2016/679 of the European Parliament and of the Council of 27 April 2016. https://eur-lex.europa.eu/legal-content/EN/TXT/?uri=uriserv:OJ.L_.2016.119.01.0001.01.ENG&toc. Last access 7 July 2019

F-Secure, (2018) Incident Response Report. Available at: https://fsecurepressglobal.files.wordpress.com/2018/02/f-secure-incident-response-report.pdf. Accessed 13 July 2018

Falk C (2014) Gray hat hacking: morally black and white, CERIAS tech report, 2004–20. Center for Education and Research in Information Assurance and Security, Purdue University, Lafayette

Freeman R (1984) Strategic management: a stakeholder approach. Pittman, Boston

Freeman R, Gilbert D (1989) Corporate strategy and the for ethics. Prentice Hall, Englewood Cliffs

Freeman R, Gilbert R (1992) Business, ethics and society: a critical agenda Bus Soc 31:9–1

Freeman R et al (2010) Stakeholder theory: state of the art. Cambridge University Press, Cambridge/New York

Gilligan C (1982) In a different voice: psychological theory and women's development. Harvard University Press, Cambridge

Ismail N (2018) Ransomware costs European SMEs £71M in downtime, reveals report. https://www.information-age.com/ransomware-costs-european-smes-71m-downtime-reveals-report-123470721/. Last access 7 July 2019

Anton Ivanov, David Emm, Fedor Sinitsyn, Santiago Pontiroli (2016) Kaspersky security bulletin https://securelist.com/kaspersky-security-bulletin-2016-story-of-the-year/76757/. Last access 7 July 2019

Kaspersky Lab (2018) Ready… Or not: balancing future opportunities with future risks. A global survey into attitudes and opinions on IT security. https://media.kaspersky.com/documents/business/brfwn/en/The-Kaspersky-Lab-Global-IT-Risk. Last access 7 July 2019

Leiwo J, Heikkuri S (1998) An analysis of ethics as foundation of information security in distributed systems. In: Proceedings of the thirty-first Hawaii international conference on system sciences, vol VI: Organizational systems and technology track, Watson HJ (ed) IEEE Computer Soc, Los Alamitos, pp 213–222

McReynolds P (2015) How to think about cyber conflicts involving non-state actors. Philos Technol 28(3):427–448. https://doi.org/10.1007/s13347-015-0187-x

National Audit Office (2017) Investigation: WannaCry cyber attack and the NHS. https://www.nao.org.uk/wp-content/uploads/2017/10/Investigation-WannaCry-cyber-attack-and-the-NHS.pdf. Last access 7 July 2019

No More Ransom (2018) No more ransom. https://www.nomoreransom.org/en/about-the-project.html. Last access 7 July 2019

PECB (2017) Projected cyber attacks in 2018: a matter of when, not if? https://pecb.com/article/projected-cyber-attacks-in-2018%2D%2D-a-matter-of-when-not-if. Last access 7 July 2019

Radziwill, Nicole & Romano, Jessica & Shorter, Diane & Benton, Morgan. (2015). The Ethics of Hacking: Should It Be Taught?

Sullivan S (2016) Got ransomware? Negotiate. https://labsblog.f-secure.com/2016/08/10/got-ransomware-negotiate. Last access 7 July 2019

Tavani H (2013) Ethics & Technology. Controversies, questions, and strategies for ethical computing, 4th edn. s.l.:Wiley

Wenger F et al (2017) Canvas white paper 3 – Attitudes and opinions regarding cybersecurity. https://ssrn.com/abstract=3091920. Last access 7 July 2019

Wicks A, Gilbert D, Freeman R (1994) A feminist reinterpretation of the stakeholder concept. Bus Ethics Q 4(4):475–497

Yaghmaei E et al (2017) Canvas white paper 1 – cybersecurity and ethics. https://papers.ssrn.com/sol3/papers.cfm?abstract_id=3091909. Last access 7 July 2019

# Chapter 7
# Cybersecurity in Health Care

**Karsten Weber and Nadine Kleine**

**Abstract** Ethical questions have always been crucial in health care; the rapid dissemination of ICT makes some of those questions even more pressing and also raises new ones. One of these new questions is cybersecurity in relation to ethics in health care. In order to more closely examine this issue, this chapter introduces Beauchamp and Childress' four principles of biomedical ethics as well as additional ethical values and technical aims of relevance for health care. Based on this, two case studies—implantable medical devices and electronic Health Card—are presented, which illustrate potential conflicts between ethical values and technical aims as well as between ethical values themselves. It becomes apparent that these conflicts cannot be eliminated in general but must be reconsidered on a case-by-case basis. An ethical debate on cybersecurity regarding the design and implementation of new (digital) technologies in health care is essential.

**Keywords** Autonomy · Beneficence · Electronic health cards · Implants · Justice · Nonmalefience · Principlism

## 7.1 Introduction: The Value of Health

In the preface of his book *The value of life* (1985: xv) bioethicist John Harris writes, with a dash of sarcasm, that

> [n]ot very long ago medical ethics consisted of two supremely important commandments. They were: do not advertise; and avoid sexual relations with your patients. At about the same time as doctors were doing their best to obey these commandments, moral philosophers were more concerned with the meaning of words than with the meaning of life. Now,

K. Weber (✉)
OTH Regensburg, Regensburg, Germany
e-mail: Karsten.Weber@oth-regensburg.de

N. Kleine
Universität Osnabrück, Osnabrück, Germany
e-mail: Nadine.Kleine@uni-osnabrueck.de



M. Christen et al. (eds.), *The Ethics of Cybersecurity*, The International Library of Ethics, Law and Technology 21,
https://doi.org/10.1007/978-3-030-29053-5_7

> not just doctors but all health care professionals are interested in ethical questions as they relate to medical practice […].

The questions Harris addresses are of fundamental character: the value of life, the beginning and end of life, euthanasia, and the like. Most astonishingly, health is not mentioned at all in the table of contents, although the whole book is dedicated to providing arguments that protecting the life and health of their patients is the most important responsibility of physicians and other health care professionals, since health is seen as the most important prerequisite of a good life.

In Western culture, at least since the time of ancient Greece, there has been a great deal of thought given to the value of health for a good and successful life. Even after more than 2500 years, the Hippocratic Oath still has an important significance for medical action; the value of health, not only throughout Western intellectual history, is a recurring theme. It is probably no exaggeration that health, despite all the problems inherent in a precise definition of this term, enjoys high priority worldwide. Given this importance, it cannot be surprising that in order to protect health, the WHO has formulated access to it as a central human right.

If health actually is an important, if not the most important, value to human beings, then a health care system being able to provide effective and efficient help in case of medical problems also is most valuable—from an individual as well as societal point of view. That immediately raises the question of who must be obliged to provide for the necessary resources to maintain an effective health care system (e.g. Daniels 1985; Harris 1988). Although we do not discuss the benefits and burdens or moral justifications of different ways to maintain and finance an effective and efficient health care system, justice and fairness will be an important issue in what follows. The provision and maintenance of cybersecurity in health care can be very resource-intensive; this raises the question of who has to pay for these resources.

Health care systems most obviously need huge amounts of resources—according to the WHO in 2015, US $7.2 trillion worldwide was spent on health care. This amounts to 10% of the 2015 global GDP. At the same time, in many countries providing these resources is becoming more difficult because political or economic factors, as present in most countries with aging populations, make it difficult to finance their respective health care system. Therefore, as Nancy Lorenzi (2005: 2) puts it, "[a]lmost every major economy in the world experiences the effects of the high cost of health care, and many, if not most, national and regional governments are in some stage of health care reform". Although this was being said more than a decade ago it is still valid—and it is to be expected that it still will be valid in the years to come.

Attempts to reform existing health care systems most often include the development and implementation of Information and Communication Technology (ICT) in order to support the provision of effective and efficient health care services. In other words, ICT shall be employed to reduce or at least stabilise the costs of health. One of the main purposes of ICT systems in health care is the administration of information about patients and treatments that "[…] is a vital but complex component in the modern health care system. At a minimum, health care providers need to know a patient's identity and demographic characteristics, recent and distant medical history, current medications, allergies and sensitivities, chronic conditions, contact information, and legal preferences." (McClanahan 2007: 69) However, McClanahan also stresses that "[t]he increased use of electronic medical records has created a substantial tension between two desirable values: the increased quality and utility of patient medical records and the protection of the privacy of the information they contain".

At the same time, "[i]mprovements in the health status of communities depend on effective public health and health care infrastructures. These infrastructures are increasingly electronic and tied to the Internet. Incorporating emerging technologies into the service of the community has become a required task for every public health leader". (Ross 2003: v) In other words, stakeholders (see Chap. 6 for an example of a comprehensive stakeholder identification) such as patients, health care professionals, health care providers, or insurance companies are confronted with competing or even contradictory aims such as increasing efficiency, reducing costs, improving quality, and keeping information secure and confidential (cf. Fried 1987). Employing new technologies in health care therefore creates new value conflicts (see Chap. 3) or at least makes old conflicts and problems more visible or increases their urgency.

Simultaneously, other moral values also shall be protected and supported, either as fundamental moral values in European societies and/or as moral values (see Chap. 3), which are constitutive for the relationship between patients on the one side and health care professionals on the other. Conflicting or even contradictory aims and values raise moral concerns, since it has to be decided which aim and which value should be prioritised. To illustrate this, studying the conflict between beneficence and autonomy—both are important moral values within and outside the medical sphere —can be of assistance: When ICT is deployed in the health sector, it shall be aimed at ensuring that patients themselves determine when which information is revealed to whom—password protection and encryption are common measures to achieve this aim. However, in emergencies, when patients are no longer able to make this decision, there is now a risk that important medical information will no longer be accessible.

Moreover, it might be very helpful to share medically relevant patient information widely among health care professionals to improve the quality and efficiency of treatment. The goal of protecting patients' privacy and autonomy, however, may be at odds with this aim. In addition, in scholarly debates it is often mentioned that to provide cybersecurity it might be necessary to compromise privacy (see also Chap. 10). This can occur, for example, when non-personal health information on the Internet is only accessible if potential users of this information have to disclose their identity. It is argued that the respective platforms are better protected against attacks because the identity of the attackers could be determined. The problem here, however, is that anonymous searching, for example for information on diseases that are socially stigmatised, would then no longer be possible.

Such conflicting aims raise particular concern because it is obvious that both the protection of patients' privacy as well as the security of information systems and patient data must be important objectives in health care. Without privacy, trust among patients and health care professionals necessary for medical treatment is jeopardised (cf. Beauchamp and Childress 2009: 288ff.) and without the certainty that patient data will not be tampered with or stolen, treatment itself is at risk.

Approaching cybersecurity in health, in the second section we first discuss the relevant moral principles, values and technical aims relevant for the health domain. To illustrate the complexity of these issues, in the third section we present case studies from health practice. We furthermore explain in detail the conflicts that have emerged, which are examples of the broad spectrum of existing conflicts and trade-offs in health care. Finally, we outline the relationship between moral values and cybersecurity in health care. In the fourth section, we draw a brief conclusion.

## 7.2 Principles, Moral Values and Technical Aims

### *7.2.1 Principlism as a Starting Point of Ethical Analysis*

Those involved in scholarly and professional debates concerning biomedical ethics will be familiar with autonomy, beneficence and justice: Together with nonmaleficence these values—or more accurately 'principles'—can be seen as core moral aims, as particularly emphasised in Beauchamp and Childress' considerations on the foundations of biomedical ethics (see also Chap. 4). Their book *Principles of Biomedical Ethics* (2009) first published in 1977 is a groundbreaking text. The core features of their approach—'principlism'—involves four moral principles, namely autonomy, nonmaleficence, beneficence and justice, which are pertinent to a particular moral situation; furthermore, they use their specification, balancing and (deductive) application to create a bridge between the moral situation and the relevant principles.

It must be stressed that principlism is far from an indisputable tenet in biomedical ethics; its weaknesses include neglect of emotional and personal factors that are inherent in specific decision situations, oversimplification of the moral issues, and excessive claims of universality (e.g. Clouser and Gert 1990; Hine 2011; McGrath 1998; Sorell 2011). Nevertheless, principlism remains highly influential for scholarly thinking about ethical issues arising (not only) in the health domain (e.g. Reijers et al. 2018). Hence, we use principlism as the starting point of our ethical analysis concerning cybersecurity in health.

As already mentioned, Beauchamp and Childress' four principles of biomedical ethics are *respect for autonomy*, *nonmaleficence*, *beneficence* and *justice,* the definitions of which can be briefly summarized as follows (cf. Loi et al. 2019):

- *Respect for autonomy* as a negative obligation means avoiding interfering in other people's freely made decisions. Understanding respect for autonomy as a positive obligation means informing people comprehensibly and thoroughly about all aspects of a decision, for example about its consequences. Respect for autonomy also may "[…] affect rights and obligations of liberty, privacy, confidentiality, truthfulness, and informed consent [...]" (Beauchamp and Childress 2009: 104).

- The principle of *nonmaleficence* is derived from the classic quote "above all, do no harm" which is often ascribed to the Hippocratic Oath. As Beauchamp and Childress (2009: 149) state, "[...] the Hippocratic oath clearly expresses an obligation of nonmaleficence and an obligation of beneficence". At the heart of this principle is the imperative not to harm or ill-treat anyone, especially patients.
- *Beneficence* must be distinguished from nonmaleficence. According to Beauchamp and Childress (2009: 197), "[m]orality requires not only that we treat persons autonomously and refrain from harming them, but also that we contribute to their welfare." Consequently, care must always be taken to ensure that actions that are intended to be benevolent do indeed contribute to a benefit; the advantages and disadvantages, risks and opportunities as well as the costs and benefits of those actions must therefore be weighed up.
- *Justice* as a principle is even more difficult to grasp than the other three principles, since the different existing theories of justice produce very different results. For the purposes of our considerations, justice is to be translated as a guarantee of fair opportunities and the prevention of unfair discrimination, for instance based on gender or ethnicity. Justice also means that scarce resources should not be wasted; in addition, these resources often have to be provided by others, for example by the insured (cf. McCarthy 1987), so that economic use is required.

As Beauchamp (1995: 182) emphasises, "[t]he choice of these four types of moral principle as the framework for moral decision making in health care derives in part from professional roles and traditions." Hence, it should be considered that it might have repercussions on the principles as a framework for moral decision making in health care if professional roles and traditions change in time. It is most obvious that new technologies contribute to such changes.

### 7.2.2 Technical Aims Mapping to Ethical Principles

Despite justified criticism, we chose to use principlism as a starting point of our ethical analysis because its four moral principles can be mapped to the important aims of the employment of ICT in health care, which are *efficiency and quality of services*, *privacy of information and confidentiality of communication*, *usability of services* and *safety* (this idea was first developed by Christen et al. 2018; see also Fig. 7.1). The definitions of these four aims can be summarised as follows:

- *Efficiency and Quality of Services:* One of the main purposes of ICT systems in health care is the administration of information in order to increase the *efficiency* of the health care system and to reduce its costs. Improvements in health care in *qualitative* terms refer, for instance, to new services that provide treatment or processes with better health-related outcomes. Big Data the collection and sharing of as much health related data as possible, might be used to establish new

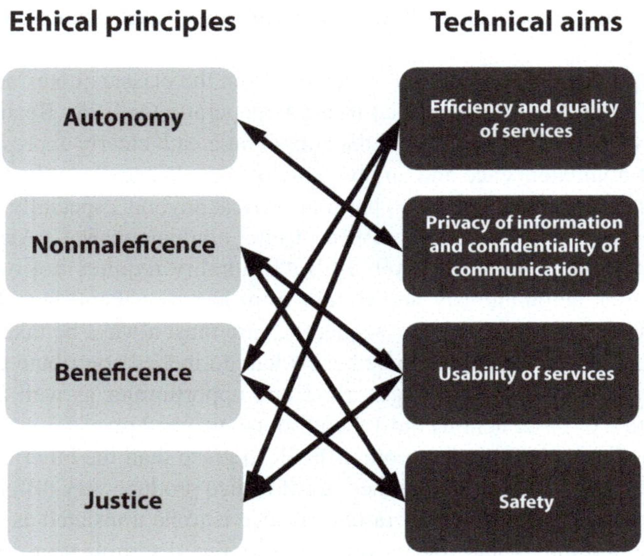


**Fig. 7.1** Technical aims mapping to ethical principles

insights regarding diseases and possible treatments (e.g. Vayena et al. 2016). In this regard, *quality and efficiency of services* map to the *principle of beneficence*. *Efficiency of services* map also to the *principle of justice* insofar as services contribute to the economic use of resources, in this way diminishing the risk of unfair allocations.

- *Privacy of Information and Confidentiality of Communication:* Using ICT to process patient data creates a moral challenge in terms of quality on the one hand and *privacy* and *confidentiality* on the other hand—yet both are important aims in health care. In particular, privacy is often seen as a prerequisite of patients' autonomy and therefore *privacy* maps to the *principle of autonomy*. Privacy and confidentiality are also foundations of trust among patients on the one hand and health care professionals on the other.
- *Usability of Services: Usability* can be defined as "[…] the degree of effectiveness, efficiency, and satisfaction with which users of a system can realize their intended task" (Roman et al. 2017: 70). With regard to health, users can be patients, medical staff and/or administrators, which have different degrees of ICT competences, depending on personal attitudes and socio-demographic variables (Kaplan and Litewka 2008). *Usability of services* map to the *principle of nonmaleficence* since poor usability can hurt people (e.g. Magrabi et al. 2012; Viitanen et al. 2011). Thus, usability, quality and efficiency are interrelated since reduced usability may compromise quality and efficiency. *Usability of services* additionally maps to the *principle of justice* in that usability for all kinds of users increases the accessibility of services.

- *Safety: Safety* can be defined as the reduction of health-threatening risks. Safety, quality, efficiency and usability are interrelated, but they do not align, because safety measures might reduce the efficiency and usability of services and therefore quality. *Safety* maps to the *principle of nonmaleficence* as well as to the *principle of beneficence*.

The four technical objectives mentioned above are composed of various subgoals. For instance, accessibility, availability, responsibility and transparency can be considered part of safety. Another example is universal design as "design-for-all, barrier-free design, transgenerational design, design-for-the-broader-average, or design-for-the-nonaverage" (Sandhu 2000: 80) that can be understood as part of usability. A detailed ethical analysis of case studies requires a very thorough examination of what subgoals make up the above mentioned technical aims in each case—this can be understood as a "specification" in the sense that Beauchamp and Childress understand it in relation to their ethical principles. This kind of specification is important not only for the technical requirements, but—as will become apparent—also for the identification of moral values that could be affected by technical aims.

### 7.2.3 Other Moral Values

The findings of an extensive structured literature search (Christen et al. 2017; Yaghmaei et al. 2017: 9–17) show that, beside the four principles, additional moral values are affected by cybersecurity in health care. These values may often have a connection to Beauchamp and Childress' principles, but, to different extents, they go beyond them. The most relevant ones with regard to cybersecurity in health care are *freedom and consent*, *privacy and trust*, *dignity and solidarity*, and *fairness and equality*.

- *Privacy and Trust:* Privacy plays a crucial role, not least because of the use of constantly growing amounts of data (Big Data). Privacy of patients shall be guaranteed, also with particular regard to the sensitive nature of health-related data. Risks such as uncontrolled access by third parties, disclosure of data and the like are to be eliminated. Patients must be able to trust new health technologies, professionals and the health care system in general. In other words, they must be certain to be protected from harm, which is connected to the *principle of nonmaleficence*.
- *Freedom and Consent:* Freedom includes both the unrestricted choice of (non-) use of new technologies as well as the unhindered choice of how and for which purposes new technologies are being used. To achieve this, patient consent must be recognised as an important factor in health care. This refers, in contrast to presumed consent, to informed consent. The idea of informed consent and the general freedom of use and freedom of choice emphasises the *principle of autonomy*.

- *Fairness and Equality:* An important value in terms of health is fairness in treatment. This includes access for all patients to all types of treatment, regardless of, for instance, their ethnicity and social background. This is closely linked to the principle of justice, but emphasises the protection against subtle unfair treatments, e.g. special consideration for people with a lack of skills, knowledge or abilities: Patients with limited health and technical literacy should be treated equally compared to those who know how to operate health technology. Everybody must be protected from unfair treatment, discrimination and stigmatisation; vulnerable groups shall not be excluded. Fairness and equality are closely linked to the *principle of justice*.
- *Dignity and Solidarity:* Human dignity is a major democratic and European value. Dignity must always be maintained, regardless of technical innovations, necessary moral compromises and limited resources. While dignity in its abstract form is difficult to grasp and primarily addresses the individual, solidarity describes a societal value in a more concrete way: the interpersonal commitment of individuals and groups who have both responsibility and benefits as a community, e. g. in a health insurance system and public welfare. Both dignity and solidarity, especially in relation to health and cybersecurity, are tied to the *principle of beneficence*.

These ethical principles and additional values are often both interlinked and in conflict with each other. In addition, there is the different use of terms: Privacy, for example, appears as part of an ethical principle, a technical aim and a moral value. Privacy as technical aim refers to data protection whereas Beauchamp and Childress consider privacy as a specification of the principle of autonomy. This ambiguity again demonstrates the importance of a detailed analysis of moral principles and values on the one hand and technical aims on the other.

## 7.3 Case Studies

### *7.3.1 Cardiac Pacemakers and Other Implantable Medical Devices*

#### 7.3.1.1 Brief Description of the Case

Implantable medical devices (IMDs) are employed with the intention of improving the quality of a patient's life. Implants such as cardiac pacemakers, insulin pumps, biosensors and cochlear implants offer therapeutic, monitoring and even life-saving benefits: medical treatment can be made more precise, efficient, customised and flexible (Burleson and Carrara 2014, 1 f.; Ransford et al. 2014, 157/167 f.). An increasing number of IMDs are wirelessly networked and can be connected to other devices to, for example, monitor functionality, set parameters, exchange data or install software updates.

However, for some years, there have been reports about the dangers of implantable medical devices. In addition to the risk of unintentional loss of function due to defects, the connectivity of IMDs leaves them open to malicious attacks. Examples of such possible attacks are (Baranchuk et al. 2018: 1285 f.; Coventry and Branley 2018: 48 f.; Mohan 2014: 372, Ransford et al. 2014: 158/161 f.)

- Unauthorised access to sensitive data, and their manipulation or further misuse such as identity theft.
- Spread of malware and viruses to interconnected devices and system networks.
- Manipulations of the devices to, for instance, modify the automatic insulin output or the impulse rate of a cardiac pacemaker.
- Switching off devices, which can endanger the health or, in the worst case, even the life of the person carrying the device.

Although there have been no real incidents known to date, for years, hackers, security experts, and scientists have been illustrating the vulnerabilities of IMDs: Jerome Radcliffe presented a talk at the Black Hat conference in 2011 at which he explained how he was able to get access to implanted insulin pumps through reverse engineering (Radcliffe 2011); Barnaby Jack showed his successful hack in order to control pacemakers (Burns et al. 2016: 70); and Pycroft et al. (2016) discussed the actual possibilities of 'brainjacking' neurological implants. In 2017, the FDA published a safety communications issue in which it announced that almost half a million cardiac pacemakers must get a software update "[…] to reduce the risk of patient harm due to potential exploitation of cybersecurity vulnerabilities […]" (FDA 2017). In one of the most recent cases, Billy Rios and Jonathan Butts explained in the abstract of their Black Hat 2018 presentation that they "[…] provide detailed technical findings on remote exploitation of a pacemaker systrm [sic!], pacemaker infrastructure, and a neurostimulator system. Exploitation of these vulnerabilities allow for the disruption of therapy as well as the ability to execute shocks to a patient." (Rios and Butts 2018) Already some years ago, this issue received special public attention when the media widely reported that the wireless function of then US Vice President Dick Cheney's pacemaker was deactivated due to security risks (e.g. Vijayan 2014).

Although dangers posed by attacks on IMDs should not be underestimated, their occurrence is, due to the complexity of such attacks, not yet too realistic: First, depending on the type of data transmission, a short distance may be required, not least because of the already difficult energy provision of IMDs. Second, the motivation to potentially risk the lives of implant users need to be given; if it was a matter of financial gain through access to personal data, other cyberattacks would serve a better purpose. Experts expect a greater risk of malware and viruses affecting medical networks including connected implants (Baranchuk et al. 2018, 1287; Burleson and Carrara 2014, 2–5; Coventry and Branley 2018: 49–51).

Different factors contribute to the lack of security. In addition to the risks posed by interconnectivity, there are other technical difficulties: Digital implants are supposed to have a long lifetime circle to minimise invasive treatment. Therefore, and due to the required small size and lightweight of medical devices, battery capacity and storage space are very limited, which often results in weak or missing encryption; outdated, weak or even no virus protection; and/or in the lack of regular software updates. The latter in particular creates the risk of endangering patients' health and/or life caused by malfunctions or breakdowns of a device due to the problem of outdated and insecure software used with IMDs (Burleson and Carrara 2014: 1/4; Fu and Blum 2013: 36; Mohan 2014, 372 f.; Ransford et al. 2014: 162/166–169). The development of effective regulations to improve the security of IMDs has proven to be difficult as well: Several administrative bodies (e.g. the FDA, see Woods 2017) have been working on such regulations and on certification systems for years without successfully covering all eventualities. Due to the complex combination of various technical factors and different actors, the definition of responsibilities and requirements regarding IMDs seems to be quite difficult and often comes with a huge time delay with regard to technical improvements (Burns et al. 2016: 70 f.; Cerminara and Uzdavines 2017: 311 f.; Coventry and Branley 2018: 48).

#### 7.3.1.2 Conflicting Ethical Values

The following analysis of possible moral conflicts demonstrates that there are not just management problems that contributes to these conflicts but that competing moral values or different value hierarchies on the part of stakeholders increase the insecurity of IMDs. Furthermore, as already pointed out, moral values can also conflict with technical requirements.

IMDs serve the primary aim of increasing the physical safety of patients. Wireless IMDs are designed to enable the continuous monitoring of vital parameters and faster communication with health care professionals both routinely and in emergency cases. While this faster access aims to enable health care professionals to use medical data more quickly, efficiently and flexibly to perform successful treatment, lack of transparency about who and under what circumstances can access what information does not ensure patient consent and control (Mohan 2014: 372). In addition, a key problem is that patients do not have direct access to information stored in IMDs, particularly in the case of so-called 'closed-loop-devices', although these data could inform them about their own body and health status (Alexander 2018; Ransford et al. 2014: 165–167).

If patients think that they might have little or no control over their own health-related data, that could, in the long run, contribute to a loss of confidence in health technology as well as in health care professionals. Because IMDs can be attacked and personal data stolen, patients may perceive danger for themselves and their data and thus for privacy and trust. Furthermore, there is the risk that implant users will be discriminated against as a consequence of unauthorised access to sensitive data, their uncontrollable use and disclosure to third parties. (Burleson and Carrara 2014: 1f; Coventry and Branley 2018: 48, Ransford et al. 2014: 158).

Another possible negative effect on patients' trust is the lack of a clear attribution of (moral) responsibility to the various stakeholders involved (e.g. manufacturers and designers, health care professionals and insurance companies, legislators and regulators), who pursue different interests and are not always primarily focused on patients' well-being (Alexander 2018; Baranchuk et al. 2018: 1285 f.; Burns et al. 2016: 72).

If patients were to decide who exactly has access to their IMD or if the access would be at least (through technical or regulatory measures) more protected, however, other problems (in addition to the ones mentioned above) would arise:

> Requiring users to authenticate to a device before altering its functionality is a boon for security, but it introduces risks in case of an emergency. A medical professional may need to reprogram or disable a device to effectively treat a patient. […] [E]ncryption or other strong authentication mechanisms could make such emergency measures impossible if the patient is unconscious or the facility does not possess a programming device with a required shared secret. (Ransford et al. 2014: 170).

In this case, the effective use and safety of the IMD would be in jeopardy. The conflict between usability and security does not only occur with the use by health care professionals. In the case of an open-loop system in which patients have access to the information stored in the device, their literacy level must be considered to ensure that patients with little technical knowledge and understanding for security do not suffer disadvantages. The degree of dependency and the level of risk must also be considered (Alexander 2018; Ransford et al. 2014: 164 f.).

## 7.3.2 *Electronic Health Card (eHC) in Germany and Elsewhere*

### 7.3.2.1 Brief Description of the Case

Conflicts with regard to cybersecurity are often related to privacy and data protection (e.g. Fernández-Alemán et al. 2013; see also Chap. 10). However, there are other types of conflicts. For instance, reaching a high level of cybersecurity might be very expensive. In a health care system financed on a solidarity basis, as it exists, for instance, in many European states, such costs would be passed on to all insured persons and thus potentially make the health care system more expensive for all. In health care systems where every person insures her own risk, as in the United States for example, it could be the case that only those who are willing and able to pay for expensive security would be able to enjoy the benefits of appropriately secured technology. This might raise concerns regarding social justice. As mentioned above, cybersecurity can also conflict with usability and accessibility. Despite these potential difficulties, there are high hopes for the use of ICT in health care, in particular regarding electronic health records and electronic health cards. This is demonstrated with reference to the German eHealth Card (eHC):

> As part of the German health-care reform, the current health insurance card is being upgraded to an electronic health card. On it, data on patient investigations, drug regulations, vaccinations and emergency data are stored. The aim is among other things to improve medical care and the prevention of drug incompatibilities and duplication of investigations. (Jürjens and Rumm 2008)

The development of an eHC in Germany was already discussed for the first time in 2004. Technical development then began in 2006, but in 2009 the project was halted (Tuffs 2010) because it was feared that the costs and benefits were no longer in reasonable proportion to each other. There was also a great deal of resistance, particularly on the side of physicians. Now, in 2019, the nationwide introduction of the German eHC has yet to begin (cf. Stafford 2015).

In particular, German physicians are quite sceptical with regard to the eHC, since it is feared that its deployment will result in huge costs and increase the workload of physicians and health care personnel: "The cost-benefit factor plays an important role in the implementation process, because—in the opinion of many physicians—the financial effort for acquiring and maintaining the system does not sufficiently outweigh the resulting benefit" (Wirtz et al. 2012: 659). As Ernstmann et al. (2009: 185) write, "[…] the ratings of perceived usefulness are rather low, i.e. physicians are not aware of useful aspects of the new technology or do not judge the established aspects as useful in their practice."

It is difficult to make accurate statements about whether this dissatisfaction has improved, as there is little practical experience with the eHC to date. A large-scale study (Schöffski et al. 2018) shows that many practitioners are still sceptical about the benefits. Although it is emphasised that the validity of the insurance status can be determined more reliably by the eHC—which is an important (cyber)security aspect—the administrative effort has not decreased. Since the functional capabilities of the eHC have also been very limited to date, it is still not possible to prove any medical benefit. Some scholars (Deutsch et al. 2010; Klöcker 2014) assume that these attitudes result from the perception of different aims on the part of the stakeholders; this would strengthen the assumption that technical, medical and ethical values or principles often compete or conflict with each other, especially in the health care sector. Although not discussed in detail here, it should be added that economic considerations play a dominant role in this particular case, which may also compete with other goals and values.

This rather sceptical attitude changes if it is assumed that the functional scope of the eHC is supplemented by the storage of a so-called emergency dataset, which, for example, would make it considerably easier for emergency physicians to provide first aid more accurately (Born et al. 2017). Since the medical benefit for physicians and, of course, for patients is most obvious, other considerations such as privacy, data protection and the like seem to be pushed into the background.

At the same time, at least to some stakeholders, benefits such as increased security are less obvious: "The efficiency of the system is considered as critical by the physicians, particularly in terms of data security and potential misuse of data. The primary concern of the physicians is the unauthorised access of a third party to stored data." In addition, "[r]egarding the introduction of the eHC to date, most physicians have criticized the very opaque communication and poor instruction on the subject" (Wirtz et al. 2012: 651). Or, to put it in other words (Ernstmann et al. 2009: 181): "Primary care physicians rate their involvement in the process of the development of the technology and their own IT expertise concerning the technological innovation as rather low."

The German eHC is based on a decentralised ICT infrastructure; its security features are strongly dependent on online network connections between end-user terminals and servers. Only if such connections are available all security features can be fully used—two-factor authentication with PIN and eHC, for example, only works if there is an online connection between the terminal and the server. Without being online, end-user terminals can still be used, but with reduced security. In such cases the application of the eHC comes with a potential conflict of (cyber-)security on the one hand and usability on the other (Jürjens and Rumm 2008). Since the provision of mobile Internet has improved since 2008, this problem may have been mitigated. The example shows, however, that cybersecurity builds on infrastructures that are not always and universally available—this might raise questions of social justice.

#### 7.3.2.2 Conflicting Ethical Values

In addition to the obvious conflicts of moral values that could arise from the high infrastructural costs for the introduction of the eHC, this brief description already illustrates that there are other areas of conflict that should be examined in more detail.

Beyond the issue of unfair distributed economic burdens, which raise moral concern with regard to social justice, the deployment of the German eHC as well as similar ICT infrastructures in other countries might be accompanied with another issue concerning discrimination. Due to security considerations, e.g. to protect medical data against misuse and unauthorised access, most of these infrastructures employ encryption and password protection of sensitive data. Laur (2014) mentions that "[w]hile some people have already difficulty remembering a PIN (especially elderly and disabled people), having many more passwords that are intended to protect them could put them at risk of disclosure, loss or stealing."

Although Laur refers to electronic health records in general, the problem also applies to the German eHC in particular: The eHC not only consists of a database, but its core components are a PIN and a credit card-sized chip card for two-factor authentication. Patient data (apart from the emergency dataset) can only be accessed if the chip card and PIN are used simultaneously. For elderly and/or handicapped people, for instance the visually impaired, using the eHC could be difficult. It is very likely that the persons concerned will create their own work-arounds, for example by writing PINs on the eHC or by disclosing them to health care personnel, which will certainly reduce the level of data protection, privacy and security of those persons. In such cases, a personal relationship of trust, which was originally intended to be replaced by technology, regains importance. From an ethical perspective, this does not necessarily have to be evaluated negatively, but it demonstrates that security measures can have ambivalent consequences and might raise concerns with regard to equality. Furthermore, it must be considered that in the large study of Schöffski et al. (2018), usability was not really examined. This raises questions regarding the consideration of stakeholder groups such as handicapped or elderly people and their needs.

### 7.3.3 *Cybersecurity and Ethics in Health: A Tentative Summing-Up*

It must be stressed that there is a long history behind the collection, storage and use of patient data. During that time, moral rules or moral orders developed to manage this data conscientiously and according to the interests of all stakeholders, but these rules related to data storage in paper files. The introduction of new technologies for storing and processing patient data, such as the electronic patient record or the eHC, will undoubtedly affect traditional moral and legal rules "governing health records, for example, consent and access rules, responsibility for data quality, liability for negligence, mistakes and accidents" (Garrety et al. 2014: 72); they will certainly be called into question by the new possibilities. In the future, we will have to prove whether these changes should be called "disruption of moral orders" (Garrety et al. 2014). Nevertheless, (digital) technologies and their possibilities force us to pay more attention to how moral rights and obligations change with the use of technology.

The case studies described above should already demonstrate that in terms of cybersecurity, the design and application of new technologies in health care affect numerous principles, goals and moral values that are in competitive, conflicting or exclusive relationships. Without striving for completeness, the conflicts among technical aims and moral values and/or among different moral values should be briefly mentioned again: security vs. usability, safety and usability vs. privacy and trust, efficiency and quality of service vs. freedom and consent, and security vs. beneficence. It is likely that in many cases, conflicts can be mitigated or even completely resolved by skilful technical design or by adapting organisational processes. However, it is equally likely that in some cases no such simple solutions are available. Beauchamp and Childress have often been criticised for not providing a clear hierarchy of principles; this, as often denounced, leaves the prioritisation of principles to the discretion of the decision-makers. However, it could well be that in many conflicts this is all that can be achieved. It is therefore one of the most important tasks of the value-based design of technology to make considerations transparent that lead to a decision. This makes it possible for decisions to be reconstructed, questioned and, if necessary, revised later on. In addition, there is often a demand that as many stakeholders as possible be involved in the value-based design of technology so that their expectations, demands and fears could be considered (Hennen 2012). However, it should be kept in mind that the participatory design of technology itself raises moral concerns that cannot always be answered adequately (Saretzki 2012).

## 7.4 Conclusion

Verbeek (2006: 362) writes that "[l]ike a theater play or a movie [...] technologies possess a "script" in the sense that they prescribe the actions of the actors involved. Technologies are able to evoke certain kinds of behaviour [...] Technological artefacts can influence human behaviour, and this influence can be understood in terms of scripts." Verbeek (2006: 361) thus stresses that it is necessary to explore technology's normative aspects because "[w]hen technologies coshape human actions, they give material answers to the ethical question of how to act. This implies that engineers are doing 'ethics by other means': they materialize morality." As a consequence, we must learn that "[...] information systems are intentionally or unintentionally informed by moral values of their makers. Since information technology has become a constitutive technology which shapes human life it is important to be aware of the value ladenness of IT design." (van den Hoven 2007: 67).

The statements above aim to provide an initial insight into how moral values can conflict with each other in the design and use of medical technology, as well as how technical design decisions can come into competition with moral values. It is to be expected that an investigation of further case studies would reveal other and more conflicts not considered here. Following the concepts of 'value sensitive design' (VSD, e.g. Friedman 1996; Friedman et al. 2013) and 'responsible research and innovation' (RRI, i.e. Burget et al. 2017; Stahl et al. 2014), every research and development project must therefore ensure that a comparable detailed analysis takes place in order to detect and then avoid such conflicts.

**Acknowledgments** The chapter was created with funding from the European Union's Horizon 2020 research and innovation programme under grant agreement No 700540.

## References

Alexander N (2018) My Pacemaker is tracking me from inside my body. The Atlantic. https://www.theatlantic.com/technology/archive/2018/01/my-pacemaker-is-tracking-me-from-inside-my-body/551681/. Last access 7 July 2019

Baranchuk A, Refaat MM, Patton KK (2018) Cybersecurity for cardiac implantable electronic devices: What should you know? J Am Coll Cardiol 71(11):1284–1288. https://doi.org/10.1016/j.jacc.2018.01.023

Beauchamp TL (1995) Principlism and its alleged competitors. Kennedy Inst Ethics J 5(3):181–198. https://doi.org/10.1353/ken.0.0111

Beauchamp TL, Childress JF (2009) Principles of biomedical ethics, 6th edn. Oxford University Press, New York

Born J, Albert J, Bohn A et al (2017) Der Notfalldatensatz für die elektronische Gesundheitskarte: Die Sicht von Notfallmedizinern und Rettungsdienstpersonal. Notfall + Rettungsmedizin 20(1):32–37. https://doi.org/10.1007/s10049-016-0197-y

Burget M, Bardone E, Pedaste M (2017) Definitions and conceptual dimensions of responsible research and innovation: a literature review. Sci Eng Ethics 23(1):1–19. https://doi.org/10.1007/s11948-016-9782-1

Burleson WP, Carrara S (2014) Introduction. In: Burleson WP, Carrara S (eds) Security and privacy for implantable devices. Springer, New York, pp 1–11

Burns AJ, Johnson ME, Honeyman P (2016) A brief chronology of medical device security. Commun ACM 59(10):66–72. https://doi.org/10.1145/2890488

Cerminara KL, Uzdavines M (2017) Introduction to regulating innovation in healthcare: protecting the public or stifling progress? Nova Law Rev 31(3):305–312

Christen M, Gordijn B, Weber K et al (2017) A review of value-conflicts in cybersecurity. ORBIT J 1(1). https://doi.org/10.29297/orbit.v1i1.28
Christen M, Loi M, Kleine N et al (2018) Cybersecurity in health – disentangling value tensions. Paper presented at the Ethicomp 2018, SWPS University of Social Sciences and Humanities, Sopot/Poland, September 24–26, 2018
Clouser KD, Gert B (1990) A critique of principlism. J Med Philos 15(2):219–236. https://doi.org/10.1093/jmp/15.2.219
Coventry L, Branley D (2018) Cybersecurity in healthcare: a narrative review of trends, threats and ways forward. Maturitas 113:48–52. https://doi.org/10.1016/j.maturitas.2018.04.008
Daniels N (1985) Just health care. Cambridge University Press, Cambridge
Deutsch E, Duftschmid G, Dorda W (2010) Critical areas of national electronic health record programs—is our focus correct? Int J Med Inform 79(3):211–222. https://doi.org/10.1016/j.ijmedinf.2009.12.002
FDA (2017) Firmware update to address cybersecurity vulnerabilities identified in Abbott's (formerly St. Jude Medical's) implantable cardiac pacemakers: FDA safety communication. https://www.fda.gov/MedicalDevices/Safety/AlertsandNotices/ucm573669.htm. Last access 7 July 2019
Fernández-Alemán JL, Señor IC, Lozoya PÁO et al (2013) Security and privacy in electronic health records: a systematic literature review. J Biomed Inform 46(3):541–562. https://doi.org/10.1016/j.jbi.2012.12.003
Fried C (1987) The primacy of the physician as trusted personal advisor and not as social agent. In: Brody BA, Engelhardt HT Jr (eds) Bioethics: readings & cases. Prentice-Hall, Englewood Cliffs, pp 221–225
Friedman B (1996) Value-sensitive design. Interactions 3(6):16–23. https://doi.org/10.1145/242485.242493
Friedman B, Kahn PH, Borning A et al (2013) Value sensitive design and information systems. In: Doorn N, Schuurbiers D, van de Poel I (eds) Early engagement and new technologies: opening up the laboratory, vol 16. Springer, Dordrecht, pp 55–95. https://doi.org/10.1007/978-94-007-7844-3_4
Fu K, Blum J (2013) Controlling for cybersecurity risks of medical device software. Commun ACM 56(10):35–37. https://doi.org/10.1145/2508701
Garrety K, McLoughlin I, Wilson R et al (2014) National electronic health records and the digital disruption of moral orders. Soc Sci Med 101:70–77. https://doi.org/10.1016/j.socscimed.2013.11.029
Harris J (1985) The value of life. Routledge, London/New York
Harris J (1988) More and better justice. In: Bell JM, Mendus S (eds) Philos med welfare. Cambridge University Press, Cambridge, pp 75–96
Hennen L (2012) Why do we still need participatory technology assessment? Poiesis Prax 9(1–2):27–41. https://doi.org/10.1007/s10202-012-0122-5
Hine K (2011) What is the outcome of applying principlism? Theor Med Bioeth 32(6):375–388. https://doi.org/10.1007/s11017-011-9185-x
Jürjens J, Rumm R (2008) Model-based security analysis of the German health card architecture. Methods Inf Med 47(5):409–421. https://doi.org/10.3414/ME9122
Kaplan B, Litewka S (2008) Ethical challenges of telemedicine and telehealth. Camb Q Healthc Ethics 17(04):401–416. https://doi.org/10.1017/S0963180108080535
Klöcker P (2014) Understanding stakeholder behavior in Nationwide electronic health infrastructure implementation. In: 2014 47th Hawaii international conference on system sciences. IEEE, Waikoloa, HI, pp 2857–2866. https://doi.org/10.1109/HICSS.2014.357
Laur A (2014) Fear of e-health records implementation? Med Leg J 83(1):34–39. https://doi.org/10.1177/0025817214540396

Loi M, Christen M, Kleine N et al (2019) Cybersecurity in health – disentangling value tensions. J Inform Commun Ethics Soc. https://doi.org/10.1108/JICES-12-2018-0095
Lorenzi NM (2005) Introduction. In: Lorenzi NM, Ash JS, Einbinder J et al (eds) Transforming health care through information, 2nd edn. Springer, New York, pp 2–6
Magrabi F, Ong M-S, Runciman W (2012) Using FDA reports to inform a classification for health information technology safety problems. J Am Med Inform Assoc 19(1):45–53. https://doi.org/10.1136/amiajnl-2011-000369
McCarthy C (1987) The money we spend and its sources. In: Brody BA, Engelhardt HT Jr (eds) Bioethics: readings & cases. Prentice-Hall, Englewood Cliffs, pp 206–213
McClanahan K (2007) Balancing good intentions: protecting the privacy of electronic health information. Bull Sci Technol Soc 28(1):69–79. https://doi.org/10.1177/0270467607311485
McGrath P (1998) Autonomy, discourse, and power: a postmodern reflection on principlism and bioethics. J Med Philos 23(5):516–532. https://doi.org/10.1076/jmep.23.5.516.2568
Mohan A (2014) Cyber decurity for personal medical devices internet of things. In: 2014 IEEE international conference on distributed computing in sensor systems. IEEE, Marina Del Rey, CA, USA, pp 372–374. https://doi.org/10.1109/DCOSS.2014.49
Pycroft L, Boccard SG, Owen SLF et al (2016) Brainjacking: implant security issues in invasive neuromodulation. World Neurosurg 92:454–462. https://doi.org/10.1016/j.wneu.2016.05.010
Radcliffe J (2011) Hacking medical devices for fun and insulin: breaking the human SCADA system. White paper. Black Hat Conference 2011, USA, https://media.blackhat.com/bh-us-11/Radcliffe/BH_US_11_Radcliffe_Hacking_Medical_Devices_WP.pdf. Last access 7 July 2019
Ransford B, Clark SS, Kune DF et al (2014) Design challenges for secure implantable medical devices. In: Burleson WP, Carrara S (eds) Security and privacy for implantable devices. Springer, New York, pp 157–173
Reijers W, Wright D, Brey P et al (2018) Methods for practising ethics in research & innovation: a literature review, critical analysis and recommendations. Sci Eng Ethics 24(5):1437–1481. https://doi.org/10.1007/s11948-017-9961-8
Rios B, Butts J (2018) Understanding and exploiting implanted medical devices. https://www.blackhat.com/us-18/briefings.html#understanding-and-exploiting-implanted-medical-devices. Last access 7 July 2019
Roman LC, Ancker JS, Johnson SB et al (2017) Navigation in the electronic health record: a review of the safety and usability literature. J Biomed Inform 67:69–79. https://doi.org/10.1016/j.jbi.2017.01.005
Ross DA (2003) Foreword. In: O'Carroll PW, Yasnoff WA, Ward ME (eds) Public health informatics and information systems. Springer, New York, p vvi
Sandhu JS (2000) Citizenship and universal design. Ageing Int 25(4):80–89. https://doi.org/10.1007/s12126-000-1013-y
Saretzki T (2012) Legitimation problems of participatory processes in technology assessment and technology policy. Poiesis Prax 9(1–2):7–26. https://doi.org/10.1007/s10202-012-0123-4
Schöffski O, Adelhardt T, Brunner, S et al (2018) VSDM Ergebnisphase: LG 15: Evaluationsgutachten (inklusive LG 14: Statistische Auswertungen). https://www.evaluation-egk.de/wordpress/wp-content/uploads/2018/03/ORS1-WEV-VSDM_LG15_Evaluationsgutachten_inkl.-LG14_v1.0_final.pdf. Last access 7 July 2019
Sorell T (2011) The limits of principlism and recourse to zheory: the example of telecare. Ethical Theory Moral 14(4):369–382. https://doi.org/10.1007/s10677-011-9292-9
Stafford N (2015) Germany is set to introduce e-health cards by 2018. BMJ 350(jun01 1):h2991–h2991. https://doi.org/10.1136/bmj.h2991
Stahl BC, Eden G, Jirotka M (2014) From computer ethics to responsible research and innovation in ICT: the transition of reference discourses informing ethics-related research in information systems. Inf Manag 51(6):810–818. https://doi.org/10.1016/j.im.2014.01.001

Tuffs A (2010) Germany puts universal health e-card on hold. BMJ 340(Jan 12 2):c171. https://doi.org/10.1136/bmj.c171
van den Hoven J (2007) ICT and value sensitive design. In: Goujon P, Lavelle S, Duquenoy P et al (eds) The information society: innovation, legitimacy, ethics and democracy. In honor of Professor Jacques Berleur S.J, vol 233. Springer, Berlin, pp 67–72. https://doi.org/10.1007/978-0-387-72381-5_8
Vayena E, Gasser U, Wood A, O'Brien D, Altman M (2016) Elements of a new ethical framework for big data research. Wash Lee Law Rev 72(3):420–441
Verbeek P-P (2006) Materializing morality: design ethics and technological mediation. Sci Technol Hum Values 31(3):361–380. https://doi.org/10.1177/0162243905285847
Viitanen J, Hyppönen H, Lääveri T, Vänskä J, Reponen J, Winblad I (2011) National questionnaire study on clinical ICT systems proofs: physicians suffer from poor usability. Int J Med Inform 80(10):708–725. https://doi.org/10.1016/j.ijmedinf.2011.06.010
Vijayan J (2014) DHS investigates dozens of medical device cybersecurity flaws. Informationweek. http://www.informationweek.com/healthcare/security-and-privacy/dhs-investigates-dozens-ofmedical-device-cybersecurity-flaws-/d/d-id/1316882. Last access 7 July 2019
Wirtz BW, Mory L, Ullrich S (2012) eHealth in the public sector: an empirical analysis of the acceptance of Germany's electronic health card. Public Adm 90(3):642–663. https://doi.org/10.1111/j.1467-9299.2011.02004.x
Woods M (2017) Cardiac defibrillators need to have a bulletproof vest: the national security risk posed by the lack of cybersecurity in implantable medical devices. Nova Law Rev 41(3):419–447
Yaghmaei E, van de Poel I, Christen M, et al (2017, October 4) Canvas white paper 1 – cybersecurity and ethics. https://doi.org/10.2139/ssrn.3091909. Last access 7 July 2019

# Chapter 8
# Cybersecurity of Critical Infrastructure

**Eleonora Viganò, Michele Loi, and Emad Yaghmaei**

**Abstract** This chapter provides a political and philosophical analysis of the values at stake in ensuring cybersecurity for critical infrastructures. It presents a review of the boundaries of cybersecurity in national security, with a focus on the ethics of surveillance for protecting critical infrastructures and the use of AI. A bibliographic analysis of the literature is applied until 2016 to identify and discuss the cybersecurity value conflicts and ethical issues in national security. This is integrated with an analysis of the most recent literature on cyber-threats to national infrastructure and the role of AI. This chapter demonstrates that the increased connectedness of digital and non-digital infrastructure enhances the trade-offs between values identified in the literature of the past years, and supports this thesis with the analysis of four case studies.

**Keywords** Critical infrastructures · Cybersecurity · Ethical issues · National security · Value conflict

---

E. Viganò (✉)
Digital Society Initiative and Institute of Biomedical Ethics and History of Medicine, University of Zurich, Zurich, Switzerland
e-mail: eleonora.vigano@uzh.ch

M. Loi
Digital Society Initiative, University of Zurich, Zurich, Switzerland

Institute of Biomedical Ethics and History of Medicine, Zurich, Switzerland
e-mail: michele.loi@uzh.ch

E. Yaghmaei
Faculty of Technology, Policy and Management, Technical University of Delft, Delft, The Netherlands
e-mail: E.Yaghmaei@tudelft.nl



M. Christen et al. (eds.), *The Ethics of Cybersecurity*, The International Library of Ethics, Law and Technology 21,
https://doi.org/10.1007/978-3-030-29053-5_8

## 8.1 Introduction

One of the first duties of a national state is defending national security, which is the protection of its citizens, economy and institutions. Originally, national security pertained protection from military threats, but nowadays its scope is broader and includes security from terrorism and crime, security of economy, energy, environment, food, critical infrastructure, and finally cybersecurity. In this chapter, we tackle the ethical challenges posed by cybersecurity in national security and, in particular, the security of critical infrastructures. The critical infrastructures of a state are the physical, non-physical and cyber resources or services that are fundamental to the minimum functioning of a society and its economy. Reliable ICT networks and their services, which are critical infrastructures, are crucial in ensuring public welfare, economic stability, law enforcement and defence operations. Societies increasingly depend on public ICT networks and their services. The stability, safety and resiliency of the cyberspace is a national security issue, as the vulnerabilities of the cyberspace can be exploited to impair or destroy the critical infrastructures of a state, which highly rely on ICT networks and services.

In the national security sphere, state actors such as the police and national security agencies have privileged access to ICT services, in order to enforce the law and carry out defence operations and countermeasures to terrorism. However, the privileged access of government agencies to ICT services may endanger values that are pivotal for contemporary societies. Cybersecurity measures at the national level may create a condition of discrimination by affecting people's access to some resources or services, have economic implications that affect fairness, influence freedom of expression, limit people's autonomy and violate privacy (see also Chaps. 3 and 4). For this reason, the identification and discussion of the ethical issues and value conflicts involved in cybersecurity at the national level is fundamental to assist national security organisations. In this contribution, we answer this need by providing the main ethical issues and potential value conflicts that should be considered by every national security organisation when carrying out cybersecurity initiatives, with a specific focus on the vulnerabilities to which critical infrastructures are subject. The aim of this chapter is to raise awareness about cybersecurity values, and to stimulate idea generation and discussion regarding values of cybersecurity in the national security domain.

## 8.2 Review of the Literature on Cybersecurity in the National Security Domain

We identified the ethical issues at stake in cybersecurity in the national security domain in the papers selected in the literature review on cybersecurity and ethics by Yaghmaei et al. (2017). We then constructed a network of the ethical values involved and of their possible tensions within the network. As a starting point, we categorised the papers by identifying value conflicts of cybersecurity initiatives. We further marked ethical issues and values that were either supportive or in conflict with security, as the latter is the core value of cybersecurity. On the basis of that categorisation, we delineated a set of ethical issues and conflicting values.

In our review of the papers on cybersecurity in the national security domain, two topics are mostly investigated. The first is the urgency for nations to develop strategies, frameworks, and suitable legal policies to defend and protect from cyber-attacks. The second topic is the difficulty and complexity of handling cyber-attacks countermeasures, which is because cyber-attacks overcome national borders and because interconnectivity, even though it boosts economic growth and makes people's life easier, nonetheless makes ICT networks and systems more vulnerable to attacks.

In the papers reviewed, cybersecurity is considered the top priority in dealing with terrorism and a necessary complement to national security strategies. Much of the literature indicates that national cybersecurity strategies need to be mindful of national cultures and ethical and technical values and at the same time compatible with international strategies and the global nature of the Internet.

The main ethical issues and conflicting values in national cybersecurity strategies that the authors of the reviewed papers have identified are shown in Table 8.1.

**Table 8.1** The main ethical issues and value conflicts in the literature on national cybersecurity strategies

| Ethical issue | Core value | Conflicting value |
|---|---|---|
| "Technology that was considered as a key contributor in progress of any country has evolved into a nightmare in form of cyber crimes" (Adeel et al. 2005) | Security (against cyber crime) | Connectivity |
| "Growing pressure for government to develop capacities to fight cyber wars" (Deibert 2011) | Security (against cyber terrorism/ cyber wars) | Protection of data |
| "Cyberspace enables cooperation and conflict in nearly equal measure" (Demchak 2011) | Security | Equity |
| "Focus on state's security crowds out consideration for security of an individual resulting in detrimental effect of the whole system" (Dunn Cavelty 2014) | Individual security | State security |
| "lawyers face dilemma because of the insufficient and vague cyber legislations are incompatible to deal with cyber crimes" (Faqir 2013) | Security (against cyber-crime) | Legality |
| "Infrastructure is owned and operated by private rather than public entities" (Hiller and Russell 2013) | Security | Surveillance |
| "Growth of criminal activities with the increased use of Internet and information technology" (Hui et al. 2007) | Security (against digital crime) | Accessibility |
| "Value of information increase so as well the efforts of criminals is more convenient" (Lehto 2013) | Security (against criminals) | Accessibility |
| "Information and communication technologies go beyond national boundaries" (Phahlamohlaka 2008) | Security | Protection of data |

In the next sections, we provide a detailed list of ethical issues and conflicting values regarding cybersecurity in national security that were found and discussed in Yaghmaei et al. (2017).

### 8.2.1 Ethical Issues That Emerged in the Literature

***Cyber Terrorism/Cyber Warfare*** Sekgwathe and Talib (2011: 171) argue that "Cyber-crime is typically understood to consist of accessing a computer without the owner's permission, exceeding the scope of one's approval to access a computer system, modifying or destroying computer data or using computer time and resources without proper authorisation. Cyber-terrorism consists essentially of undertaking these same activities to advance one's political or ideological ends." There is a twofold link between terrorism and the Internet. First, the Internet has become a forum for terrorist groups and individual terrorists, both to spread their messages of hate and violence, as well as to communicate with one another and their sympathisers. Second, individuals and groups have tried to attack computer networks, including those on the Internet; these acts are described as cyber terrorism or cyber warfare (Bucci 2012). Phahlamohlaka (2008) argues that the security risks associated with information and communication technologies, which go beyond national boundaries, are not fully in line with the value of data protection of all states. To avoid cyber warfare, the author contends that there is a need to develop and implement agile security-related ICT policies that mitigate the value conflict between data protection and security in the national security domain. Building on this value conflict, Deibert (2011) discusses the growing pressure on governments to develop capacities to fight cyber wars. He observes (2011: 1) that "today's deteriorating cyber-environment poses immediate threats to the maintenance of online freedom and longer-term threats to the integrity of global communications networks".

***Cyber-Espionage*** Cyber espionage is the use of electronic capabilities to illegally gather information from a target. For all nations, the information technology revolution quietly changed the way governments operate. The asymmetrical threat posed by cyber-attacks and the inherent vulnerabilities of cyberspace constitute a serious security risk confronting all nations. The achievements of cyber espionage—to which law enforcement and counterintelligence have found little answer—hint that more serious cyber-attacks on critical infrastructures are only a matter of time (Geers 2010a). Nevertheless, national security planners should address all threats with method and objectivity. As dependence on IT and the Internet grows, governments should make proportional investments in network security and incident response to the cyber espionages (Geers 2010b; Lehto 2013).

***Lack of Cyber Law*** The literature review reveals that legality problems play an important role in cybersecurity in the national security domain. Lawyers are faced with insufficient and vague cybersecurity legislations, which are incompatible with the requirements for effectively dealing with cyber-crimes (Faqir 2013; see also Chap. 5), as we will see in the case study of Exodus in the final section of this chapter. At the same time, cyber laws have become more critical than before in data and information security, as one can see in the growth of cyber-criminal activities. Hui et al. (2007: 11) argue that "... digital crimes (e-crimes) impose new challenges on prevention, detection, investigation, and prosecution of the corresponding offences". Widely accessible systems should be made in a manner that enables one to detect and investigate digital crimes in a more efficient and effective way.

***Cyber Awareness*** Raising awareness about cyber-security threats and vulnerabilities and their impact on society has become vital, but it seems to be missing in the society, if compared to the leadership that the governments of nations try to establish. By raising awareness, individual and corporate users can learn how to behave in the online world and protect themselves from typical risks. Awareness activities occur on an ongoing basis and use a variety of delivery methods to reach broad audiences. The awareness raising, however, varies across countries. Security awareness activities may be triggered by different events or factors, which may be internal or external to an organisation. Major external factors include recent security breaches, threats and incidents, new risks, updates of security policy and/or strategy. Examples of the internal factors are new laws and new governments.

***Profiling*** In profiling, people are approached, judged or treated in a certain way because they have characteristics that fit a certain profile and are associated with certain other traits. Profiling is not addressed explicitly in the identified literature, but it is implicitly mentioned in four papers. Profiling is used for a wide range of purposes and by various actors. It is employed by police or security agencies to find criminals or terrorists, by airport security to decide whom to check more carefully, by companies to target certain consumers, and by banks in deciding to whom to give a loan. As these examples already suggest, sometimes profiling serves security objectives. At the same time, profiling may inflict all kinds of undeserved harm on people, from nuisance to false accusations to even, in extreme cases, unjustified imprisonment. Thus, profiling can create tension between values such as non-discrimination and absence of bias, on the one hand, and security, on the other. Although profiling may involve privacy violations—as personal information is gathered to fit somebody into a profile—the main issue at stake is not privacy. Rather, the issue is that a generalisation is made on the basis of limited information about a person. This generalisation is based on statistical information regarding a group to which a person belongs. However, in virtue of the probabilistic nature of such information, the latter may say nothing about a person. As a consequence, profiling may lead to stereotyping and discrimination, as has occurred in the use of facial recognition technologies by the police and security: such systems are less accurate for certain groups (Klare et al. 2012) and may lead to the discriminatory treatment of people (Introna and Wood 2004; Garvie et al. 2016), as we will see in the third case study that we present.

### 8.2.2 Value Conflicts Identified in the Literature

***Privacy/Protection of Data ↔ Security*** A critical issue in cyberspace lies in the inability of companies and private businesses to exchange information with the government. This causes insufficient information collection, skews analysts' results, and prevents the states from collecting sufficient data on cyber-attacks and developing better defenses (McNally 2013). The cyber-attacks on Google illustrate the vulnerability of information stored in the cloud, online surveillance and private sector collaboration with government agencies against global terrorism. Hiller and Russell (2013) argue that cyber infrastructure is mainly owned and operated by private entities instead of public ones. Therefore, the states should select the most effective cybersecurity strategy and regulate the private sector to reduce overall cybersecurity risk and address the privacy concerns on cyberspace. We delve into this value conflict in the case study of Exodus. Furthermore, counter-terrorism measures and tools that tackle cyber-crime often invade privacy in the most brutal ways. At the same time, lack of personal online security leads to breaches of privacy. Security is thus an essential part of enabling privacy in the national security domain, especially with regards to data security, data protection, data ownership, access control, and information and computer security.

***State Security ↔ Individual Security*** Dunn Cavelty (2014) discusses a lack of focus on individuals in the efforts of states to achieve security in the building of ICT and other critical infrastructures. As a result, he argues, state security is not aligned with individual security. In fact, the focus on state's security crowds out consideration for the security of individuals. The result is a detrimental effect of the whole system: the state actors militarise cyber-security and override the different security needs of individuals in the cyberspace.

***Connectivity ↔ Security*** The urgency for nations to develop strategies, frameworks or suitable legal policies to defend and protect from cyber-attacks is discussed in several papers. At the same time, as mentioned, it is often contended that cyber-attacks beyond borders are increasingly difficult and complex to handle.

***Accessibility ↔ Security*** With lower costs associated with information accessibility and retrieval, more consumers and producers have access to global markets and transnational communication. Many Internet users, however, are not fully aware of cyber threats and they are not trained to protect themselves against these threats, thus becoming vulnerable to online exploits and increasing insecurity in cyberspace.

***Connectivity ↔ Equity of Access*** Globally interconnected digital information and communication underpin almost every facet of modern society and its critical infrastructure. However, not everyone in society has the same degree of access to information and communication technology. From the literature review, it emerged that inclusion and equity of access, consumer and producer accessibility to global markets, transnational communication, learning, and entertainment should be guaranteed to all, without causing exclusion, along with connectivity.

***Confidentiality ↔ Trust*** Confidentiality prevents the disclosure of information to unauthorised individuals or systems. The impact of cyber-threats could reduce public confidence and damage reputation of Internet transactions. Thus, assuring a trusted and resilient information and communications infrastructure is needed to protect privacy.

### *8.2.3 The Gap in the Literature*

We observed that the examined literature fails to emphasise to a sufficient degree that cybersecurity in national security involves numerous conflicting values. By contrast, the literature generally tends to focus on only one value (e.g. security, privacy, connectivity). Moreover, two topics that are highly relevant for ethics in cybersecurity at the national level are overlooked in the articles we reviewed: limitation of democratic values and creation of power imbalances.

With regards to the risk that cybersecurity may limit democratic values, on several occasions, governments and security agencies have required access to encrypted communication such as that on WhatsApp for security reasons, e.g. to detect and avoid potential terrorist attacks. Opponents of such access do not only point to privacy considerations but also to the fact that encrypted communication that cannot be accessed by governments and their agencies might be important for the democratic process and support opposition movements in countries with totalitarian or suppressive regimes. A similar issue has arisen in relation to the Tor network. The latter is a free software and an open network that supports users in protecting themselves against traffic analysis, which is a form of network surveillance that threatens freedom and privacy. In the aftermath of the hacking of the Democratic Party during the U.S. elections, it transpired that a Dutch private Tor server had probably been used in the hacking. The Tor server was owned by Rejo Zenger, an employee of Bits of Freedom. Bits of Freedom is a Dutch digital rights organisation which focuses on privacy and freedom of communications in the digital age. Although Zenger recognises that Tor servers can be misused by hackers, and are in that sense a threat to cybersecurity, he believes that this is a price worth paying, not only for reasons of privacy but also because these servers may be crucial for whistle blowers to reveal abuses. Again, the value that is at stake here is not just privacy but also a range of civil liberties that are seen as crucial for democracy and the democratic process.

The second value issue that is neglected in the literature but relevant for cybersecurity in the national security domain regards economic and political power imbalances. Economic monopolies or oligarchies are often considered undesirable, and in democracies, the balance of the political power between citizens and their government is a fundamental goal. It is acknowledged that maintaining certain power balances is important for a healthy economy and for democratic politics. What seems to be less recognised is that the possession of information about others and their behaviour is an increasing source of power in the information age. In fact, organisations that collect or possess large amounts of (personal) data may increasingly have power over other actors, which may lead to the disruption of existing power balances and the creation of new ones. The alteration of power balances pertains to companies such as Google or Facebook that collect large amounts of data about users and consumers, but also to governments and security agencies that may collect large amounts of data about citizens, and to providers of cybersecurity technologies, as these activities may involve accessing highly sensitive data. It should be noted that the accumulation of large amounts of data in the hands of a few may lead to power imbalances and may be problematic even if such data are anonymised, or if people have given their informed consent for the collection, storage, and use of their data. Consequently, even when privacy concerns are properly addressed, the accumulation of large amounts of data in the hands of a few may be considered problematic for economic as well as political reasons.

## 8.3 Cybersecurity of Critical Infrastructure

There are many definitions of critical infrastructures, which mirror cultural trends and historically evolving political needs (Office of the [US] President 2003; Federal Register 1996; Maglaras et al. 2018; Moteff and Parfomac 2004; Commission of the European Communities 2006). The common features of all these definitions include the idea that infrastructures are *general purpose means* to different kinds of human activities, in particular economic activities, but also activities necessary to protect security and health. One could compare critical infrastructures to the skull and bones of a body, to its blood vessels, to its nervous system: in short, to its vital organs, which need to be in place and work well for every action of the human body to be performed efficiently and painlessly.

Although nowadays all the systems that are comprised in critical infrastructure rely on ICT networks and services, they are not equally sensitive to attacks through cyber means. For example, hospitals and telecommunication systems, energy, banking and finance, and postal sectors, all rely on cyberinfrastructure to a such a degree that makes them obvious targets to an attacker.

We find that the definition of what counts as a cyber-attack to infrastructure is ambiguous, hence we introduce a classification of attacks by means of two orthogonal conceptual distinctions, leading to four distinct kinds of cyber-attacks to infrastructure. The types of attacks to critical infrastructure can be distinguished on the basis of the means of attack, as mere cyber-attacks vs. attacks with a physical component (physical or cyber-physical) and on the basis of the outcome damage, which can be physical (or physical and functional) vs. purely functional (see Table 8.2). We now describe the four possible combinations of means of attack and damage and all kinds of cyber-attacks.

**Table 8.2** Types of attacks on critical infrastructure

| Damage → | 1. Physical or physical-functional | 2. Merely functional |
|---|---|---|
| Means of attack ↓ | | |
| A. Physical or cyber-physical | A1 | A2 |
| B. Merely cyber | B1 | B2 |

First, in terms of the damage caused by the attack, we can distinguish physical or physical-functional (1) from merely functional attacks (2). In our definition, when the attack is *merely* functional (2), the only object that gets destroyed is information. Although malfunctioning and disruption of services may follow from the attack, there is *no* physical damage. In a physical attack (1), the attacked object is "persons, property or infrastructure attacked *through* cyberspace" (Roscini 2017: 103). We can make this distinction more precise by appealing to a criterion that has been suggested in the law of armed conflict. According to this criterion, a cyber operation counts as a physical attack if "restoration of functionality requires replacement of physical components" (Schmitt 2013: 108). The criterion is controversial in its original legal function as a measure of attack severity legitimising a military response, because it treats as an attack the physical destruction of a single server but not the incapacitation of an object (e.g. civilian power station) for days (Roscini 2017). However, our question here does not concern the justification of acts of wars, thus the distinction is far less problematic in our context. We merely need it to rigorously distinguish purely functional (2) from physical attacks, which typically have *functional consequences* (thus the label physical or physical-functional, in 1). Any attack that causes physical damage to infrastructure belongs to the column 1, irrespective of the means of attack (which can be also be purely software-based, as in the Stuxnet case, see below).

Second, in terms of means of attack, we shall distinguish a 'merely cyber' attack (B), for example through a virus or trojan, from a physical attack (A). Ordinary physical attacks to physical infrastructure causing physical damage (A1), e.g. shooting a missile to bring down a bridge or throwing poison in the water pipes may not belong to the realm of *cyber*security. However, some such attacks do, for example, the use of drones hacked or guided by malicious AI to carry explosives in the proximity of a dam. An instance of A2 (physical attack without physical damage) can be the use of graphite bombs, which spread extremely fine carbon filaments over electrical components that cause fully recoverable physical damage to the infrastructure: a short-circuit and a disruption of the electrical supply (Roscini 2017). This clearly counts as a cybersecurity threat, and it may not count as a physical attack according to our definition, as it is possible that no physical component needs replacement. An example of B1 is Stuxnet, the virus targeting the Siemens software that operated the uranium enrichment facility in Iran, in which the attacked objects were the turbines themselves, not just the information in the system. In this case, the means of the attack, unlike the case involving drones, were merely informational (a piece of software), but the goal was to physically damage the turbines. Cell B2 comprises attacks that disrupt the informational infrastructure of a country, without causing physical damage as defined. This includes, for example, DDoS attack that disrupt the processes of critical systems as well as the use of social media bots to spread dissent and convey political messages (Brundage et al. 2018). Any substantial and long perpetuated attack of the functioning of the Internet, when it does not cause physical damage to machineries or people, falls in category B2. An example is the sustained DDoS attack against the Chinese national domain name resolution registry on 25 August 2013, which interrupted or slowed down connectivity (Roscini 2017) without any lasting physical damage.

Therefore, the same critical infrastructure, e.g. the Internet, can be attacked by causing physical or merely functional damage, i.e. by targeting respectively its *hardware* or *software* components (Roscini 2017). The Internet is also vulnerable to both physical and 'merely cyber' means of attacks, e.g. missiles destroying servers and DDoS attacks, respectively. In *all* cases, the main impact on the population is that Internet connectivity is reduced, slowed down or made sloppy.

In all four kinds of attack to critical infrastructures, the vulnerable attack surface gets broader and broader due to digitisation—which means increased data availability and connectedness—and the development of AI—which obviously leads to augmenting the technological infrastructure for data collection and data analysis. We discuss two phenomena that are related to this issue, in the next section: first, the embedding of industrial control systems into public communication infrastructures. The traditional relative isolation and peculiar constitution of these information and communication systems has declined as business has turned to exploit peer-to-peer communications, real time monitoring, and lately, smart grids built through the Internet of Things and other services provided through the Internet (Maglaras et al. 2018). This has implications for cybersecurity, as we will see. The second phenomenon is the diffusion of AI, which has three implications for the cybersecurity of national infrastructure. First, the widespread availability of new cyber-physical systems, which can be exploited by novel attacks, for example causing self-driving cars to crash (Brundage et al. 2018); this is typically a physical and functional attack; second, the vulnerability that follows from the embedding of AI in critical infrastructures itself, which makes them vulnerable to both functional and physical-functional (*à la* Stuxnet) attacks; third, the possibility of using AI to enhance the scale and/or sophistication of attacks (both purely cyber as well as cyber-physical) against the critical infrastructure itself.

### *8.3.1 Cybersecurity of Industrial Control Systems*

The threat of cyber-attacks to infrastructure is capable of motivating the state to enhance its cyber capabilities. Unfortunately, some countermeasures of the state do not lead to enhancing the country's cyber defences directly, but rather enhancing investigative and retaliatory capabilities. State officials may recognise that there are structural limits that prevent improving the cyber defences of some critical infrastructures to the degree needed by national security objectives, or at least, there are such limits for any society that is not ready to renounce the efficiency advances brought by increased connectedness through ICT and AI. As Maglaras et al. point out, these limits are due to the current industrial control system network, which is a "unique environment, that combines large scale, geographically distributed, legacy and proprietary system components" (Maglaras et al. 2018 43). In a sense, the combination in the same network of ad hoc programmable logical controllers and proprietary systems (unconventional solutions) with well-documented protocols and off-the-shelf hardware solutions (conventional solutions) is the worst of all worlds from the point of view of cybersecurity. While unconventional solutions (which are still in place) may be poorly understood by cybersecurity specialists, the use of conventional ones threatens to undermine the obscurity of previous configurations, which are used to protect them from simple attacks (Maglaras et al. 2018). The combination of both solutions in the same network means that although the benefit of obscurity may be significantly reduced, it will still be very costly to guarantee high levels of security to such systems, as it requires ad hoc solutions.

The challenge in improving the strictly defensive cybersecurity programme of industrial control systems may lead, as a logical response by concerned politicians, to enhancing the capabilities of attack and surveillance by state agencies. This can be considered a strategy of *prevention* of attacks to critical infrastructure, and perhaps even *retaliation*, which appears all the more necessary since its *protection* is so challenging from a technical and financial perspective. The enhancement of *prevention,* which is achieved through surveillance, is, however, in a trade-off with citizen's privacy. The development of *retaliation* capabilities is in tension with the prospects of long-term cyber peace. Moreover, the technology risks escaping from direct control of the government and may create inequities in citizens' capacity to protect privacy and render privacy a luxury good. In other words, our hypothesis is that, considering national security as an integrated socio-technical system, the following socio-political chain (C) of events may be in place:

*C1. Enhanced connectivity of critical infrastructure ➔ increased vulnerability of critical infrastructure ➔ increased political incentive to enhance prevention against internal (e.g. domestic terrorists) and external (e.g. enemy states) threats*

Furthermore, the causal chain may continue in two distinct branches, one domestic and one that starts with foreign and may have domestic implications as well:

*C1A. Increased political incentive to enhance prevention against internal threats ➔ greater threats to citizens' privacy and freedom ➔ increased inequity in the protection from surveillance*

*C1B. Increased political incentive to enhance prevention against external threats ➔ cyber-offensive capabilities to be used against foreign enemies ➔ increased distrust between states*

C1B may in turn lead to a causal chain that reinforces the nefarious effects of C1A, namely:

*C1C. Increased distrust between states ➔ development of cyber-offensive capabilities (e.g. zero-day exploits) ➔ possible misuse of cyber-offensive capabilities ➔ greater threats to citizen's privacy and freedom ➔ increased inequity in the protection from surveillance*

In conclusion, there appears to be a trade-off between, on the one hand, the efficiency granted by embedding industrial control systems in larger and more general-purpose networks and by using off-the-shelf and more general-purpose information technology and, on the other, the capability to protect such systems from attacks. This conflict leads to further trade-offs if the states decide to protect infrastructure by developing preventive and retaliation offensive cyber capabilities.

### 8.3.2 AI and Cybersecurity of Critical Infrastructure

AI enhances the capabilities of attackers to affect the informational infrastructure of a society, as AI technologies are in general dual use (Brundage et al. 2018). For example, face-recognition and the ability to generate synthetic pictures and audios, or to manipulate existing ones, can be used to disrupt, among others, political processes. Recently, the literature on cybersecurity has turned its attention to the cyber vulnerabilities emerging from: (a) the increased use of AI in cyber-physical systems that, if hacked or repurposed, can pose novel threats to critical infrastructure; (b) the increased use of AI in critical infrastructure itself; and (c) the use of new AI-powered tools to launch more powerful attacks against critical infrastructure (Brundage et al. 2018).

An instance of (a) is the use of self-driving cars. Their AIs create opportunities for attacks through adversarial examples that cause crashes. If the attack is of sufficiently wide scope, it can be configured as an attack to a country's road networks, which are a critical infrastructure. Another example is the repurposing of commercial AI systems as physical weapons against infrastructure. For example, commercial drones and self-driving cars could be used to deliver explosives against physical infrastructures such as the electric grid, dams, hospitals, schools, etc. (Brundage et al. 2018). These attacks all fall into case A1 in our fourfold classification. Examples of type (b) derive from the fact that AI-augmented services are vulnerable to AI-specific attacks such as adversarial examples (Brundage et al. 2018). One case concerning a specific critical infrastructure, namely hospitals, is the possibility of adversarial attacks against diagnostic tools employing AI (Finlayson et al. 2019). These are instances of B2 in our classification. Finally, example of type (c) concerns the use of AI to enhance attacks against critical infrastructure. The autonomy of AI increases the potential damage that a single person may be able to cause (Brundage et al. 2018). The literature describes cases of both A1 and B2 cyber-attacks. Distributed attacks by networks of coordinated robotic systems (swarming attacks) such as drone swarms may be enabled by multi-agent swarming networks, which are an instance of AI (Brundage et al. 2018). Face-recognition, navigation and planning algorithms are similar enhancements of robotic systems (Brundage et al. 2018), which can be used to launch physical attacks (A1) to infrastructures. Moreover, AI can be used to enhance the search of software vulnerabilities (Brundage et al. 2018; King et al. 2019), thus increasing the scale or sophistication of attacks to the software embedded in infrastructure. The effect can be functional disruption (B2) or physical damage (A1) when the infrastructure in question relies on information and communication technology for its functioning or safety.

In conclusion, the widespread availability of AI, which is a dual use technology, enhances the capabilities of attackers, by "alleviating the trade-off between scale and efficacy of attacks" (Brundage et al. 2018: 6) and by enabling new kinds of attacks, such as swarming attacks coordinated by AI frameworks.

### 8.3.3 Value Conflicts in the Use of AI in Cybersecurity in the National Security Domain

As discussed in the previous section, AI is taking both an attacking and defensive role in cybersecurity. One of the clearest demonstrations was the DARPA Cyber Grand Challenge of 2016, with AI systems able to both identify and patch vulnerabilities (King et al. 2019; Taddeo 2019). Some AI cybersecurity defences are familiar, such as spam filters and malware detectors. Other examples are defence drones and the use of AI in criminal investigations and terrorism (Brundage et al. 2018). The recent literature has identified three significant value conflicts concerning AI: (1) security vs. privacy, (2) non-discrimination vs. security, and (3) short-term security vs. long-term security in cybersecurity between nation states.

The first value conflict concerns the use of AI-empowered technology such as facial recognition or social network analysis (Brundage et al. 2018) for purposes of national security defence. The employment of AI in a defensive and preventive role may enable a faster identification and response to threats, but it will not protect society from the threat of authoritarian abuse of the cyber domain by states (Brundage et al. 2018). As AI is more pervasively used for image, video and text recognition by state agencies, the traditional trade-off of cybersecurity mentioned in Sect. 8.2.2 (*Privacy/Protection of Data ↔ Security*) is exacerbated. Moreover, AI can be employed to better identify and profile citizens in relation to their online behaviour, for example through biometric profiles based on the way in which users move their mice (Taddeo 2019).

The conflict between non-discrimination and security is due to the biases and discriminations in AI, by which one means either *indirect discrimination/disparate impact*, which leads to certain groups (e.g. races, religions) being negatively affected by the outcome of the facially neutral algorithms, or *unequal accuracy*, which is the different balance in false positive/false negative rates for different groups (Zafar et al. 2017; Chouldechova and Roth 2018). All kinds of systems employed for profiling dangerous individuals and predicting threats are affected by indirect discrimination and/or unequal accuracy. This is not due exclusively to biases in data collection, but also to unavoidable trade-offs between different kinds of biases (Chouldechova 2016; Kleinberg et al. 2016) and between bias-removal techniques and the accuracy or efficiency of the prediction, or classification, in question (Berk et al. 2017; Corbett-Davies et al. 2017). We examine a case study of the ethical conflict between non-discrimination and security in the next session.

The third value conflict is a tension between the short-term goal of enhanced security, which may be *also* promoted by cyber defences (Brundage et al. 2018), and the negative side-effects of such reliance in the long-term (Brundage et al. 2018; King et al. 2019; Taddeo 2019). While the current confidence of experts in these systems is low (Brundage et al. 2018), improving such systems has been recommended (Brundage et al. 2018), and it may be speculated that the AI testing of cybersecurity will greatly enhance cybersecurity and reduce the value of zero-day exploits (Taddeo 2019). Among the side-effects is, first, the fact that AI-based defences may also have unattended vulnerabilities (Brundage et al. 2018). Second, if AI testing of cybersecurity proves more accurate than the human testing in the short term, then a human deskilling problem follows, namely the risk that "delegating testing to AI could lead to a complete deskilling of experts [which] would be imprudent" (Taddeo 2019: 188). Third, there is the risk that AI-enabled cyber weapons will be used in national active cyber defence strategies, i.e. in order to retaliate or create deterrence (Taddeo 2019). Some scholars have argued that the use of AI-enabled cyber weapons by states, for purposes of retaliation and deterrence, will lead to a cyber arms race from which all involved parties will lose in terms of their national security (Taddeo and Floridi 2018). Thus, scholars have advocated the adoption of an international regime of norms regulating state behaviour in cyber space (Taddeo 2018; Taddeo and Floridi 2018). However, consensus on such norms for the specific case of AI is unlikely to be reached soon, witnessing the failure of governmental actors to agree on more general principles of cyberspace behaviour (see Chap. 18). For at least two decades, governments and scholars alike have been advocating a regime of responsible behaviour in cyberspace (see Chap. 18) of which norms concerning AI can be considered an extension. Similar proposals include common norms of collaboration and information sharing between states (see Chap. 13), in order to build and strengthen trust, and/or higher investments in the security and resilience of digital infrastructure, which reduce the benefit that can be derived from such attacks. In a similar vein, Lucas (in this volume) has placed emphasis on creating the conditions for the emergence of practices and customs that confer more stability and predictability of the behaviour of states in the cyber domain. This could be facilitated, he suggests, by promoting public-private partnership in cyberspace and investing in international cooperation, to identify malevolent cyber actors.

## 8.4 Case Studies of Cybersecurity in the National Security Domain

In what follows, we illustrate four case studies that are related to one or more ethical issues in cybersecurity at the national level that we tackled in this chapter. First, we present a case of cyber retaliation against a critical infrastructure, which threatens cyber peace (see also Chap. 13). Subsequently, we describe two cases of surveillance technologies that governments are pursuing to enhance their cyber capabilities, which may be misused against the governed. Finally, we address the case of some morally problematic cybersecurity threats exploited by governments against enemy states or internal opponents.

### 8.4.1 *Iranian Attack to the US Power Grid System (Counter-Measure to Stuxnet)*

In 2013, some hackers breached the control system of a dam near New York through a cellular modem and infiltrated the U.S. power grid system, gaining enough remote access to control the operations networks of the power system. The hackers targeted Calpine Corporation, a power producer with 82 plants operating in 18 states and Canada. Opening a pathway into the networks running the U.S. power grid was not difficult as the infrastructure was outdated and its ICT network was not sufficiently protected (Thompson 2016). Previously, various cyber-attacks from Russia and China to networks tied to the U.S. power grid were discovered, but in the case of the dam near New York, the hackers gathered much more data: passwords to connect remotely to the power grid's networks and detailed engineering drawings of networks and power stations from New York to California. Potentially they would have been able to shut down generating stations and cause blackouts, but their infiltration was discovered before they started damaging the power grid. The digital clues that were gathered pointed to Iranian hackers (Thompson 2016). In the same period, hackers linked to the Iranian government attacked American bank websites. These attacks were Iran's retaliation for Stuxnet.

It is likely that the infiltration into Calpine's network was part of the Iranian counter-attack and thus it can be considered a case of cyber warfare. The Calpine case shows that the exploit of vulnerabilities in the ICT systems by governments produces a cyber arms race. In fact, while the Stuxnet attack did not harm innocent civilians, the data gathered by the hackers attacking Calpine would have harmed civilians, if the plan had been completed. Furthermore, the aim of the Stuxnet attack was considered a worthy one by the majority of the international community, as it consisted in preventing Iran from acquiring nuclear weapons, even though it raised several moral concerns (Baylon 2017). A final ethical issue that characterises the Calpine case is the tension between resource investment and security: enhancing the network security of energy infrastructures is a costly operation that requires significant investments.

### 8.4.2 Hacking of Citizens' Telephone with Exodus

In many countries in Europe and in the U.S., law enforcement and investigation can legally hack the devices of targets if required by a court order. In Italy, the police used Exodus, which is a spyware for smartphones, to gather data from criminals' cell phones (e.g. their telephone book, call and browsing history, GPS position, text messages, audio recordings of the phone's surroundings, etc.) and to send commands to the infected cell phone via a port and a shell. Exodus was uploaded in more than 20 Android applications on the official Google Play Store, which were mostly apps to receive promotions and marketing offers or to improve the smartphone's performance. Thus, these apps attracted and were downloaded by innocent people. Their phone was infected because Exodus installed itself on any phone without validating that the target was legitimate, whereas it should have checked the devices' IMEI to verify if the phone was intended to be targeted. Moreover, the port that was opened by Exodus could be exploited by anyone on the same Wi-Fi network, thus enabling the hacking of the infected phone to third parties. Google declared that less than 1000 mobile phones of Italian customers were infected (Franceschi-Bicchierai and Coluccini 2019).

In such a case we see, first, the opposition between national security in the form of the fight against crime, which is the aim pursued by the Italian state police and magistrates, versus the practical realisation of this aim. The latter involved innocent people and the violation of their privacy for no legitimate reason, since they were not under investigation. Furthermore, these people were rendered more vulnerable, as following the infection their mobile phone could be hacked by potentially everyone. Second, we observe a tension between legality and security, as the Italian legal framework on cybersecurity is not keeping pace with the new technologies adopted in criminal surveillance. The 2017 Italian law regulating legal spyware and its 2018 integration are too vague and do not address the need to protect the overall security of a targeted telephone. The results of such legal framework is that Exodus could be equated with old physical surveillance devices such as hidden microphones, whereas it is much more invasive (Franceschi-Bicchierai and Coluccini 2019). The society that the State police hired to develop Exodus is to be held responsible for infecting non-targeted people, as it deliberatively uploaded the apps with Exodus on Play Store, most likely in order to use innocent customers as oblivious experimental subjects for its software. Thus, it is likely that Exodus's failure to check the target's IMEI was not a programming error. Finally, Apple adopts filters that prevent malware from slipping onto its store that are stricter than those employed by Google. Apple's higher level of control protects its customers but has repercussions on the prices of Apple devices. This means that citizens' privacy is not equally protected: citizens with more economic resources can afford Apple's devices and be more protected.

### 8.4.3 'Biased' Face Recognition Systems

Face recognition systems (FRSs) are software used by police departments and airport security to respectively identify suspects and collect information regarding passengers with criminal records. The main reason why FRSs are increasingly employed by state agencies is that the task of finding a 'face in the crowd' or identifying a suspect from pictures of known offenders is a difficult task that requires effort. The FRSs automate this task and thus free government employees for more valuable tasks. FRSs are highly desirable as a biometric for digital surveillance as they are silent, non-invasive, and above all they are the only biometric techniques currently used by law enforcement that do not require the explicit consent of the subject. However, the performance of FRSs is highly reduced in an uncontrolled 'face-in-the-crowd' environment, in the case of a large database, and if there is an elapsed time between the database image and the probe image (Introna and Wood 2004).

The first ethical issue raised by the implementation of FRSs in general is the reduction of citizens' privacy, as FRSs can use the data from any CCTV camera system, for the sake of security. The second ethical issue is that FRSs were found to have lower performances on certain demographic groups: females, Afro-Americans, and young people (Klare et al. 2012), thus generating a form of discrimination. In the U.S., the criminal justice system and law enforcement are already affected by racial disparities, as black people are more scrutinised than white people by the police. FRSs may exacerbate this disparity as they increase the frequency that an innocent Afro-American suspect will come under police scrutiny (McCullon 2017). FRSs are increasingly employed by state agencies even because they should not be subject to the biases of human vision; they should be neutral, as they are technological artefacts. However, they are designed by humans in a specific sociotechnical context. This means that the biases of the algorithms of FRSs can be present in every phase of the algorithm design, from the selection of the data to the translation of the goal of the algorithm into mathematical constructs, to the selection of the tests that verify the performance of the algorithm (Loi et al. 2019). Hence, intentional attention to fairness in algorithm design is required for systems to overcome human biases and really achieve the equal treatment of individuals before the law.

### 8.4.4 Government Buying Zero-Day Exploits

Nowadays, cyber warfare comprises the practice of government agencies in buying zero-day exploits in the grey market. Prominent buyers of zero-day exploits are the governments of the U.S., Brazil, U.K., India and Israel. As these transactions occur in the grey markets and governments buy them in order to attack other countries or opponents, these purchases are secret, and mentioning a specific real case is not possible. However, it is possible to delineate the dynamics of such transactions, thanks to the disclosures of hackers trading with government agencies (Perlroth and Sanger 2013).

The zero-day exploits can be used as a form of weapon, as they can disrupt and destroy computers and their network. The targets can be critical infrastructure and services vital to the economy, public health and national security of a country. Government buying vulnerabilities protect their national security by threatening that of other countries. The paradoxical consequence is that if each government seeks the vulnerabilities of the other governments in order to protect itself, in the long run each one will be less secure. This practice is an instance of the conflict between short-term security and long-term security (the third value trade-off of AI in national cybersecurity). The zero-day exploits can also be used by governments to monitor the activity of political dissenters, thus violating the privacy of these persons. The zero-day exploits *per se* are not harmful (Dunn Cavelty 2014); it is the purpose of their use that can be moral or immoral. A further ethical tension regarding governments buying vulnerabilities is between the hackers' business aim to maximise profits and the government's duty to ensure adequate cyber defence (Baylon 2017). Furthermore, cybersecurity should be a public good, but the governments buying zero-day exploits have to follow the logic of market. Lastly, as zero-day exploits are kept secret, they may benefit few people and empower institutions that are already powerful.

## 8.5 Conclusion

This chapter provided a political and philosophical analysis of the values at stake in ensuring cybersecurity for critical infrastructure. We applied a bibliographic analysis of the literature until 2016 to identify and classify cybersecurity value conflicts and ethical issues in national security. We then interpreted the recent literature as suggesting that the increased connectedness of digital and non-digital infrastructure enhances the trade-offs between the values we identified in the literature of the past few years. This is due primarily to two phenomena: first, the embeddedness of an individual control system in conventional networks and technological solutions and, second, the diffusion of AI, which broadens the attack surface (e.g. self-driving cars and other robots) and enhances the capabilities of hackers and crackers. We presented four case studies that show the trade-offs involving security in cybersecurity at the national level—which is the core value of cybersecurity—and the values that most frequently conflict with that: non-discrimination, equity, privacy, and long-term security.

**Acknowledgments** The chapter was created with funding from the European Union's Horizon 2020 research and innovation programme under grant agreement No 700540 and the Swiss State Secretariat for Education, Research and Innovation (SERI) under contract number 16.0052-1.

## References


Adeel M, Chaudhry A, Shaikh R et al (2005) Taxonomy of cyber crimes and legislation in Pakistan. In: Proceedings of 1st international conference on information and communication technology, ICICT 2005, p 350

Baylon C (2017) Lessons from Stuxnet and the realm of cyber and nuclear security: implications for ethics in cyber warfare. In: Taddeo M, Glorioso L (eds) Ethics and policies for cyber operations. Springer, Cham, pp 213–229 https://doi.org/10.1007/978-3-319-45300-2_12

Berk R, Heidari H, Jabbari S et al (2017) A convex framework for fair regression. ArXiv:1706.02409. http://arxiv.org/abs/1706.02409. Last access 7 July 2019

Brundage M, Avin S, Clark J et al (2018) The malicious use of artificial intelligence: forecasting, prevention, and mitigation. ArXiv:1802.07228. http://arxiv.org/abs/1802.07228. Last access 7 July 2019

Bucci S (2012) Joining cybercrime and cyberterrorism: a likely scenario. In: Reveron DS (ed) Cyberspace and national security: threats, opportunities, and power in a virtual world. George Town University Press, Washington, DC, pp 57–68

Chouldechova A (2016) Fair prediction with disparate impact: a study of bias in recidivism prediction instruments. ArXiv:1610.07524. http://arxiv.org/abs/1610.07524. Last access 7 July 2019

Chouldechova A, Roth A (2018) The frontiers of fairness in machine learning. ArXiv:1810.08810. http://arxiv.org/abs/1810.08810. Last access 7 July 2019

Commission of the European Communities (2006) Communication from the Commission on a European Programme for Critical Infrastructure Protection. https://eur-lex.europa.eu/LexUriServ/LexUriServ.do?uri=COM:2006:0786:FIN:EN:PDF. Last access 7 July 2019

Corbett-Davies S, Pierson E, Feller A et al (2017) Algorithmic decision making and the cost of fairness. ArXiv 1701.08230. https://doi.org/10.1145/3097983.309809

Deibert R (2011) Tracking the emerging arms race in cyberspace. Bull At Sci 67(1):1–8. https://journals.sagepub.com/doi/pdf/10.1177/0096340210393703

Demchak CC (2011) Wars of disruption and resilience: cybered conflict, power, and national security. University of Georgia Press, Athens

Dunn Cavelty M (2014) Breaking the cyber-security dilemma: aligning security needs and removing vulnerabilities. Sci Eng Ethics 20(3):701–715

Faqir RSA (2013) Cyber crimes in Jordan: a legal assessment on the effectiveness of information system crimes law no (30) of 2010. Int J Cyber Crim 7(1):81–90

Federal Register (1996) Executive order 13010 – critical infrastructure protection. 61(138): 37347–37350

Finlayson S, Bowers JD, Ito J et al (2019) Adversarial attacks on medical machine learning. Science 363(6433):1287–1289. https://doi.org/10.1126/science.aaw4399

Franceschi-Bicchierai, L, Coluccini R (2019, March 29) Researchers find Google Play Store Apps were actually government malware. Vice. https://www.vice.com/en_us/article/43z93g/hackers-hid-android-malware-in-google-play-store-exodus-esurv. Last access 7 July 2019

Garvie C, Bedoya AM, Frankle J (2016, October 18) The perpetual line-up. Unregulated police face recognition in America. Georgetown Law Center on Privacy & Technology. https://www.perpetuallineup.org. Last access 7 July 2019

Geers K (2010a) The challenge of cyber attack deterrence. Comput Law Secur Rev 26(3):298–303

Geers K (2010b) The cyber threat to national critical infrastructures beyond theory. J Digit Forensic Pract 3(2/4):124–130

Hiller JS, Russell RS (2013) The challenge and imperative of private sector cybersecurity: an international comparison. Comp Law Secur Rev 29(3):236–245

Hui LCK, Chow KP, Yiu SM (2007) Tools and technology for computer forensics: research and development in Hong Kong. In: Dawson E, Wong DS (eds) Information security practice and experience, ISPEC 4464, pp 11–19

Introna L, Wood D (2004) Picturing algorithmic surveillance: the politics of facial recognition systems. Surveill Soc 2(2/3):177–198

King TC, Aggarwal N, Taddeo M et al (2019) Artificial intelligence crime: an interdisciplinary analysis of foreseeable threats and solutions. Sci Eng Ethics:1–32. https://doi.org/10.1007/s11948-018-00081-0

Klare BF, Burge MJ, Klontz JC et al (2012) Face recognition performance: role of demographic information. IEEE Trans Inf Forensics Secur 7(6):1789–1801

Kleinberg, J, Mullainathan S, Raghavan M (2016) Inherent trade-offs in the fair determination of risk scores. ArXiv:1609.05807. http://arxiv.org/abs/1609.05807

Lehto M (2013) The ways, means and ends in cyber security strategies. In: Kuusisto R, Kurkinen E (eds) Proceedings of the 12th European conference on information warfare and security, pp 182–190

Loi M, Ferrario A, Viganò E (2019) Transparency as design publicity: explaining and justifying inscrutable algorithms. SSRN scholarly paper ID 3404040. https://doi.org/10.2139/ssrn.3404040

Maglaras LA, Kim K, Janicke H et al (2018) Cyber security of critical infrastructures. ICT Express 4(1):42–45. https://doi.org/10.1016/j.icte.2018.02.001

McCullon R (2017, May 17) Facial recognition technology is both biased and understudied. Undark. https://undark.org/article/facial-recognition-technology-biased-understudied/. Last access 7 July 2019

McNally J (2013) Improving public-private sector cooperation on cyber event reporting. In: Hart D (ed) Proceedings of the 8th international conference on information warfare and security, pp 147–153

Moteff J, Parfomac P (2004) Critical infrastructure and key assets: definition and identification. Congressional report ADA454016. Library of Congress Washington DC Congressional Research Service. https://apps.dtic.mil/dtic/tr/fulltext/u2/a454016.pdf. Last access 7 July 2019

Office of the [US] President (2003) The National strategy for the physical protection of critical infrastructure and key assets, US White House Office. https://www.hsdl.org/?view&did=1041. Last access 7 July 2019

Perlroth N, Sanger DE (2013, July 13) Nations buying as hackers sell flaws in computer code. The New York Times. https://www.nytimes.com/2013/07/14/world/europe/nations-buying-as-hackers-sell-computer-flaws.html. Last access 7 July 2019

Phahlamohlaka J (2008) Globalisation and national security issues for the state: implications for national ICT policies. In: Avgerou C, Smith ML, van den Besselaar P (eds) IFIP international conference on human choice and computers, Social dimensions of information and communication technology policy 282, pp 95–107

Roscini M (2017) Military objectives in cyber warfare. In: Taddeo M, Glorioso L (eds) Ethics and policies for cyber operations: a NATO cooperative cyber defence centre of excellence initiative, Philosophical studies series. Springer, Cham, pp 99–114. https://doi.org/10.1007/978-3-319-45300-2_7

Schmitt MN (2013) Tallinn manual on the international law applicable to cyber warfare. Cambridge University Press, Cambridge

Sekgwathe V, Talib M (2011) Cyber crime detection and protection: third world still to cope-up. In: Yonazi JJ, Sedoyeka E, Ariwa E, El Qawasmeh E (eds) e-Technologies and networks for development, Communications in Computer and Information Science, ICeND 2011 171, pp 171–181. https://link.springer.com/chapter/10.1007/978-3-642-22729-5_15

Taddeo M (2018) Deterrence and norms to foster stability in cyberspace. Philos Technol 31(3):323–329. https://doi.org/10.1007/s13347-018-0328-0

Taddeo M (2019) Three ethical challenges of applications of artificial intelligence in cybersecurity. Mind Mach 29(2):187–191. https://doi.org/10.1007/s11023-019-09504-8

Taddeo M, Floridi L (2018) Regulate artificial intelligence to avert cyber arms race. Nature 556(7701):296–298. https://doi.org/10.1038/d41586-018-04602-6

Thompson M (2016, March 26) Iranian Cyber Attack on New York Dam shows future of war. Time. https://time.com/4270728/iran-cyber-attack-dam-fbi/. Last access 7 July 2019

Yaghmaei E, Van de Poel I, Christen M (2017) Canvas white paper 1 – cybersecurity and ethics, SSRN scholarly paper ID 3091909. Social Science Research Network, Rochester. https://papers.ssrn.com/abstract=3091909

Zafar M, Bilal H, Valera I et al (2017) Fairness beyond disparate treatment & disparate impact: learning classification without disparate mistreatment. ArXiv 1610.08452:1171–1180. https://doi.org/10.1145/3038912.3052660

# Chapter 9
# Ethical and Unethical Hacking

**David-Olivier Jaquet-Chiffelle and Michele Loi**

**Abstract** The goal of this chapter is to provide a conceptual analysis of ethical hacking, comprising history, common usage and the attempt to provide a systematic classification that is both compatible with common usage and normatively adequate. Subsequently, the article identifies a tension between common usage and a normatively adequate nomenclature. 'Ethical hackers' are often identified with hackers that abide to a code of ethics privileging business-friendly values. However, there is no guarantee that respecting such values is always compatible with the all-things-considered morally best act. It is recognised, however, that in terms of assessment, it may be quite difficult to determine who is an ethical hacker in the 'all things considered' sense, while society may agree more easily on the determination of who is one in the 'business-friendly' limited sense. The article concludes by suggesting a pragmatic best-practice approach for characterising ethical hacking, which reaches beyond business-friendly values and helps in the taking of decisions that are respectful of the hackers' individual ethics in morally debatable, grey zones.

**Keywords** Cracker · Black hats · Hacking · Hacktivism · Script kiddies · Pentesters · Taxonomy · True hackers · White hats

## 9.1 Introduction

The goal of this chapter is to provide a conceptual analysis of ethical hacking. The chapter begins (Sect. 9.2) with a historical introduction, describing how the term hacking and different denominations for different varieties of hacking have been

D.-O. Jaquet-Chiffelle (✉)
University of Lausanne, Lausanne, Switzerland
e-mail: david-olivier.jaquet-chiffelle@unil.ch

M. Loi
Digital Society Initiative, University of Zurich, Zurich, Switzerland

Institute of Biomedical Ethics and History of Medicine, Zurich, Switzerland
e-mail: michele.loi@uzh.ch

 
M. Christen et al. (eds.), *The Ethics of Cybersecurity*, The International Library of Ethics, Law and Technology 21,
https://doi.org/10.1007/978-3-030-29053-5_9

introduced in everyday, journalistic and technical language. Section 9.3 introduces our proposal of a systematic classification, one that fulfils adequate descriptive purposes and that maps salient moral distinctions into the different denominations of hacker types. It does so by proposing an initial taxonomy (inspired by common usage) and subsequently revising it by adding further nuances, corresponding to further evaluative dimensions. Section 9.4 discusses the concept of ethical hacking, revealing a fundamental ambiguity in the meaning of 'ethical' as an attribution to hacking. It presents our main thesis, namely that 'ethical hacking' refers to a limited view of ethics which assumes the pre-eminence of business-friendly values and that hacking that is ethical, all things considered, may not be 'ethical hacking' according to the common usage of the term. We recognise, however, that in terms of assessment, it may be quite difficult to determine who is an ethical hacker in the 'all things considered' sense, while society may agree more easily on the determination of who is one in the 'business-friendly' limited sense.

## 9.2 What Actually Is a 'Hacker'?

Almost every week mass media communicates about *hackers* having stolen thousands of passwords and other sensitive private information. It is commonplace to read articles about hackers having taken advantage of system vulnerabilities to bypass security barriers in order to fraudulently access private and company networks. The current understanding of the term 'hacker' is influenced by the news, and this twists the original definition of what a hacker is (Fig. 9.1).[1]

Today's perception of the term 'hacker' tends to be reduced to 'black hat' and 'cyber-criminal'. This has not always been the case, and the term 'hacker' conveys a much broader meaning.

### *9.2.1 Hackers in the Early Days*

In the 1960s and 1970s, typical hackers were not really driven by malicious intent. They were often supportive of strong (ethical) values, broader than computer security issues, such as democracy or freedom of speech. At the same time, computers, not to mention networks, were still in an early stage of development. The economic weight of computer related business was trifling in comparison to today's influence of GAFAMs[2] in the global market. Criminal opportunities were limited. Early

[1] As C.C. Palmer wrote: "Instead of using the more accurate term of 'computer criminal', the media began using the term 'hacker' to describe individuals who break into computers for fun, revenge or profit. Since calling someone a 'hacker' was originally meant as a compliment, computer security professionals prefer to use the term 'cracker' or 'intruder' for those hackers who turn to the dark side of hacking." (Palmer 2001: 770)

[2] The GAFAM acronym stands for Web main players, namely, **G**oogle, **A**pple, **F**acebook, **A**mazon and **M**icrosoft.

Fig. 9.1 Word cloud around 'hackers'

hackers were often students with special programming skills. They were dreaming of a world where information would be free and openly shared, a world where hackers would belong to a fair community and would collaborate to build a better and more secure digital environment. They could be enthusiastic and appreciative about the aesthetic and the inherent beauty of an optimal programming code (e.g. using the least amount of memory). They were playing pranks and challenging each other, hoping for peer recognition. Cracking the passwords of their institution was not seen as an illegal activity (and usually was not illegal at that time), but as a playful challenge with no malicious intent. They were adept at the so-called *hacker ethic*—including sharing information, mistrusting centralised authorities, and using computers to make a better world—which is not to be confused with what is called 'ethical hacking' nowadays. We sometimes refer to these early hackers as adherent to the programming subculture, or as *true hackers*.

### 9.2.2 *Hackers in the 2000s*

With the development of computers, networks, the Internet and our modern information society, information has become one of the most valuable assets. Information is the raw resource that boosts Google and Facebook. Information leads to knowledge and new forms of identities, which, in turn, allow targeted advertisement. Such valuable assets create new criminal opportunities and incentives, and need to be protected. The time when computers were a safe playground for geeks with

**Fig. 9.2** Shift in the hackers' incentives

insignificant economic consequences at stake seems far away. Hacking has become a business; a very serious one at that.

From the 1960s to the 2010s, we can therefore observe a shift in the nature of hacking incentives: ideological incentives have been replaced by economic ones (Fig. 9.2).

Ethical values at stake have evolved accordingly. In the 1960s, they were essentially described by the so-called hacker ethic. With the development of the Internet, of e-commerce and the increasing economic weight of information, freely shared information as well as many early ideological ethical values entered into conflict with economic-related ethical values, in particular regarding the protection of information ownership.

### *9.2.3 Modern Hackers*

Modern computer hackers are usually defined as skilled programmers and computer experts who focus on software, computer and network vulnerabilities. There is a plethora of terms available to distinguish them: white hats, black hats, grey hats, pen testers, ethical hackers, crackers and hacktivists, to mention the most important ones. Some categories of modern hackers do not even require significant expertise. Indeed, *script kiddies* are non-expert hackers who run programs and scripts developed by other, more expert hackers (Barber 2001). Modern hackers are categorised not only according to their expertise, but also according to the (ethical) values they adhere to or not. Legal values are often implicitly emphasised in this classification (see also Fig. 9.3).

Early hackers were categorised according to their expertise through peer recognition, and were adherent to values described in the hacker ethic. Today, 'hacktivists' still consider IT vulnerabilities as opportunities to promote a cause, a political opinion or an ideology. The group *Anonymous* is a typical heterogeneous group of hacktivists. In her best-seller (Olson 2013), Parmy Olson shows a large variety of profiles and incentives within *Anonymous*. However, most modern hackers use IT vulnerabilities for malicious purposes to commit fraud and make money. Some modern hackers strictly conform to applicable laws, whereas the majority does not really care.

Modern hackers can have a broad spectrum of incentives for their activities. According to Richard Barber, white hats are "[s]ecurity analysts and intrusion detection specialists […] [who] spend their time—just as police or intelligence analysts do—researching the technologies, methodologies, techniques and practices of hackers, in an effort to defend information assets and also detect, prevent and track hackers" (Barber 2001: 16). White hats do respect applicable laws. In a dichotomic world, they are the good guys. Their incentive is to protect software,

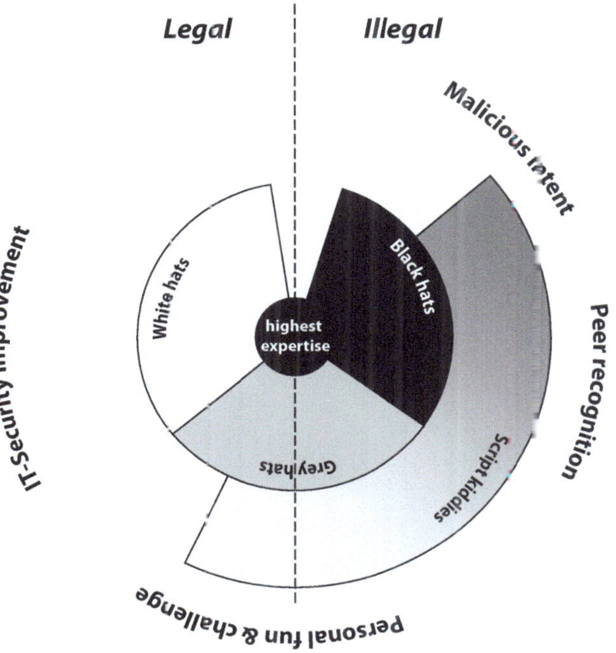


**Fig. 9.3** White hats, black hats, grey hats and script kiddies (Note that the outer layer refers to one predominant motivation (not the exclusive one). For example, not only grey hats, but also white hats as well as black hats may have fun in doing their activities or enjoy taking a challenge. White hats might also look for peer recognition)

computers, networks and the IT infrastructures from the bad guys, the so-called black hats or crackers.

According to Sergey Bratus, by contrast, black hats "act for personal gain and without regard for possible damage" (2007: 72). According to Technopedia (n.d.), a black hat is "a person who attempts to find computer security vulnerabilities and exploit them for personal financial gain or other malicious reasons". They might also have other motivations such as cyber vandalism for example. Their values lead to illegal activities.

*Grey hats* are hackers whose intentions are not fundamentally malicious, but who accept irregular compliance with the law to reach their objectives, which distinguishes them from white hats. Contrary to black hats, greed is not their typical main incentive.

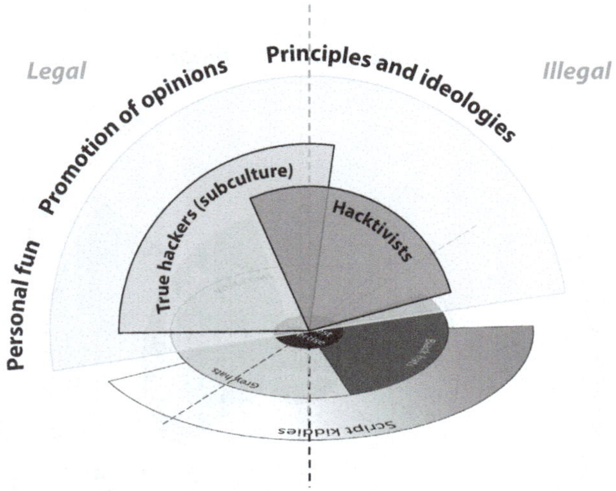


**Fig. 9.4** A third dimension to represent true hackers and hacktivists

Grey hats might also share some incentives with white hats and so-called true hackers: personal fun, peer recognition, intellectual challenges, etc. However, they do not really share the original hacker ethic.

To represent true hackers, as well as hacktivists, we need a third perpendicular dimension where the legal perspective only plays a secondary role (Fig. 9.4).

Many different definitions are used for terms categorising modern hackers. These definitions are not always fully compatible. They bring different nuances. There is a need for a more systematic classification.

### 9.2.4 Today's Hackers

We have already emphasised a shift in hackers' incentives from the 1960s to the 2010s. Since the beginning of the 2000s, information grew as a valuable asset and created new economic incentives for cyber-criminals. In our modern interconnected society, we now observe a new shift: information tends to also increasingly become a societal asset too (Fig. 9.5).

Nowadays, our whole society heavily depends on information and information technologies: transport and communication systems, medical facilities, SCADA control systems, electrical grid, nuclear plants and other critical infrastructures,

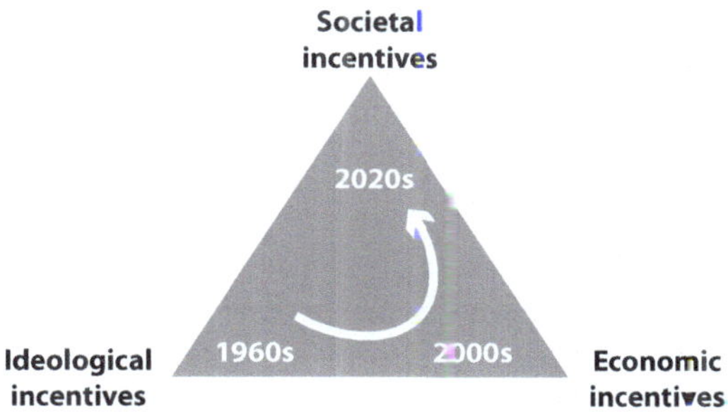


**Fig. 9.5** A societal dimension in hackers' incentives

government activities and voting systems, commercial exchanges and payment infrastructures, security-oriented surveillance technologies, or even military control systems.

With the advent and the development of smart cars, autonomous drones, smart medical devices and the Internet of Things, our physical world is becoming even more intertwined with the virtual one. To mimic a famous slogan,[3] what happens on the Internet does not necessarily stay on the Internet anymore. Lives are at stake. The very functioning of our society now relies on the Internet. A disruption of Internet services and other information infrastructure can paralyse a whole country. This creates a new paradigm and extra incentives for hacking activities. As a direct consequence, we observe the emergence of new categories of hackers: *state-sponsored hackers*, *spy hackers* or even *cyber-terrorists*. The target can be an individual, a company, a facility, an infrastructure or even a state. Whereas black hats foster cyber-crime and cyber-security countermeasures, state-sponsored hackers or cyber-terrorists have given rise to new concepts such as cyber-war, cyber-defence and cyber-peace.

## 9.3 Towards a More Systematic Hackers' Classification

As pointed out, different meanings of the term 'hacker' coexist in the context of computerised systems. The term seems to have evolved since the 60s and describes very different realities nowadays. True hackers, adept at the so-called hacker ethic, are disappointed by today's mainstream usage of the term 'hacker'. They do not want to be considered in the same category as security breakers and cyber-criminals.

However, in the earliest known appearance of the term 'hacking' in the context of computerised systems (Lichstein 1963)—which appeared in the MIT student newspaper *The Tech* on 20 November 1963—the pejorative connotation is already present.

[3] What happens in Vegas stays in Vegas!

Traditional dictionaries are of limited assistance in refining the meaning of the term 'hacker' in the context of computerised systems. In fact, this word has numerous different meanings in the English language. The Merriam-Webster dictionary provides four definitions for a hacker ("Hacker | Definition of Hacker by Merriam-Webster" n.d.):

1. : one that hacks[4]
2. : a person who is inexperienced or unskilled at a particular activity (a tennis hacker)
3. : an expert at programming and solving problems with a computer
4. : a person who illegally gains access to and sometimes tampers with information in a computer system

Curiously, the second definition seems completely opposite to the typical common understanding as it emphasises the *inexperience* of the hacker at a particular activity.

The last two definitions better capture the main meanings in the context of this chapter. The third one is general and covers most of the modern categories of hackers, whereas the last one is close to what we call a black hat or a cracker.

The American Heritage dictionary gives similar definitions for a hacker ("American Heritage Dictionary Entry: Hacker" n.d.):

1. (a) One who is proficient at using or programming a computer; a computer buff.
(b)One who uses programming skills to gain illegal access to a computer network or file.

2. One who demonstrates poor or mediocre ability, especially in a sport: *a weekend tennis hacker.*

Those definitions only describe large categories of hackers. We need to delve deeper into subtle differences to distinguish between the many terms used nowadays to characterise hackers in the context of computerised systems and eventually to precisely define what an ethical hacker is.

A more systematic classification requires, as a first step, a *taxonomy*, i.e. the creation and definition of classes with clear identities. A second stage of classification is *ascription*, i.e. placing each hacker into its class. Ascription corresponds to the identification of a hacker as belonging to a specific class. Identification itself is a "decision process attempting to establish sufficient confidence that some identity-related information describes a specific entity in a given context, at a certain time" (Pollitt et al. 2018: 7). When the entity is a person, i.e. for people identification, the identification process relies on authentication technologies in order to corroborate

[4]The verb 'to hack' has numerous meanings. According to the Merriam-Webster dictionary, the first definition is "*to cut or sever with repeated irregular or unskillful blows*" which has nothing to do with computer hacking.

(or to exclude) the fact that the given identity-related information describes this person in the given context, at the time of reference, with sufficient confidence.

Authentication technologies are classified themselves into four categories, namely:

- Something you know
- Something you are
- Something you do
- Something you have

A key aim of this paper is to develop a classification of (modern) hackers, related to categories of authentication technologies.

### 9.3.1 A First Taxonomy

In order to reach a new systematic classification of (modern) hackers, different perspectives can be chosen. A first approach consists in defining classes according to hacker's expertise (its scope and its level) and to hacker's values (his/her objectives and moral principles). Expertise can be seen as a collection of internal resources—something that the hacker *knows*—while values followed by the hacker can be seen as an internal attitude—something that the hacker *is*. Those classes are defined in compliance with the first two categories of authentication technologies (Table 9.1).

Hacker's expertise is defined by both its scope and its level. It corresponds to what the hacker knows and is able to do. The scope considers the expertise environments (OS, protocols, network, etc.), the objects covered by this expertise—those being physical (computers, phones, medical devices, smart cars, drones, etc.) or virtual (websites)—as well as the tools and programming languages mastered. The level of expertise appears to be a decisive criterion within hackers' communities to grant access to peer recognition. Next to their technical skills, some hackers might possess social engineering expertise. This might appear to be useful for black hats in order to bypass physical or logical security measures.[5] Social engineering can be

**Table 9.1** A first classification based on expertise and legal goals

| | High expertise | Low expertise |
|---|---|---|
| Legal goals | White hats | – |
| Illegal goals | Black hats | Script kiddies |
| Unlegal[a] goals | Grey hats | |
| | True hackers | |
| | Hacktivists | |

[a]*Unlegal* qualifies a value that is neither legal nor illegal

[5] Social skills may also be useful for white hats, when testing again the possibility of black hat hackers' intrusions.

used to gain a first internal access into a company computer network, for example. However, social engineering requires significant social skills, and not all hackers are social engineering experts. Hackers can be geeks. In his book (Marshall 2008: 1), Angus Marschall humourously defines a geek as "a nerd with social skills, and an extrovert geek looks at *your* shoes when he/she is talking to you." Conversely, most social engineering experts are not hackers. However, they can work together, typically under the direction of the same entity, a conductor.

Hacker's values encompass both his/her objectives and his/her moral principles. Hacker's objectives can be noble: make the digital realm a better and more secure place; they can be ideological: promote political views and ethical values (freedom of speech, democracy); they can be self-oriented (fun, personal intellectual challenge, peer recognition); and they can be malicious (information theft, money extortion, vandalism). Hacker's moral principles define the limits, if any, that they respect while trying to reach their objectives. These limits can be legal and/or ethical. They can also be personal or related to a particular community.

To give an example based on this first classification, we only consider both the expertise level (high or low) and the legal nature of hacker's goals. We use *illegal* to qualify a goal which is *not legal*—typically a value related to malicious intentions—and *unlegal* to qualify a goal which is neither legal, nor illegal in nature, for example 'to have fun' or 'to make the world a better place'.

### 9.3.2 A Second Taxonomy

We can extend the first taxonomy to develop a finer classification (Table 9.2). In our attempt to determine a more systematic classification of modern hackers, a second approach consists in considering not only the internal resources (expertise) and the internal attitude (values), but also external attitudes, as well as the external resources hackers have access to. Following the analogy with authentication technologies, the external attitude corresponds to something the hacker does and the external resources to something that he or she has.

The external attitude describes the modus operandi. Hackers' modi operandi are numerous. Actions can be potential or actual. Some hackers will act according to what they are able to do, as long as this is compatible with their goals. Others will stop as soon as their actions could become illegal or incompatible with some moral principles. Hackers' targets belong either to the physical world (smart objects, computers, networks, critical infrastructures, banks) or to the virtual one (e-commerce,

**Table 9.2** Analogy between authentication technologies and criteria to classify hackers

| | Resources | Attitude |
|---|---|---|
| Internal | *Something you know* | *Something you are* |
| | **Expertise** | **Values** |
| External | *Something you have* | *Something you do* |
| | **Tools** | **Modus operandi** |

e-banking, websites, crypto-currencies). These targets span from individual properties, to companies or even to country-level assets. Hackers can work alone, in (criminal) networks or in state-sponsored groups. They can work for themselves or as mercenaries on behalf of a conductor.

In the economic paradigm, hackers can be classified according to three categories, namely what they know (their expertise, i.e. their internal resources), what they are (their values, i.e. their internal attitude) and what they do (their modi operandi, i.e. their external attitude). In the societal paradigm, hackers are also characterised by what they have (their tools), i.e. the external resources they have access to. Indeed, state-sponsored hackers can have access to classified information and weaponised zero-days, to sneaking, eavesdropping or deep packet inspection tools. More traditional hackers usually do not have access to these resources. Some state-sponsored hackers might even have privileged access to specific locations: Internet backbone or other key physical IT-infrastructures. State-sponsored hackers can work directly for a government, e.g. if they belong to a government agency. Alternatively, they might work for official companies selling hacking products and services to governments. Eventually, they might also belong to mercenary groups selling their services to governmental or non-governmental organisations.

In this second taxonomy (see also Fig. 9.6), a *white hat* is a skilled programmer and computer expert who looks for vulnerabilities in software, protocols, OS, computers and servers, in other physical or virtual devices, and in network systems in order to improve the IT-security of a system. As a principle, he or she abides by applicable laws. He or she will stop any action as soon as it has the possibility of becoming illegal. A white hat might work alone and disclose vulnerabilities to the legitimate owner of the targeted system, with or without a financial compensation. Most of the time, white hats are professional hackers employed by IT-security companies, the clients of whom are other companies that need their own IT-security to be assessed. *Pen testers* are white hats specialised in penetration tests using the client's IT-infrastructure. All pen testers are white hats, but not all white hats are pen testers. Indeed, a white hat might decide to analyse the code of some specific open source software without being mandated by its developer or by any third party.

*Black hats* are skilled programmers and computer experts who look for vulnerabilities in software, protocols, OS, computers and servers, in other physical or virtual devices, and in network systems in order to support their malicious intentions. They do not abide by ethical values and do not respect laws. Black hats typically use bugs and exploits to gain unauthorised access to a computer system or an IT-infrastructure with both malicious intent and, typically, illegal means. They aim to steal sensitive information, and personal or corporate data. They attempt to trick users or companies in order to get money transferred to accounts they have access to. They might work alone, belong to professional criminal networks or act as mercenaries by selling their services to such networks or a conductor (crime-as-a-service). All black hats are cyber-criminals, but not all cyber-criminals are black hats. Indeed, many cyber-criminals do not have much expertise. They are not hackers themselves; rather, they buy and use tools or services developed by black hats.

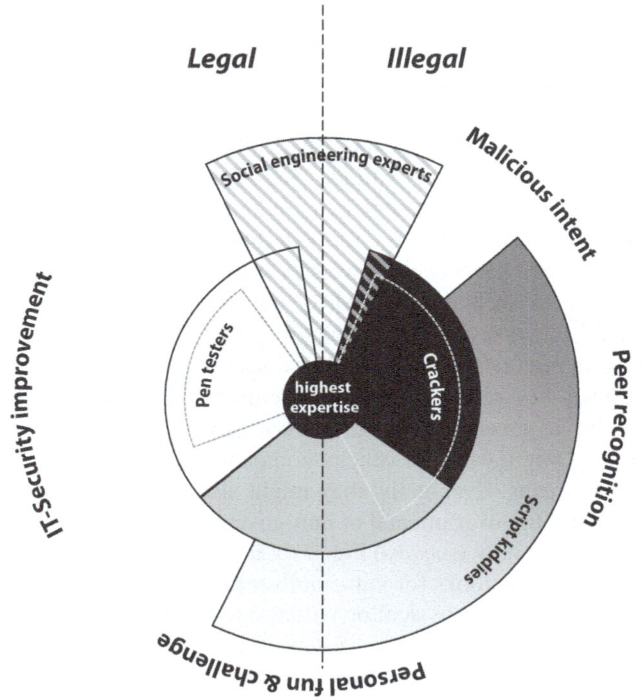


**Fig. 9.6** Crackers, pen testers and social engineering experts

*Grey hats* are skilled programmers and computer experts who look for vulnerabilities in software, protocols, OS, computers and servers, in other physical or virtual devices, and in network systems in order to have fun, to play around, to solve a challenge, to be granted peer recognition, or to improve the IT-security of a system. Usually their intentions are not malicious and financial gain is not their main incentive. They might comply with their own moral principles that can differ from the original hacker ethic. They do not necessarily respect applicable laws, which distinguishes them from white hats.

Below we select the level of abstraction to describe the intentions and voluntary constraints of the different types of hackers at the right level of abstraction in order to distinguish them more analytically. For example, a hacktivist may share attributes with a black hat or a grey hat if he/she breaks the law, while pursuing ideological objectives (not personal gain). Grey hat hackers may also pursue apparently malicious goals, ideological or personal objectives (e.g. fun, etc.) while disregarding law altogether, but who, unlike black hats, do not aim at committing crimes. One possible way to distinguish white, grey and black hats is in terms of their relation to the law and organisations or individuals:

- A white hat acts legally and tries to be trustworthy for companies or other organisations that (may) purchase his or her services.
- A black hat acts both illegally and maliciously, e.g. against a victim (a company or another organisation or an individual), either alone or within a criminal network.
- A grey hat does not attempt to be trustworthy for companies or organisations: he or she may act illegally when required to pursue his or her goal. However, he or she does not act maliciously and attempts to minimise harm and avoid unnecessary harm.

For example, a grey hacker motivated by ideological goals (e.g. the love of justice) may illegally break the security system of a political party to highlight inadequate privacy protections, but refrains from downloading data, publishing them and causing (serious) harm. Nonetheless, he acts illegally (in most jurisdictions) because he lacks the consent of the attacked party and may also cause some harm (e.g. reputational harm for the party), which is 'offset' by the broader benefit for the party members' deriving from the awareness of the vulnerability, so the act could be seen as being prevalently benevolent.

*Crackers*[6] are black or grey hats who perform computer and system break-ins without permission. As a consequence, their activities are illegal. *Phreakers* are phone crackers.

Note that such descriptions correspond to hackers described as *personae*, or social roles, not to flesh and bone individuals. It is logically possible for the same individual to sometimes act as a white hat and sometimes as a grey hat hacker *in incognito*. However, such an individual would have to keep those identities—corresponding to the different persona, the white and the grey hat—completely separated for the public eye. Indeed, the reputation as a grey hat hacker undermines all grounds for trustworthiness that are essential to being employed as a white hat hacker. Of course, it is also theoretically possible for an individual to transact from one personae to another one: e.g. from being a black hat to becoming a white hat hacker. To be credible, however, such role changes would have to be understood as a 'full conversion' by others—a change in the overall motivational set of the individual. Moreover, the conversion may not be sufficient to make the individual trustworthy. Indeed, many security companies would not hire a former black hat. For example, at least until 2001, IBM had a policy to "not hire ex-[black hat]-hackers" (Palmer 2001: 772).[7] The television series 'Mr Robot' (Mr. Robot n.d.) tells the story

[6] Some authors consider black hats and crackers as equivalent terms. We introduce here some distinctions. In particular, we consider that crackers might be grey hats acting for fun with no malicious intent.

[7] This may have been the case up to 2001; the authors were not able to determine if a change of policy occurred since then.

of an individual who routinely switches between the roles of a white-, grey- and even black-hat hacker, even in the course of the same day. However, the character has an unstable personality and is schizophrenic.

### 9.3.3 Ethical Hacking

*Ethical hackers*[8] are white hats mandated by clients (companies) who want their own IT-security to be assessed. They abide by a formal set of rules that protect the client, in particular its commercial assets. All pen testers are ethical hackers, but ethical hackers do not limit themselves to penetration tests. They can use other tools or even social engineering skills to stress and evaluate their client's IT-security (see also Fig. 9.7).

An ethical hacker will try to act similarly to a black hat but without causing any tort to the company. He will look for vulnerabilities that could be exploited by malicious hackers, both in the physical world and in the virtual one. In ethical hacking, the conductor of the attack is the target itself or, more precisely, the target's representative who mandated the ethical hacker to stress and assess the target's IT-security. In comparison, the conductor of a black hat's attack is never the target itself, but either the black hat or a third party—different from the target—if the black hat acts as a mercenary.

Ethical hackers adopt a strict code of conduct that protects their relationship with their clients and their client's interests. Such a code of conduct sets a frame for their attitude. It describes rules that the ethical hacker must abide by. These rules prevent the ethical hacker from taking any personal advantage of his relationship with his client. This fosters the creation of a trusted relationship similar to the special relationship between a medical doctor and his or her patients, or between a lawyer and his or her clients. The client's trust is of utmost importance in order for the ethical hacker to get the contract and to be granted permission to maybe successfully penetrate the system. Indeed, during the course of such an attack, the ethical hacker might discover trade secrets or other very sensitive data about his or her client's activities, as well as personal data about employees. The company needs to trust that the ethical hacker will not misuse his or her potential privileged access into its IT-infrastructure in order to introduce backdoors or to infringe privacy, neither during the mandate, nor after the contract is fulfilled.

The typical content of such a code of conduct contains rules which guarantee that the ethical hacker:

- will get *written permission* prior to stressing and assessing his or her client's IT-security
- will act *honestly* and stay within the scope of his or her *client's expectations*

[8] Some authors consider white hats, pen testers and ethical hackers as equivalent terms. In this chapter, we introduce some slight distinctions.

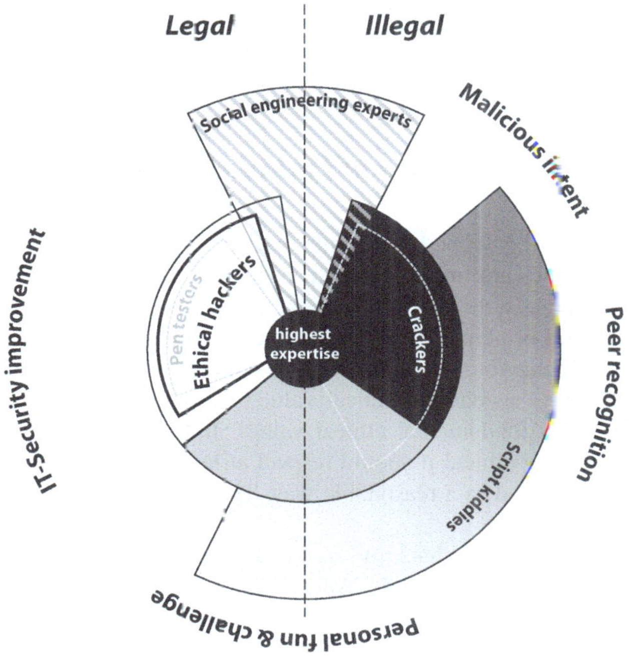


**Fig. 9.7** Ethical hackers

- will *respect* his or her client's as well as its employees' *privacy*
- will use *scientific*, state-of-the-art and *documented processes*
- will *transparently communicate* to his or her client all the *findings* as well as a transcript of all his or her *actions*
- will remove his or her traces and will *not introduce* or keep any *backdoor* in the system
- will *inform* software and hardware vendors about *found vulnerabilities* in their products

These rules also aim at protecting the ethical hacker and making his or her work legal de facto. Different curricula even propose training and certifications in order for a hacker to become a certified ethical hacker (CEH).

## 9.4 Is 'Ethical Hacking' Ethical?

Ethical issues are evaluated according to a collection of ethical values and moral principles in regards to objectives and behaviours in a specific context.

### 9.4.1 *Inethical, Unethical and Ethical Hacking*

*Inethical hacking* can be defined as hacking that does not abide by any ethical value. Inethical hacking does not imply *unethical* behaviour, but removes ethical barriers and in doing so increases the risk of actual unethical behaviour. Greed is not an ethical value or a moral principle. Black hats typically perform inethical hacking that leads to unethical behaviour. However, what is *ethical hacking* fundamentally? Is it hacking that respects at least an ethical value? Certainly not, as such a hacking might infringe other fundamental ethical values. Indeed, intuitively, in order for hacking to be deemed ethical it should respect at least the most important ethical values at stake, balanced in a reasonable way. Therefore, non-inethical hacking is not necessarily ethical.

Precisely defining 'ethical hacking' in a fundamental, context-independent way is not a trivial matter, if even possible. We could start to define *prima facie unethical hacking* as hacking that infringes at least one ethical value or moral principle in an actual context. Prima facie means that the hacking seems unethical, although it may cease to appear so after a thorough examination of the issue. By contrast, the *ultima facie* ethical or unethical choice considers all relevant reasons, also those pulling in opposite directions, and tries to determine what is best *all things considered.* The 'all things considered' best act is the choice that is supported by most reasons, or by the strongest 'undefeated' reason, including all moral reasons, if any, bearing on the matter (Scanlon 1998). Under this logic, *non-prima facie unethical hacking* would be hacking that respects all ethical values and moral principles in that context. It makes sense to consider that any non-*prima facie* unethical hacking is *ethical.* However, should we require hacking to be non- *prima facie* unethical in order to be deemed ethical? This would lead to an overly restrictive definition. Indeed, with such a restrictive definition of ethical hacking, almost no hacking could be deemed ethical. In practice, we often face competing ethical values. Not all ethical values can be respected simultaneously; they need to be prioritised in regards to objectives and behaviors in a specific context. Therefore, a general concept of *ethical hacking* should not be reduced to non-*prima facie* unethical hacking as it would lead to a useless definition.

The *prima facie* unethical category can be further sub-divided into three categories:

1. Morally problematic: when at least one value is violated; however, the action may be justified 'all things considered'.
2. Non (ethically) optimal (*weakly* unethical): when the action is not the best one, considering all ethical reasons bearing on the issue.

3. Ethically impermissible (*strongly* unethical): when there is a strong moral reason not to perform the action; e.g. the action violates an important moral duty (what Immanuel Kant refers to as a 'perfect duty'), e.g. the duty corresponding to another person's moral right.[9]

This distinction is mirrored in terms of a normative moral psychology, specifying the emotions that a morally decent person should feel in correspondence to each category of cases: hacking that is morally wrong in the strong sense (i.e. impermissible) should evoke feelings of blameworthiness by others and moral guilt by the moral agent. Morally problematic hacking may not even be unethical *ultima facie*, and may reasonably lead to no moral blame and no feelings of moral remorse; however, some have argued that it may lead to some kind of moral regret (Williams 1981, 27–28). Non-ethically optimal hacking is unethical (*ultima facie*) but in a *weaker* sense compared to ethically impermissible hacking; it may then justifiably lead to moral remorse and regret.

We have mentioned the idea of the *all things considered* (morally) best choice. Note that in a case of value conflict, a pluralist society may not agree with a single way of balancing and resolving trade-offs between values in practice. As an example of disagreement on balancing, consider *supporting trust in cybersecurity* vs. *achieving justice*. Both values could be in conflict when a white hat hacker discovers proof of unethical behaviour, or possible signs of crimes by a company during pen testing. In order to be trustworthy, the hacker should not act in any way against the interest of the company and cannot, for example, blackmail the company, in order to induce it to stop *a weakly* unethical practice. Moreover, a white hat should avoid any investigation—even pursuing the signs of a possible crime—which is out of the scope of his or her mandate. Moreover, such an investigation might lead to discoveries that further reinforce the conflict between promoting justice and being trustworthy, e.g. the discovery of a *strongly* unethical practice by the company. We can assume that companies would have a counter-incentive to hire the services of penetration testers unless they trust them to promote their own interests in any circumstance, creating a trusted relationship similar to the relationship between a medical doctor and a patient, or between a lawyer and her client. We might also claim that widespread and protected trust in the services of white hat hackers is necessary to achieve good levels of cybersecurity for society at large, which is ethically desirable, in utilitarian terms.

It could be argued that this 'favouring trust between white hat hackers and companies' should include companies that do not have a perfectly blank sheet in terms of ethics and legal behaviour. This is in conflict with another strong value: the goal of achieving immediate justice and of protecting possible victims of a crime or of a strongly unethical treatment. Therefore, it is not clear if a penetration tester should always reveal strongly unethical behaviour or clues of crimes to the public, or if he

[9] An imperfect moral duty is a duty like the duty to do charity. Wheres—Kant maintained—we all have a duty to charity, the duty is not perfect in the sense that we have discretion concerning when, how, and to whom we act charitably. Act-utilitarianism rejects the distinction between perfect and imperfect duties, because according to act-utilitarianism the acts that maximise aggregate utility are both right and dutiful and all other acts are wrong and impermissible in the context.

or she should at least threaten to do it, in order to give the company an incentive to address the problem.

The way the term ‘ethical hacking’ is used appears to presuppose a clear and unilateral solution to the problem of value balancing: the solution that gives the highest priority to (a) refraining from acting against the interests of the company hiring the services of the hacker, (b) only acting within boundaries that have been explicitly consented to, and (c) fulfilling the expectations of the client in a way that preserves the white hat hacker’s reputation for trustworthiness.[10] It seems that these three conditions do not conflict in practice. A so-called ‘ethical hacker’ enjoys the contractual freedom to act in ways that would be illegal if they had taken place without the consent of the party hiring his or her services. He/she acts in a trustworthy way because, in addition to that, he or she acts conscientiously towards the party placing trust in him or her (Becker 1996). We may add to this ‘respecting the law’; respecting all law in the pertinent jurisdictions, not only the law of private property.

As mentioned above, an ‘ethical’ hacker could face situations involving a trade-off between, on the one hand, preserving trust in himself or herself and white hat hackers in general and, on the other hand, achieving justice or other ethical values directly, in the short term. Note that the trade-off between trustworthiness and other ethical values could be solved differently depending on the legal framework in which the white hat hacker operates. Suppose that the hacker operates in a jurisdiction with a law that mandates the white hacker to violate a confidentiality agreement should he or she establish proof of serious crimes. In this case, the individual choice of the hacker to act against the interest of the company hiring him or her, e.g. by revealing proof of strongly unethical behaviour (which happens to also be illegal), would not in itself undermine trust. Indeed, trust relies on rational expectations and we could claim that a company could not rationally expect a hacker to protect its interests when this is explicitly prohibited by the law. Note, however, that the legal framework itself would make some companies less likely to *rely* on white hat hackers to enhance their cybersecurity, since some companies may prefer to run cybersecurity risks rather than giving others legal opportunities to reveal their illegal and/or strongly unethical activities.

To maximise the incentive to rely on white hat hackers, society could pass laws allowing and requiring them, like lawyers, priests and medical doctors, to maintain confidentiality about all behaviours, including crimes, discovered in the course of their professional activities. In such a context, a hacker would undermine trust by revealing clues, or even proof of illegal activities by firms. Note, however, that this is not the same as acting *strongly unethically*: the severity of the unethical behaviour discovered could make it the case that *all things considered,* the choice involving a breach of trust is the most ethical (ethically optimal), or even the *only* ethical (morally required) choice. Nothing guarantees that the (most, or only) ethical way to act is always the legal way to act.

It should also be noted that in choosing between these two legal frameworks, society, or its elected representatives, have to choose a trade-off point between

[10] For the link between trust, trustworthiness and reputation see (Pettit 1995).

different, equally legitimate, social values. The choice involves a balance between, on the one hand, maximising incentives to rely on white hat hackers or, on the other hand, discovering some serious crimes in the short term. Societies may make this choice based on their understanding of where the utilitarian optimum lies, but some societies may also adopt legislation reflecting non-utilitarian considerations. For example, the public discussion of a case in which a white hat hacker had a legal *duty* to keep an ugly crime confidential may turn public opinion against confidentiality protection, irrespective of whether it is the utility-maximising solution. A society may be moved by moral indignation to adopt legislation less protective of companies, even if the rationally expected result is that unethical companies will not hire ethical hackers and thus expose their clients to more risks.

In the previous section, we presented the well-established concept of ethical hackers (white hats mandated by clients who want their own IT-security to be assessed, and who abide by a formal set of rules that protect the client, in particular its commercial assets.) Ethical assessment in this context prioritises honesty towards the client, as well as legal and commercially-oriented values. However, other ethical values could interfere with these prioritised values. If the company which IT-security is assessed has some *ultima facie* (weakly or strongly) unethical activities, is it ethical to reinforce its IT-security? What about if its core business is deemed to be *ultima facie* unethical, in the strong sense (morally impermissible)? This shows the limit of an automated analysis of ethical behaviour based on a standard set of rules. So-called ethical hackers might perform ethical hacking in the context of their trusted relationships with their clients, while this same ethical hacking appears unethical (weakly or strongly) if we take a broader perspective.

This ethical problem cannot be solved by simply prescribing absolute respect of the law of a country. As highlighted above, nothing in the world guarantees that the 'all things considered' best act is always compatible with the laws of the country in which the ethical hacker operates.

Legislation might prioritise trust relations between hackers and companies above all other values.[11] However, it is possible—at least logically—that considerations of trust and trustworthiness do not override, or defeat, any other consideration in every context.[12] Hence, the 'all things considered' best act may sacrifice trust and trustworthiness.[13] Therefore, a hacker who is ethical—in the sense of doing the best 'all things considered' act—is not necessarily an 'ethical hacker' according to the ordi-

[11] Maybe, it (correctly) identifies this policy as the one promoting the utilitarian optimum—maximum aggregate utility—in the long term.

[12] Even if preserving trustworthiness maximises long-term utility, for it may even be the case that the best moral view is not utilitarian.

[13] If the ultimately *right* morality is *not* utilitarian morality, the morally right act can be one that violates a policy that has a rule-utilitarian justification (the policy that would optimise utility in the long run). It is even conceivable that the morally best/right act for *social* morality (the morality behind laws and public policies) and for *individual* morality are *different* acts, because the two moralities differ, due to constraints (e.g. of impartiality, objectivity, inter-subjectivity, integrity) that apply with different force in the two cases. If this unfortunate moral hypothesis is correct, individuals in high-stake roles are condemned to face hard-to-solve moral dilemmas occasionally. See Sect. 4.2.

nary definition, which presupposes both actions to be lawful and acting in a way that proves trustworthiness *to mandating firms*.

Actually, the well-established concept of an 'ethical hacker' is misleading. In some ways, it is a misappropriation of the term 'ethical'. The expression 'trustworthy for business and lawful hacker' would fit better. Indeed, the rules that the ethical hacker has to abide by are fundamentally business-oriented. They foster economic-compliant ethical behaviour,[14] and they create a clear trust-enabling distinction between ethical hackers and black hats. They also protect ethical hackers in making their activities legal de facto. However, these rules do not consider the possibility of ethical issues competing with the need of a trusted relationship and a protection of economic interests. Often, ethical hackers essentially agree to stay faithful to their client whatever the client's activity is. This creates an inviolable trusted relationship similar to the relationship between a lawyer and his or her client, or between a priest and his faithful. Is it ethical to keep secret (and protect) the illegal activities of a client? In utilitarian terms, it depends on the existence or not of a greater public interest to improve companies' IT-security even at the cost of covering critical non-ethical behaviours. Even if it were not a matter of public interest, covering critical non-ethical behaviour may simply be irreconcilable with reasonable individual moralities (e.g. of a more deontological type). Some ethical hacking companies introduce a provision allowing them to report observed illegal activities, at least if questioned by the police in the course of an investigation.

Any practical definition of ethical hacking should incorporate the existence of possible competing ethical values, even within a fixed context (see also Chap. 3). In other words, hacking could be deemed ethical when it sufficiently respects ethical values and moral principles at stake in regards to objectives and behaviours in a specific context. This provides a practical definition of *ethical hacking*. We are not suggesting that this definition should replace the ordinary one. The most important purpose fulfilled by having a new definition is to distinguish both concepts. One possibility would be to use 'trustworthy for business and lawful hacker' and 'ethical hacker' to distinguish both of them. An alternative would be to use 'ethical hacker' in the usual (business-oriented) way and invent some other label for the sufficiently 'all things considered' ethical hacker instead. This new definition—as well as ethical assessment actually—is intrinsically vague, subject to interpretation and context-dependent. This emphasises the fact that ethical evaluation cannot be reduced to an *a priori* assumption that business-oriented values should take priority, and the qualification of ethical should not be limited to a narrow definition of professional ethics.

[14] This behavior may, or may not, be optimal in utilitarian terms (it is often very difficult to determine what maximises utility in the long term and some economic behavior may be harmful, all things considered). Even if it is optimal in utilitarian terms, it may not be ethical, if, as many people think, utilitarianism is not the right ethical theory.

### 9.4.2 Competing Ethical Values

Ethical evaluation, like any evaluation process, produces values that can be fed into a decision process (Pollitt et al. 2018: 8). The values resulting from an evaluation process are not restricted to numbers. They can be impressions, feelings, opinions or judgments. In her axiological sociology essay (Heinich 2017), Nathalie Heinich identifies three ways to attribute a value: measurement, attachment, judgement. An ethical evaluation is typically of the third kind: some form of judgement. The decision process following an ethical evaluation usually allows or does not allow an action, an activity or a behaviour to be pursued.

A priori, the ethical assessment of relevant ethical values related to hacking could perform an ethical evaluation of all four criteria used to classify hackers (see also Table 9.2):

- hacker's expertise
- hacker's tools
- hacker's values
- hacker's modus operandi

However, a hacker's expertise is knowledge. It is ethically neutral and does not carry out direct ethical issues. Tools available to the hacker are not relevant from an ethical standpoint either. This does not mean that hacking tools do not create ethical issues. Indeed, *the creation or not* of some hacking tools, e.g. weaponised zero-days, leads to important ethical issues at a societal level: on the one-hand, weaponised zero-days allow countries to develop cyber-weapons to dissuade potential enemies, on the other hand, unpatched vulnerabilities—if discovered by or made available to black hats—can endanger large scale IT-systems. The WannaCry worldwide ransomware attack that shut down UK hospitals and numerous systems in May 2017 shows the impact of such a weaponised zero-day falling into criminal hands (Mohurle and Patil 2017).

Eventually, only the hacker's values and modus operandi need to be ethically assessed by the evaluator. Note that the evaluator can be either the hacker or another person.

The result of an ethical evaluation depends on the evaluator's expertise, on the available information, and on his or her way of handling and processing this information, as well as on his or her own criteria and values' prioritisation and interpretation. State-sponsored hackers, for example, might be deemed ethical if the evaluator prioritises values of the sponsoring state, whereas these same hackers might be considered simultaneously unethical by evaluators living in the targeted country. The interpretation of the facts (state-sponsored actors do not necessarily follow traditional white hats' rules; they typically try to introduce and keep backdoors in the targeted system; they might use zero-days and not divulge them to the developers) really depends on the evaluator's perspective, interpretation and prioritised values.

Ethical evaluation parameters also present similarities with the four classes of authentication technologies (Table 9.3).

**Table 9.3** Similarities between authentication technologies and ethical evaluation parameters

| | Resources | Attitude |
|---|---|---|
| Internal | *Something you know* | *Something you are* |
| | **Expertise** | **Values prioritisation** |
| External | *Something you have* | *Something you do* |
| | **Available information** | **Information processing** |

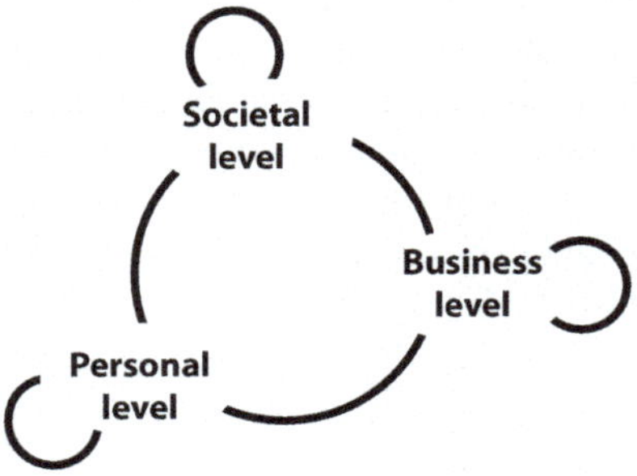


**Fig. 9.8** Potential conflicts between collections of possibly competing ethical values

The evaluator's level of expertise allows a distinction to be made between an ethical opinion and an ethical expert evaluation (Heinich 2017). The information available to the evaluator might change over time, possibly resulting in new conclusions. This is in particular true when a so-called ethical hacker penetrates his or her client's infrastructure and discovers ethically sensitive new information. The way the evaluator processes the information relates to quality procedures and best practices; it influences the confidence in the conclusion. The core of the evaluation resides in the evaluator's own prioritisation of (competing) values at stake.

When addressing ethical hacking, we should consider at least three collections of possibly competing ethical values (see also Fig. 9.8): one at a personal level (hacker's own perspective), one at a business level (company's perspective) and one at a societal level (global perspective). Ethical conflicts can happen within one of these collections or between some of them.

So-called ethical hackers can ethically evaluate their own attitude, i.e. their values and their modus operandi, and they probably will because they chose not to use their expertise for malicious purpose. The code of conduct that ethical hackers have to abide by strongly focuses on the collection of values at a business level. Therefore, these values must belong to the own hacker's ethical values and moral principles. Already at this stage, competing ethical values can appear if, for example, protecting an employee's privacy (whose emails reveal that he is blackmailed by a competitor's board member) conflicts with transparently communicating all the findings to the mandating client. Generally speaking, it will be easier to assess if a hacker is ethical in the narrow (and usual) sense of the term, which assumes the priority of business-oriented moral values.

Ethical hackers also have their own values and moral principles at a personal level. They might share some of the original hacker ethic. If their ethical values conflict with those at a business level, their ethical evaluation of the situation will depend on the prioritisation of the values. A strong personal ethical value or a well-established important societal value might prevail on any other business-related value and lead to breaking the code of conduct. This is in particular true if the ethical hacker unveils critical non-ethical behaviours within the company. In this case, the evaluation of whether the hacker is ethical will be significantly more complex. It is likely to achieve reasonable disagreement, even between equally well-informed persons, concerning what is the ethically optimal act in a given context. There might be no pre-established harmony between values—e.g. no way to maximise fairness and aggregate well-being at the same time—(Berlin 1991; Nagel 1991; Raz 1986) Moreover, even individuals who rely on monistic moral views (e.g. utilitarianism, which recognises only utility, understood as well-being) and single-rule based moralities (e.g. again utilitarianism: maximise aggregate well-being in the long term) may disagree on what the actual best choice turns out to be (see also Chap. 4 for a discussion of ethical frameworks in cybersecurity).

Note that our argument does not rely on a rejection of ethical realism or cognitivism. Realism is entailed by the view that the question concerning 'the all things considered best choice' can be objective, because it is determined by moral objective facts existing independently of mental states (beliefs, attitudes, emotions) about the choice in question. Cognitivism is entailed by the view that these objective moral reasons, or facts, are not facts about what (all, or the majority) of people actually *want* to be the case. The key point is that, even conceding that morality is grounded in objective facts independent of will of any agent, it may be *in fact* extremely difficult to determine what the *morally best* choice is.

### 9.4.3 A Pragmatic Best Practice Approach

Pen-test companies and other IT-security hiring white hats face a competing values dilemma (see also Chap. 15). On the one hand, they need to create a trusted relationship with their clients. On the other hand, they need to respond and even anticipate their employees' ethical expectations. There is certainly no perfect solution to solve this dilemma, as ethical evaluation has an intrinsic personal component, is subject to interpretation and is context-dependent.

As explained above, companies hiring ethical hackers develop a code of conduct that reinforces the business-related ethical behavior of their employees, guarantees that their hacking activities are compliant with applicable laws and fosters a trusted relationship with their clients.

As already mentioned, some ethical hacking companies have introduced a provision allowing them to report observed illegal activities, at least if questioned by the police in the course of an investigation.

To minimise the inherent risks related to the competing values dilemma, an active European pen-test company with about 40 employees created an internal ethical committee. This ethical committee is composed of three employees, freely elected by all employees. Company board members are not allowed to be elected in order to avoid business-related biases in the ethical evaluation. Any employee can submit his or her ethical concerns about an upcoming project if this employee fears that participating in such a project could create a conflict with his or her own values or moral principles, or with other societal ethical values. Members of the ethical committee are in a position to make an independent ethical evaluation. Their decision is binding and cannot be challenged, neither by the direction nor by the other employees. If the committee decides to block a project, the company will stop it independently from having financial consequences.

This example illustrates a possibility to anticipate potential competing ethical values in order to avoid employees breaking their code of conduct or leaving the company. Such an approach enriches and strengthens the concept of ethical hacking and goes beyond a rule-based definition. It promotes an ethical evaluation that is not reduced to an automated process or a checklist, and allows a fine interpretation of the context and a more subtle ethical evaluation, as well as context-dependent decisions.

## 9.5 Conclusion

The term 'hacker' has many different meanings, even within the context of computerised systems. It should not be amalgamated with that of a cybercriminal only. In this chapter, in order to capture a much broader perception of the term and to describe its nuances more faithfully, we developed a new systematic and neutral classification based on four categories: the hacker's expertise (his or her internal resources), the hacker's own values and moral principles (his or her internal attitude), the hacker's modus operandi (his or her external attitude), and the tools and information that he or she has access to (his or her external resources). These four categories can be related to the four categories of authentication technologies: something that the hacker knows, something that the hacker is, something that the hacker does, and something that the hacker has.

The term 'ethical hacker' in its wide acceptance appears to be misleading and a misappropriation of the term 'ethical'. Particular pluralist societies, those that recognise that different ethical values are valid and there is no single simple way of measuring or ranking them, are likely to disagree on what is the morally best behaviour for a hacker to adopt in every given circumstance. The expression 'business-oriented ethical hacker' would fit better. Moreover, it gives the false impression that it is sufficient for hacking activities to abide by a list of fixed rules in order to be deemed ethical. Ethical evaluation *cannot* and *should not* be reduced to a checklist of rules to abide by those rules that are legal and/or ethical. This is especially true in contexts where at-the-edge hacking opportunities are sometimes in a grey zone which is not covered by current laws, e.g. for spy and state-sponsored hacking activities.

The creation of a code-of-conduct with rules to abide by is a welcome and necessary step in order to support ethical hacking. However, it is not sufficient. Other mechanisms—such as internal ethical committees—have to be created within the pen-test companies or the Gov-CERT units in order to allow a finer interpretation of each context, a more subtle ethical evaluation, and context-dependent decisions

**Acknowledgments** The authors would like to thank their colleagues Eoghan Casey and Olivier Ribaux, who reviewed a draft version of this document, for their fruitful comments. The chapter was created with funding from the European Union's Horizon 2020 research and innovation programme under grant agreement No 700540 and the Swiss State Secretariat for Education, Research and Innovation (SERI) under contract number 16.0052-1.

## References

American Heritage Dictionary Entry Hacker (n.d.) https://www.ahdictionary.com/word/search.html?q=hacker. Last access 7 July 2019

Barber R (2001) Hackers profiled—who are they and what are their motivations? Comput Fraud Secur 2001(2):14–17

Becker LC (1996) Trust as noncognitive security about motives. Ethics 107(1):43–61

Berlin I (1991) The crooked timber of humanity: chapters in the history of ideas. In: Hardy H (ed) Knopf: distributed by Random House, New York

Bratus S (2007) What hackers learn that the rest of us don't: notes on hacker curriculum. IEEE Secur Priv 5(4):72–75

Heinich N (2017) Des Valeurs. Une Approche Sociologique. Editions Gallimard, Paris

Lichstein H (1963) Telephone hackers active. The Tech, MIT. http://tech.mit.edu/V83/PDF/V83-N24.pdf. Last access 7 July 2019

Marshall AK (2008) Digital forensics: digital evidence in criminal investigations. Wiley-Blackwell, London

Mohurle S, Manisha Patil (2017) A brief study of Wannacry threat: Ransomware At-tack 2017. Int J Adv Res Com Sci Udaipur 8(5). https://search.proquest.com/docview/1912631307/abstract/DEF9AE2FF2924E35PQ/1. Last access 7 July 2019

Mr. Robot (n.d.). http://www.imdb.com/title/tt4158110/. Last access 7 July 2019

Nagel T (1991) Mortal questions. Cambridge University Press, Cambridge

Olson P (2013) We are anonymous: inside the hacker world of LulzSec, anonymous, and the global cyber insurgency. Back Bay Books, New York

Palmer CC (2001) Ethical hacking. IBM Syst J 40(3):769–780. https://doi.org/10.1147/sj.403.0769

Pettit P (1995) The cunning of trust. Philos Public Aff 24(3):202–225. https://doi.org/10.1111/j.1088-4963.1995.tb00029.x

Pollitt M, Casey E, Jaquet-Chiffelle D-O, Gladyshev P (2018) A framework for harmonizing forensic science practices and digital/multimedia evidence. OSAC.TS.0002. OSAC Task Group on Digital/Multimedia Science. OSAC/NIST. https://doi.org/10.29325/OSAC.TS.0002

Raz J (1986) The morality of freedom. Oxford University Press, Oxford
Scanlon T (1998) What we owe to each other. Belknap Press of Harvard University Press, Cambridge, MA
Techopedia.Com (n.d.) What is a black hat hacker? – definition from Techopedia. https://www.techopedia.com/definition/26342/black-hat-hacker. Last access 7 July 2019
Williams B (1981) Moral luck: philosophical papers 1973–1980, 1st edn. Cambridge University Press, Cambridge

# Chapter 10
# Cybersecurity and the State

**Eva Schlehahn**

**Abstract** This chapter provides an overview on state actor's opinions and strategies relating to cybersecurity matters. These are addressed on the EU level as well as on the level of the individual European Member States while the focus is on legislation, policy and political approaches to cybersecurity. In this context, many different measures and approaches are taken both in the Union and nationally to streamline knowledge, resources, and measures to combat cybercrime. Furthermore, the role of the new European data protection framework is addressed, and it is explained why data protection has a close relationship to security matters. The main tensions and conflicts in relation to IT and cybersecurity are depicted, which evolve primarily around the frequently negative effect of IT and cybersecurity measures on the rights of data subjects. However, the issue of governmental surveillance is also addressed, with its implications for the fundamental rights of European citizens. Solution approaches to align the two domains of data protection and cybersecurity are explored, since cybersecurity incidents often involve the loss or compromise of an individual's personal information. To this end, overlaps and synergies are examined that seem promising for a more holistic approach to cyber threats. For instance, this could be achieved by applying principles such as data protection by design and default in IT more thoroughly. In addition, methodologies of data protection impact assessments as well as a more broad deployment of technical and organisational measures while using well-known information security best practices and standards can help to enhance cybersecurity across the European Union.

**Keywords** European Union · General data protection regulation · State actors · Surveillance

E. Schlehahn (✉)
Unabhängiges Landeszentrum für Datenschutz (Independent Centre for Privacy Protection), Kiel, Schleswig-Holstein, Germany
e-mail: uld67@datenschutzzentrum.de



M. Christen et al. (eds.), *The Ethics of Cybersecurity*, The International Library of Ethics, Law and Technology 21,
https://doi.org/10.1007/978-3-030-29053-5_10

## 10.1 Introduction

Within the European Union, the EU Member States have a crucial role in maintaining and fostering Cybersecurity by policy regulations and institutional work. It has been widely acknowledged that Cybersecurity needs to be addressed in earnest to mitigate the risks of the increasing digitisation nationally, as well as within Europe and globally. These risks mostly affect European citizens in their everyday lives, but can also affect industries and nation states alike. Notably, the North Atlantic Treaty Organization (NATO) countries published in July 2016 a *Cyber Defense Pledge*, which recognises security threats and reaffirms the support and enhancement of the cyber defenses of their national infrastructures and networks.[1] This chapter provides an overview on the correlating cybersecurity opinions and presents various state actor's strategies to address cybersecurity on EU as well as on the national level within the European Union (see also Chap. 5). In this context, state actors are understood here as official governmental institutions at EU and EU member state levels. Furthermore, solution approaches for cybersecurity issues are examined, which do not aim only to address merely the security perspective but also to integrate the data protection perspective. As for the research methodology for this chapter, only little insight could be drawn from literature and studies. Therefore, our sources consist mostly of legislation, policy documents, official statements and other information directly coming from the above-mentioned state actors.

## 10.2 Cybersecurity Strategies at the European Union Level

Cybersecurity threats are a global issue, a fact that was recognised by the EU and its individual institutions relatively early. Furthermore, it was accepted that this issue can only be addressed via global responses, necessitating international communication, harmonised legislation and effort coming from both the public and private sectors. Nonetheless, cybersecurity matters have a quite complex nature, making a unified approach sometimes difficult. Working towards resolving this difficulty, the European Commission issued a communication already in 2001 addressing Europe's transition to an information society. This communication referenced a number of already existing approaches and proposed some further action items in order to protect information and communication infrastructures. It called for a comprehensive policy initiative, a unified definition of cybercrime, more in-depth communication with different stakeholders, and more R&D funding to address such threats.

---

[1] NATO (2016): This pledge entails a general commitment of NATO to allocate adequate resources nationally, foster interaction of stakeholders and improve awareness and understanding of cybersecurity threats overall, including in education and training of NATO and Alliance forces. It is meant to reinforce collaboration and better exchange of best practices across the Alliance, including with the EU.

With the drafting of its *Cyber Security Strategy* in 2013, the EU had detailed its earlier position regarding cooperation and communication related to cybersecurity matters (European Commission, COM 7 Feb 2013). Based on this position, the Commission committed itself to launching a new public-private partnership on cybersecurity with industry to better equip Europe against cyber-attacks and to strengthen the competitiveness of its cybersecurity sector. This occurred as a common platform, called the 'NIS Platform' (platform on network and information security solutions), in order to develop incentives for the adoption of secure ICT solutions and to increase the cybersecurity performance of ICT products used in Europe. This platform was most active in 2013 and 2014, where it involved the European Agency for Network and Information Security (ENISA) as well as various public and private stakeholders. Its purpose was to achieve insight into possible technical guidelines, recommendations, industry standards and general information exchange to enhance cybersecurity.

More concrete legislative action by the European Union followed, such as Directive 2008/114/EC on the identification of European critical infrastructures, or a directive on the security of network and information systems, which got adopted in 2016.[2] While the former is aimed at critical information infrastructure protection, the latter foresees rules, preconditions, and measures meant to ensure a high common level of NIS across the Union. Furthermore, the European Commission encouraged the European member states to make the most of the NIS coordination mechanisms enabled by this legislative act (COM 2016). So far, the NIS Directive has been addressed for national transposition in a multitude of European Member States.[3]

In 2015, the European Commission released its Digital Single Market Strategy, which also reinforced the importance of trust and security in digital services and in the handling of personal data (COM 2015). In the outcome of its mid-term review published May 2017, the Commission identified cybersecurity challenges as one of three main areas where further EU action would be needed.[4] Therefore, the Commission adopted a cybersecurity package in 2017. This package consists of a number of various recommendations and calls for action. An example would be recommendations related to the establishment of stronger and better networked institutions concerned with cybersecurity on EU level as well as on national EU Member States level. Moreover, it entails the endorsement of an EU-wide cybersecurity certification scheme, ideas for optimised incident responses, a call for legislation and frameworks focused on combatting fraud and counterfeiting of non-cash means of payment in order to reduce cyber-crime, as well as joint EU responses to malicious

[2] Directive (EU) 2016/1148 of the European Parliament and of the Council of 6 July 2016 concerning measures for a high common level of security of network and information systems across the Union. This is in the following abbreviated as *NIS Directive*.

[3] See for more detail the Directive 2008/114/EC overview page of the EUR-Lex: https://eur-lex.europa.eu/legal-content/EN/NIM/?uri=CELEX:32008L0114

[4] European Commission, press release: '*Digital Single Market: Commission calls for swift adoption of key proposals and maps out challenges ahead*', Brussels, 10 May 2017. The other two areas in need of being addressed are the fostering of the European data economy and promoting online platforms.

cyber activities on diplomatic level. Moreover, the Commission calls for better international cooperation on cybersecurity (including EU and NATO), fostering the development of cybersecurity skills both for civilian and military professionals, and for a set-up of a cyber-defence training and education platform (COM 2017: 2).

Based on these recommendations, the ENISA, founded in 2004, is endorsed as a core European Union Cybersecurity Agency to play a crucial role mainly by providing information and guidance, e.g. on cyber crisis management.[5] In June 2019, the EU Cybersecurity Act came into force which establishes a permanent mandate for the ENISA with increased responsibilities and resources. Moreover, this legislative act reinforces the previously proposed EU-wide cybersecurity certification framework for ICT products and regulates its governance.[6] Alongside the European Commission and ENISA, the Cybercrime Convention Committee (T-CY) of the Council of Europe[7] represents the state parties to the Budapest Convention on Cybercrime. The consultation of the T-CY aims at facilitating the effective use and implementation of the Convention, the exchange of information and the consideration of any future amendments. The T-CY has published a number of different assessments and reports on cybercrime.[8] All these institutions at the European level aim to achieve comprehensive and harmonised governance of cybersecurity-related issues, whereby efforts are undertaken in various areas, such as policy/legislation, finances and operational measures. Yet, those institutions still struggle with divisive factors on the national, pan-European and extra-European/transatlantic level, mostly caused by the diverging willingness of the EU member states to commit resources, the lack of clarity regarding the understanding of cybersecurity and cybercrime, and partially significant disparities in governance strategies and focus. The European Union has acknowledged those difficulties already by beginning several initiatives to address cyber threats. Therein, a strong focus lies on strengthening the resilience of democracy, especially by measures to enhance the security of the electoral infrastructure and campaign information systems. Moreover, guidance on the application of EU data protection law will be pursued further as well as legislative proposals to foster EU Member States coordination on cybersecurity matters (COM 2018: 1). For example, on 12 September 2018, the European Commission made a proposal for a regulation to pool resources and expertise in cybersecurity technology, which involves creating a network of National Coordination Centres for cybersecurity cooperation, research and innovation (COM 2018b).

[5] See e.g. the ENISA overview of recommended publications on that matter: https://www.enisa.europa.eu/topics/cyber-crisis-management?tab=publications

[6] Regulation (EU) 2019/881 of the European Parliament and of the Council of 17 April 2019 on ENISA (the European Union Agency for Cybersecurity) and on information and communications technology cybersecurity certification and repealing Regulation (EU) No 526/2013 (Cybersecurity Act).

[7] The Council of Europe (CoE) is not an official EU body, but a human rights organisation that was established in 1949 after World War II. It now comprises 47 member states, 28 of which belong to the European Union. See their website here: http://www.coe.int/en/web/about-us/who-we-are

[8] https://www.coe.int/en/web/cybercrime/tcy

## 10.3 Cybersecurity Strategies at the National Level

At the national level, the EU member states have developed their own cybersecurity strategies, the goals of which correlate with those of the EU strategy, with varying detail and a focus on specific aspects. For example, Luxembourg's cybersecurity strategy foresees a number of important objectives for the country, plus an additional action plan naming in detail the responsible authorities, as well as the anticipated timeframe for realisation. These objectives include strengthening national cooperation (also with the academic and research sphere), increasing the resilience of digital infrastructures, the determination of measures to fight cybercrime, the implementation of norms, standards certificates, labels and frames of references for government and critical infrastructure requirements. Furthermore, this strategy recommends and calls for the information, training, and awareness of cyber risks (Luxembourg 2015: 23ff). In an update in 2018, this was emphasised further, demanding that measures be taken to strengthening public confidence in the digital environment and that digital infrastructures get protected better (Luxembourg 2018: 15ff). Therein, the Luxembourg 2018 strategy is one of the few newer ones in comparison to other EU Member countries.[9]

As an example of a larger country, France's cybersecurity strategy focuses on specific details in some areas, such as increasing the security of state information systems (including the development of cybersecurity requirements for public contracting and support), providing local assistance to victims of cyber-malevolent acts, measuring cybercrime, and protecting the digital lives, privacy and personal data of French citizens. Moreover, France's approach to eliminate and mitigate cybersecurity threats includes operational mechanisms for international administrative assistance and educational measures, the support of security services and products, and knowledge transfer including the education of the general public. However, for the individual objectives mentioned, the French strategy does not provide action items as detailed as the Luxembourg one (France 2015: 15, 21ff, 26f, 31ff).

As already mentioned, it is proving difficult that many countries still have a different understanding of what the terms 'cybersecurity' and 'cybercrime' mean and convey in scope, if they have such a tangible understanding at all. For instance, Spain has a rather strong focus on the country's capability to investigate and prosecute cyber terrorism and cybercrime, yet its cybersecurity strategy does not specify which kind of acts and deeds are exactly considered a cybercrime (Spain 2013: 11, 29). As for Croatia's cybersecurity strategy, it provides a definition of cybercrime, yet this definition is rather broad and vague (Croatia 2015: 16). Thus, there are large differences in the level of detail and commitment made in those national cybersecurity strategies. This issue will probably require some time, additional pan-European communication and a stronger harmonisation effort for remedy.

[9] For direct comparison per country, the ENISA provides an interactive EU map with detail information and links to the individual documents: https://www.enisa.europa.eu/topics/national-cyber-security-strategies/ncss-map

Most of the EU member states have established institutions dedicated to cybersecurity issues, such as for example the German BSI (Federal Office for Information Security). This institution is tasked with investigating current IT security risks and creates yearly situation reports of the IT security landscape in Germany. It also functions as a cyber-defence centre and reporting office for security incidents. Together with another institution, the BBK (Federal Office of Civil Protection and Disaster Assistance), the BSI provides an Internet platform for the protection of critical infrastructures.[10] The German operators of critical infrastructures in the sectors of energy, information technology and telecommunications, water and nutrition, are required to report security incidents to the BSI and to demonstrate legal compliance every 2 years by providing a detailed protection concept corresponding with the state of the art.[11] Other operators (not active in the aforementioned sectors) can make such reports on a voluntary basis.

Besides institutions like the BSI, many EU countries have national expert groups focusing on security incidents, which are organised in computer emergency response teams (CERTs), sometimes also called computer emergency readiness teams or computer security incident response teams (CSIRTs). They are cross-linked globally and across the EU, offering warnings and problem resolution on security issues, especially involving product security teams from the government, commercial and academic sectors.[12]

However, when it comes to addressing cybersecurity nationally and on institutional level, there are many open questions with regard to coherent policy and strategy decisions (see also Chap. 18). For example, there might be issues of competence area conflicts and institutional mission dichotomies in relation to the German BSI, which pursues both offensive as well as defensive goals. Moreover, other institutions have been established by the German government in 2017 and 2018 that are now tasked with developing offensive as well as defensive cybersecurity strategies and measures. For example, the German government established the 'Zentrale Stelle für Informationstechnik im Sicherheitsbereich (Zitis)' in August 2017, which aims to develop new tools for law enforcement and intelligence (Beuth 2017). Furthermore, in August 2018, it was announced that a new cybersecurity agency will be established that will be concerned with research on cybersecurity and key technologies (Hegemann 2018). Whereas Germany, as only one of many EU countries, serves just as an example here, this illustrates how governments struggle with effectively determining, coordinating and institutionally streamlining potentially overlapping or even conflicting competence areas.

---

[10] https://www.bsi.bund.de/EN/TheBSI/Functions/functions_node.html

[11] Artikel 8a Gesetz über das Bundesamt für Sicherheit in der Informationstechnik (BSI-Gesetz or BSIG).

[12] See the information website of the global CERT association platform FIRST (Forum of Incident Response and Security Teams): https://www.first.org/about

## 10.4 The EU Data Protection Framework Addressing Cybersecurity

Already in 2013, the European Data Protection Supervisor (EDPS) Peter Hustinx commented both the *European Cyber Security Strategy* and the NIS Directive in an opinion, highlighting that a high level of Internet security will also improve the security of personal information. Nonetheless, the EDPS highlighted that there is a threat of cybersecurity measures interfering with individuals' rights to privacy and the protection of their personal data. He called for ensuring that every cybersecurity measure deployed complies with article 52(1) of the Charter of Fundamental Rights of the European Union. Thus, all relevant fundamental rights should be considered in the EU's Cybersecurity Strategy, which includes all its implementing actions (EDPS 2013: 4). In 2015, the following EDPS in office, Giovanni Buttarelli, further emphasised this demand in a follow-up opinion on the topic of national security in 2015 (EDPS 2015: 3).

By that time, the EU has also acknowledged that the protection of individual's personal information needs to be improved. This is a major reason why the EU triggered its reform process for its data protection framework, while a new regulation on privacy and electronic communications is still underway. By the time of writing this book chapter, the legislative proposal of the Commission and the amendments suggested by the Parliament and the Council are still within the Trilogue process, without any clear progress forecast.[13]

As for the European data protection reform so far, the 2009 Treaty of Lisbon and the now binding EU Charter of Fundamental Rights[14] enabled the European Commission to trigger a legislative reform process in January 2012. With the intention of harmonising the fragmented legal data protection framework across the European Union (COM 2012), this data protection reform produced two instruments coming into force on 27 April 2016, namely the:

- Regulation (EU) 2016/679 of the European Parliament and of the Council of 27 April 2016 on the protection of natural persons with regard to the processing of personal data and on the free movement of such data, and repealing Directive 95/46/EC (General Data Protection Regulation)[15]
- Directive (EU) 2016/680 of the European Parliament and of the Council of 27 April 2016 on the protection of natural persons with regard to the processing of personal data by competent authorities for the purposes of the prevention, investigation, detection or prosecution of criminal offences or the execution of criminal penalties, and on the free movement of such data, and repealing Council Framework Decision 2008/977/JHA[16]

---

[13] The draft proposal has been made by the European Commission on 10 January 2017. For more information, see: https://ec.europa.eu/digital-single-market/en/proposal-eprivacy-regulation

[14] Charter of Fundamental Rights of the European Union, OJ C 364, 18.12.2000, pp. 1–22.

[15] The General Data Protection Regulation (EU) 2016/679 is the main framework directly applicable in the EU member states. It is in the following abbreviated as *GDPR*.

[16] In contrast to the GDPR, the regulatory instrument for the police and justice sectors comes in form of a directive, which needs to be transferred into correlating national law by the European countries. It is in the following abbreviated as *Directive (EU) 2016/680*.

Both the GDPR, as well as Directive (EU) 2016/680, became applicable by 25 May 2018.

From a data protection perspective, the responsibilities of the data controllers are most relevant in the context of cybersecurity. According to Art. 4 no. 7 GDPR, controllers are those entities determining the purposes and means of the processing. These responsibilities include the legal obligation of controller(s) and processor(s) to effectively implement appropriate technical and organisational measures to protect the personal information they intend to collect and process (GDPR, Art. 24(1) and 28(1); Directive (EU) 2016/680, Art. 19(1) and 22(1)).

The individually necessary technical and organisational measures may vary depending on the case, situation and state of the art in specific areas. Thereby, they can entail preventive as well as reactive security measures such as access control, encryption, data separation, records of processing activities, technical and organisational procedures for backup and restore, or data breach notification procedures, while this list is not conclusive. Typical standards already known in classical IT security, such as ISE/IEC 27001, can also be considered.

Especially noteworthy are Article 32 GDPR and corresponding, Article 29 in Directive (EU) 2016/680, which manifest specified requirements to ensure the security of processing. These also mention exemplary measures, such as e.g. pseudonymisation or measures to ensure the confidentiality, integrity, availability, and resilience of systems and services in the context of personal data processing.

Furthermore, under certain circumstances, the responsible controller has to conduct a data protection impact assessment (DPIA, see Art. 35 GDPR and Art. 27 Directive (EU) 2016/680). Yet it is very important to note that while the risks assessment as known classical in IT security, the data protection perspective is very different. For example, IT security departments of companies are used to assess risks based on which financial or reputation damage for the company could be expected. But in a proper data protection based risk assessment, the perspective of the concerned data subject is paramount. A number of aspects play a role, such as the nature, scope, context and purpose of the processing, the inherent risks of varying likelihood and severity for the rights and freedoms of the concerned data subjects, as well as the state of the art and implementation costs of the needed measures. In cases where the processing is deemed to result in a high risk to the rights and freedoms of natural persons, an additional data protection impact assessment must be conducted (GDPR, Art. 35; Directive (EU) 2016/680, Art. 27).

Based on these assessments, the controller is required to determine the concrete technical and organisational measures needed to sufficiently protect the personal data. Specific examples of technical and organisational measures are also made in both legal frameworks in various places, such as pseudonymisation, encryption, the proper documentation of processing operations, access control and logging.[17] Such

[17] See for those examples in the GDPR: Articles 6 (4) e (Lawfulness of processing), 30 (Records of processing activities), while the Directive (EU) 2016/680 has in parts even more technically specific requirements e.g. for logging, access control and other security measures, cf. Articles 25 (Logging) and 29 (Security of processing).

measures can also be part of a data protection by design and by default approach as also demanded by the respectively applicable legal frameworks (GDPR, Art. 25; Directive (EU) 2016/680, Art. 20).

Beyond the preventive and reactive technical and organisational measures to protect the data, controllers and processors are required to make data breach notifications under certain circumstances and within specific timeframes. According to Article 4 (12) GDPR, *'personal data breach' means a breach of security leading to the accidental or unlawful destruction, loss, alteration, unauthorized disclosure of, or access to, personal data transmitted, stored or otherwise processed.* Therefore, the GDPR directly refers to security incidents with a negative effect on the protection of personal data, which may also play a role within the cybersecurity domain. According to Article 33 GDPR, a notification of a personal data breach to the supervisory authority is required no later than within 72 h, unless a risk to the rights and freedoms of natural persons is unlikely. However, if there is a high risk (see Art. 34 GDPR), the notification must also be made directly to the data subject without undue delay, unless specific technical and organisational measures are in place to render the personal data unintelligible to any person who is not authorised to access it, such as encryption. Moreover, a notification may be omitted if the controller has taken subsequent measures to ward off this high risk, or if the notification would involve disproportionate effort. However, in the latter case, a public communication or similar measure may be required of the controller nonetheless.

In contrast to the formerly applicable Directive 95/46/EC, non-compliance is now more likely to lead to negative consequences for the controllers, since they are now required to demonstrate compliance with the legal framework.[18] The competent data protection supervisory authorities now have increased enforcement powers due to the new legal framework, which includes a broader range for fine amounts. Therefore, it might be advisable for each data controller to establish an effective data protection management procedure within the own organisation. Moreover, making use of yearly security checks, audits and best practices in technology, such as penetration tests and performance indicators, seems to be reasonable to demonstrate compliance.

## 10.5 Tensions Between Cybersecurity and Data Protection

Cybersecurity is a matter of concern not only in the context of police and national security, or solely for EU-located state actors. Instead, it is a global issue, motivating private and state actors alike to think about optimal cybersecurity strategies in order to mitigate risks (see e.g. Atlantic Council 2017). Therein, governmental strategies and policies relating to cybersecurity matters strongly concern the European citizens in such a way as cybersecurity incidents often involve the loss, compromise, or unauthorised disclosure of their own personal information.

[18] See e.g. articles 24 (1), 25 (1) + (2), 28 (1) + (3) (e), 30 (1) (g) + (2) (d), 32 (1) GDPR.

With regard to cybersecurity challenges in general, the European Union Agency for Network and Information Security (ENISA) developed a taxonomy classifying different threat types and individual threats at various level of detail. The purpose of this taxonomy is to establish a point of reference in a living structure (ENISA 2016a). According to this document, a number of high-level threat types have been identified, such as physical attacks, unintentional damage/loss of information or IT assets, disaster (natural, environmental), failures/malfunction, outages, eavesdropping/interception/hijacking, nefarious activity/abuse and legal. Many of these threats are closely linked to the cyber domain, for example hacking, Internet of Things (IoT), botnets, ransomware or doxxware (ENISA 2016a, p 8ff).

The World Economic Forum (WEF), a Swiss non-profit foundation committed to bringing business, political, academic and other leaders together for dialogue on global, regional and industry agendas, has also taken a stance on cybersecurity. From their perspective, incidents can cover a very wide spectrum, ranging from e.g. hacking and blackmail encryption to data or identity theft. They can be caused by the most diverse entities for a number of different reasons, and with varying, often unforeseeable impact. Furthermore, the WEF identified in its Global Risk Report 2017 twelve key emerging technologies playing a role in the cybersecurity landscape of the future. These are: 3D printing, advanced materials and nanomaterials, artificial intelligence and robotics, biotechnologies, energy capture, storage and transmission, blockchain and distributed ledger, geoengineering, ubiquitous linked sensors, neuro-technologies, new computing technologies such as quantum computing or neural network processing, space technologies, and virtual and augmented realities (WEF 2017: 42).

An example of a typical cybersecurity incident affecting a broad range of the world population could be the so-called Mirai botnet. This malware was created and distributed in 2016 by students in the US who originally wanted to gain advantages in the online game Minecraft by creating a large-scale distributed denial of service (DDoS) attack. However, the botnet got out of control and infected a large number of IoT devices worldwide, such as IP cameras and home routers. This attack and the distribution of the malware was possible because Mirai exploited the fact that customers and users of IoT devices rarely change the manufacturer's default usernames and passwords on their newly bought machines. Once infected, an IoT device would become part of the botnet, being remotely controlled for large-scale network attacks. In October 2016, the attack got to a point where it almost completely brought down the Internet in the entire eastern United States. The device owners themselves seldom noticed the malware infection because the machine continued to function normally, except for some lagging response time and increased usage of Internet bandwidth.

Therefore, many different technology areas both in the civilian as well as in the governmental spheres are affected by cybersecurity incidents, making appropriate responses crucial in order to succeed in ensuring the availability, integrity and confidentiality of those technologies.[19] This also includes the personal data of

[19] This was explicitly acknowledged by the European Union in COM (2013, p. 3).

individuals which is being collected and processed by digital technologies, and which may be exposed to risks.

While private actors may conduct cyberattacks for monetary or social motives, governmental activities usually extend to wider dimensions, which include Law Enforcement Agency (LEA) cyberspace activities for purposes of crime investigation or prevention, as well as further intelligence activities focused on national security (see also Chap. 12). The targeted entities can also be varied: whereas the attack of critical infrastructure is to be considered the most concerning for all countries worldwide, closely followed by attacks on the governmental structures themselves, e.g. by various types of election fraud (see also Chap. 11).

When focusing on governments specifically as potential cybersecurity attackers, the use of so-called surveillance-oriented security technologies (SOSTs) plays a significant role. Many states, also within the EU, allow to varying degrees and with different preconditions the deployment of such technologies (e.g. Pietrosanti and Aterno 2017), which is often criticised by the media and human rights activists.[20] Media reports about technology used by governments to infiltrate citizen's devices brought into discussion their inherent risks of misuse and bias, usually coming along with a severe lack of transparency.

One example is the governmental deployment of software that infiltrates citizen's devices to gain access to communications and files. In Germany, a Trojan Horse malware (named 'Bundestrojaner', translated: 'Federal Trojan' or 'State Trojan') was discovered by the German Chaos Computer Club (CCC) in 2011 which employed surveillance functionalities on targeted devices. The software was enabled for backdoor remote control and was proved to generally weaken the security of the targeted device. The revelation of the use of this malware triggered a significant public debate around the legality of such technologies in democratic societies (CCC 2011; see also Chap. 15).

Also criticised often by medias and civil rights organisations is the use of so-called zero-day exploit acquisition by governmental institutions to gain leverage in the field of domestic as well as foreign intelligence. Such approaches have received critical attention due to making the whole IT landscape more insecure, while leaving security loopholes open for the obtainment and potential exploitation not only by agencies with lawful national security interests, but also by malicious outsiders.[21]

In this context, also relevant is the general debate around so-called 'lawful access' of police as well as intelligence agencies. Many such institutions have long been demanding access to encrypted devices via backdoor functionalities. Thereby, legal obligations imposed on companies to implement such access might in future affect all types of software and even hardware. Furthermore, the impact of weakened

[20] Cf. Amnesty International (2017). The report heavily criticises the digital surveillance of European governments as negatively affecting the cybersecurity of citizens' devices.

[21] A recent example is the theft of some of the US National Security Agency's most powerful espionage tools by the Shadow Brokers group. These were hoarded by the NSA's TAO (Tailored Access Operations) department, yet outsiders from the mentioned hacking group published them in August 2016, causing significant media reaction. See e.g. Nakashima (2016).

encryption permeates all deployment sectors, including the financial sector, due to the increasing use of cryptocurrencies such as Bitcoin. Similar to zero-day exploits, there is some risk of proliferation beyond the LEA sphere. Furthermore, the legal and factual preconditions for the access to encrypted information are not always clear, requiring clarification. Among security experts, there seems to be a growing recognition of the need to establish mandatory warrants and additional safeguards against misuse (Bellovin et al. 2014). However, even beyond the mere scientific area, encryption has been acknowledged as presenting a number of different challenges for the criminal justice sector.

In November 2016, the Council of the European Union[22] proposed the launch of a reflection process on such challenges, led by the European Commission (Council of the European Union Presidency 2016: 7). Encryption was then further addressed in the Council Meeting on the 8th and 9th December 2016, at which the Ministers acknowledged that this is an area to be approached carefully to take into account the risks to privacy and cybersecurity.[23] Furthermore, the ENISA published an opinion paper on encryption in December 2016, coming to the conclusion that weakening encryption to enable lawful interception is not an optimal approach. The ENISA explicitly warned of unintended consequences, e.g. weakening digital signatures, and recommended some further benefits and risks analysis, as well as a more in-depth exploration of alternatives before any legislative actions should be taken (ENISA 2016a: 5). Similarly, the European Group on Ethics in Science and New Technologies (EGE)[24] published an opinion already in 2014 on security and surveillance technologies, highlighting the dangers of such technologies. It highlighted that whereas foreign state actors may pose a problem, it should not be forgotten that the deployment of intrusive surveillance technologies domestically is risky as well. Therefore, European and democratic principles and values must be considered carefully (EGE 2014: 87ff).

Therefore, specifically in the national security context, it ultimately comes back to the question of boundaries and which goals domestic surveillance should be allowed to pursue, considering the necessity and proportionality of measures (Austin 2015). This however, is not an issue reserved exclusively to the matter of backdoors in encryption but to all governmental activities involving SOSTs. Especially with the increasing use of Big Data analysis tools by LEAs, there is much concern related

[22] The *Council of the European Union* is an official EU body, whose members are the ministers from each EU country, based on the respective policy areas that are addressed. It should not be confused with the *European Council*, which is another EU body consisting of the 28 EU member state government leaders, the European Council President and the President of the European Commission. The European Council defines the EU's strategic short- and long-term policy agenda. For the sake of completeness, confusion should also be avoided with the *Council of Europe (CoE)* that was mentioned above in this chapter.

[23] Outcome of the 3508th Council meeting, document 15391/16 and press release 67 by the Justice and Home Affairs department, section '*Criminal justice in Cyberspace*', Brussels, 8th and 9th December 2016, p. 7.

[24] The European Group on Ethics in Science and New Technologies is an independent advisory body of the President of the European Commission.

**Fig. 10.1** Simplified overview of cybersecurity issues

to citizens having only limited possibilities to defend themselves against any mistreatment or security risks based on algorithmic-founded suspicion. The same counts not only for LEA activity in the context of specific crime prevention or investigation, but also for intelligence in the interest of national security.

Naturally, all intelligence institutions aim to use IT vulnerabilities to target individuals and organisations endangering national security. However, depending on their competences and objectives, these institutions may sometimes have several, contradicting goals. For instance, it appears doubtful whether both SIGINT[25] and COMSEC[26] missions can be pursued by the very same institutions without triggering unexpected internal dichotomies regarding cybersecurity issues.

In conclusion, discrepancies between offensive and defensive strategies are particularly striking with regard to any legislative acts requiring technology to generally undermine the privacy and security of citizen's computers and communications. This is evident when observing the on-going political and public debate around governments collecting personal information of their citizens (see also Fig. 10.1). Examples are the EU-level and national controversies around data retention, counter-terrorism legislation, and the expansion of intelligence services' competences and cooperation. Combating crime and terrorism definitely plays a role in the political and legislative landscape of the European member countries and will continue to do so.

## 10.6 Recommended Realignment and Solution Approaches

It is increasingly acknowledged that the cybersecurity issues landscape can change very fast, leaving policy-makers, data protection and cybersecurity experts at a strategical and operational disadvantage. The increase of interconnectedness in the digital era also means an increase of involved actors and recipients of data, with ever greater networks of entities and stakeholders involved. More data also leads to more

[25] Signals Intelligence, for example getting access to the content of people's emails.

[26] Communications Security, with the ultimate goal of protecting communications, e.g. of government officials.

possibilities of analysis with big data tools, thus scaling up risks of re-identification of individuals, profiling and disrupted power balances. Furthermore, there is a growing recognition that cybersecurity risks do not only come from the outside, but malicious insiders may cause significant damage as well.[27] Within the cybersecurity domain, the effectiveness of offensive measures taken mostly by governmental actors is often questioned. This is due to doubtful allocation of cybersecurity attacks and related insecurities regarding accurate forensic evidence to target the true attackers for retaliation purposes.[28] Therefore, some cybersecurity experts advise focusing more on defensive strategies in order to protect valuable assets. This is where the above-mentioned implementation of technical and organisational measures required by new European data protection framework may contribute to better protected devices and systems.

The responsibilities of the controller and processor entities as well as principles such as data protection by design and default (GDPR, Art. 25; Directive 2016/680, Art. 20) are focused strongly on either eliminating or at least mitigating any risks for the personal information of individuals, regardless of the type of attack. This is a considerable approach because even though the cybersecurity domain provides much collaboration and information on the national level of the EU member countries, it still lacks a clear, organised mandate to enforce the implementation of protective measures on the European level.

Against this background, the national DPAs publish their own statements and opinions on cybersecurity issues to bring in their perspective. In 2015, the French national data protection authority Commission Nationale de l'Informatique et des Libertés (CNIL) published an analysis of personal data protection in the context of cybersecurity. It found that privacy is a crucial aspect in the digital era and that a more holistic approach to both cybersecurity and privacy is sorely needed, while baseline security rules have not yet been sufficiently established (CNIL 2015: 14ff; see also Chap. 14). In July 2017, the CNIL published its stance on encryption, stating that the protection of the confidentiality of communications is essential to maintain the balance between the protection of an individual's personal data, technological innovation and monitoring. Especially with regard to the Edward Snowden NSA mass surveillance revelations, robust encryption solutions would contribute to the security of the whole digital ecosystem, whereas backdoors would endanger citizens, organisations and states alike (CNIL 2017). In 2018, the CNIL published a guideline related to the security of personal data, giving recommendations related to specific technical and organisational measures that controllers and processors may take (CNIL 2018). In Italy, the Italian DPA strives for better cooperation with other Italian governmental institutions concerned with cybersecurity.[29] The Information

---

[27] See ENISA Threat Landscape Report (2018a), subchapter 3.9 about insider threats, pages 64ff.

[28] This was explicitly acknowledged by many cybersecurity experts, also abroad, see as an example the cybersecurity policy/approach of the US Obama administration (Marks 2017).

[29] See the following article on askanews.it: '*Cyber security, protocollo Garante-Dis su dati personali*', 6 October 2017, http://www.askanews.it/cronaca/2017/10/06/cyber-security-protocollo-garante-dis-su-dati-personali-pn_20171006_00134/

Commissioner of the United Kingdom (ICO UK) also focuses on information security, detailing on his website the relevant technical and organisational measures required by the national and EU data protection frameworks.[30] Moreover, the ICO UK regularly publishes current data security incident trends, covering various issues relating to information security in the cyber domain. Therein, the ICO differentiates per sector, such as justice, education, finance, insurance and credit, general business, local government, legal, and health sector. Examples of issues mentioned are cryptographic flaws (e.g. failure to use HTTPS), exfiltration of data, key-logging software, phishing, cybersecurity misconfiguration (e.g. inadvertent publishing of data on website), loss/theft of an only copy of encrypted data or the loss/theft of an unencrypted device, diverse DDoS and others.[31]

Many institutions within the EU, at both national and European levels, recommend taking initial steps for IT systems and networks with the definition of processes, the close monitoring of their execution, supplemented by preventive and reactive measures compliant with the state of the art.[32] This includes the consideration of information security best practices and standards, such as ISO, COBIT or ITIL. From a data protection perspective, the above-mentioned technical and organisational measures often correlate and their implementation should be much more prevalent in many areas and sectors.

Essential from data protection perspective is the conduct of a data protection impact assessment (DPIA) in advance of certain intended personal data processing operations. The GDPR regulates in Article 35 (1) that a DPIA is required when "*a type of processing in particular using new technologies, and taking into account the nature, scope, context and purposes of the processing, is likely to result in a* ***high risk to the rights and freedoms of natural persons*** *[…]*". Many national DPAs in the EU have developed own DPIA methodologies.[33] However, some of these methodologies have their own shortcomings and weaknesses. For example, some fail to properly determine what a risk actually is, or reduce the assessment to a mere risk-based IT security approach which lacks the fundamental rights perspective required by the EU data protection laws. An example of a methodology integrating this perspective is the German Standard Data Protection Model (SDM), which has a strong fundamental rights underpinning and which has been acknowledged by all national

[30] See the ICO website information: https://ico.org.uk/for-organisations/guide-to-the-general-data-protection-regulation-gdpr/security/

[31] These examples come from the reports of the July–September 2016 period (https://ico.org.uk/action-weve-taken/data-security-incident-trends/) and of the Q4 2017/18 (https://ico.org.uk/action-weve-taken/data-security-incident-trends/).

[32] This is also reflected in the private sector as well, reacting to the governmental encouragement. See for example the recommendations of the industry-sector-driven ECSO (2016, chapter 6).

[33] See e.g. the ICO UK guidelines on their website: https://ico.org.uk/for-organisations/guide-to-the-general-data-protection-regulation-gdpr/accountability-and-governance/data-protection-impact-assessments/ or the methodology explanations by the French CNIL: https://www.cnil.fr/en/privacy-impact-assessment-pia

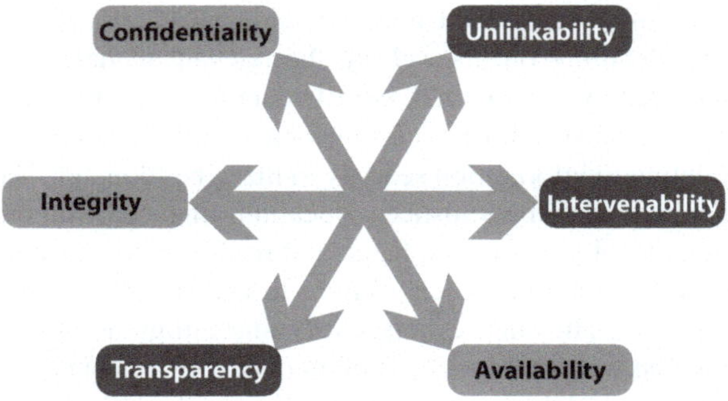


**Fig. 10.2** Data protection goals (darker grey) integrating the IT security goals (lighter grey) that require balancing. The classical IT security goals are described from an individual data subject perspective; unlinkability includes data minimisation

data protection supervisory authorities in Germany.[34] It is based on protection goals that build and extend upon classic IT security goals[35] (see also Chap. 2), but can still be linked directly to the applicable data protection framework.[36] The underlying concept was developed much earlier than the GDPR (Hansen et al. 2015) yet it still provides a methodology that is based on the GDPR directly and thus is useable all across the EU. Briefly summarised, three additional data protection goals supplement the IT security focused ones, namely: *unlinkability* (data minimisation), *intervenability* and *transparency* (see also Fig. 10.2).

These additional, privacy-focused goals can be used together with the classic IT security goals to assess and evaluate data protection and data security objectives and risks. The objective is to map the (often rather vague and broad) legal requirements of the European data protection framework to more concrete functional and organisational requirements. Therefore, the above mentioned SDM approach for a DPIA seems to be a candidate methodology to broaden the view of IT security and to be aligned with the perspective of personal data protection.

Howsoever, regardless of which DPIA methodology is being used, it must always be aimed at determining the necessary operational measures to resolve data protection issues (GDPR, Art. 35(7)). Furthermore, it requires the responsible entity to consider the whole processing lifecycle, including all data, formats, IT systems, processes and functions.

While addressing both security and data protection, it appears reasonable not to invent the wheel anew but to refer to known standards and instruments such as ISO/IEC 27001 and/or code of conducts, as well as to process-oriented approaches (plan, do check, act). Since technological and security challenges are continuously evolving,

---

[34] See Germany (2016) – Unanimously and affirmatively acknowledged (under abstention of Bavaria) by the 92. Conference of the Independent Data Protection Authorities of the Bund and the Länder in Kühlungsborn on 9–10 November 2016. See for a very first English version: https://www.datenschutzzentrum.de/sdm/. A second and improved English version is currently in the works.

[35] The classic '*CIA triad*' (abbreviation for the protection goals confidentiality, integrity, and availability).

[36] Germany (2016), see the pages 23 ff. for the direct linkage of the individual protection goals to the requirements of the GDPR.

it is advisable to earnestly assess the whole lifecycle of IT product manufacturing processes. Such processes usually range from design, development, testing, procurement, operation, management, and to the product phase-out and deployment. All of these stages need to be subjected to security risk assessments and countermeasures deployment (ENISA 2018a: 21). To this end, an effective assignment of clear responsibilities, time periods, as well as a prioritisation of measures implementation should be the primary goal. To plan, implement and evaluate processes, procedures and measures in an optimal way, a data protection management system should always make clear cross-references to an eventually already existing IT security management system (ISMS) to avoid divergences, conflicts, contradictions and unnecessary overlaps.

Moreover, a close observation of the still active legislative process for the future ePrivacy Regulation is advisable since it will be relevant for the area of electronic communications. The original European Commission draft[37] has been criticised significantly by relevant stakeholders in the data protection domain, such as the Article 29 Working Party[38] and the European Data Protection Supervisor (EDPS 2017) What might matter most in the context of cybersecurity and more general IT security issues is that the draft has been found faulty for vagueness in the scope definition. Also, for having weakened requirements in relation to information about security risks and data breaches, as well as regarding privacy by design and by default in comparison to the GDPR. Thus, it provides a lack of consistency.[39]

**Acknowledgments** The chapter was created in the context of the research project CANVAS (Constructing an Alliance for Value-driven Cybersecrutiy), with funding from the European Union's Horizon 2020 research and innovation programme under grant agreement No 700540. This work was co-supported (in part) by the Swiss State Secretariat for Education, Research and Innovation (SERI) under contract number 16.0052-1.

## References

Amnesty International (17 Jan 2017) Dangerously disproportionate: the ever-expanding national security state in Europe. https://www.amnesty.org/en/documents/eur01/5342/2017/en/. Last access 7 July 2019

Article 29 Working Party (2017) Opinion 01/2017 on the proposed regulation for the ePrivacy Regulation (2002/58/EC). Adopted on 4 April 2017 (WP247). http://ec.europa.eu/newsroom/document.cfm?doc_id=44103. Last access 7 July 2019

---

[37] European Commission: '*Proposal for a Regulation on Privacy and Electronic Communications*', https://ec.europa.eu/digital-single-market/en/news/proposal-regulation-privacy-and-electronic-communications

[38] The Article 29 Working Party, set up on account of Article 29 EU Data Protection Directive 95/46/EC, was an independent advisory group counselling the European Commission in data protection and privacy issues. Since 25 May 2018, the European Data Protection Board is its successor entity.

[39] See the Article 29 Working Party: '*Opinion 01/2017 on the Proposed Regulation for the ePrivacy Regulation (2002/58/EC)*', adopted on 4 April 2017, WP247, pages 3 and 24. Furthermore, see the '*Opinion 6/2017 EDPS Opinion on the Proposal for a Regulation on Privacy and Electronic Communications (ePrivacy Regulation)*', April 24th 2017, pages 3, 12 ff., 19, 22 f., and 34 f

Austin LM (2015) Surveillance and the rule of law. Surveill Soc J 13(2). http://ojs.library.queensu.ca/index.php/surveillance-and-society/article/viewFile/law_rule/law_rul. Last access 7 July 2019
Bellovin SM, Blaze M, Clark S et al (2014) Lawful hacking: using existing vulnerabilities for wiretapping on the internet. Northwest J Technol Intellect Prop 12:1. http://scholarlycommons.law.northwestern.edu/njtip/vol12/iss1/1. Last access 7 July 2019
Beuth P (30 Aug 2017) Bundeshacker im Verzug. Zeit Online. https://www.zeit.de/digital/datenschutz/2017-08/zitis-eroeffnung-thomas-de-maiziere-bundeshacker. Last access 7 July 2019
CCC (2011) Chaos computer club: 'Chaos Computer Club analyzes government malware'. 8 October 2011. Available at: https://www.ccc.de/en/updates/2011/staatstrojaner. Last access 7 July 2019
Charter of Fundamental Rights of the European Union (2000) OJ C 364, 18 December 2000. http://eur-lex.europa.eu/legal-content/EN/TXT/?uri=CELEX%3A32000X1218 (01), pp 1–22
CNIL (2015) Commission Nationale de l'Informatique et des Libertés: 36th activity report 2015. https://www.cnil.fr/sites/default/files/atoms/files/cnil_rapport_2015_gb.pdf. Last access 7 July 2019
CNIL (18 July 2017) Commission Nationale de l'Informatique et des Libertés: Encryption: security element of information assets. https://www.cnil.fr/en/what-cnils-position-terms-encryption. Last access 7 July 2019
CNIL (4 Apr 2018) Commission Nationale de l'Informatique et des Libertés: Security of personal data. https://www.cnil.fr/sites/default/files/atoms/files/cnil_guide_securite_personnelle_gb_web.pdf. Last access 7 July 2019
COM (26 Jan 2001) European Commission: Creating a safer information society by improving the security of information infrastructures and combating computer-related crime. Communication COM/2000/890 final, Brussels. http://eur-lex.europa.eu/legal-content/EN/TXT/?uri=CELEX:52000DC0890. Last access 7 July 2019
COM (2012) Safeguarding privacy in a connected world – a European data protection framework for the 21st century
COM (7 Feb 2013) European Commission: Cyber security strategy of the European Union: an open, safe and secure cyberspace. Joint communication JOIN/2013/1 final, Brussels. http://eur-lex.europa.eu/legal-content/EN/TXT/?uri=CELEX:52013JC0001. Last access 7 July 2019
COM (2015) European Commission: A digital single market strategy for Europe. Communication from the Commission to the European Parliament, the Council, the European Economic and Social Committee and the Committee of the Regions. COM/2015/192 final. https://eur-lex.europa.eu/legal-content/EN/TXT/?uri=COM:2015:192:FIN. Last access 7 July 2019
COM (5 July 2016) European Commission: Strengthening Europe's cyber resilience system and fostering a competitive and innovative cybersecurity industry. Communication COM/2016/410 final, Brussels, 5 July 2016. http://eur-lex.europa.eu/legal-content/EN/TXT/?uri=CELEX:52016DC0410. Last access 7 July 2019
COM (2017) European Commission: Resilience, deterrence and defense: building strong cybersecurity in Europe. Fact sheet on the cybersecurity package. 19 September 2017. https://ec.europa.eu/digital-single-market/en/news/resilience-deterrence-and-defense-building-strong-cybersecurity-europe. Last access 7 July 2019
COM (2018a) European Commission: Communication from the commission to the European Parliament, the European Council and the Council – sixteenth progress report towards an effective and genuine security union. Brussels, 10 October 2018. COM (2018) 690 final. https://ec.europa.eu/home-affairs/sites/homeaffairs/files/what-we-do/policies/european-agenda-security/20181010_com-2018-690-communication_en.pdf. Last access 7 July 2019
COM (2018b) European Commission: Proposal for a regulation of the European Parliament and of the Council establishing the European Cybersecurity Industrial, Technology and Research Competence Centre and the Network of National Coordination Centres. Brussels, 12 November 2018. COM(2018) 630 final. 2018/0328 (COD). https://ec.europa.eu/commission/sites/beta-political/files/soteu2018-cybersecurity-centres-regulation-630_en.pdf. Last access 7 July 2019

Consolidated Version of the Treaty on the Functioning of the European Union (2012) OJ C 326, 26 October 2012, pp 47–390. http://eur-lex.europa.eu/legal-content/EN/TXT/?uri=celex%3A12012E%2FTXT. Last access 7 July 2019

Council Decision 2009/371/JHA of 6 April 2009 establishing the European Police Office (EUROPOL) (2009) OJ L121/37, 15 May 2009, pp 37–66. http://eur-lex.europa.eu/eli/dec/2009/371/oj. Last access 7 July 2019

Council Directive 2008/114/EC of 8 December 2008 on the identification and designation of European critical infrastructures and the assessment of the need to improve their protection. OJ L 345, 23 December 2008, pp 75–82. https://eur-lex.europa.eu/legal-content/EN/TXT/?uri=CELEX:32008L0114. Last access 7 July 2019

Council Framework Decision 2006/960/JHA of 18 December 2006 on simplifying the exchange of information and intelligence between law enforcement authorities of the Member States of the European Union (2006) OJ L 386/89, 29 December 2006, pp 89–100. http://eur-lex.europa.eu/eli/dec_framw/2006/960/oj. Last access 7 July 2019

Council Framework Decision 2008/977/JHA of 27 November 2008 on the protection of personal data processed in the framework of police and judicial cooperation in criminal matters (2008) OJ L 350, 30.12.2008, pp 60–71. http://eur-lex.europa.eu/eli/dec_framw/2008/977/oj. Last access 7 July 2019

Council of the European Union – Justice and Home Affairs department (2016) Outcome of the 3508th Council meeting, Document 15391/16, section 'Criminal justice in Cyberspace and Press release 67, Brussels, 8 and 9 December 2016. http://data.consilium.europa.eu/doc/document/ST-15391-2016-INIT/en/pdf. Last access 7 July 2019

Council of the European Union Presidency (2016) Encryption: challenges for criminal justice in relation to the use of encryption – future steps – progress report. Note 14711/16 to the Permanent Representatives Committee/Council, Brussels, 23 November 2016. http://data.consilium.europa.eu/doc/document/ST-14711-2016-INIT/en/pdf. Last access 7 July 2019

Croatia (2015) The national cyber security strategy of the Republic of Croatia. Official Gazette No. 108/2015, Zagreb, 7 October 2015. https://www.enisa.europa.eu/topics/national-cyber-security-strategies/ncss-map/CRNCSSEN.pdf. Last access 7 July 2019

Directive 2002/58/EC of the European Parliament and of the Council of 12 July 2002 concerning the processing of personal data and the protection of privacy in the electronic communications sector (Directive on privacy and electronic communications) (2002) OJ L 201, 31 July 2002, p 37. http://eur-lex.europa.eu/legal-content/en/ALL/?uri=CELEX:32002L0058. Last access 7 July 2019

Directive (EU) 2016/680 of the European Parliament and of the Council of 27 April 2016 on the protection of natural persons with regard to the processing of personal data by competent authorities for the purposes of the prevention, investigation, detection or prosecution of criminal offences or the execution of criminal penalties, and on the free movement of such data, and repealing Council Framework Decision 2008/977/JHA. OJ L 119, 4 May 2016, pp 89–131. http://eur-lex.europa.eu/eli/dir/2016/680/oj. Last access 7 July 2019

Directive (EU) 2016/1148 of the European Parliament and of the Council of 6 July 2016 concerning measures for a high common level of security of network and information systems across the Union. (2016) OJ L 194/1 (NIS Directive). http://data.europa.eu/eli/dir/2016/1148/oj. Last access 7 July 2019

ECSO (June 2016) European Cyber Security Organisation: European Cybersecurity Strategic Research and Innovation Agenda (SRIA) for a contractual public-private-partnership (cPPP). http://www.ecs-org.eu/documents/ecs-cppp-sria.pdf. Last access 7 July 2019

EDPS (14 June 2013) European Data Protection Supervisor (Peter Hustinx): Opinion on the Joint Communication of the Commission and of the High Representative of the European Union for Foreign Affairs and Security Policy on a "Cyber security strategy of the European Union: an open, safe and secure cyberspace", and on the Commission proposal for a Directive concerning measures to ensure a high common level of network and information security across the Union. Brussels. https://edps.europa.eu/sites/edp/files/publication/13-06-14_cyber_security_en.pdf. Last access 7 July 2019

EDPS (15 Dec 2015) European Data Protection Supervisor (Giovanni Buttarelli): Opinion 8/2015 on dissemination and use of intrusive surveillance technologies. Brussels. https://edps.europa.eu/sites/edp/files/publication/15-12-15_intrusive_surveillance_en.pdf. Last access 7 July 2019

EDPS (24 Apr 2017) European Data Protection Supervisor: Opinion 6/2017 EDPS opinion on the proposal for a regulation on privacy and electronic communications (ePrivacy Regulation). https://edps.europa.eu/sites/edp/files/publication/17-04-24_eprivacy_en.pdf. Last access 7 July 2019

EGE (2014) European Group on Ethics in Science and New Technologies: Ethics of security and surveillance technologies. Opinion No. 28, Brussels, 20 May 2014. Available at: https://bookshop.europa.eu/en/ethics-of-security-and-surveillance-technologies-pbNJAJ14028/. Last access 7 July 2019

ENISA (Dec 2016a) European Union Agency for Network and Information Security: ENISA's opinion paper on encryption – strong encryption safeguards our digital identity. https://www.enisa.europa.eu/publications/enisa-position-papers-and-opinions/enisas-opinion-paper-on-encryption. Last access 7 July 2019

ENISA (Jan 2016b) European Union Agency for Network and Information Security: ENISA threat taxonomy – a tool for structuring threat information. Initial Version 1.0. https://www.enisa.europa.eu/topics/threat-risk-management/threats-and-trends/enisa-threat-landscape/etl2015/enisa-threat-taxonomy-a-tool-for-structuring-threat-information. Last access 7 July 2019

ENISA (Jan 2018a) European Union Agency for Network and Information Security: ENISA threat landscape report 2017. Final Version 1.0. https://www.enisa.europa.eu/publications/enisa-threat-landscape-report-2017. Last access 7 July 2019

ENISA (31 Jan 2018b) European Union Agency for Network and Information Security: Looking into the crystal ball – a report on emerging technologies and security challenges. Version 1.0. https://www.enisa.europa.eu/publications/looking-into-the-crystal-ball. Last access 7 July 2019

France (2015) République française. French National Digital Security Strategy. https://www.ssi.gouv.fr/en/actualite/the-french-national-digital-security-strategy-meeting-the-security-challenges-of-the-digital-world/. Last access 7 July 2019

Germany (2016) The standard data protection model – a concept for inspection and consultation on the basis of unified protection goals. German Data Protection Authorities, Kühlungsborn, 9–10 November 2016. https://www.bfdi.bund.de/DE/Datenschutz/Themen/Technische_Anwendungen/TechnischeAnwendungenArtikel/Standard-Datenschutzmodell.html. Last access 7 July 2019

Hansen M, Jensen M, Rost M (2015) Protection goals for privacy engineering. Security and privacy workshops (SPW), IEEE, 2015, pp 159–166. https://doi.org/10.1109/SPW.2015.13. Last access 7 July 2019

Hegemann L (29 Aug 2018) Deutschland bekommt eine Agentur für innere Netzsicherheit. Zeit Online. https://www.zeit.de/digital/internet/2018-08/cybersicherheit-bundesregierung-innovation-cyberagentur-netzpolitik. Last access 7 July 2019

High Representative of the European Union for Foreign Affairs and Security Policy (2013) Cybersecurity strategy of the European Union – an open, safe and secure cyberspace. Joint Communication to the European Parliament, the Council, the European Economic and Social Committee and the Committee of the Regions Brussels 7 February 2013. JOIN (2013) 1 final. http://eeas.europa.eu/archives/docs/policies/eu-cyber-security/cybsec_comm_en.pdf. Last access 7 July 2019

Luxembourg (27 Mar 2015) Gouvernement du Grand-Duché de Luxembourg. National Cybersecurity Strategy II. https://www.enisa.europa.eu/topics/national-cyber-security-strategies/ncss-map/Luxembourg_Cyber_Security_strategy.pdf. Last access 7 July 2019

Luxembourg (26 Jan 2018) Gouvernement du Grand-Duché de Luxembourg. National Cybersecurity Strategy III. https://hcpn.gouvernement.lu/dam-assets/fr/publications/brochure-livre/national-cybersecurity-strategy-3/national-cybersecurity-strategy-iii-en-.pdf. Last access 7 July 2019

Marks J (17 Jan 2017) Obama's cyber legacy: he did (almost) everything right and it still turned out wrong. nextgov.com. http://www.nextgov.com/cybersecurity/2017/01/obamas-cyber-legacy-he-did-almost-everything-right-and-it-still-turned-out-wrong/134612/. Last access 7 July 2019

Nakashima E (16 Aug 2016) Powerful NSA hacking tools have been revealed online. https://www.washingtonpost.com/world/national-security/powerful-nsa-hacking-tools-have-been-revealed-online/2016/08/16/bce4f974-63c7-11e6-96c0-37533479f3f5_story.html?utm_term=.61735c899442. Last access 7 July 2019

NATO (8 July 2016) North Atlantic Treaty Organization. Cyber defense pledge. Press release (2016) 124. http://www.nato.int/cps/en/natohq/official_texts_133177.htm. Last access 7 July 2019

Pietrosanti F, Aterno S (15 Feb 2017) Italy unveils a legal proposal to regulate government hacking. https://boingboing.net/2017/02/15/title-italy-unveils-a-law-pro.html. Last access 7 July 2019

Regulation (EU) 2016/679 of the European Parliament and of the Council of 27 April 2016 on the protection of natural persons with regard to the processing of personal data and on the free movement of such data, and repealing Directive 95/46/EC (General Data Protection Regulation) (2016) OJ L 119/1. http://data.europa.eu/eli/dir/2016/1148/oj. Last access 7 July 2019

Regulation (EU) 2019/881 of the European Parliament and of the Council of 17 April 2019 on ENISA (the European Union Agency for Cybersecurity) and on information and communications technology cybersecurity certification and repealing regulation (EU) No 526/2013 (Cybersecurity Act) (2019) OJ L 151/15. https://eur-lex.europa.eu/eli/reg/2019/881/oj. Last access 7 July 2019

Spain (3 Jan 2013) Gobierno de España. National cyber security strategy. https://www.enisa.europa.eu/topics/national-cyber-security-strategies/ncss-map/NCSS_ESen.pdf

The Atlantic Council of the United States (2017) A nonstate strategy for saving cyberspace, Atlantic Council Strategy Paper No. 8, January

The H Security blog (11 Sept 2012) Federal Commissioner unable to audit Federal Trojan source. http://www.h-online.com/security/news/item/Federal-Commissioner-unable-to-audit-Federal-Trojan-source-1704460.html. Last access 7 July 2019

Treaty of Lisbon amending the Treaty on European Union and the Treaty establishing the European Community. Signed at Lisbon, 13 December 2007. OJ C 306, 17 December 2007, pp 1–271. Available at: http://eur-lex.europa.eu/legal-content/EN/TXT/?uri=celex%3A12007L%2FTXT. Last access 7 July 2019

WEF (2017) World economic forum: global risks report 2017, 12th edn, published within the framework of The Global Competitiveness and Risks Team

# Chapter 11
# Freedom of Political Communication, Propaganda and the Role of Epistemic Institutions in Cyberspace

**Seumas Miller**

**Abstract** This article provides definitions of fake news, hate speech and propaganda, respectively. These phenomenon are corruptive of the epistemic norms, e.g. to tell the truth. It also elaborates on the right to freedom of communication and its relation both to censoring propaganda and to the role of epistemic institutions, such as a free and independent press and universities. Finally, it discusses the general problem of countering political propaganda in cyberspace and argues, firstly, that there is an important role for epistemic institutions in this regard and secondly, that social media platforms need to be redesigned since, as they stand and notwithstanding the benefits which they provide, they are a large part of the problem.

**Keywords** Applied ethics · Epistemic institutions · Epistemic norms · Fake news · Hate speech · Knowledge · Objectivity · Propaganda · Social media

## 11.1 Introduction

Social media platforms, such as Facebook and Twitter, are used by billions of communicators worldwide, as are search engines such as Google The advent of these tech giants, or at least of the technology upon which they rely, has enabled the moral right to communication to be exercised on a scale hitherto undreamt of and, as a consequence, led to unprecedented flows of information and opinion, globally as well as locally. However, these developments have gone hand in hand with an exponential increase in the spread of fake news, hate speech and propaganda (Cocking

S. Miller (✉)
Charles Sturt University, Canberra, Australia

TU Delft, The Hague, The Netherlands

University of Oxford, Oxford, UK
e-mail: semiller@csu.edu.au



M. Christen et al. (eds.), *The Ethics of Cybersecurity*, The International Library of Ethics, Law and Technology 21,
https://doi.org/10.1007/978-3-030-29053-5_11

and van den Hoven 2018; see also Chap. 12). Of particular relevance to this article on political communication, the advent of the tech giants has enabled extremist political groups, such as Islamic State to flourish, facilitated interference in the democratic process by foreign powers (e.g. in the US presidential elections by Russia), and turbo-charged virulent politically motivated hate speech leading, in some instances, to murder and mayhem, as in the recent case of attacks on Rohingya Muslims following hate speech on Facebook that emanated from the Myanmar military.

Recent revelations concerning data firm Cambridge Analytica's illegitimate use of the data of millions of Facebook users highlight the ethical issues arising from the use of machine learning techniques in relation to social media for political purposes. Cambridge Analytica is, or was—the revelations brought about its demise—a firm that used machine learning processes to try to influence elections in the US and elsewhere by, for instance, targeting 'vulnerable' voters in marginal seats with political advertising (Grassegger and Krogerus 2016). Of course, there is nothing new about political candidates and parties employing firms to engage in political advertising on their behalf, but if a data firm has access to the personal information of millions of voters, and is skilled in the use of machine learning techniques, then it can develop detailed, fine-grained voter profiles that enable political actors to reach a whole new level of manipulative influence over voters. The ethical consequences are potentially far reaching. One set of ethical issues pertains to privacy and confidentiality; illegitimate access on the part of Cambridge Analytica to private information and, in the case of Russian hackers hacking into the democratic party's emails, to confidentiality. Another set of ethical issues pertains to institutional corruption; corruption of the democratic process. A further set of ethical issues pertains to national security; the use of machine learning techniques by foreign powers, such as Russia, to favour one candidate over another in the service of their own political agenda, e.g. to sow discord in liberal democratic polities. Such manipulative political influence over users of social media utilising a combination of new technological tools, such as machine learning, and psychologically based, manipulative marketing techniques raises more directly the emerging ethical issue of the tension in cyberspace between freedom of communication, on the one hand, and the need to restrict certain forms of political propaganda on the other.

It is agreed by all that the dissemination of fake news, hate speech and extremist propaganda on the Internet and on social media in particular is a bad thing and should be curtailed, if not prohibited, albeit giving effect to this is easier said than done. However, a host of difficult practical ethical problems arise at this point. Who ought to decide what is fake news and what is fact—the tech giants themselves? Who ought to decide what counts as hate speech, and on the basis of what criteria? Should all political propaganda be prohibited and, if not, which should be prohibited, which permitted and on what basis? Doubtless, Islamic State's YouTube video clips of beheadings and incitements to murder should be prohibited, but what of the propaganda disseminated by right wing groups who might not advocate the overthrow of the state or the murder of innocents but, nevertheless, do disseminate political perspectives at odds with liberal democratic values, such as tolerance of minorities, and in doing so rely heavily on false claims, half-truths and racial and other long standing prejudices—thereby undermining liberal democratic institutions, including epistemic institutions.

What do I mean by epistemic institutions (Miller 2010)? The term 'episteme' refers, of course, to knowledge. Therefore, epistemic institutions are those institutions that have as a principal institutional purpose the acquisition and/or dissemination of knowledge (understood broadly so as to include factual knowledge, reasoning processes such as induction and deduction, evidence-backed economic, political and ethical perspectives, and understanding). Accordingly, epistemic institutions include schools, universities and media organisations responsible for news/comment. They also include private or government research laboratories, think tanks and, for that matter, intelligence agencies.

These practical ethical questions mentioned above presuppose answers to some more fundamental theoretical questions. For instance, can the distinction between politically motivated fake news, hate speech and propaganda, on the one hand, and, on the other hand, factual and other objective claims and perspectives actually be sustained? What is the nature and extent of the moral right of freedom of communication? Who ought to be the decision-makers in relation to determining what is fake news, hate speech and political propaganda in cyberspace. More specifically, who ought to be the decision-makers in relation to determining when such communications ought to be prohibited?

In this article, my concern is with countering politically motivated fake news, hate speech and propaganda while respecting the moral right to freedom of communication. In the first section, I offer definitions of fake news, hate speech and propaganda respectively. As we shall see, these phenomena have at least one important feature in common; they are not truth-aiming (in a certain sense). In the second section, I elaborate on the right to freedom of communication and its relation to epistemic institutions. In the third and final section, I discuss the general problem of countering political propaganda in cyberspace and the role of epistemic institutions and social media platforms in this enterprise.

## 11.2 Fake News, Hate Speech and Propaganda

The definition of fake news is contested and, therefore, the following definition is necessarily somewhat stipulative (Lynch 2016a). News by definition purports to be true or, in the case of visual images and the like, purports to be an accurate representation of reality, even if it is in fact false. However, news items are frequently disseminated on the Internet by persons who do not endorse them; indeed, on occasion, by persons who explicitly state at a later time that they are false. Here I use the term 'fake news' to refer to news that is in fact false and not believed by its originator—as opposed to subsequent disseminators—to be true. Accordingly, on this definition, news that is false and believed to be false by its originator is fake news, but so is news that is false and neither believed nor disbelieved by its originator is to be true.

This is because news by definition—and whether it is in fact true or false—purports to be true. Thus, whatever its originator believes or does not believe, he or she presents the news item as being true.

Fake news is problematic for at least two reasons. Firstly, it is false and yet, given the communicative reach of the Internet, and of social media—and the use of automated dissemination techniques, e.g. bots—it is likely to be believed by many, even if disbelieved by many others (or, at least, their beliefs are suspended). I note that somewhat paradoxically the credibility of fake news on social media platforms, notably Facebook, is enhanced by the co-presence on these platforms of objective news emanating from high quality news outlets, such as the New York Times. Secondly, especially in the case of an ongoing series of mutually supportive, politically motivated, fake news items, there are likely to be untoward political consequences arising from large numbers of people believing such news items, including potentially the undermining of democratic processes that rely on voters making judgments based on facts rather than falsehoods.

It is sometimes suggested that ultimately there is no important distinction between fake news and factual news and, as a corollary, politicians, academics, news media and other disseminators cannot provide objective communicative content of high quality since the notion of such objective truth or of a fact of the matter independent of representations is itself meaningless or hopelessly naïve; accordingly, one media or other report cannot be of higher quality than another by virtue of being correct or more accurate or more balanced. It is further suggested that the reasons for this are manifold, and they include: the fact that communicative content is a representation and, as such, always reflects a standpoint; that mechanisms of media communication necessarily mediate, and therefore distort; that quality is simply in the eye of the beholder; and so on. There is not the space to deal with all these kinds of arguments in detail, though it is not difficult to show that they do not demonstrate the strong position they are intended to (Bok 1978). Suffice it to say here that the notion that we cannot aim at truth, and on occasion approximate to it, and the notion that every piece of analysis and comment is as good as every other, is self-defeating and, if accepted, would render communication pointless. It is a presupposition of communication in general, including both linguistic communication and visual representation, that there is a truth to be communicated or some fact of the matter to be represented, and that on many occasions this is achieved. If this were not so, communication of news would be rendered pointless and cease to take place. Thus, it would be pointless, because not objectively true, to report that on 9/11 two planes were flown by terrorists into the Twin Towers building in New York City killing some 3000 people. Likewise, it would be pointless to show footage of the planes flying into the towers and the subsequent collapse of the towers; pointless because (allegedly) there was no fact of the matter. Moreover, it is a presupposition of comment and analysis that not every piece of analysis and comment is as good as every other one, since there is always as least one which is regarded by the communicator as inferior, namely that which is the negation of the one put forward, e.g. that terrorists did not fly and planes into Twin Towers and did not kill anyone.

While the distinction between fake news and factual claims is relatively clear-cut, notwithstanding claims to the contrary, distinctions, firstly, between politically motivated hate speech and strident pejorative criticism, and, secondly, between, political propaganda and political comment/opinion, are more problematic.

The definition of hate speech is contested. Let us, assume however, that it is speech that incites hatred against some group (Waldron 2012)—or, at least, is intended to do so and has some reasonable chance of doing so. Accordingly, hate speech is to be distinguished from strident pejorative criticism insofar as the latter is truth-aiming, i.e. has truth as an end in itself. By contrast, hate speech is not truth-aiming in this sense; the truth is only of interest in so far as it can serve to incite hatred.

Hate speech does not necessarily incite violence or other serious crimes, albeit these may well be longer term, indirect consequences of hate speech. The hate speech of interest to us here is politically motivated hate speech; speech that incites hatred against a target group and is performed in order to serve some political purpose, e.g. a right-wing politician seeking to get elected by vilifying immigrants belonging to a minority ethnic group. Naturally, politically motivated hate speech, often features abusive language, and manifestly incites hatred against the target group. However, sometimes it is couched in moderate language and consists in advocating particular policies ostensibly based on facts ('facts' which turn out to be false or highly misleading). In the latter cases context is all important if the speech in question is properly to be regarded as hate speech. Consider for instance, a right-wing politician's speech advocating that immigrants from a certain racial group should be sent back to their homeland and that there should be a ban on any further immigrants from that group, on the grounds that, as he falsely claims, the immigrants in question are mostly criminals and/or welfare recipients. Suppose this speech is disseminated via social media and on a targeted basis to members of an audience likely to be receptive to these views in part because of their pre-existing prejudice. The speech is racially discriminatory and, given its pattern of dissemination and its ultimate intention, i.e. to incite racist sentiment in the service of a political agenda (let us assume), it arguably constitutes hate speech.

In the light of this definition of hate speech as speech intended to incite hatred, and having a reasonable chance of doing so, it is clear that politically motivated hate speech is potentially harmful not only to individual and groups who are the object of its attack, and not only because it is likely to be false, but because it is likely to sow discord in a liberal democratic polity and, for that matter, in authoritarian states. As is the case with fake news, hate speech in cyberspace is especially problematic, given the communicative reach of the Internet and social media platforms in particular.

Political propaganda is, I suggest, communication in the service of a political ideology (Ellul 1973). Therefore, political ideology is the more fundamental concept. Accordingly, we need a serviceable account of political ideology and one that enables a distinction to be maintained between ideology, on the one hand, and the more generic notion of systems of political ideas, on the other.

Firstly, it is important to note that in order for something to be an ideology it must comprise a set of systematically connected beliefs, assumptions or claims.

Moreover, this systematically connected set of beliefs or claims must if it is an ideology be susceptible of instantiation; and if it is instantiated it must be instantiated in the minds of a group of people. Such a group must constitute a community (of sorts) and not simply a set of unrelated individuals. The notion of an (instantiated) ideology, then, is the notion of a shared set of beliefs and claims. Furthermore, the key constitutive elements of the system are beliefs and claims cannot be too strongly emphasised, since it is sometimes supposed that the key constitutive elements are actions, at other times appearances, and at still other times that these elements are words or concepts. However, an ideology cannot consist of actions, social practices and the like per se since unlike beliefs or claims, actions are not about the world and are not true or false; but it is a constitutive feature of an ideology that it be about the world, and that it be true or (more likely) false. Nor can an ideology comprise appearances per se, even though the way the world appears to be may bring about false beliefs and indeed ideological beliefs. Here a perceptual analogy may be useful. A stick placed in water has the appearance of being bent and may cause the perceiver to believe that it is in fact bent. Yet from the fact that the world appears to a subject to be a certain way it does not follow that the subject believes that the world is the way it appears to be. We do not, for example, believe that the stick is bent, although it certainly appears to us to be bent. However, if appearances are not necessarily accepted as true by a subject then they cannot be constitutive of ideologies, for if someone adopts an ideology then the person accepts its content as being true. Again, it is surely clear that it is only beliefs and claims, as opposed to unitary items such as words or concepts, that constitute commitments to this or that view of the world, and as such can be true or false. By contrast, words and concepts as such do not constitute such commitments and make no truth claims. Thus, the word 'unicorn' is consistent with there being or not being unicorns; however, the belief 'there are unicorns' is a commitment to the world being a certain way and is true if the world is that way and false if it is not.

Secondly, I suggest that for any systematically connected set of shared beliefs to count as an ideology it must have a certain kind of origin. In particular, the existence of the ideology cannot ultimately be caused by the world being as the ideology says it is. Thus a particular systematically connected set of beliefs (say liberalism) would qualify as an ideology on our definition if it were brought into existence not by the world being as liberalism says it is, but rather was fashioned as an expedient account of things by the economically ascendant classes.

Thirdly, I suggest that to count as a political ideology, a set of beliefs must serve some kind of political purpose. It might, for example, have the purpose of undermining or, alternatively, of preserving the political status quo.

Finally, it should be noted that there is a high probability that an ideology will be false, given that its causal origin cannot be the world being the way the ideology says it is, and given that it must serve some or other political purpose. That said, it is important to keep in mind that political ideologies typically consist in part in truths, as well as falsehoods and half truths, and rely in part on legitimate grievances. If not, they are likely to have little or no credibility.

However, core or constitutive elements of a political ideology are likely to be false or fanciful, e.g. the classless society, the Caliphate. Moreover, the propagation of an ideology relies on falsehoods, half-truths and hate speech. Modern propaganda is likely to rely on a suite of psychologically based, manipulative marketing techniques and fake news disseminated on the Internet. Aside from the constitutively ideological components of an ideology, i.e., its content, ideology impacts itself causally on communication and thought, by way of permeation, by implication, and by being presupposed. Accordingly, and notwithstanding what was claimed above, actions, practices, appearances and so on can be used to convey ideological content.

Sometimes processes of permeation, implication and presupposition enable the ideology to influence while going undetected. Consider an advertisement consisting of a video clip of a well-dressed, handsome man ostentatiously smoking an identifiable brand of cigarette, standing next to an expensive car, and making the statement 'That is a fine car'. Here, there may be an (as it were) non-political-ideological core belief: the conviction that in virtue of its being mechanically sound and fuel-efficient, the car is fine. However in addition to this non-ideological core belief, and overlaying it, may be ideological beliefs, such as the belief that the car is fine, not simply in virtue of being mechanically sound but also in virtue of being socially prestigious because expensive. Here a core of non-ideological meaning is permeated by ideological meaning: in effect, a consumerist ideology is being sold. In addition, of course, there is the implication that smoking this particular brand of cigarette goes hand in glove with having prestige.

A further kind of example entails the notion of a presupposition as well as implication, albeit there is no attempt to conceal the ideological message. Consider for instance the statement, 'all Crusaders are mortal' uttered in the context of an extremist jihadist diatribe. Here there is a crude ideology presupposed, viz. that the world is divided up into Christians who are loathsome and Muslims who are not. In addition, the reference to mortality implies that Christians can and should be killed.

A final important point needs to be kept in mind. Propaganda on its own has little political effect. If it is to undermine, for instance, a liberal democracy it needs to be a component of an integrated package comprising the existence of a felt grievance against some group, such as injustice suffered at the hands of the political elite, a technological means for wide dissemination, (e.g. printed matter, social media) and, at least in conflict situations, some form of kinetic capacity (e.g. armaments), and strategy (e.g. terrorism) (Ingram 2016). Needless to say, as is the case with fake news and hate speech, the unprecedented communicative reach afforded by the Internet and social media platforms to propagandists have greatly increased the potential impact of political propaganda.

## 11.3 Freedom of Communication, Truth and Liberal Democracy

Notwithstanding the individual, collective and institutional harms caused by politically motivated fake news, hate speech and propaganda—not to mention their inherent epistemic and moral undesirability—there are good reasons not to enact laws to prohibit them entirely, although these reasons are consistent with placing some legal restrictions on them. For instance, most would agree that there should be laws against incitements to violence. Naturally, it does not follow from this that there should not be individual, collective and, indeed, institutionally based opposition to fake news, hate speech and propaganda. The historically most important reason for not enacting laws to prohibit fake news, hate speech and propaganda is the moral right to freedom of communication (Schauer 1981).

There are two especially salient arguments for freedom of communication and, relatedly, freedom of intellectual inquiry, the first associated with the English philosopher John Stuart Mill (1869), the second (loosely) associated with the German philosopher Immanuel Kant (1956). (I do not mean to imply that these arguments are the only ones advanced by these philosophers, much less that the versions of them I propound below are precise renderings of the work of these philosophers.)

According to Mill, new knowledge will only emerge in a free marketplace of ideas. If certain ideas are prevented from being investigated or communicated then the truth is not likely to emerge, since those suppressed ideas may in fact be the true ones. I note that the notion of a market place in play here might need to be somewhat loosely construed so that, for instance, Wikipedia might be understood as a market place in so far as there are no barriers to participation by adding or correcting information, although there are no buyers and sellers in the conventional sense. I take it that Wikipedia involves a form of collective epistemic action or, as I term it, joint epistemic action (Miller 2018). It relies on the epistemic (knowledge) contribution of multiple actors.

Let us look more closely at this argument, restricting ourselves to political ideas in the sense of politically relevant factual claims, hypotheses, unsubstantiated claims, interpretations and theories, the epistemic resolution of which call for occasionally complex processes of reasoning and justification to be undertaken in a public forum such as, in recent times, the Internet and social media platforms. Here, Mill appears to rely on a distinction between rational inquiry and justification on the one hand—a possibly solitary activity—and freedom of communication on the other.

This argument needs to be unpacked (Miller 2000). I suggest the following rendering of it.

(1) Freedom of communication is necessary for rational inquiry.
(2) Rational inquiry is necessary for knowledge.
Therefore: (3) Freedom of communication is necessary for knowledge.

The argument is valid and premise (2) is plausible in relation to the sort of knowledge at issue here. What of premise (1)?

The justification for (1) is evidently that rational inquiry requires: (i) a number of diverse views or perspectives (possessed by different persons and different interest groups) and; (ii) a substantial amount of diverse evidence for/against these views (available from different sources). Moreover, (iii) regarding (i) and (ii), there is no single (a) infallible and (b) reliable authority.

Note that Mill's argument for freedom of inquiry—understood as rational inquiry in a context of freedom of communication—is instrumentalist or means/end in its form. The claim is not that freedom of inquiry is good in itself, but rather that it is a means to another good, namely knowledge and, it should be added, the knowledge of interest to us here and, for that matter, to Mill is collective knowledge generated by joint epistemic action. The notion of collective knowledge in play here is (roughly speaking) that of knowledge shared among members of a population, be the population a polity, a global audience or, for that matter, an academic community (which is probably a segmented global community). (It is then an open question—as far as Mill's argument is concerned—whether or not knowledge is an intrinsic good, or merely a means to some other good. By contrast, I assume that knowledge is an intrinsic good.) To this extent, the moral weight to be attached to freedom of inquiry is weaker than it would be by the lights of an argument, which accorded freedom of inquiry the status of an intrinsic good or fundamental moral right.

The second argument for freedom of inquiry is not inconsistent with the first but is nevertheless quite different. Specifically, it accords freedom of inquiry greater moral weight by treating it as having the status of a fundamental moral right. This second argument—or at least my own neo-Kantian rendering of it—relies on a wider sense of freedom of intellectual inquiry, one embracing not only freedom of thought and reasoning but also freedom of communication and discussion. The argument begins with the premise that freedom of intellectual inquiry thus understood is a basic, as opposed to derived, moral right. Here the term 'intellectual' is intended to be taken in its original Latin-based sense of pertaining to understanding, as opposed to its modern rarefied sense of pertaining to those matters that can only be understood by experts or 'intellectuals'. Intellectual inquiry is a human practice that should not be the preserve only of academics and other experts. This is not to say that academics and others with specialist or more developed levels of understanding ought not to be accorded due respect as epistemic authorities. Climate scientists are a case in point.

Thus conceived, freedom of intellectual inquiry is not an individual right of the ordinary kind. Although it is a right which attaches to individuals, as opposed to groups per se, it is not a right which an individual could exercise by him/herself. Communication, discussion and intersubjective methods of testing are social, or at least interpersonal, activities. However, it is important to stress that they are not activities, which are necessarily relativized to certain designated social groups. In principle, intellectual interaction can and ought to be allowed to take place between individuals in interpersonal and communal, including on-line, settings irrespective of whether they belong to the same social, ethnic or political group. In short, freedom of intellectual inquiry, or at least its constituent elements, is a basic moral right. Note that being a basic moral right it can, at least in principle, override collective interests and goals, including national economic interests and goals. Hence, the dilemmas that can arise between, for instance, security and freedom of communication.

If freedom of intellectual inquiry is a basic moral right then, like other basic moral rights such as the right to life and to freedom of the person, it is a right that all humans possess and it is a right that should be protected in liberal democracies in particular. Here, we need to be clearer on the relationship between the basic moral right to freely engage in intellectual inquiry on the one hand, and knowledge or truth on the other.

The term 'knowledge', as used in this context, embraces not only information but also understanding. Note also that in order to come to have knowledge in this sense, one must possess rational capacities, i.e. capacities that enable not only the acquisition of certain kinds of information, e.g. via a Google search, but especially the development of understanding. Here the term 'rational' is broadly construed. It is not, for example, restricted to deductive and inductive reasoning. This point holds irrespective of whether the communicative context is offline or online, the coffeehouse or Twitter, and notwithstanding the advantages and disadvantages—and ultimate intellectual upsides and downsides (Lynch 2016b)—of some of these modes of communication over others, e.g. lengthy single speeches to a small audience versus brief tweets to thousands.

Freedom of intellectual inquiry and knowledge, in this extended sense of knowledge, are not simply related as means to end, but also conceptually. To freely inquire is to seek the truth by reasoning. Truth is not an external contingently connected end which some inquiries might be directed towards if the inquirer happened to have an interest in truth, rather than, say, an interest in falsity or (a la Derrida) playfulness. Rather, truth is internally connected to intellectual inquiry. An intellectual inquiry, which did not aim at the truth, would not be an intellectual inquiry, or at least would be defective qua intellectual inquiry. Moreover, here aiming at truth is aiming at truth as an end in itself. (This is not inconsistent with also aiming at truth as a means to some other end.) In other words, an alleged intellectual inquiry which only aimed at truth as a means to some other end would not be an intellectual inquiry or would be defective qua intellectual inquiry, since for such a pseudo-inquirer truth would not be internal to his/her activity. Such a pseudo-inquirer is prepared to abandon—and indeed would have in fact abandoned—truth-aiming if, for example, it turns out, or if it had turned out, that the means to his or her end was not after all truth, but rather falsity.

Furthermore, to engage in free intellectual inquiry in my extended sense involving communication with, and testing by, others, is to freely seek the truth by reasoning with others. Intellectual inquiry in this sense is not exclusively the activity of a solitary individual. Moreover, here reasoning is broadly construed to embrace highly abstract formal deductive reasoning at one end of the spectrum and informal (including literary) interpretation and speculation at the other. Furthermore, it embraces ordinary political discourse among non-specialists as well as technical discourse among experts, and discourse attempting to bridge these divides, e.g. between scientists and ordinary citizens on climate change.

There are, of course, methods of acquiring knowledge which do not necessarily, or even in fact, involve free inquiry, e.g. my knowledge that I have a toothache, or my knowledge that the object currently in the foreground of my visual field is a table, but these taken in themselves are relatively unimportant items of knowledge as far as public discourse is concerned, and certainly as far as epistemic institutions such as the press and universities are concerned. (Obviously, other items of knowledge of the same species can be very important in the context of some intellectual inquiry e.g. an inquiry into whether a recently developed drug eases pain or an inquiry into ordinary perception.)

Given that freedom of intellectual inquiry is a basic moral right, and given the above described relationship between intellectual inquiry and truth (or knowledge), we can now present our second argument in relation to freedom of intellectual inquiry (Miller 2000). This argument in effect seeks to recast the notion of freedom of intellectual inquiry in order to bring out the potential significance for liberal democratic polities, in particular, of the Kantian claim that freedom of intellectual inquiry is a basic moral right.

(1) Freedom of intellectual inquiry is a basic moral right.
(2) Freedom of intellectual inquiry is (principally) freedom to seek the truth by reasoning with others.
(3) Freedom to seek the truth by reasoning with others is a basic moral right.

Our discussion has yielded the following plausible propositions. First, the kind of knowledge in question is typically attained by reasoning with others (whether conducted offline or on-line, whether in the coffee house or via Twitter etc.). Second, to engage in free intellectual inquiry is to seek truth (or knowledge) for its own sake. Third, freely seeking the truth (or knowledge) for its own sake, and by reasoning with others, is a basic moral right.

Let us grant the existence of a basic moral right to freely pursue the truth by reasoning with others. The political implications of this are threefold. Firstly, liberal democracies, in particular, need to ensure that this moral right of members of the citizenry is respected, indeed cultivated. As Mill stressed, the ability to exercise this right, and the habit of exercising it, are preconditions of liberal democracy. Secondly, liberal democracies need to ensure that this right is institutionally embedded in epistemic institutions in particular. For instance, the exercise of the moral right to freely pursue the truth by reasoning with others is a central feature of universities (Miller 2010). Naturally, the truths in question are sometimes ones difficult to acquire without intellectual training of various kinds, e.g. empirical methods. Again, the moral right to pursue the truth by reasoning with others is a central feature of media organisations functioning as the so-called Fourth Estate (Miller 2010) or, at the least, ought to be a central feature of these organisations even if it is often not (Gore 2007). Naturally, the truths in question pertain to matters of public interest and are often subject to political contestation. Thirdly, liberal democracies need to ensure that public discourse, including in cyberspace, is conducted in accordance with the conventions in part constitutive of the exercise of the moral right to freely pursue the truth by reasoning with others, e.g. the convention to aim at the truth, conventions governing evidence collection and analysis. Here, there is a need for qualifications when the communication in question is understood to be of an informal or casual kind, e.g. between Facebook friends, or when the communicators are, say, children. I note that fake news, hate speech and propaganda flout these conventions—although they are parasitic on them (see below)—and are antithetical to the proper exercise of the right itself (the right to freely pursue the truth with others) . Accordingly, the question that now arises is how political propaganda (including politically motivated fake news and hate speech) is to be countered.

## 11.4 Epistemic Institutions, Market-Based Social Media Platforms and Combating Propaganda

Effectively countering political propaganda—including political propaganda impregnated with fake news and hate speech—is a complex undertaking. For one thing, as noted above, determining what is propaganda and what is not is problematic, especially given that, as shown above, non-ideological content often only implies or is permeated by ideology. For another thing, it is inconsistent with the liberal democratic value of freedom of communication to prohibit all propaganda, all fake news or even all hate speech. Moreover, as is to be expected, different liberal democracies take a different view on where to draw the line here. The US does not prohibit hate speech (unless it directly incites serious crimes such as violence) whereas many EU jurisdictions do (Waldron 2012). This is, of course, not to say that propaganda might not be curtailed (with necessarily being prohibited), as is the case with advertising. Cigarette advertising, for instance, is curtailed without being prohibited in many jurisdictions, e.g. no cigarette ads on TV or on sites accessed by children.

However, even if the legal issues could be contended with (on the basis, in part, of cogent ethical analysis) and agreed to nationally, and perhaps globally —since international regulations might be required for certain platforms and content—there remains the enforcement problem. Consider extremist jihadist propaganda that incites violence and, as such, is prohibited. According to J. M. Berger, for instance, extremist jihadist propaganda has three dimensions: content; dissemination methods; identity (Berger 2017). Accordingly, in the case of extremist jihadist propaganda, social media sites can be quickly taken down, undermining that particular dissemination method. On the other hand, terrorist attacks themselves continue to be widely reported in the local and global media, thereby giving oxygen to terrorists. Moreover, there are more sophisticated and, potentially, more effective methods of dissemination of propaganda. For example, the targeting of 'vulnerable' groups by state actors such as Russia. As mentioned above, these can make use of large data banks and machine learning techniques to build profiles and target the vulnerable. Such methods are not so easy to counter, although providing adequate protection of personal information held by social media companies, such as Facebook, would be a good start.

Directly countering content with counter-messaging, e.g. counter-messaging espousing liberal democratic values, may have a limited effect on those susceptible to propaganda, whether fundamentalist Muslims or those with extreme right views. After all, it is these groups' felt alienation from liberal democracy that is in part the source of the problem. Successful propaganda, as was suggested above, is always anchored in part in reality (but is also vulnerable to the communication of reality, i.e. facts inconsistent with its content—inconvenient truths" [Gore 2007]). Accordingly, there is likely to be a need to address felt grievances, at least to the extent that they are justified, e.g. if in part based on economic injustice. Naturally, propaganda can be countered by counter-propaganda, disinformation campaigns and the like, as frequently happens in war-time, for instance. However, there is something inherently morally problematic in liberal democracies eschewing a commitment to truth (notably facts), evidence-based rational inquiry and open discussion, in favour of propaganda, i.e. fake news, half-truths, manipulation, hate speech(?) etc. Moreover, this strategy might ultimately be counter-productive and simply end up devaluing the liberal democratic currency.

What of identity? Certainly an appeal to national, religious, ethnic, racial, class or other identity and an attempt to drive a wedge between 'them' and 'us' is an important feature of political propaganda. The propaganda in question might or might be unlawful, depending on the nature of it and the jurisdiction in which it is disseminated. Given legal limitations or enforcement problems what is the way forward here? Naturally, if a polity has processes and pursues policies that are just (both procedurally and substantively), inclusive (e.g. of marginalised groups) and effective (i.e. have beneficial outcomes) then this will mitigate the harms of identity focused propaganda. However, as is the case with other strategies, this strategy while necessary is not sufficient. It is not a silver bullet. Moreover, when the identities in question are national identities and the 'us-them' wedge is being driven by their own governments, e.g. the Russian government in the Baltic states, the Chinese government in respect of foreign states who oppose its policies in the South China Sea, or the United States under the Trump administration's 'America First' policy, then this strategy is unlikely to succeed even if it can be implemented to some extent.

In the context of the legal limitations and/or enforcement problems confronting the enterprise of countering political propaganda (including politically motivated fake news and hate speech), and assuming that counter-propaganda, disinformation and the like are not a morally acceptable option, I want to suggest a different strategy; a strategy which should be seen as complementary to the other strategies already mentioned. In doing so, I draw attention to three somewhat neglected, related, underlying conditions that facilitate political propaganda, namely: (1) the strength of epistemic norms in a population targeted by propaganda; (2) the intellectual health of the epistemic institutions in that population, and; (3) their degree of embeddedness in, and influence on, the population that hosts them.

I note at the outset the importance of maintaining not only the distinction insisted upon above between propaganda and knowledge acquisition/dissemination (typically a species of joint epistemic action), but also between knowledge acquisition/dissemination and entertainment, e.g. soap operas, cartoons. The latter does not generally purport to be true. However, the emergence in recent decades of infotainment, including in cyberspace, is corrosive of this distinction; a point I cannot pursue further here. While insisting on the distinction between propaganda and knowledge acquisition/dissemination, it is also important to draw attention to a central aspect of their relationship; propaganda is parasitic on knowledge acquisition/dissemination and the epistemic norms that underpin it. Fake news, for instance, purports to be true; otherwise, it would have little effect. However, while pretending to comply with the epistemic norm of aiming at the truth, it flouts it; it is not required by its originator to be true and, indeed, its originator often knows it is false—it is a lie.

As with many parasites, propaganda undermines the health of its host while simultaneously relying on the continued existence of its host. Accordingly, propaganda is a species of corruption: institutional corruption (Miller 2017). If successful, propaganda corrupts epistemic norms within a population and may also corrupt epistemic institutions, notably media organisations responsible for news/comment which lack independence from an authoritarian government or which are subject to powerful and pervasive financial pressures tending to cause them to espouse, for instance, a virulent form of capitalist ideology. On the other hand, propaganda, being parasitic on epistemic norms, is susceptible to criticism for failing to live up to the epistemic and, importantly, moral standards it purports to be complying with. It purports to be true and hence is discredited when shown to be false. Propagandists fail to meet moral standards not simply because they fail to comply with epistemic standards by being incorrect or insufficiently attentive to the evidence, but because they are dishonest; they pretend to be aiming at the truth while actually telling lies. Accordingly, propagandists can be criticised not only for being incorrect, but also for being dishonest; indeed, for being corrupt. The charge of corruption is more likely to generate moral disapproval and, ultimately, rejection among members of a population than are purely epistemic offences.

In a liberal democratic polity, epistemic institutions, notably the free and independent press, and schools and universities, have a key role in combating propaganda, or so I suggest. Epistemic institutions, such as schools and universities, have a key role in building resilience to propaganda, whether it be on-line or off-line propaganda, by cultivating the skills and habits of rational inquiry and, relatedly, the development of well-informed, rationally defensible, political perspectives among children and adults. Moreover, epistemic institutions, such as a free and independent press and universities, have a key role in not only ensuring that the citizenry is reflective and well informed, but also in helping to ensure that public discourse, whether on-line or off-line, is conducted in accordance with the epistemic norms constitutive of free and open rational inquiry; consistent with the proper exercise of the right to freely pursue the truth by reasoning with others. For instance, experienced investigative journalists based in well-resourced newspapers, such as the *New York Times*, are the source of much of the important news to enable informed opinions on the part of voters. Moreover, those responsible for politically motivated fake news, hate speech and, more generally, propaganda can be held to account by a free and independent press. Consider, in this connection the *British Broadcasting Commission* (BBC). The BBC is both independent of government and, as a public broadcaster, independent of private sector companies. Moreover, its news division is a well-resourced, epistemically sound, genuinely public communicator, as opposed to an epistemically suspect or narrowcast communicator—or platform facilitating the dissemination of epistemically suspect, narrowcast content. It is a genuinely public communicator by virtue of having a UK national and a global audience composed in part of most of the key national and international opinion makers and most of the other influential public communicators. As such, it is well-positioned to hold governments and powerful private sector actors alike to account.

Here I note that the widely held view that the advent of the Internet and of social media platforms, such as Facebook, Google, Twitter and the like, has rendered traditional epistemic institutions, such as a free and independent press, redundant has proven to be incorrect. Contrary to this view, the advent of global social media platforms, such as Facebook, Twitter and YouTube has led, as mentioned above, to an exponential increase in the spread of fake news, hate speech and propaganda and, as a consequence has undermined the practice of rational inquiry and the existence of well-informed political perspectives among the citizenry, and done so in part by undermining epistemic norms and in part by undermining the strength and influence of epistemic institutions e.g. by enabling the dissemination of propaganda, fake news and hate speech on a vast scale. Moreover, these giant tech companies have failed to adequately self-regulate in a manner that ensures that the content on their platforms complies with epistemic norms. Indeed, the tech giants often disavow responsibility for these untoward developments by arguing that they are merely platforms and not publishers of the noxious content in question. More generally, the commercial interests of the tech giants tend in practice to override their stated commitments to the public good and, in particular, to upholding epistemic norms in respect of the content their platforms support.

There are at least four salient features of the developments just described. First, the social media platforms are in fact platforms rather than publishers. They provide communication infrastructure and, in this respect, they are akin to telephone companies. An important consequence of this is that they can escape legal liability for illegal content supported by their platforms. Second, there is the extraordinary communicative reach of the technology. Third, there is the global institutional character of the tech companies. Fourth, there is the embeddedness of these technology platforms that ought to serve the collective good in market-based institutions whose business model is to provide 'free' access in return for the provision of private data that can be exploited commercially.

What is called for at this point is a strategy for the institutional redesign of the giant tech companies. Here there are a number of guiding principles. These principles should be understood against a background assumption that the tech companies and the technology they use have provided enormous communicative and epistemic benefits and these should not be sacrificed; the baby should not be thrown out with the bathwater. In so far as the giant tech companies are to remain market-based companies, they need to respect the principles of free and fair competition; accordingly, they might need to be downsized to achieve this, although the presence of Chinese-based tech giants, such as Tencent and Baidu, complicates matters here. In so far as they are infrastructure providers of platforms then each must be redesigned to ensure that it provides the required public good; commercial considerations cannot be allowed to trump its provision of the public good, as is allowable in the case of an ordinary commercial enterprise considered on its own (as opposed to as one actor in a market-based industry (Miller 2010)). This may require them to be transformed into public utilities. Thirdly, regulation of content to ensure compliance with epistemic norms is a task that cannot be left to the tech giants themselves or, at least, cannot be left to them in the absence of legal liability in the circumstance that they fail adequately to ensure this compliance, i.e. in the absence of their having the legal status of publishers. Arguably, this task needs to be performed by an external, independent institution, albeit it is a task that should be paid for by the tech companies themselves and/or their advertisers or others who use their platforms. Here it is important to distinguish between holding someone and/or some organisation legally liable for publishing illegal content—and, in the absence of a publisher other than the tech giants providing the platforms, this might need to be the tech giants themselves—and ensuring the compliance of communicative content with epistemic norms by means of, for instance, an editorial process. The latter process of epistemic quality assurance includes more than ensuring that legal requirements are met. A final point concerns the business model that involves the provision of a service in return for handing over one's private information. Recent EU regulation (General Data Protection Regulation) has been enacted, among other reasons, to ensure informed consent on the part of those who might be asked to provide private information in return for a service. Such legislation might ultimately undermine this business model.

## 11.5 Conclusion

In this article, I provided definitions of fake news, hate speech and propaganda, respectively. These phenomena are corruptive of epistemic norms. I also elaborated on the right to freedom of communication and its relation both to censoring propaganda and to the role of epistemic institutions. Finally, I discussed the general problem of countering political propaganda in cyberspace and argued, firstly, that there was an important role for epistemic institutions in this regard and, secondly, that social media platforms needed to be redesigned since, as they stand and notwithstanding the benefits that they provide, they are a large part of the problem.

## References

Berger JM (2017) Defeating is propaganda. sounds good, but what does it really mean? International Centre for Counter-Terrorism – The Hague. https://icct.nl/publication/defeating-is-ideology-sounds-good-but-what-does-it-really-mean/. Last access 7 July 2019
Bok S (1978) Lying: moral choice in public and private life. Pantheon Books, New York
Cocking D, van den Hoven J (2018) Evil on-line, Wiley-Blackwell, Hoboken
Ellul J (1973) Propaganda: the formation of men's attitudes (trans: Kellen K, Lerner J). Random House/Vintage, New York
Gore A (2007) The assault on reason. Penguin, New York
Grassegger VH, Krogerus M (3 Dec 2016) Ich habe nur gezeigt, dass es die Bombe gibt. Das Magazin. https://www.dasmagazin.ch/2016/12/03/ich-habe-nur-gezeigt-dass-es-die-bombe-gibt/. Last access 7 July 2019
Ingram HJ (2016) A brief history of propaganda during conflict. International Centre for Counter-Terrorism – The Hague. https://icct.nl/publication/a-brief-history-of-propaganda-during-conflict-a-lesson-for-counter-terrorism-strategic-communications/. Last access 7 July 2019
Kant I (1956) Groundwork of the metaphysics of morals (trans: Paton HJ). Harper Collins
Lynch M (2016a) Fake news and the internet shell game. New York Times. https://www.nytimes.com/2016/11/28/opinion/fake-news-and-the-internet-shell-game.html. Last access 7 July 2019
Lynch M (2016b) The internet of us. Liveright, New York
Mill JS (1869) On liberty. Longman, Roberts and Green, London
Miller S (2000) Academic autonomy. In: Coady T (ed) Why universities matter. Allen and Unwin, St Leonards
Miller S (2010) The moral foundations of social institutions. Cambridge University Press, Cambridge
Miller S (2017) Institutional corruption. Cambridge University Press, Cambridge
Miller S (2018) Joint epistemic action: some applications. J App Philos 35(2):300–318
Schauer F (1981) Free speech: a philosophical inquiry. Cambridge University Press, Cambridge
Waldron J (2012) The harm in hate speech. Harvard University Press, Cambridge, MA

# Chapter 12
# Cybersecurity and Cyber Warfare: The Ethical Paradox of 'Universal Diffidence'

**George Lucas**

**Abstract** In lieu of the present range of rival and only partial ethical accounts, this essay proposes an underlying interpretive framework for the cyber domain as a Hobbsean state of nature, with its current status of unrestricted conflict constituting a 'war of all against all'. The fundamental ethical dilemma in Hobbes's original account of this "original situation" was how to bring about the morally required transition to a more stable political arrangement, comprising a rule of law under which the interests of the various inhabitants in life, property and security would be more readily guaranteed. Hobbes described opposition to this morally requisite transition as arising from 'universal diffidence', the mutual mistrust between individuals, coupled with the misguided belief of each in his or her own superiority. His is thus a perfect moral framework from which to analyse agents in the cyber domain, where individual arrogance often seems to surpass any aspirations for moral excellence. With this framework in place, it is briefly noted that the chief moral questions pertain to whether we may already discern a gradual voluntary recognition and acceptance of general norms of responsible individual and state behaviour within the cyber domain, arising from experience and consequent enlightened self-interest (As, for example, in the account of emergent norms found in Lucas (The ethics of cyber warfare. Oxford University Press, New York, 2017)), or whether the interests of the responsible majority must eventually compel some sort of transition from the state of nature by forcibly overriding the wishes of presumably irresponsible or malevolent outliers in the interests of the general welfare (the moral paradox of universal diffidence).

**Keywords** Cyber conflict · Cyber vandalism · Cyber warfare · State-sponsored hacktivism · Stuxnet

---

G. Lucas (✉)
U.S. Naval Academy & Naval Postgraduate School, Annapolis, MD, USA



M. Christen et al. (eds.), *The Ethics of Cybersecurity*, The International Library of Ethics, Law and Technology 21,
https://doi.org/10.1007/978-3-030-29053-5_12

## 12.1 Introduction

> ….in the nature of man, we find three principall causes of quarrel. First, Competition; Secondly, **Diffidence**; Thirdly, Glory. …Nature hath made men so equall, in the faculties of body and mind; as that though there bee found one man sometimes manifestly stronger in body, or of quicker mind then another; yet when all is reckoned together, the difference between man, and man, is not so considerable, as that one man can thereupon claim to himself any benefit, to which another may not pretend, as well as he. … For such is the nature of men, that howsoever they may acknowledge many others to be more witty, or more eloquent, or more learned; Yet they will hardly believe there be many so wise as themselves:….from this diffidence of one another, there is no way for any man to secure himself… till he see no other power great enough to endanger him…. (Thomas Hobbes (1651/1968, 183–185))

In this essay, I set out a case that our cybersecurity community is its own worst enemy, and that our security dilemmas, including serious moral dilemmas, have arisen mostly because of our flawed assumptions and methodology (modus operandi). These include what Hobbes (1651/1968) termed "universal diffidence"—a devastating flaw shared by many individuals in the "state of nature" (which the cyber domain certainly is)—combined with a smug antipathy towards ethics and moral reasoning as irrelevant or unimportant dimensions of cybersecurity.

The cybersecurity communities of democratic and rights-respecting regimes encompass some of the most intelligent, capable and dedicated public servants one could imagine. However, our community is also rife with jealousy, competitiveness, insularity, arrogance and a profound inability to listen and learn from one another, as well as from the experiences of mistaken past assumptions. I wish to outline the specific impact of all of these tendencies on self-defence, pre-emptive defence, attribution and retaliation in inter-state cyber conflict, alongside vulnerabilities introduced in the Internet of Things (IoT) (arising especially from the inability to foster robust cooperation between the public/governmental and private spheres, and from the absence of any coordinated government or intergovernmental plan to foster such cooperation, leading to increasing reliance on civil society and the private sector to take up the security slack) (Washington Post 2018).

My discussion briefly ranges across vandalism, crime, legitimate political activism, vigilantism and the rise to dominance of state-sponsored hacktivism. I briefly examine cases of vulnerabilities unknowingly and carelessly introduced via the IoT, the reluctance of private entities to disclose potential 'zero-day' defects to government security organisations; financial and 'smart' contractual 'blockchain' arrangements (including bitcoin and Ethereum, and the challenges these pose to state-regulated financial systems); and issues such as privacy, confidentiality and identity theft. The goal is to enable a productive and constructive dialogue among both contributors and readers of this volume on this range of important security and ethics topics. I begin by commenting on the discipline and concerns of ethics itself and its reception within the cybersecurity community, including my earlier treatment of ethics in the context of cyber warfare.

## 12.2 Ethics and Individuals in the Cyber Domain

At first blush, nothing could seem less promising than attempting to discuss ethics in cyber warfare. Even apart from the moral conundrums of outright warfare, the cyber domain in general is often described as a 'lawless frontier' or a 'state of nature' (in Hobbes's sense), in which everyone seems capable in principle of doing whatever they wish to whomever they please without fear of attribution, retribution or accountability. When it comes to human behaviour and the treatment of one another, human behaviour within the cyber domain might aptly be characterised, as above, as a 'war of all against all'.

Upon further reflection, however, that grim generalisation is no more or less true than Hobbes's own original characterisation of human beings themselves in a state of nature. The vast majority of actors in the cyber domain are relatively benign: they mind their own business, pursue their own ends, do not engage in deliberate mischief, let alone harm, do not wish their fellow citizens ill, and generally seek only to pursue the myriad benefits afforded by the cyber realm: access to information, goods and services, convenient financial transactions and data processing, and control over their array of devices, from cell phones, door locks, refrigerators and toasters to voice assistants such as Alexa and Echo, and even swimming pools.

Beyond this, there are some 'natural virtues' and commonly shared definitions of the Good in the cyber domain: anonymity, freedom and choice, for example, and a notable absence of external constraints, restrictions and regulations. These are things that cyber activists, in particular, like to champion, and seem determined to preserve against any encroachments upon them in the name of the 'rule of law'. In essence, we might characterise the cyber domain as being colonised by libertarians and anarchists who, if they had their way, would continue to dwell in peace and pursue their private and collective interests without interference.

Like all relatively ungoverned frontiers, however, this Rousseauvian bliss is shattered by the malevolent behaviour of even a few 'bad actors'—and there are more than a few of these in the cyber domain. As portrayed in the forthcoming book by Australian cybersecurity experts Seumas Miller and Terry Bossomaier (2019), the principal form of malevolent cyber activity is criminal in nature: theft, extortion, blackmail, vandalism, slander and disinformation (in the form of trolling and cyber bullying), and even prospects for homicide (see also Chap. 11). The widespread chaos and disruption of general welfare wrought by such actors in conventional frontier settings (as in nineteenth century North America and Australia, for example) led to the imposition of various forms of 'law and order'. These ranged from the formation of a posse of ordinary citizens armed with legal authority, engaging in periodic retaliation against criminals, to the election of a Sheriff (or the appointing by government officials of a Marshal) to enforce the law and imprison law-breakers. The eventual outcome of such procedures and interim institutions ultimately led to the more familiar and stable institutions and organisations such as police, courts and prisons to effect punishment, protect the general population from wrong-doers and generally to deter crime.

The control of such malevolent actors and the provision of security against their actions is not primarily a matter of ethics or moral argument (although important moral issues, such as interrogation, torture and capital punishment, do arise in the pursuit of law enforcement). Rather, as Aristotle first observed, for those lacking so much as a tincture of virtue, there is the law. Law, on Aristotle's account, defines the minimum standard of acceptable social behaviour, while ethics deals with aspirations, ideals and excellences that require a lifetime to master. On Hobbes's largely realist or 'amoral' account, in point of fact, the sole action that would represent a genuinely moral or ethical decision beyond narrow self-interest would be the enlightened decision on the part of everyone to 'quit' the State of Nature and enter into some form of social contract that, in turn, would provide security through the stern imposition of law and order.

However law and order, let alone legal institutions such as the police, judges and courts, are precisely what the rank and file individual actors and non-state organisations (such as 'Anonymous') in the cyber domain wish to avoid. This is a very stubborn illustration of widespread 'diffidence' on the part of cyber denizens. I look forward to seeing how Miller and Bossomaier (2019) address this dilemma.

## 12.3 Ethics and Inter-State Relations in the Cyber Domain

When we turn to international relations (IR), we confront the prospect of cyber warfare. The malevolent actors are primarily rogue nations, terrorists and non-state actors (alongside organised crime). The reigning theory of conflict in IR generally is Rousseau's metaphorical extension of Hobbes from individuals to states: the theory of international anarchy or 'political realism'. There is one significant difference. Although the 'state of nature' for individuals in Hobbes's account is usually understood as a hypothetical thought experiment (rather than an attempt at a genuine historical or evolutionary account), in the case of IR, by contrast, that condition of ceaseless conflict and strife among nations (as Rousseau first observed) is precisely what is actual and ongoing.

Conflict between international entities on this account naturally arises as a result of an inevitable competition and collision of interests among discrete states, with no corresponding permanent institutional arrangements available to resolve the conflict beyond the individual competing nations and their relative power to resist one another's encroachments. In addition, borrowing from Hobbes's account of the amoral state of nature among hypothetical individuals prior to the establishment of a firm rule of law, virtually all political theorists and IR experts assume this condition of conflict among nations to be immune to morality in the customary sense of deliberation and action guided by moral virtues, an overriding sense of duty or obligation, recognition and respect for basic human rights, or efforts to foster the common good.

However we characterise conventional state relationships, the current status of relations and conflicts among nations and individuals within the cyber domain perfectly fits this model: a lawless frontier, devoid (we might think) of impulses towards virtue or concerns for the wider common good. It is a 'commons' in which the advantage seems to accrue to whomever is willing to do anything they wish to anyone they please whenever they like, without fear of accountability or retribution. This seems, more than conventional domains of political rivalry, to constitute a genuine war of all against all, as we remarked above, and yet this was the arena I chose to tackle (or perhaps more appropriately, the windmill at which I decided to tilt) in *Ethics & Cyber Warfare* (Lucas 2017). As Miller and Bossomaier note in their discussion of that work, I made no pretence of taking on the broader issues of crime, vandalism or general cybersecurity. The book itself was actually completed in September 2015. I predicted then, as Miller and Brossomaier do now, that much would change during the interim from completion to publication. That was certainly true from the fall of 2015 to the fall of 2018. The realm of cyber conflict and cyber warfare appears to most observers to be much different now than portrayed even a scant 2 or 3 years ago.

In the summer of 2015, while wrapping up that project, I noted some curious and quite puzzling trends that ran sharply counter to expectations. Experts and pundits had long predicted the escalation of 'effects-based' cyber warfare and the proliferation of cyber weapons such as the Stuxnet virus. The major fear was the enhanced ability of rogue states and terrorists to destroy dams, disrupt national power grids, and interfere with transportation and commerce in a manner that would, in their devastation, destruction and loss of human life, rival conventional full-scale armed conflict (see also Chap. 18). Those predictions preceded the discovery of Stuxnet, but that discovery (despite apparent U.S. and Israeli involvement in the development of that particular weapon as part of 'Operation Olympic Games') was taken as a harbinger of things to come: a future cyber 'Pearl Harbor' or cyber Armageddon.

However, by and large, this is *not* the direction that international cyber conflict has followed (see also Chap. 13) Instead of individuals and non-state actors becoming progressively like nation-states, I noticed that states were increasingly behaving like individuals and non-state groups in the cyber domain: engaging in identity theft, extortion, disinformation, election tampering and other cyber tactics that turned out to be easier and cheaper to develop and deploy, while proving less easy to attribute or deter (let alone retaliate against). Most notably, such tactics proved themselves capable of achieving nearly as much if not more political 'bang for the buck' than effects-based cyber weapons (which, like Stuxnet itself, were large, complex, expensive, time-consuming and all but beyond the capabilities of most nations).

In an article published in 2015 (Lucas 2015), I labelled these curious disruptive military tactics 'state-sponsored hacktivism' (SSH) and predicted at the time that SSH was rapidly becoming the preferred form of cyber warfare. We should consider it a legitimate new form of warfare, I argued, based upon its political motives and effects. It fit Karl von Clausewitz's definition of warfare as politics pursued by other means. We were thus confronted with not one but *two* legitimate forms of cyber warfare: one waged conventionally by large, resource- and technology-rich nations seeking to emulate kinetic effects-based weaponry; the second pursued by clever, unscrupulous but somewhat less well-resourced rogue states designed to achieve the overall equivalent political effects of conventional conflict. I did not maintain that this was perfectly valid, pleading only (with no idea what lay around the corner) that we simply consider it, and in so doing accept that we might be mistaken in our prevailing assumptions about the form(s) that cyber conflict waged by the militaries of other nations might eventually take. We might simply be looking in the wrong direction or over the wrong shoulder.

Then the Russians attempted to hack the 2016 U.S. presidential election. The North Koreans downloaded the 'Wannacry' software—stolen from the U.S. National Security Agency—from the 'dark web' and used it to attack civilian infrastructure (banks and hospitals) in European nations who had supported the U.S. boycotts launched against their nuclear weapons programme. Really! How stupid were we victims capable of being? SSH had become the devastating 'weapon of choice' among rogue nations, while we had been guilty of clinging to our blind political and tactical prejudices in the face of overwhelming contradictory evidence. We had been taken in; flat-footed; utterly by surprise.

At the same time, readers and critics had been mystified by my earlier warnings regarding SSH. No one, it seems, knew what I was talking about. My editor at Oxford even refused me permission to use my original subtitle for the book: *Ethics & The Rise of State-Sponsored Hacktivism.* This analysis had instead to be buried in the book chapters. I managed, after a fashion, to get even! When the book was finally published in the immediate aftermath of the American presidential election in January of 2017, I jokingly offered thanks to my (unintentional) "publicity and marketing team": Vladimir Putin, restaurateur Yevgeny Prigozhin, the FSB, PLA Shanghai Unit 61384 (who had stolen my personnel files a few years earlier, along with those of 22 million other U.S. government employees), and the North Korean cyber warriors, who had by then scored some significant triumphs at our expense. State-sponsored hacktivism had indeed, by that time, become the norm.

Where, then, is the ethics discussion in all this? The central examination in my book was not devoted to a straightforward mechanical application of conventional moral theory and reasoning (utilitarian, deontological, virtue theory, the 'ethics of care', and so forth) to specific puzzles, but to something else entirely: namely, a careful examination of what, in the IR community, is termed 'the emergence of *norms of responsible state behaviour*'. This, I argued, was vastly more fundamental than conventional analytic ethics. Such accounts are not principally about deontology, utility and the ethical conundrum of colliding trolley cars. They consist instead of a kind of historical moral inquiry that lies at the heart of moral philosophy itself, from Aristotle, Hobbes, Rousseau and Kant to Rawls, Habermas —and the book's principal intellectual guide, the Aristotelian philosopher, Alasdair MacIntyre.

The great puzzle for philosophers is, of course, *how* norms can be meaningfully said to '*emerge*?' Not just where do they come from or how do they catch on but *how can such a historical process be valid* given the difference between normative and descriptive guidance and discourse? The entire discussion of norms in IR seems to philosophers to constitute a massive exercise in what is known as the 'naturalistic fallacy'. In its original formulation by the Scottish Enlightenment philosopher

David Hume, the fallacy challenges any straightforward attempt to derive duties or obligations straightforwardly from descriptive or explanatory accounts—in Hume's phraseology, one cannot (that is to say) derive an 'ought' straightforwardly from an 'is'.

This is precisely what the longstanding discussion of emergent norms in IR does: it claims to discern action-guiding principles or putative obligations for individual and state behaviour merely from the prior record of experiences of individuals and states. This central conception of IR regarding what states themselves do, or tolerate being done, is thus a massive fallacy. That is to say, states may in fact be found to behave in a variety of discernible ways, or likewise, may in fact be found to tolerate other states behaving in these ways. Certain such behaviours—such as, famously, the longstanding practice of granting immunity from punishment or harm to a foreign nation's ambassadors—may indeed come to be regarded as 'customary'. However, that set of facts alone tells us nothing about what states *ought* to do, or to tolerate. We might claim to be *surprised* if a nation suddenly turns on an adversary state's ambassadors by killing or imprisoning them. However, there are no grounds in the expectations born of past experience alone for also expressing *moral outrage* over this departure from customary state practice. Yet, these kinds of incidents (departure from custom) occur all the time, and the offending state usually stands accused of violating an 'international norm of responsible state behaviour'. Perhaps they have, but there is nothing in the customary practice itself that provides grounds for justifying it as a norm—not, at least on Hume's objection, unless there is something further in the way of evidence or argument to explain how the custom comes to enjoy this *normative* status.

Perhaps my willingness to take on this age-old question and place it at the heart of contemporary discussions of cyber conflict is why so few have bothered to read the book! Who (we might well ask) cares about all that abstract, theoretical stuff? It seems more urgent (or at least, less complicated and more interesting) either to discuss all the latest 'buzz' concerning zero-day software vulnerabilities in the IoT, or else to offer moral analysis of specific cases in terms of utility, duty, virtue and those infamous colliding trolley cars—merely substituting, perhaps, driverless, robotic cars for the trolleys (and then wondering, "should the autonomous vehicle permit the death of its own passenger when manoeuvring to save the lives of five pedestrians", and so forth).

In any event, in order to make sense of this foundational theory of emergent norms in IR, I found it necessary to discuss the foundations of just war theory and the morality of exceptions or exceptionalism (i.e. how do we justify sometimes having to do things we are normally prohibited from doing?), as well as the IR approach to 'emergent norms' itself, as in fact, dating back to Aristotle, and his discussion of the cultivation of moral norms and guiding principles within a community of practice, *characterised by a shared notion of the good* (what we might now call a shared sense of purpose or objectives). Kant, Rawls and Habermas were invoked to explain how, in turn, a community of common practice governed solely by individual self-interest may nevertheless evolve into one characterised by the very kinds of recognition of common moral values that Hobbes had also implicitly invoked to explain the transition from a "nasty, brutish" state of nature to a well-ordered commonwealth.

I believe that these historical conceptions of moral philosophy are important to recover and clarify, since they ultimately offer an account of *precisely the kind of thing we are trying to discern now within the cyber domain.* That is, the transition (or rather, the prospect for making one) from a present state of reckless, lawless, selfish and ultimately destructive behaviours towards a more stable equilibrium of individual and state behaviour within the cyber domain that contributes to the common good, and to the emergence of a shared sense of purpose. Kant called this evolutionary learning process 'the Cunning of Nature', while the decidedly Aristotelian philosopher Hegel borrowed and tweaked Kant's original conception under the title, 'the Cunning of History'. Their argument is very similar to that of Adam Smith and the 'invisible hand': namely, that a community of individuals merely pursuing their individual private interests may come nevertheless, and entirely without their own knowledge or intention, to engage in behaviours that contribute to the common good, or to a shared sense of purpose.[1]

Finally, in applying a similar historical, experiential methodology to the recent history of cyber conflict from Estonia (2007) to the present, I proceeded to illustrate and summarise a number of norms of responsible cyber behaviour that, indeed, seem to have emerged, and caught on—and others that seem reasonably likely to do so, given a bit more time and experience. Even the turn away from catastrophic destruction by means of kinetic, 'effects-based' cyber warfare (of the catastrophic kind so shrilly predicted by Richard Clarke and others) and instead towards SSH as the preferred mode of carrying out international conflict in cyber space, likewise showed the emergence of these norms of reasonable restraint. Such norms do far less genuine harm, while achieving similar political effects—not because the adversaries are 'nice', but because they are clever (somewhat like Kant's 'race of devils', who famously stand at the threshold of genuine morality).

This last development in the case of cyber war is, for example, the intuitive, unconscious application by these clever 'devils' of a kind of proportionality criterion, something we term in military ethics the 'economy of force', in which a mischievous cyber-attack is to be preferred to a more destructive alternative, when available—again, not because anyone is trying to 'play nice', but because such an attack is more likely to succeed and attain its political aims without provoking a harsh response. However, such attacks, contrary to Estonia (we then proceed to reason) really should be pursued only in support of a legitimate cause, and not directed against non-military targets (I am not happy about the PLA stealing my personnel files, for example, but I am—or was, after all—a federal employee, not a private citizen—and in any case, those files may be more secure in the hands of the PLA than they were in the hands of the U.S. Office of Personnel Management). And thus is the evolutionary emergence of moral norms, Kant's 'cunning of nature' (or

[1] It bears mention that MacIntyre himself explicitly repudiated my account of this process, even when applied to modern communities of shared practices, such as professional societies. I detail his objections and our discussions in the book itself.

Hegel's 'cunning of history') at last underway. Even a race of devils can be brought to simulate the outward conditions and constraints of law and morality—if only they are 'reasonable' devils. (I apologise if I find the untutored intuitions and moral advances of those 'reasonable' and clever devils more morally praiseworthy than the obtuse incompetence of my learned colleagues in both moral philosophy and cybersecurity, who should already know these things!)

## 12.4 Privacy, Vulnerability and the 'Internet of Things'

Oddly, and despite all the hysteria surrounding the recent Russian interference in the electoral affairs of western democracies, this makes cyber warfare among and between nations, at least, look a lot more hopeful and positive from the moral perspective than the broader 'law and order' problem in the cyber domain generally. Reasonably responsible state actors and agents with discernable, justifiable goals, finally, act with greater restraint (at least from prudence, if not morality), than do genuinely malevolent private, criminal actors and agents (some of whom apparently just want to see the world burn). Here, what might be seen as the moral flaw or failing of 'universal diffidence' is the reckless, thoughtless manner in which we enable such agents and render ourselves vulnerable to them through careless, unnecessary and irresponsible innovations within the IoT.

What I mean is this: technically, almost any mechanical or electrical device can be connected to the Internet: refrigerators, toasters, voice assistants like Alexa and Echo, 'smart' TVs and DVRs, dolls, 'cloud puppets' and other toys, baby monitors, swimming pools, automobiles and closed-circuit cameras in the otherwise-secure corporate board rooms—*but should they be? Do they really need to be?* Moreover, does the convenience or novelty thereby attained justify the enhanced security risks those connections pose, especially as the number of such nodes on the IoT will soon vastly exceed the number of human-operated computers, tablets and cell phones? This appears to be a form of incipient, self-destructive madness.

Miller and Bossomaier, in their forthcoming book on cybersecurity, offer the amusing hypothetical example of GOSSM: the "Garlic and Onion Storage and Slicing Machine". This imaginary device is meant to be stocked with raw onions and garlic, and will deliver chopped versions of such conveniently, on demand, without tears. The device's design engineers seek to enhance its utility and ease of use by connecting it via the Internet to a cell phone app, providing control of quantities in storage in the machine, fineness of chopping, etc. The app connects via the cellphone to the Internet. When the owner is in the supermarket, GOSSM alerts the owner via text message if more garlic or onions should be purchased. The device is simple and handy, and costs under $100 and thus typifies the range of devices continually being added (without much genuine need or justification) to the Internet.

However, in order to provide all that web-based functionality at low cost, the machine's designers (who are not themselves software engineers) choose to enable this Internet connectivity feature via some ready-made open-source software modules, merely tweaking them to fit. The device is not designed to operate through the owner's password-protected home wireless router. Instead, it links directly to the user's cell phone app, and hence to the Internet, via the cellular data network. Its absence of even the most rudimentary security software, however, makes it, along with a host of other IoT devices in the user's home, subject to being detected online, captured as a zombie and linked in a massive botnet, should some clever, but more unreasonable devil choose to do so.

In October 2016, precisely such a botnet constructed of IoT devices was used to attack Twitter, Facebook and other social media along with large swaths of the Internet itself, using a virus known as Mirai to launch crippling DDoS attacks on key sites, including Oracle's DYN site, the principal source of optimised Domain Name Servers and the source of dynamic Internet protocol addresses for applications such as Netflix and LinkedIn. More recently, in April of 2018, a new Mirai-style virus known as 'Reaper' was detected, compromising IoT devices in order to launch a botnet attack on key sites in the financial sector.[2]

Such events are little more than nuisances, however, when compared with prospects for hacking and attacking driverless cars, or even the current smart technology on automobiles, aircraft and drones. Meanwhile, a new wave of industrial espionage has been enabled through hacking into the video cameras and smart TVs used in corporate boardrooms throughout the world to listen in to highly confidential and secret deliberations ranging from corporate finances to innovative new product development. We have done all this to ourselves, with hardly a thought other than the rush to make exotic functionality available immediately (and leaving the security dimensions to be backfilled afterwards).

Meanwhile, the advent of quantum computing (QC) technology is liable to have an enormous impact on data storage and encryption capacities. Should QC become a reality, the density of storage will increase dramatically, enabling vast amounts of data (even by today's standards) to become available for analysis and 'data mining', while vastly increased process speeds will enable hackers to break the codes of even the most sophisticated encryption software presently available. Encrypted *https://* sites, currently the backbone of Internet commerce, will quickly become outmoded and vulnerable. E-commerce itself, upon which entire commercial sectors of many of the most developed nations depend at present, could grind to a halt.

One likely victim of new security breaches attainable by means of these computational advances would likely be the 'blockchain' financial transactions carried out with cryptocurrencies such as *Bitcoin*, along with the so-called 'smart contracts' enabled by the newest cryptocurrency, *Ethereum*. The latter, for example, is an open-source, public, blockchain-based distributed computing platform and operating system featuring smart contract (scripting) functionality, which delivers payments when some third-party, publicly verifiable condition is met.

---

[2]Zack Whittaker for Zero Day (5 April 2018): https://www.zdnet.com/article/new-mirai-style-botnet-targets-the-financial-sector/ (last access July 7 2019)

This newest cryptocurrency claims to offer total financial transparency and a consequent reduction in the need for individual trust in financial transactions, eliminating (on the one hand) any chance of fraud, censorship or third-party interference. However, as implied above, the opportunities for hacking and disruption of such transactions, creating instability in the currencies and enabling fraud and theft, are likely when increased use of such currencies and transactions are combined with the enhanced power of quantum computing. Preventing that sort of cybercrime, however, would rely on a much more robust partnership between the private and government sectors, which would, in turn, appear to threaten users' privacy and confidentiality. Thus, the prospective solution to the new vulnerabilities would paradoxically impede one of the main present benefits of these cyber alternatives to conventional banking and finance.

Interestingly, we have witnessed Internet firms such as Google, and social media giants such as Facebook and Twitter, accused in Europe of everything from monopolistic financial practices to massive violations of privacy and confidentiality. However, these same private firms, led by Amazon and Google in particular, have taken a much more aggressive stance on security strategy than have many democratic governments in Europe and North America. Meanwhile, for its part, the U.S. government sector, from the FBI to the National Security Agency, has engaged in a virtual war with private firms such as Apple to erode privacy and confidentiality in the name of security by either revealing or building in encryption 'back doors' through which government agencies could investigate prospective wrong-doing. The private firms have been understandably reluctant to reveal their own 'zero-day' vulnerabilities in new software and products, lest doing so undermine public confidence in (and market for) their products.

Their reluctance to do so has only increased in light of a growing complaint that the entire international government sector (led by the U.S. under President Trump) seems to have abandoned the task of formulating a coherent and well-integrated strategy for public and private security. A coherent cyber policy would require, at minimum, a far more robust public-private partnership in cyber space (as noted above), as well as an extension of the kind of international cooperation that was achieved through the 2001 Convention on Cyber Crime (CCC), endorsed by some sixty participating nations in Bucharest in 2001. We need that kind of public-private partnership extended across national boundaries to enable the identification, pursuit and apprehension of malevolent cyber actors, including rogue nations as well as criminals. In the absence of such a collaborative agreement at present, trolls, hackers, vigilantes, and rogue nations are enjoying a virtual field day.

Instead, in an effort to counter these tendencies and provide for greater security and control, European nations have, as mentioned, simply sought to crack down on multinational Internet firms such as Google, while proposing to reassert secure national borders within the cyber domain itself. Generating border controls in this featureless and currently nationless domain is presently possibly only through the empowerment of each nation's CERT (computer emergency response team) to construct Internet gateway firewalls. Such draconian restrictions on cyber traffic across national borders are presently the tools of totalitarian regimes such as China, Iran and North Korea, which do indeed offer ‘security’ entirely at the expense of individual freedom and privacy.

All of the concerns sketched above number among the myriad moral and legal challenges that accompany the latest innovations in cyber technology, well beyond those posed by war fighting itself.

## 12.5 Our Own Worst Enemy

In light of this bewildering array of challenges, it is all too easy to lose sight of the chief aim of ‘the Leviathan’ (strong central governance) itself in Hobbes’s original conception. That goal was not simply to contain conflict but to establish a secure peace. It is perhaps one of the chief defects of the current discussion of cyber conflict that the metaphor of war (as well as the discussion of possible acts of genuine warfare) has come to dominate that discourse (see also Chap. 13). However, our original intention in introducing the ‘state of nature’ image was to explore the prospects for peace, security and stability—outcomes which hopefully might be attained without surrendering all of the current virtues of cyber practice that activists and proponents champion.

But if peace is ultimately what is desired in the cyber domain, our original Hobbesean problem or paradox remains its chief obstacle: namely, how are we to transition from the state of perpetual anarchy, disruption, and the ‘war of all against all’ within the cyber domain in a manner that will simultaneously ensure individual privacy, security, and public confidence? In that domain, as we have constantly witnessed, *the basic moral drive to make such a transition from a state of war to a state of peace is almost entirely lacking*. Advocates of greater law and order are metaphorically ‘shouted down’ by dissidents and anarchists (such as the vigilante group, *Anonymous*) or their integrity called into question and undermined by the behaviour of organisations such as *WikiLeaks*.

For my part, I have not been impressed with the capacities of our most respected experts, in their turn, to listen and learn from one another, let alone to cooperate or collaborate in order to forge the necessary alliances to promote and foster the peace that Hobbes promised through the imposition of law and order. Instead, as in the opening epigram from the *Leviathan* on diffidence, each such expert seems to think himself or herself to be the wisest, and to seem more interested in individual glory through competition with one another for the limelight than in security and the common good.

The case of the discovery of Stuxnet provides a useful illustration of this unfortunate inclination. Who was the first to finally discover the escape of this worm from Nantez Laboratories? Was it cybersecurity expert Ralph Langner (as he claimed in September 2010),[3] VirusBlokADA’s Sergey Ulasen 3 months earlier (as most

[3] See Langner’s TED Talk in 2011 for his updated account: https://www.ted.com/speakers/ralph_langner (last access July 7 2019).

accounts now acknowledge),[4] Kaspersky Labs (as Eugene Kaspersky still claims),[5] Microsoft programming experts (during a routine examination of their own Programmable Logic Controller [PLC] software)[6] or Symantec security experts (who, to my mind, have issued the most complete and authoritative report on the worm; Fallieri et al. 2011)? All have gone on record as having been the first to spot this 'worm in the wild' in 2010.

Furthermore, what about the phenomenon of state-sponsored hacktivism? It belatedly garnered attention as a strategy and policy following the U.S. election interference, but had been ongoing for some time prior. Cybersecurity experts in Western countries utterly missed this advent, and did not know at first what to make of it when it was discovered, as they continued to hysterically hype the coming 'Cyber Armaggedon'. No planes have fallen from the sky as the result of a cyber-attack, nor have chemical plants exploded or dams burst in the interim—but lives have been ruined, elections turned upside down and the possible history of humanity forever altered. In my own frustration at having tried for the past several years to call attention to this alteration of tactics by nation-state cyber warriors, I might well complain that the cyber equivalent of Rome has been burning while cybersecurity experts have fiddled.[7]

How many times must we fight the wrong war, or be looking over the wrong shoulder, before we learn to cooperate rather than compete with one another for public acclaim? Each of us may think himself or herself the wisest, but wisdom itself seems to lurk in the interstices of the cyber domain: in the shadows, among those who act and those who humbly discern instead. We can and must do better. The fate of the welfare of human kind—certainly a moral imperative worthy of consideration—hangs in the balance.

---

[4] See the account, for example, on the "Security Aggregator" blog: http://securityaggregator.blogspot.com/2012/02/man-who-found-stuxnet-sergey-ulasen-in.html (last access July 7 2019).

[5] See the Kaspersky Labs video presentation detailing their discovery and analysis of the worm, released in 2011: https://video.search.yahoo.com/yhs/search;_ylt=AwrCwogmaORb5lcAScMPxQt.;_ylu=X3oDMTByMjB0aG5zBGNvbG8DYmYxBHBvcwMxBHZ0aWQDBHNlYwNzYw%2D%2D?p=eugene+kaspersky+on+stuxnet+virus&fr=yhs-pty-pty_maps&hspart=pty&hsimp=yhs-pty_maps#id=29&vid=4077c5e7bc9e96b32244dbcbc0c04706&action=view (last access July 7 2019).

[6] See the account offered in the Wikipedia article on Stuxnet: https://en.wikipedia.org/wiki/Stuxnet#Discovery (last access July 7 2019).

[7] In April 2017, only a few weeks after the appearance of my own book on this transformation (n. 1), General Michael Hayden (USAF Retired), former head of the CIA, NSA, and former National Security Adviser, offered an account of the months of consternation within the Executive branch during the period leading up to the U.S. presidential election of November 2016, acknowledging that cybersecurity experts did not at the time no what to make of the Russian attacks, nor even what to call them. I had just finished a 7-year stint in federal security service teaching and writing on this topic for the members of that community, evidently to no avail. His 2017 annual Haaga Lecture at the University of Pennsylvania Law School's "Center for Ethics and the Rule of Law" (CERL) can be found at: https://www.law.upenn.edu/institutes/cerl/media.php (last access July 7 2019).

## References

Fallieri N, Murchu LO, Chien E (2011) W32.Stuxnet Dossier (version 4.1, February 2011). https://www.symantec.com/content/en/us/enterprise/media/security_response/whitepapers/w32_stuxnet_dossier.pdf. Last access 7 July 2019

Hobbes T (1651/1968) Leviathan, Part I, Ch XIII [61] (Penguin Classics edn, Macpherson CB (ed)). Penguin Press, New York

Lucas G (2015) Ethical challenges of disruptive innovation. State sponsored hacktivism and 'soft' war. In: Blowers EM (ed) Evolution of cyber technologies and operations to 2035. Springer International Publishers, Basel, pp 175–184

Lucas G (2017) The ethics of cyber warfare. Oxford University Press, New York

Miller S, Bossomaier T (2019) Ethics & cyber security. Oxford University Press, Oxford

Washington Post (Saturday 25 Aug 2018) A11

# Chapter 13
# Cyber Peace: And How It Can Be Achieved

**Reto Inversini**

**Abstract** This contribution investigates elements of cyber conflicts and attacks to determine the current state of cyber peace. The first section examines the current state of the Internet and whether or not it is in a state of cyber war. It analyses the classical concept of peace and war and determines which elements can be adapted to the digital sphere and where such a transformation can be problematic. The term 'cyber peace' is then defined and the components that make such a state possible identified. The last section discusses the different roles and their responsibilities to reach and preserve a state of peace in the digital sphere, coming to the conclusion that the Internet is not in a state of cyber war but more in a state of negative or unstable peace. To protect the Internet as a critical infrastructure from being abused as a new battleground, this chapter suggests moving towards a state of stable peace, and proposes increasing the security and resilience on a technical level and building up trust between all actors, ranging from the individual to the state level.

**Keywords** Attribution · Collaboration and information sharing · Confidence-building measures · Cyber conflict · Cyber espionage · Cyber war · Digital sabotage · State-sponsored actors · Trust and confidence

## 13.1 Cyber Conflicts of Today

Cyber war is an often-used term in current media and scientific publications. There is much controversy regarding whether it is something real or likely to happen in a near future or if it is a chimera originating from a misunderstanding of the digital sphere.

R. Inversini (✉)
Computer Emergency Response Team (GovCERT) of the Swiss Government, Bern University of Applied Science, Bern, Switzerland
e-mail: reto.inversini@lab42.ch



M. Christen et al. (eds.), *The Ethics of Cybersecurity*, The International Library of Ethics, Law and Technology 21,
https://doi.org/10.1007/978-3-030-29053-5_13

Richard A. Clarke argues that the preparation for cyber war has already begun and that powers such as the U.S., China or Russia are making efforts to plan for such actions:

> It is cyberspace and war in it about which I speak. On October 1, 2009, a general took charge of the new U.S. Cyber Command, a military organization with the mission to use information technology and the Internet as a weapon. Similar commands exist in Russia, China, and a score of other nations. (Clarke 2010, p. x–xi)

Thomas Ridd, in contrast, argues that cyber war did not take place and is unlikely to happen soon:

> It is meant rather as a comment about the past, the present, and the likely future: cyber war has never happened in the past, it does not occur in the present, and it is highly unlikely that it will disturb our future. (Rid 2013: xiv)

Both authors use well-known events such as the Distributed Denial of Service (DDoS) attacks in Estonia in 2007 (Schmidt 2013), but come to different conclusions. Both lines of arguments have their strengths but also their shortcomings. However, we neither have a clear definition of what cyber war is nor do we know enough about the implications such a war would have. Therefore, we prefer to use the term 'cyber conflict'.

Whether events from the past such as the DDoS attacks in Estonia, digital sabotage such as Stuxnet (de Falco 2012) or ransomware outbreaks such as NotPetya[1] are already warlike situations is not the crucial question. In contrast, it is of pivotal concern how we avoid such incidents or even more devastating attacks in the future. In the following, we introduce a concept to make the Internet a more secure and peaceful place.

We can divide the moral aspects of war roughly into one of these three categories: Pacifism, Real-ism and Just War (Walzer 1978; Orend 2006). Pacifism denies any morality to war, and a pacifist must refrain from any involvement in a war. Realism believes that war by itself is something amoral and we can neither judge war, nor can it be guided by moral principles. The Just War theory claims that under certain circumstances, a war may be justified and there are rules to follow to start and lead a war in a morally acceptable way. It goes back to Greek and Roman philosophers and lawyers and since then has evolved and was influenced by Christian theology. There have been many wars that did not fulfil the Just War principles and the Just War Theory has been debated and needs adaptions (Brough et al. 2007). Nevertheless, it forms the base of current international norms such as the UN Charter, The Hague Conventions and the Geneva Convention. Therefore, we use the concept of Just War as the basis for this chapter.

[1] Crowdstrike, NotPetya Technical Analysis; https://www.crowdstrike.com/blog/petrwrap-ransomware-technical-analysis-triple-threat-file-encryption-mft-encryption-credential-theft/ (last access July 7 2019).

War would need to follow several principles[2] to be justified and not violate international law:

- There must be a cause for war that must be declared by a legitimate authority.
- War must be waged with the right intentions and a just cause.
- The probability of success must be determined; there must be a justifiable ratio between gain and loss and it must be the last resort.

These principles form the *Jus ad Bellum*, the right to go to war. The guiding principles of Jus ad Bellum are difficult to adapt to cyber space:

- In order to declare war, one must know one's enemies. This is relatively easy in the physical world even though the number of cases where states hide behind mercenary organisations is rising because it allows them to deny any direct involvement. There are more difficulties inherent in identifying the attackers in the digital sphere: Most states deny any involvement in actions that might be considered as acts of war in the cyber space. It is easy to hide behind proxies, to place false flags and to act on behalf of someone else. Attributing attacks correctly is therefore one of the most important things to address in the digital sphere.
- The Jus ad Bellum allows a country only to go to war if the chances of success are high enough, especially regarding the estimated number of casualties. The probability of success and the number of fatalities are difficult to predict as there are many unknown factors that influence the outcome and because casualties can also be indirect.
- Only national self-defence and humanitarian need are considered acceptable causes for war. To exercise the right of self-defence, a nation-state needs to prove that the event is an armed attack that threatens the state's sovereignty and independence and that another state conducted the attack. In the context of incidents in the digital domain, situations exist where the impact may be obvious such as disruptive or destructive attacks against critical infrastructures, but the problem of who is to blame for an attack remains.
- An important part of the Jus ad Bellum is the concept of territorial and political sovereignty of a state. If a state's sovereignty is in danger, the state has the right to defend itself. Political sovereignty can be easily endangered, but it is difficult to define the threshold where such attacks would justify the right of self-defence. The attackers may try to destabilise a state, e.g. by spreading wrong information or by attacking the political system. This can be done by influencing elections, either by manipulation of the infrastructure or by digitally intruding a disfavoured party. The influencing of public opinion and even elections is nothing new and has been done before the digital era. However, with the use of social media, it has become much easier to directly or indirectly influence large parts of a country. The concept of territorial sovereignty is important but difficult to adapt

[2] Beyond Intractability Knowledge Base, Jus ad Bellum, https://www.beyondintractability.org/essay/jus_ad_bellum (last access July 7 2019).

to the digital sphere, as there are no physical borders, notably when dealing with distributed systems or applications that use any kind of cloud technology. Scholars and practitioners have written The Tallin Manual on behalf of the NATO Cooperative Cyber Defence Centre of Excellence (CCDCOE; Schmitt 2017). It describes how international law can be applied to cyber conflicts. Rule 81 states that "Cyber operations are subject to geographical limitations imposed by the relevant provisions of internal law applicable during an armed conflict (Schmitt 2017: 378)." In the second part of the rule, the authors state that these restrictions may be difficult to implement: "Restrictions based on geographical limitations may be particularly difficult to implement in the context of cyber warfare. For instance, consider a cyber-attack using cloud computing techniques. Data used to prosecute the attack from one State may be replicated across servers in a number of other States, including neutral States, but only observably reflected on the systems where the attack is initiated and completed (Schmitt 2017: 378)."

If we consider the goals of a traditional war, there are some interesting differences between a traditional war and a cyber-conflict:

- A traditional war has the goal of conquering territory, accessing resources or gaining political control over the adversary.
- In the digital sphere, no defined territory exists, and digital battles are not about gaining resources. However, a digital war may be used as a supportive element of a traditional war to seize territory or resources. This may be a sign that in most cases, hostile digital actions are part of a larger scenario that also includes more traditional elements of war.
- It is possible that we will only observe actions in the digital domain when a state wants to gain political control over another state. This leads us back to the concept of political sovereignty, which will become increasingly important.

We believe it is likely that most hostile actions in the digital sphere will not take place in the context of officially declared wars. This is not a result of the ongoing digitalisation but reflects a more general trend: As Fazal states, there has been a sharp decrease of war declarations since the 1950s:

> From 1950 on, by contrast, the number of wars remained about the same, but the number of wars accompanied by declarations declined dramatically—to three. Declaring war—an institution that has typically accompanied the outbreak of hostilities since at least the Roman Empire—appears to have fallen out of states' repertoire of behaviors. (Fazal 2012: 557–558)

If we consider this and accept the difficulty of attribution beyond any reasonable doubt, we do not expect that countries will declare war formally, especially for cyber operations. Without a war declared and without an independent and accepted attribution, the prerequisites of Jus ad Bellum are not fulfilled. In the future, more situations that resemble a war or are characterised by high tensions will emerge, but they will not meet the criteria mentioned above.

This is why we include not only the case of declared war into our considerations but any action that violates the sovereignty of a state. Rule No 4 of the Tallin Manual states that no violation of the sovereignty of another state is acceptable (Schmitt 2017: 16–18): “A state must not conduct cyber operations that violate the sovereignty of another state.”

The comments to Rule No 4 describe various cases where the experts agree that a violation had occurred such as if the cyber operation damages an infrastructure on the territory of another country (Schmitt 2017: 18) or if governmental functions of a state are impaired by a cyber-operation of another state (Schmitt 2017: 22). One basic precondition of a violation of sovereignty is that it must be attributable to another state. This gets progressively complicated as governments hire mercenary groups to carry out attacks in the digital sphere. This allows a country to deny any direct involvement in a conflict.

Using so-called cyber proxies (Maurer 2018) or cyber mercenaries can be attractive to governments as they provide expertise and plausible deniability that a state has any direct involvement. In the past, we have seen two types of such actors: hacktivist and commercial organisations. Mostly, actions performed by such groups may be illegal from a penal point of view but cannot be considered as acts of war. However, there are actions that increase the tension between conflicting parties and that lead to an escalation into a warlike situation. It is likely that the use of such groups will rise as their use is too tempting for governments. They can be a cheap yet effective alternative to regular soldiers acting in the cyber space and provide more deniability in case an attack is discovered and analysed. George Lucas (2017: 28) believes that the danger of such groups is underestimated and may pose a serious threat in the future.

We believe the use of such organisations will increase the likelihood that warlike situations will be of longer duration without a formal war being declared, as such groups tend to engage in war for their own benefit (political influence or commercial interests). During wars that relied largely on mercenary armies such as the 30 Years War, at least a part of the financing of the soldiers was done by robbing civilians. Even though not directly comparable, the overlapping of digital crime and state-sponsored hacktivism resembles this situation and might get progressively important, as states could offer impunity to cyber criminals in return for digital attacks which are in the interest of the state. The authors of the Tallinn Manual explain that non-state actors cannot violate the sovereignty of a state but that the targeted state may nevertheless react to harmful attacks following international law (Schmitt 2017: 18). We believe the differentiation between state and non-state actors is becoming increasingly difficult. This uncertainty might eventually lead to situations with a high risk of escalation if a state responds with force to attacks of non-state groups and, by doing so, violates the sovereignty of another state.

Although we believe it is wrong to infiltrate other networks to gain information illegally, such attacks are not necessarily acts of war. Espionage has always existed, even during peace times and sometimes it has even helped to preserve peace: It gave the other party information about what the enemy has planned and thus improved the predictability, which helps to define the course of action. However, the uncontrolled use of espionage may destroy trust. As cyber espionage seems to become epidemic, state actors should be cautious and should refrain themselves from too-frequent spying.

## 13.2 Cyber Peace

The contrastive term of cyber war is 'cyber peace'. Often, peace is defined in a negative way as the absence of war. Boulding defines peace in both ways:

> The concept of peace has both positive and negative aspects. On the positive side, peace signifies a condition of good management, orderly resolution of conflict, harmony associated with mature relationships, gentleness and love. On the negative side, it is conceived as the absence of something, the absence of turmoil, tension, conflict and war. (Boulding 1989: 3)

We define cyber peace in a manner that considers both aspects. We should not define peace just by the absence of conflict and war, as these elements may be visible in the physical world but not in the digital sphere.

Peace can have various states that are defined in different ways, e.g. by Alexander George (1998: p. ix) as precarious, conditional and stable, by Miller (2017) as cold, normal and warm, or by Kacowicz et al. (2000) as negative peace, stable peace and pluralistic security communities. These definitions have much in common. We use the definition by Kacowicz et al. (2000: 21):

> A zone of negative peace (mere absence of war) is one in which peace is maintained only on an unstable basis and / or by negative means such as threats, deterrence or lack of capabilities to engage in violent conflict at a certain time. (…) A zone of stable peace (no expectations of violence) is one in which peace is maintained in on a reciprocal and consensual basis. (…) A pluralistic security community of nation-states, with stable expectations of peaceful change, is one in which member states share common norms, values and political institutions; sustain a common identity; and are deeply interdependent.

### *13.2.1 Current State of Cyber Peace*

The Internet is still in the zone of a negative peace: Current operations are not very violent, but there is an imminent risk of an escalation.

We may understand the current state of the Internet in a similar way as the frontier area in the Wild West. The absence of regulation, the quick emergence of new ways to earn money, and the fact that most effective security for the participants does not come from the state but from private organisations are all elements that show similarities with a booming frontier town. We have witnessed the rapid development of new technologies and the emergence of a new and global form of criminality and state sponsored espionage and even destructive attacks. However, in most cases, the damage was still limited and often it was not inflicted on purpose but was a collateral effect caused by underestimating the interconnectivity of the Internet and the low security precautions.

A good example of the uncertainty about the current state of the Internet, and whether we are already near a state of cyber war is the aforementioned NotPetya case. There has been considerable discussion over whether this attack could already be considered as an act of war. While NotPetya caused substantial damage, we believe it is not an act of war as it lacks most of the prerequisites we have mentioned above. NotPetya is a malware that is based on the leaked National Security Agency (NSA) exploit 'Eternal Blue'. One hypothesis is that NotPetya was aimed at infrastructure elements in the Ukraine. It spread like wildfire and hit many big organisations such as Merck or Maersk. This was possible because systems were neither patched against known vulnerabilities nor isolated from other networks. However, governments and media treated the case like a hostile action that was at least at the border of an act of cyber war.[3] This case displays a few interesting elements:

- If a state stores and uses 0-day vulnerabilities,[4] there is a risk that someone else uses it against e.g. critical infrastructures.
- In most cases, attackers exploit bad security practices.
- For affected organisations, it is often favourable to make the attack bigger than it was to distract attention from its own failure to secure its systems properly.

NotPetya was an attack with a big disruptive effect that endangered many organisations and—under bad preconditions—could have been the starting point of an escalation. However, this attack was only possible because organisations neglected basic security and not because the attack was remarkably skilful. We can therefore learn from this case that with proper security precautions, attacks become much harder to conduct and the risk of collateral damage drops. As many critical infrastructure elements are being connected to the Internet without appropriate security controls, offensive actions are often perilous, as no-one can limit actions to the intended target. To maintain a stable cyber peace, information and communication technology (ICT) operators must assume their responsibility for building and maintaining secure and resilient systems.

Attacks with a global impact are possible and there is a high risk associated with this. As no specific de-escalation procedures for the digital sphere are in place on the state-level, the risk of an escalation which eventually could lead to hostilities exists and we should not underestimate it. If too many unfavourable political elements come together, such an attack might be the starting point for a rapidly escalating situation that nobody ever intended but that could cause a lot of harm.

[3]The Independent, Britain has entered 'new era of warfare' with Russian cyber-attacks, Defense Secretary warns; https://www.independent.co.uk/news/uk/home-news/russia-cyber-attacks-notpetya-gavin-williamson-defense-secretary-putin-hacking-ransomware-a8212801.html (last access July 7 2019).

[4]A 0-day vulnerability is a vulnerability that has not yet been publicly disclosed and for which no security patches yet exist but that is known to persons and organisations that are willing to exploit it. Day 0 refers to the day the programmer/manufacturer of the software affected learns about the vulnerability.

The Internet is currently in a state of a negative peace. We have a good chance to move towards a stable peace if we can increase collaboration and trust between the different actors. We should act on different levels to stabilise the cyber space and to reduce the likelihood and impact of hostile actions.

### 13.2.2 How to Achieve a State of Stable Cyber Peace

It is not reasonable to believe war and conflicts can be completely avoided in the near future. However, it is possible to reduce the likelihood and the impact of conflicts, both in the real world and in the digital world, thus moving from the state of a negative peace to a stable peace. Luckily, there are already several elements in place that will help us achieve this goal (see also Chap. 18):

- All participants are highly interdependent, which leads to some degree of restraint in attacking others, as there might be a backlash on their own network.
- Common norms (the Internet protocols) and values (the Netiquette[5]) are in place and widely accepted.
- There are defensive organisations working together and trying to increase the security and stability of the Internet: Computer Emergency Response Teams (CERT) exist on various levels ranging from organisational CERTs to National CERTs. Sometimes they even form permanent, supra-national groups such as the European Government CERTs group (EGC[6]) where various national CERTs of Western Europe co-operate and share information about digital threats.

To achieve a stable peace, we must invest in defensive measures on all levels. While offensive capabilities may serve as a deterrence because the attacker fears retaliation, defensive measures reduce the likelihood and the impact of a successful attack. In the following, we highlight the two most important components of a stable cyber peace: security (including resilience) and trust.

On a technical level, security and resilience are the most important factors that help us reduce the likelihood and impact of digital attacks. The higher the security and resilience are, the more trustworthy the infrastructure is. Trust is important as the glue between the actors in the digital sphere and is important for collaboration and confidence. Based on security and trust, states have enough reason to exclude the risk of being attacked from their top priorities because enough protocols, processes and treaties are in place that form a stable peace.

[5] Netiquette RFC

[6] European Government CERT Group

## 13.3 Security and Resilience

Security defines the technical and organisational measures that are implemented to reduce the risks to the digital infrastructures of a country. Resilience is a close relative but also includes passive elements and is more geared towards withstanding and quickly recovering from attacks. While an attacker only needs to make one single, successful attack with reasonable costs and low risk, defending all the critical infrastructure of a country is extraordinarily hard to achieve. In contrast to the nuclear arms race, cyber-attacks are not that devastating, even though one should not ignore the potential impact of a cyber-attack due to collateral damage and unwanted escalation. This may lead to a much quicker and light-headed execution of such attacks and a lower rate of mutual deterrence. It is possible to recover from such an incident if proper design and planning of defence is in place. As Joseph Nye puts it: "Redundancy, resilience and quick reconstitution become crucial components of defence" (Nye JS Jr 2018: 5).

Large parts of the Internet are vulnerable to attacks, starting with routers and data centre switches that have received no security patches for years, to outdated operating systems and middleware up to content management systems and web applications that have many well-known vulnerabilities (see also Chap. 2). This gives adversaries the advantage of having many opportunities to attack systems, abusing them as jump points for their operations and thus covering their tracks. An attacker may choose between various attack vectors, infiltrate the systems and networks and achieve his goals. One single weak spot may be sufficient for the perpetrator to enter the network while the defenders need to guard many systems, often without adequate resources. We can therefore conclude that there is a disequilibrium between offense and defence; or as George Lucas (2017: 127) states: "The advantage, as the cybersecurity experts themselves admit, always lies with the offense" (see also Chap. 12).

An illustrative example is the emergence of so-called Internet of Things (IoT) devices which are mass-produced cheaply; their users often connect them to the Internet with no security measures taken (e.g. keeping default passwords active). Criminals abused the resulting attack surface to build an enormous botnet (Mirai Botnet; Antonakakis M. et al. 2017), which successfully attacked one of the largest Domain Name System (DNS) providers (DynDNS). As many companies use the DNS services DynDNS provides, the attack led to outages in the U.S. and also in Europe. This case showed two things:

- There is a huge number of vulnerable devices on the Internet that can be abused for attacks.
- The centralisation of services often leads to a large impact of a successful attack and destroys parts of the design target of having a resilient Internet.

The disequilibrium between offense and defence is true at the moment, as the attacker has to find one weakness for a successful attack while the defenders must protect a plethora of systems, some of them being legacy systems that no longer receive security patches. However, we are convinced that Joseph Nye's statement is not true in its absoluteness, as there are also advantages on the defender's side:

- We should not underestimate the complexity of the attacker's task: The defenders have a good oversight of their networks and are disposing over advanced monitoring systems. The attacker, in contrast, must peek through a keyhole (one or more infected systems) and try to sort out the interesting data and systems without making too many errors and getting discovered.
- Every attacker makes mistakes and the forensic exchange principle of Locard (Tilstone et al. 2006: 59) ("Every contact leaves a trace") is also true in the digital sphere. It is up to the defender to find these traces as fast as possible to detect the attacker before severe damage occurs.
- In case of attacks against Industrial Control Systems (ICS), the attacker must have special knowledge not only about the overall functioning but over the actual implementation as well. It is a time and money-consuming task to achieve such knowledge and attackers can only do this if the price is worth it.

The advantage of the attacker should not lead to an arms race that neglects the defence ("why invest in defence, if the offense always has the advantage?"). In contrast, we must strengthen the overall security of Internet connected devices and the resilience of critical infrastructure. In many incidents, such precautions would have prevented or at least delayed the attack. The better the security, the higher the price for successful attacks becomes and thus this makes attacks less likely. It also helps to reduce the probability and impact of collateral damage that has not been intended by the attacker but could lead to a dangerous escalation by itself.

With digital sabotage, one of the biggest advantages in the digital sphere lies in the fact that restoration of the destroyed IT infrastructure can often be done fast and without high costs. However, this requires a well-thought design of infrastructure and data as well as the usage of technologies for the rapid restoration of data. This is extremely important for critical infrastructure such as electricity, water and health services. The emphasis lies on the term *quick restoration,* as a restore procedure that would take days is often too long, notably in organisations where timely access to current data is crucial, such as hospitals. It is also essential to separate the different data stores so that an attacker who destroys (encrypts, deletes or modifies) data cannot access the second storage with the data that is going to be restored. While these requirements are challenging, there are technical options to building and operating such a system. One interesting case has been documented in a hospital in the USA where the management decided to pay the ransom even though backups would have been available.[7] However, restoring all data and systems would have taken too long, as the outbreak of the ransomware had been very widespread throughout the hospital's network. It gets more difficult if the digital attack leads to physical damage, e.g. of devices that are overloaded by the attackers. To reduce such impacts, the user

[7] Bleeping Computer, Hospital Pays $55 K Ransomware Demand Despite Having Backups, https://www.bleepingcomputer.com/news/security/hospital-pays-55k-ransomware-demand-despite-having-backups/ (last access July 7 2019).

must not blindly interconnect the digital sphere with the physical world but should have well-defined gateways. The user should always define reasonable boundaries that trigger an alert or force a system to go into a 'fail-safe' state and wait for a human intervention.

We would therefore like to emphasise the importance of building up strong and resilient infrastructures that are designed and operated by organisations with mature security processes. We believe there must be an incentive by the state to lead the development of digital technologies in the right direction as there is still too little stimulus for enterprises to write secure software. This can either be on the regulating side, by enforcing minimal security standards for every device connected to the Internet, or by having better product liability for software.

## 13.4 Trust and Confidence

Trust is a crucial element for inter-personal relationships or between smaller groups of people that share common values and follow common goals. Interpersonal relationships form the base of any stable peace in a society and between nations. The better the citizens know and trust each other, the greater the confidence between their nations is. It forms the base for security, collaboration and information sharing for their mutual benefit.

There already exist many trust relationships between persons working in the domain of cybersecurity who collaborate across national and cultural borders and are building invisible trust networks globally. To build up such a trust relationship, collaboration and sharing of information must be fostered on all levels between all participants. This raises the bar for successful attacks, thus making them more unlikely. Trust is the key precondition for collaboration and sharing of information. Without trusting someone, no-one shares valuable information and without sharing information, it is difficult to increase the trust level between individuals and organisations. We therefore propose to work together and share information in areas where a common understanding already exists. A good example is the domain of combatting cyber-crime, where we can begin to build up the trust and then also increase the collaboration in areas that are much more sensitive, such as state-sponsored activities.

The collaboration and sharing of information must take place on various levels:

- Between states: There are some promising efforts such as EGC (Group of European Government CERTs) or IWWN (International Watch and Warning Network). However, much of the collaboration happens only between partners that share the same values and often already have some kind of political alliance. This is understandable and only underlines the importance of trust. There is a broad understanding that in law enforcement an urgent need to exchange information in a much quicker way exists. There are international agreements such as the Convention of Cyber Crime of the European Council that help to improve the situation (see also Chap. 18).

- Numerous interest groups and volunteer organisations are already fostering the exchange of information between individuals, non-profit organisations and commercial organisations. We must support these efforts, as many of these persons and organisations have a deep understanding of how the digital sphere works and are the best bet for effective and efficient measures to secure the Internet.
- Critical infrastructures are crucial for the safety and stability of a society. Without a reliable provisioning of electric power, water, food and health care, societies are rapidly destabilised. We must improve information exchange between the critical infrastructures not only within a nation's border but also throughout the sectors on an international level.

Trust forms the confidence between the various actors, who can be confident that no unexpected acts of violence might occur and that there is a common perception on how actors react in certain situations. Without confidence, states and organisations are constantly on guard, watching out for hostile actions. In an area as complicated as cyber space, chances for misinterpretations and escalations are particularly high. The lack of confidence that no other nation will use digital weapons against one's own nation is also something that describes the current situation rather well. We must have a mutual basic level of confidence that no unexpected behaviour takes place. This can be achieved by defining and implementing confidence-building measures (CBMs):

> The ultimate goal of CBMs is to strengthen international peace and security by reducing and eliminating causes of mistrust, fear, misunderstanding, and miscalculations. (Healy et al. 2014)

The effects of a full-scale cyber conflict are not that clear even if the potential for damage might be huge. We should therefore not neglect the risk of an unplanned and unwanted escalation. Even though not directly comparable, we can gain important insight from the era of the Cold War, with its danger of an imminent nuclear war. Joseph Nye (2011) summaries the similarities between that era and our time of cyber conflicts as follows (Nye JS Jr 2011):

- superiority of offense over defence
- use of weapons for tactical and strategical purposes
- possibilities of first and second use scenarios
- possibility of automated responses

It is challenging to define what a digital weapon is: Although it is rather clear for the case of nuclear weapons, this is much more difficult in the digital sphere: Many things that can be considered as cyber weapons have their origins in dual-use goods (this is especially true for vulnerability scanners and similar tools).

One of the most important and successful measures implemented for reducing the likelihood of a nuclear war were CMBs. We believe that CBMs could reduce the probability of an escalation in a cyber-conflict as well. In the following, we try to deduce similarities and differences for CMBs in the digital domain:

- To avoid misunderstandings, it is important to exchange information about troops, assets and their movements. This helps to avoid incorrect assumptions about the capacities of the other party and may help to reduce the speed of an arms race. This is much more difficult to achieve in the digital world, as most nations keep their capabilities secret and as there is an overlap between intelligence services, 'traditional' troops and unofficial combatants.
- Exchange of personnel/conducting joint exercises: This helps to build up a personal relationship between the participants that supports to build up trust. To some extent, this is already being done as many cybersecurity professionals meet at regular intervals and on conferences. However, for military troops, this mostly exists between friendly countries or allies such as NATO and not between potential adversaries.
- Improving predictability helps gauge unclear and fierce situations in a better way. This reduces the likelihood of unwanted escalations and helps to contain difficult situations quickly and efficiently.
- Enhancing transparency of involved parties leads to a better understanding of a conflict and reduces the risk of inadvertent escalation. Even though satellite surveillance and other reconnaissance helped to improve transparency in large classical conflicts, there are still situations where the involvement is not clear and where parties indirectly take part in a conflict, such as during the Ukraine crisis. In the digital sphere, this is even more demanding as there it is nearly impossible to verify which parties are involved in a digital operation.
- Military actions against critical infrastructure or against civilians should be restricted. During conflicts between two states, there are many regulations in place to reduce casualties of civilians and to spare infrastructures such as hospitals. In the digital sphere, this is much more complex, as it is often unclear whether a resource belongs to a legitimate target, to a civilian or even to a hospital. We must accept that there is always a large risk of unwanted collateral damage due to the strong interdependencies on the Internet. This should lead all participants to refrain from offensive actions as much as possible.

Confidence partly relies on the capability to trace down the identity of an attacker beyond a reasonable doubt. This leads us again to the problem of attribution in cyberspace. Evidence is hard to gain and tracks often end at legislative borders. Additionally, attackers can introduce wrong traces that point to another Nation/organisation ('false flags') which may lead to false accusations and in what follows to increased tensions and even real conflicts. Therefore, it is important that parties not involved in the conflict and with enough reputation, technical skill and independence are responsible for the attribution so that the public and the involved parties both accept the verdict. This is extremely challenging. Apart from some approaches in an early stage (e.g. a proposal by Microsoft for such an attribution organisation[8]), we are far away from such a situation. A correct attribution is pivotal to respond

[8] Microsoft, an attribution organisation to strengthen trust online, https://query.prod.cms.rt.microsoft.com/cms/api/am/binary/RW67QI (last access July 72,019).

with force against the adversary, but traces are seldom obvious and unambiguous. Any attacker may insert enough information to blame someone else for the attack. This also bears the risk that state sponsored groups are more willing to attack for various reasons. If they can seed false traces, politicians might use such false flag operations to justify offensive actions during a political crisis.

Even though we have shown how difficult it is to build up higher confidence between potential adversaries in the digital sphere, first steps have been made in this direction:

- A good example is the establishment of the first multilateral cybersecurity related agreement by the Organisation for Security and Co-Operation in Europe (OSCE) in 2013.[9]
- A second set of CBMs was decided upon in 2016.[10]

It is beneficial for the security of the Internet and all its participants if policy makers continue on this path and increase their efforts to reach a stable cyber peace.

## 13.5 Roles and Responsibilities

We cannot achieve cyber peace without everyone taking their own share of responsibility. We do not describe every actor and his or her role in detail but rather mention a few cornerstones:

### *13.5.1 Policy Makers*

We need to differentiate between policy making on an international level and on a national level. On an international level, multinational organisations such as the United Nations Organisation (UNO) or Organisation for Economic Co-operation and Development (OECD) are important actors that can forge a path to a cyber peace in the longer term. For short-term and operational issues, we propose strengthening existing organisations such as the Internet Corporation for Assigned Names and Numbers (ICANN), the Regional Internet Registries (RIRs), the Internet Engineering Task Force (IETF), Forum of Incident Response and Security Teams (FIRST) and Trusted Introducer (TI). These already have a strong understanding of how the Internet works and are not subject to quickly changing political situations.

Similar to the case of nuclear weapons, one strategy could be that an increasing number of states decide to refrain from possessing digital weapons with destructive capabilities or at least to guarantee they are abstaining from the first use of such

[9] Organization for Security and Co-operation in Europe OSCE, Permanent Council Decision No. 1106; www.osce.org/pc/109168 (last access July 7 2019).

[10] Organization for Security and Co-operation in Europe OSCE, Permanent Council Decision No. 1202; www.osce.org/pc/227281 (last access July 7 2019).

weapons. Although this might be an interesting approach, it is also very difficult, as such a treaty can hardly be controlled and as there is a big overlap between the tools state-sponsored organisations and criminal groups are using. At the very least, states should define and adhere to rules of engagement in the digital world that ensure no state attacks the critical infrastructures of another state in order to avoid causing civilian casualties.

States are strongly challenged when it comes to digital crime and state sponsored actions. As these actors operate from different locations and have their infrastructure in various countries that they may change swiftly, a purely national approach is doomed to fail in most cases. The most efficient way to address these problems is via international cooperation. A step forward has been taken by the Convention on Cybercrime. Its aim, set out in the preamble, is to pursue a common criminal policy aimed at protecting society against cybercrime by adopting appropriate legislation and fostering international co-operation.[11] Initially driven by the Council of Europe, 57 other countries have signed and ratified the treaty as of 2018.

On the national level, many nations have been developing National Cybersecurity Strategies. Policy makers should try to strengthen the defence before investing in offensive capabilities. Even though many countries try to overcome their weaknesses by having offensive capabilities, we believe this is not a well-thought-out approach. It assumes that in the case of an attack it is clear who is attacking (which seldom is the case) and that striking back can solve the problem and does not lead to an escalation with much collateral damage. One of the best investments any nation can do is making the Internet, and the systems connected to it, more secure and resilient. We therefore encourage policy makers to focus on the hard groundwork of securing the Internet and not so much on building cyber commands and capabilities that cannot address the underlying problems.

The state should be in charge of providing reasonable security for everyone and free of charge by ensuring basic Internet security and resilience as well as combatting criminal groups. All citizens must be able to use the Internet free of fear and with a low risk of being the victim of an attack. This is one of the most important tasks a state must fulfil. If it fails in doing so, only persons and organisations with enough financial and/or intellectual resources can protect themselves. This would violate any principle of fairness and the state would risk losing its monopoly on the use of force, which is a basic principle of any constitutional state.

### 13.5.2 The Society

As a society, we must adapt our own perception of risks and values to the new digital era. We should be careful when we are transferring concepts of the traditional world into the cyber domain and should always question their suitability. The generations to come will have a better understanding of the risks involved, as they are

[11] Council of Europe, Treaty No. 185, https://www.coe.int/en/web/conventions/full-list/-/conventions/treaty/185 (last access July 7 2019).

growing up using these technologies. We should foster this by not only teaching the technology but also the values associated with it. Societies should try to understand the Internet as a common good of humankind and not as something restricted to state or cultural boundaries.

### 13.5.3 The Private Sector

It is difficult to draft one role for all companies, as these are very diverse. In any case, they must secure their systems according to best practices and should avoid trying to reduce costs by using insecure systems, applications and procedures.

If a company has a critical role in a society, such as being part of the health care or energy sectors, there are additional points it must adhere to: Its IT department must protect the systems and data against any kind of sabotage and disruption and fulfil requirements set up by the regulator; it needs to detect intrusions quickly and needs to provide effective security incident response and recovery procedures; and it should closely monitor the threat landscape and be capable of quickly adapting to new threats.

Companies that sell security products and services have special roles and responsibilities as well. Without commercial security companies, the Internet would be much more dangerous and unstable as they provide security products that help organisations and individuals protecting their networks and systems. However, there are companies that act as mercenary groups or that export digital weapons into areas of conflict. These groups may put a stable peace in danger. We propose having guidelines about ethical behaviour that are co-developed and complied with by security companies. We believe that self-regulation is a promising approach, but that in case of a violation of these guidelines, sanctions are also necessary.

### 13.5.4 The Individual

Due to the high degree of interconnection, every participant on the Internet has a special responsibility towards the other users. If someone does not properly secure his system or application, he or she might be abused as a first attack vector for actions that eventually lead to substantial damage. The following scenario shows a possible sequence of events:

- A poorly secured website of a local restaurant is hacked by a state-sponsored attacker group.
- Employees of a nearby-located critical infrastructure (CI) repeatedly visit this restaurant and its webpage to read the current menu.
- The attackers abuse the website as a waterhole for infecting the employees of said infrastructure.

- The intruders have now gained their first foothold in the network of the CI and they can use the server for the exfiltration of the stolen data. It is difficult for intrusion detection systems to recognise such traffic, as it is expected and already known.

As it is not a workable solution that everyone taking part on the Internet can take full responsibility for securing his or her systems, all actors on higher levels must try to absorb these risks by implementing additional safeguards.

## 13.6 Conclusion

In this chapter, we discussed the current state of the Internet as a negative yet unstable peace and demonstrated the most important components for reaching a stable peace. These components require increasing confidence and trust between all participants, which is mainly a political and psychological topic. The elements formed around security and resilience are more focused on technology but also include strategic, political and economic elements.

We can achieve a stable cyber peace if most participants consider the Internet as being a space shared with others that has comprehensible and documented rules to protect its users from damage —be it physical or digital. This leads to the need for an international system of norms, rules of engagement, best-practices and responsible behaviour of individuals, enterprises and states.

It is important to note that there are already many safeguards and processes in place. These limit the actions and the impacts of state-sponsored actors and of criminals, and help secure the Internet in approaching a state of a stable cyber peace. This multi-level approach attempts to solve the problems where the chances are highest for doing so. Shackelford describes this as a "polycentric" approach:

> Private-sector cybersecurity best practices, along with national, bilateral, and regional bodies acting as norm entrepreneurs that are identified throughout this study are together conceptualized as components of a 'polycentric' approach to promoting a global culture of cybersecurity. (Shackelford 2017: 7)

We believe it is crucial to keep and foster this approach and to extend it as much as possible to ensure peace on the Internet and to prevent actors from using it as a new battleground. It is important to not try to transfer concepts and procedures from the physical world to the digital sphere without questioning their suitability. Even though it is very unlikely that the Internet will be a sphere without conflicts, we can nonetheless make it much more secure and resilient. This reduces the likelihood of devastating attacks, which in turn could lead to a dangerous escalation. Every step we make towards a more stable peace in the digital sphere helps protect the Internet, critical infrastructures and our society as a whole.

**Acknowledgments** The chapter was created with funding from the European Union's Horizon 2020 research and innovation programme under grant agreement No 700540 and the Swiss State Secretariat for Education, Research and Innovation (SERI) under contract number 16.0052-1.

## References

Antonakakis M et al. (2017) Understanding the Mirai Botnet. https://www.usenix.org/system/files/conference/usenixsecurity17/sec17-antonakakis.pdf. Last access 7 July 2019
Boulding KE (1989) Stable peace. University of Texas Press, Austin
Brough M, Lango JW, van der Linden H (eds) (2007) Rethinking the just war tradition. SUNY series, Ethics and the Military Profession
Clarke RA (2010) Cyber war: the next threat to national security and what to do about it. Ecco
De Falco M (2012) Stuxnet fact report. Available at: https://de.scribd.com/document/181049284/De-Falco-Marco-CCDCOE-Stuxnet-Facts-Report-A-Technical-and-Strategic-Analysis-pdf. Last access 7 July 2019
Fazal TF (2012) Why states no longer declare war. Secur Stud 21(4):557–593
George A (1998) Foreword in Europe undivided: the new logic of peace in U.S.-Russian Relations
Healy J, Mallery J, Tothova Jordan K (2014) Confidence building measures in cyberspace. http://www.atlanticcouncil.org/images/publications/Confidence-Building_Measures_in_Cyberspace.pdf. Last access 7 July 2019
Kacowicz A, Bar-Siman-Tov Y, Elgström O et al (2000) Stable peace among nations. Rowman & Littlefield Publishers, Lanham
Lucas G (2017) Ethics and cyber warfare: the quest for responsible security in the age of digital warfare. Oxford University Press, New York
Maurer T (2018) Cyber mercenaries: the state, hackers, and power. Cambridge University Press, Cambridge
Miller B (2017) International and regional security: the causes of war and peace. Routledge, London
Nye JS Jr (2011) Nuclear lessons for cyber security. Strat Stud Q 5(4):18–38
Nye JS Jr (2018) Cyber power. https://www.belfercenter.org/sites/default/files/files/publication/cyber-power.pdf. Last access 7 July 2019
Orend B (2006) The morality of war. Broadview Press, Peterborough
Rid T (2013) Cyber war will not take place. C Hurst & Co Publishers Ltd, London
Schmidt A (2013) The Estonian cyberattacks. Atlantic Council, Washington, DC
Schmitt MN (ed) (2017) Tallinn manual 2.0 on the international law applicable to cyber. Cambridge University Press, Cambridge
Shackelford SJ (2017) The law of cyber peace. Chic J Int Law 18(1):Article 1
Tilstone W, Savage KA, Leigh AC (2006) Forensic science: an encyclopedia of history, methods, and techniques. Emerald Group Publishing Limited, Bingley
Walzer M (1978) Just and unjust wars. Basic Books, New York

# Part III
# Recommendations

# Chapter 14
# Privacy-Preserving Technologies

**Josep Domingo-Ferrer and Alberto Blanco-Justicia**

**Abstract** This chapter introduces privacy and data protection by design, and reviews privacy-enhancing techniques (PETs). Although privacy by design includes both technical and operational measures, the chapter focuses on the technical measures. First, it enumerates design strategies. Next, it considers privacy-enhancing techniques that directly address the *hide* strategy, but also aid in implementing the *separate*, *control* and *enforce* strategies. Specifically, it addresses PETs for: (1) identification, authentication and anonymity; (2) private communications; (3) privacy-preserving computations; (4) privacy in databases; and (5) discrimination prevention in data mining.

**Keywords** Anonymisation · Cryptography · Digital signatures · Privacy · Privacy-enhancing techniques · Statistical disclosure control

## 14.1 Introduction

Applying cybersecurity mechanisms is essential to the protection of digital assets, whether they be personal, industrial or commercial. Current cybersecurity (and safety) measures include the collection of data from several points to detect, and potentially foresee, anomalies that can be attributed to malicious behaviour (e.g. cyberattacks). Collecting these data can, in some cases, encroach on the privacy of citizens. The new General Data Protection Regulation (GDPR)[1] states that the collection and processing of personal data for cybersecurity reasons is legitimate; how-

[1] Regulation (EU) 2016/679 of the European Parliament and of the Council of 27 April 2016 on the protection of natural persons with regard to the processing of personal data and on the free movement of such data, and repealing Directive 95/46/EC (General Data Protection Regulation).

J. Domingo-Ferrer (✉) · A. Blanco-Justicia
Department of Computer Science and Mathematics, CYBERCAT – Center for Cybersecurity Research of Catalonia, UNESCO Chair in Data Privacy, Universitat Rovira i Virgili, Tarragona, Catalonia
e-mail: josep.domingo@urv.cat; alberto.blanco@urv.cat



M. Christen et al. (eds.), *The Ethics of Cybersecurity*, The International Library of Ethics, Law and Technology 21,
https://doi.org/10.1007/978-3-030-29053-5_14

ever, it is still subject to the rest of requirements of the regulation, such as consent, transparency and adequate protection (see also Chaps. 5 and 10).

This chapter introduces privacy and data protection by design and reviews privacy-enhancing techniques (PETs). Although privacy by design includes both technical and operational measures, we focus here on the technical measures.

Therefore, the analyses within this chapter can empower both cybersecurity service providers and general service providers to design systems that are compliant with the GDPR, in addition to achieving other benefits. For example, while personal data can only be held by a controller for a limited period of time, anonymised data are no longer considered personal data and thus they are outside the scope of GDPR. Hence, anonymised data can be handled much more freely: they can be shared and stored indefinitely, which in particular enables exploratory, collaborative and long-term studies.

### *14.1.1 Design Strategies*

Privacy and data protection by design can be achieved by applying certain design strategies (see also Chap. 2). We next enumerate the eight design strategies introduced by Hoepman (2014).

1. *Minimise.* System designers should ensure that only the minimal necessary personal information is collected.
2. *Hide.* This strategy implies that the confidentiality of collected data is ensured, either by encrypting, pseudonymising or anonymising data in transit or in storage.
3. *Separate.* Personal data should be stored and processed in a distributed way.
4. *Aggregate.* Storage of individualised data should be restricted as much as possible and be replaced by aggregates whenever feasible.
5. *Inform.* Respondents should be made aware of what information about them is being collected and processed and for which reasons.
6. *Control.* Respondents should be able to consult, modify and delete the information about them.
7. *Enforce.* Privacy policies should be put in place and enforced.
8. *Demonstrate.* Data controllers ought to document all collection and analysis processes conducted on personal information.

The remaining sections of this chapter enumerate privacy-enhancing techniques that directly address the *hide* strategy but also aid in implementing the *separate*, *control* and *enforce* strategies. Note that some of the techniques described render data unlinkable to individuals, that is, they turn personal data into data that are no longer personal.

## 14.2 Identity, Authentication and Anonymity

Identity, authentication and access control are central components of secure systems. It is important that data assets be accessible only to authorised parties. On the one hand, a sound authentication and authorisation infrastructure prevents data breaches. On the other hand, it allows responsibilities to be attributed in case of a breach, which contributes to a transparent data processing environment.

Several methods exist to verify the identity of individuals, that is, to authenticate them. Some of them allow for the authentication of users without disclosing their identity.

### *14.2.1 Digital Signatures*

In paper documents, handwritten signatures guarantee the authenticity of the document, and the signer cannot repudiate it. Moreover, the paper support gives some protection against manipulation: deletions and additions can be detected, at least by an expert. Digital signatures were created in order to guarantee the authenticity and integrity in the case of electronic communications, and to avoid their repudiation. Digital signatures were made possible by the deployment of public-key encryption. In addition, digital signatures and the public key infrastructure can be used to provide authentication of individuals.

If both sender and receiver share some information, an alternative to digital signatures are message authentication codes (MACs). They are based on keyed cryptographic hash functions, and they can be used to guarantee the integrity of the message. MACs are commonly used in the context of symmetric encryption communications, where sender and receiver share a secret key.

Next, we enumerate specific classes of digital signatures that enable authentication while being compatible with some user anonymity.

#### 14.2.1.1 Blind Signatures

Blind signatures (Chaum 1983) are considered particularly useful for electronic payment systems, electronic voting schemes and token-based access control mechanisms; a user may obtain a signature (e.g. a signed coin from a bank) such that the signer does not know the contents of the message and cannot produce further valid signatures.

#### 14.2.1.2 Group Signatures

In a group signature scheme (Chaum and Van Heyst 1991), a set of users, called members of the group, can issue signatures of arbitrary messages on behalf of the group. A verifier can check the validity of the signature using the group public key. The main interest in this kind of signature is that it ensures the privacy of signers against potential verifiers, because a potential verifier cannot distinguish two signers from the same group.

A requirement of group signatures is the support for membership revocation of misbehaving members without the need to update the group public key. To facilitate member revocation, some members, called group managers, are endowed with the capability to revoke membership.

#### 14.2.1.3 Identity-Based Signatures

Identity-based signature schemes, theorised in Shamir (1984) and with the first concrete protocol, based on the Weil pairing, shown in Boneh and Franklin (2001), allow public keys to be arbitrary strings of some length, called identities. These strings are associated with a user and reflect some aspect of her identity, e.g. her email address. The corresponding secret key is then computed by a trusted entity taking as input the user's identity and, possibly, some other secret information, and is sent to the user through some secure channel. Identity-based public key signature schemes offer considerable flexibility in key generation and management.

#### 14.2.1.4 Attribute-Based Signatures

Attribute-based signatures generalise identity-based signatures in that, instead of having the users' identities as credentials, they use properties, or attributes, of the users as the latters' credentials (in the attribute-based setting, the identity is one more attribute of the user). Attribute-based signatures were introduced by Shanqing and Yingpei (2008), inspired by previously existing attribute-based encryption schemes, such as the one in Goyal et al. (2006). In attribute-based signatures (and encryption) schemes, the users receive private key shares associated with their credentials, such as their name, age, country of residence, having or not a driving licence, place of work, etc. Digital signatures are produced with respect to some function of the users' credentials, typically called a *policy*.

For example, a drugstore may accept drug prescriptions only if they are issued by medical doctors or by nurses with a long working experience. In this scenario, prescriptions could be digitally signed under the policy *role = "medical doctor" OR (role = "nurse" AND experience = "10 years")*. The identity of the signer in this case is irrelevant.

### 14.2.2 Zero-Knowledge Proofs

Zero-knowledge proofs (Ben-Or et al. 1988b) allow a prover to convince a verifying party of the truth of a statement without revealing any information other than the truth of the statement. In particular, if the statement requires the prover to hold some secret information, then the verifier does not learn this information—it is possible to prove knowledge of a secret without revealing the secret itself. Statements that only prove possession of a secret are known as zero-knowledge proofs of knowledge. Proofs can be either interactive or non-interactive depending on whether the parties can communicate during the proof. In general, non-interactive proofs (Blum et al. 1988) are considered more difficult since they cannot use interactive challenge-response protocols and they require the random oracle model or a common reference string between parties. Whereas zero-knowledge proofs can be rather inefficient, non-interactive proof systems built on bilinear groups (Groth and Sahai 2008) are particularly efficient for group-dependent problems where the secrets are group elements or the exponents of a group element. As many useful cryptographic schemes are built using bilinear pairings, particularly functional encryption, such a proof system can be very useful for proving knowledge of a cryptographic secret without revealing it.

Zero-knowledge proofs can be used to authenticate users holding cryptographic devices, such as smartcards, without leaking any information about these users except that they hold a valid card.

### 14.2.3 Implicit Authentication

In implicit authentication, a server can authenticate users by checking whether their behaviour is compatible or similar enough to their past-recorded behaviour. In this context, the user's behaviour can be modelled as a combination of features such as her browsing history, usual location, keystroke patterns, usually visible cell stations, etc.

In the study of Jakobsson et al. (2009), empirical evidence was given that the features collected from the user's device history are effective to distinguish users and therefore can be used to implicitly authenticate them. The collection of these data, however, may be too privacy-invasive. Proposals such as those by Safa et al. (2014), Domingo-Ferrer et al. (2015) and Blanco-Justicia and Domingo-Ferrer (2018) make use of homomorphic encryption and secure multiparty computation to authenticate users from their past behaviour without forcing them to disclose their profiles.

## 14.3 Private Communications

This section discusses the protection of communication channels. First, it describes end-to-end encryption, which provides confidentiality of communications. It then introduces anonymous channels. Having discussed mechanisms that allow users to be authenticated without revealing their identities, it is logical to discuss communication channels that do not reveal their address, which is also part of their identity.

### *14.3.1 End-to-End Encryption*

End-to-end encryption refers to the encryption of messages exchanged by two or more parties without the intervention of a centralised server. The centralised server may exist and support the transport of the messages but all this server sees is encrypted content. This behaviour is the opposite of the traditional message exchange protocols, in which the messages are only encrypted while in transit from the parties to the central server or from the central server to the parties.

End-to-end encryption is typically supported by having all participants have a key pair from a public-key encryption scheme. The centralised server, in addition to supporting the exchange of messages, works as a public-key repository, where users can find the public keys of the users to whom they want to send messages. Once a user has obtained another user's public key, she can use this public key to encrypt the messages, which will only be decryptable by the owner of the corresponding private key. A more efficient variant is for users to exchange random session keys for symmetric encryption by enciphering them under their public-private pairs and then encrypting the messages with a symmetric encryption scheme under these random temporal session keys.

### *14.3.2 Anonymous Channels*

Anonymous channels allow users to hide their address (e.g. the IP address) to the service provider they are communicating with. Examples of anonymous channels include mixnets and onion routing.

A mix network or mixnet is a routing protocol in which each of the network nodes shuffles (and re-encrypts) all received messages before sending them to the next node (Chaum 1981). The shuffling process is kept secret by each mix server. Additionally, the sender of the message might successively encrypt the message with each of the mix servers' public keys. If that is the case, each mix server will have to decrypt each of the encryption layers (as if peeling an onion) until the final destination of the message. The ToR network (Dingledine et al. 2004) is an example of this operation.

## 14.4 Privacy-Preserving Computations

This section describes mechanisms to perform computations on data while keeping the data private. The GDPR accepts encryption as a valid protection mechanism if the decryption keys are only available to those entitled to have them. However, most data analyses are incompatible with most encryption procedures: users typically require data in clear form to analyse them.

Nonetheless, the following encryption techniques do allow some computations to be carried out directly on encrypted data, and are usually part of larger systems, such as privacy-preserving data mining.

### *14.4.1 (Partially) Homomorphic Encryption*

Some encryption schemes are homomorphic in nature. Given two ciphertexts encrypting two plaintexts, certain operations can be performed on the ciphertexts such that the result can be decrypted to produce the outcome of applying an operation (not necessarily the same) on the plaintexts themselves. Thus, some computations can be performed on encrypted data. Schemes that exhibit homomorphic properties for a specific operation are known as partially homomorphic encryption schemes. Examples of this class are those in ElGamal (1985) and Paillier (1999). On the other hand, if the set of permissible operations enable arbitrary computations to be performed, then the schemes are referred to as fully homomorphic (Gentry 2009; Gentry et al. 2013). Although fully homomorphic schemes are in principle very powerful, currently available instances also involve very substantial overhead and storage expansion. For that reason, less powerful schemes known as somewhat homomorphic, are sometimes preferred: under these schemes, the number of operations that can be performed on ciphertext before decryption will no longer succeed is limited.

### *14.4.2 Multiparty Computation*

Secure multiparty computation protocols allow a set of parties to compute a joint function of their inputs in a secure way without requiring a trusted third party. During the execution of the protocol the parties do not learn anything about each other's input except what is implied by the output itself.

A general solution for the secure computation of functions among two players was introduced in Yao (1986). The main idea of these protocols was to describe the function as a circuit, and to compute every gate of the circuit in a secure way. This idea was extended to the multi-partite setting in Goldreich et al. (1987). They showed how to create a secure multiparty computation protocol that allows playing any game and does not leak any information if the majority of the participants are honest. These protocols are computationally secure. The first unconditionally secure multi-party computation protocols were presented in Ben-Or et al. (1988a) and Chaum et al. (1988). These authors gave protocols to compute any arithmetic function in a secure way when at least two thirds of the parties are honest.

Two of the main open problems in secure multiparty computation are: (i) to relax the assumptions on the behaviour of the players, and (ii) to reduce the computational and communication costs of the protocols for interesting families of functions. It should be observed that, in the general solutions described above, the computational costs of the protocol depend on the size of the circuit defining the function.

The most important properties of secure multiparty computation protocols are privacy and correctness. Another important property is fairness. A protocol is fair if there are no differences between the players when it comes to obtaining the output. That is, a protocol is fair if either everybody receives their output, or no one does.

## 14.5 Privacy in Databases

An alternative strategy to protect data is to make them no longer linkable to individuals, that is, to anonymise them. Anonymised data are no longer considered personal, and thus the legal restrictions that apply to personal data are lifted. This section describes the state of the art in data anonymisation techniques and models.

### *14.5.1 Respondent Privacy: Statistical Disclosure Control*

Traditionally, national statistical institutes and government agencies have systematically gathered information about individual respondents, either people or companies, with the aim of using it for policymaking and also distributing it for public and private research that may benefit their country. The most detailed way to disseminate this information is by releasing a microdata set, essentially a database table, each of whose records conveys information on a particular respondent. Although these databases may be extremely useful to researchers, it is of fundamental importance that their publication does not compromise the respondents' privacy in the sense of revealing information attributable to specific individuals. Statistical disclosure control (SDC) is the discipline that deals with the inherent trade-off between protecting the privacy of the respondents and ensuring that the protected data are still useful to researchers.

Usually, a microdata set contains a set of attributes that may be classified as identifiers, key attributes (a.k.a. quasi-identifiers), or confidential attributes. Identifiers allow unequivocal identification of individuals. Examples are social security numbers or full names, which need to be removed before publication of the microdata set. On the other hand, key attributes are those attributes that, in combination, may allow linkage with external information to re-identify (some of) the respondents to whom (some of) the records in the microdata set refer (*identity disclosure*). Examples include job, address, age, gender, height and weight. Last but not least, the microdata set contains confidential attributes with sensitive information on respondents, such as salary, religion, political affiliation or health condition. Beyond protecting against identity disclosure, SDC must prevent intruders from guessing the confidential attribute values of specific respondents (*attribute disclosure*).

Several SDC methods have been proposed in the literature to protect microdata sets (Hundepool et al. 2012). Next, we briefly review the main ones.

### *14.5.2 Non-perturbative Masking*

In SDC, masking refers to the process of obtaining an anonymised data set *X'* by modifying the original *X*. Masking can be perturbative or non-perturbative. In the former approach, the data values of *X* are perturbed to obtain *X'*. In contrast, in non-perturbative masking *X'* is obtained by removing some values and/or by making them more general; yet the information in *X'* is still true, although less detailed; as an example, a value might be replaced by a range containing the original value.

Common non-perturbative methods include:

- *Sampling*. Instead of publishing the whole data set, only a sample of it is released.
- *Generalisation*. The values of the different attributes are recoded in new, more general categories such that the information remains the same, albeit less specific.
- *Top/bottom coding*. In line with the previous method, values above (resp. below) a certain threshold are grouped together into a single category.
- *Local suppression*. If a combination of quasi-identifier values is shared by too few records, it may lead to re-identification. This method relies on replacing certain individual attribute values with missing values, so that the number of records sharing a particular combination of quasi-identifier values becomes larger.

### *14.5.3 Perturbative Masking*

Perturbative masking generates a modified version of the microdata set such that the privacy of the respondents is protected to a certain extent while simultaneously some statistical properties of the data are preserved. Well-known perturbative masking methods include:

- *Noise addition*. This is the most popular method, which consists in adding a noise vector to each record in the data set. The utility preservation depends on the amount and the distribution of the noise.
- *Data swapping*. This technique exchanges the values of the attributes randomly among individual records. Clearly, univariate distributions are preserved, but multivariate distributions may be substantially harmed unless swaps of very different values are ruled out.
- *Microaggregation*. This groups similar records together and releases the average record of each group (Domingo-Ferrer and Mateo-Sanz 2002). The more similar the records in a group, the more data utility is preserved.

### 14.5.4 Synthetic Microdata Generation

An anonymisation approach alternative to masking is synthetic data generation. That is, instead of modifying the original data set, a simulated data set is generated such that it preserves some properties of the original data set. The main advantage of synthetic data is that no respondent re-identification seems possible since the data are artificial. However, if, by chance, a synthetic record is very close to an original one, the respondent of the latter record will not feel safe when the former record is released. In addition, the utility of synthetic data sets is limited to preserving the statistical properties selected at the time of data synthesis.

Some examples of synthetic generation include methods based on multiple imputation (Rubin 1993) and methods that preserve means and co-variances (Burridge 2003). An effective alternative to the drawbacks of purely synthetic data are hybrid data, which mix original and synthetic data and are therefore more flexible (Domingo-Ferrer and González-Nicolás 2010). Yet another alternative is partially synthetic data, whereby only the most sensitive original data values are replaced by synthetic values.

### 14.5.5 Privacy Models

For an anonymised data set *X'* to be safe/private enough, it needs to be sufficiently anonymised. The level of anonymisation can be assessed after the generation of *X'* or prior to it.

*Ex post* methods rely on the analysis of the output data set and, therefore, it is possible to generate a data set that is not safe enough according to a certain criterion; several iterations with increasingly strict privacy parameters and decreasing utility may be needed. The most commonly used *ex post* approach is masking followed by record linkage. Protection is sufficient high only if there is a sufficiently low proportion of masked records that can be linked to the respective original records they come from.

On the other hand, the *ex ante* approach relies on *privacy models* that allow selecting the desired privacy level before producing *X'*. In this way, the output data set is always as private as specified by the model, although it may fail to provide enough utility if the model parameters are too strict.

#### 14.5.5.1 k-Anonymity and Extensions

A well-known privacy model is *k*-anonymity (Samarati and Sweeney 1998), which requires that each tuple of key-attribute values be shared by at least *k* records in the database. This condition may be achieved through generalisation and suppression mechanisms, and also through microaggregation (Domingo-Ferrer and Torra 2005).

Unfortunately, while this privacy model prevents identity disclosure, it may fail to protect against attribute disclosure. The definition of this privacy model establishes that complete re-identification is unfeasible within a group of records sharing the same tuple of perturbed key-attribute values. However, if the records in the group have the same value (or very similar values) for a confidential attribute, the confidential attribute value of an individual linkable to the group is leaked.

To fix this problem, some extensions of *k*-anonymity have been proposed, the most popular being *l*-diversity (Machanavajjhala et al. 2006) and *t*-closeness (Li et al. 2007a). The property of *l*-diversity is satisfied if there are at least *l* 'well-represented' values for each confidential attribute in all groups sharing the values of the quasi-identifiers. The property of *t*-closeness is satisfied when the distance between the distribution of each confidential attribute within each group and the whole data set is no more than a threshold *t*.

#### 14.5.5.2 Differential Privacy

Another important privacy model is differential privacy (Dwork 2006). This model was originally defined for queryable databases and consists in perturbing the original query result of a database before outputting it. This may be viewed as equivalent to perturbing the original data and then computing the queries over the modified data. Thus, differential privacy can also be seen as a privacy model for microdata sets.

An ε-differentially private algorithm is one that, when run on two datasets that differ in a single record, performs similarly (up to a power of ε) in both cases. That is, the presence or the absence of any single record does not significantly alter the output of the algorithm. Typically, ε-differential privacy is attained by adding Laplace noise with zero mean and parameter $\Delta(f)/\varepsilon$, where $\Delta(f)$ is the sensitivity of the algorithm (the maximum change in the algorithm output that can be caused by a change in a single record in the absence of noise) and ε is a privacy parameter; the larger ε, the less privacy.

#### 14.5.5.3 Permutation Model for Anonymisation

The permutation model (Domingo-Ferrer and Muralidhar 2016) views all anonymisation methods as being functionally equivalent to a two-step procedure consisting of a permutation step (mapping the original data set to the output of a reverse mapping procedure [Muralidhar et al. 2014]) plus a noise addition step (adding the difference between the reverse-mapped output and the anonymised data set). Since the ranks in the reverse-mapped version and in the anonymised version are the same by construction, the noise added in the second step needs to be small, since otherwise ranks would change. This shows that any anonymisation method basically amounts to permutation.

The most interesting feature, however, is that each subject/respondent can check whether a privacy model called *(d,v)*-permuted privacy is satisfied for his or her original record by the anonymised data set for some $d$ and $v$ of her choice; in plain words, each subject can check whether his or her response has been permuted enough in the anonymised data set. The subject only needs to know his or her original record and the anonymised data set.

### *14.5.6 Redaction and Sanitisation of Documents*

Document redaction consists of removing or blacking out sensitive terms in plain textual documents. Alternatively, when sensitive terms are replaced (instead of removed) by generalisations (e.g. AIDS → disease), the process is more generically referred to as document sanitisation (Bier et al. 2009). Document sanitisation is more desirable than pure redaction, since the former better preserves the utility of the protected output. Moreover, in document redaction, the existence of blacked-out parts in the released document can raise awareness of the document's sensitivity to potential attackers (Bier et al. 2009), whereas sanitisation gives no such clues.

In both cases, two tasks should be performed: (i) the detection of textual terms that may cause disclosure of sensitive information, and (ii) the removal or obfuscation of those entities. Traditionally, the detection of sensitive terms has been tackled in a manual way. This requires a human expert who applies certain standard guidelines that detail the correct procedures to sanitise sensitive entities (National Security Agency 2005). Manual redaction has proven to be quite time-consuming and it does not scale to currently required levels of information outsourcing (Chakaravarthy et al. 2008; Bier et al. 2009).

In recent years, numerous automatic redaction methods have been proposed. Some approaches rely on specific or tailored patterns to detect certain types of information based on their linguistic or structural regularities (e.g. names, addresses and social security numbers) (Sweeney 1996; Tveit et al. 2004; Douglass et al. 2005). Schemes such as Douglass et al. (2005) and Tveit et al. (2004) use more specific patterns to remove sensitive terms from medical records. These patterns are designed according to the HIPAA 'Safe Harbor' rules (Department of Health and Human

Services, USA 1996) that specify eighteen data elements which must be eliminated from clinical data in order to anonymise a clinical text. As an alternative to manually-specified patterns, several authors have proposed using trained classifiers that recognise sensitive entities. Yet others present a tool that focuses on the sanitisation of documents directly linked to certain companies (Cumby and Ghani 2011). The data to be detected include words and phrases that reveal the company the document belongs to.

Abril et al. (2011) propose a general scheme that uses a trained classifier for Named Entity Recognition (NER) (i.e. the Stanford NER [Finkel et al. 2005]) to automatically recognise entities belonging to general categories such as person, organisation and location names. This mechanism suggests generalising sensitive entities instead of removing them from the sanitised document. The goal is to achieve a certain degree of privacy while preserving some of the semantics. Jiang et al. (2009) provide a theoretic measure ('t-plausibility') that guides the sanitisation process in order to balance the trade-off between privacy protection and utility preservation. Their scheme tries to preserve the utility of sanitised documents by generalising terms based on general-purpose ontology/taxonomy. Finally, Sánchez et al. (2013) present a system that relies on information theory to quantify the amount of information conveyed by each term of the document. The latter work builds on Sánchez et al. (2012), where sensitive terms are generalised.

### 14.5.7 Data Stream Anonymisation

A data stream is a sequence of data items that become available over time. This type of dynamic data is common in some environments, such as sensor networks, web logs, etc. Data streams are quite different from static data sets. In particular, streams are potentially infinite, may be fast flowing and may require fast processing for anonymisation. Because of these particularities, anonymisation methods that target dynamic data must be specifically designed. Whereas there is a large body of SDC methods for static data, the disclosure risk control literature on data streams is limited. The existing proposals follow three main approaches: perturbative masking, non-perturbative masking and counterfeiting.

In the perturbative masking approach, some noise is added to conceal the real value of the records. Li et al. (2007b) devised a method by which the correlation and the autocorrelation of multivariate data streams is tracked in an attempt to identify a good trade-off between privacy and utility. Differential privacy has also been used to anonymise data streams in some constrained scenarios. In Dwork et al. (2010), a differentially private counter of the number of 1's in a data stream is released at each step. This method was generalised in Bolot et al. (2013) to compute differentially private sums over restricted windows.

In the non-perturbative masking approach, one seeks to hide each record in the stream within a group of records. In the static data setting, $k$-anonymity and its extensions are well-known privacy models that follow this approach. In the work of

Cao et al. (2011a) and (2011b) these privacy models are adapted to streams. Since to make groups we need to accumulate records, this approach necessarily introduces some delay in the release of the anonymised stream. Quite recently, a perturbative adaptation of $k$-anonymity for streams, based on a primitive called steered microaggregation, has been introduced by Domingo-Ferrer and Soria-Comas (2017).

In the counterfeiting approach, a record is attempted to be hidden within a group of records. By hiding each record within a group of fake records, we avoid the delay inherent to the previous approach Kim et al. (2014). The main drawback is the overhead introduced by the addition of fake records.

### *14.5.8 Owner Privacy: Privacy-Preserving Data Mining*

Privacy-Preserving Data Mining (PPDM) tries to solve the following question: *can we develop accurate data mining models without access to the data at the record level?* Therefore, it consists of techniques for modifying the original data in such a way that the private data remain private even after the mining process (Verykios et al. 2004).

There are two radically different approaches to PPDM, namely, *PPDM based on perturbation* and *PPDM based on Secure Multiparty Computation* (SMC). The first was introduced by Agrawal and Srikant (2000) in the database community. Its idea is that respondents (who do not wish to reveal the exact value of their respective answers/records) or controllers (who wish to engage in joint computation with other controllers without disclosing their respective data sets to each other) compute modified values for sensitive attributes in such a way that accurate statistical results can still be obtained on the modified data. PPDM based on perturbation is largely based on statistical disclosure control techniques.

PPDM based on SMC, which was introduced by Lindell and Pinkas (2000) in the cryptographic community, addresses the problem of several entities holding confidential databases who wish to run a data mining algorithm on the union of their databases, without revealing unnecessary information. This type of PPDM is equivalent to data mining in distributed environments, where the data are partitioned across multiple parties. Partitioning can be vertical (each party holds all records on a different subset of attributes), horizontal (each party holds a subset of the records, but each record contains all attributes) or mixed.

Using SMC protocols based on cryptography (many of these resort to homomorphic encryption) or on sharing perturbed information in ways that do not alter the final results often requires changing or adapting the data mining algorithms. Hence, each cryptographic PPDM protocol is designed for a specific data mining computation and, in general, is not valid for other computations. For example, a secure scalar product protocol based on cryptographic primitives is applied to privacy preserving $k$-means clustering over a distributed dataset by Vaidya and Clifton (2003) and Jagannathan and Wright (2005). Similarly, Du et al. (2004) and Karr et al. (2009)

propose different ways (none of them based on encryption) to securely compute matrix products, which permits obtaining privacy-preserving linear regressions.

A different PPDM scenario arises when a data controller wants to leverage the storage and also the computational power of untrusted clouds to process her sensitive data. This setting was studied in the H2020 project 'CLARUS' (http://clarussecure.eu) and solutions based on cleartext data splitting across several clouds have been proposed. Furthermore, protocols to compute scalar products and matrix products with minimum controller involvement and maximum cloud involvement have been given by Domingo-Ferrer et al. (2018).

### 14.5.9 User Privacy: Private Information Retrieval

Finally, we address the privacy of the users querying a database. A history of queries to a database, or to a web search engine, can be used by the database owner to learn the interests of users, that is, to profile them. In this scenario we seek to protect users from unrequested profiling by database owners. Mechanisms to achieve this goal are collectively referred to as private information retrieval (PIR).

Initial works on PIR, such as Chor et al. (1995), model databases as vectors of entries. Users requesting information from the database do so by providing an index or a set of indices of the database vector. In this setting, PIR techniques aim to hide the indices provided by the users. However, these initial approaches have several shortcomings. First, they require collaboration from the database owner, something that cannot be ensured unless database owners have a clear incentive to do so. Second, to perfectly hide the queried database indices one would need to query *all* entries in the database and then filter the results locally, which is clearly inefficient for moderately sized databases and certainly unfeasible for big databases. Finally, modelling a database as a vector and assuming that the user knows the indices where the desired information is stored is not applicable to most real databases, let alone web search engines.

Several solutions have been proposed to overcome such shortcomings. Domingo-Ferrer et al. (2009) propose a system named Goopir in which user queries are locally complemented with terms of similar frequency in the language (connected by OR operations). The responses are then filtered locally. TrackMeNot (Howe and Nissenbaum 2009) is a browser extension which periodically sends fake queries to web search engines so that the distribution of interests of the user is flattened and no useful profile can be extracted. Finally, other proposals such as the one by Reiter and Rubin (1998) make use of a P2P network in which users submit queries generated by other users to the web search engine, thus achieving the same results as TrackMeNot (flattened interest distributions) but without overloading the web search engines with fake queries.

## 14.6 Discrimination Prevention in Data Mining

Other than privacy implications, automated data collection and processing may have a secondary negative impact, which is discrimination. Automated data mining is used in several services to derive association and classification rules, which are then applied to a variety of decisions, such as loan granting, personnel selection, insurance premium computation, etc. While an automated classifier may be seen as a fair decision-making tool, if the training data are inherently biased, the generated rules will result in potentially discriminatory decisions.

Some works tackle this issue by pre-processing the training data using techniques akin to those from statistical disclosure control, but aimed at reducing the inherent bias in the data. Others act directly on the automatically mined rules, either by eliminating some of them or by generalising some of the conditions of these rules (Hajian and Domingo-Ferrer 2013; Hajian et al. 2014, 2015).

**Acknowledgments and Disclaimer** The following funding sources are gratefully acknowledged: European Commission (H2020–700540 CANVAS), Government of Catalonia (ICREA Acadèmia Prize to J. Domingo-Ferrer and 2017 SGR 705) and Spanish Government (project RTI2018–095094-B-C21 'Consent'). The views in this paper are the authors' own and do not necessarily reflect the views of UNESCO or any of the funders.

## References

Abril D, Navarro-Arribas G, Torra V (2011) On the declassification of confidential documents. International conference on modeling decisions for Artificial Intelligence. Springer, pp 235–246

Agrawal R, Srikant R (2000) Privacy-preserving data mining. ACM 29(2). Available at: https://dl.acm.org/citation.cfm?id=335438. Last access 7 July 2019

Ben-Or M, Goldreich O, Goldwasser S, Håstad J, Kilian J, Micali S, Rogaway P (1988b) Everything provable is provable in zero-knowledge. In: Conference on the theory and application of cryptography. Springer, pp 37–56

Ben-Or M, Goldwasser S, Wigderson A (1988a) Completeness theorems for non-cryptographic fault-tolerant distributed computation. In: Proceedings of the twentieth annual ACM symposiumon Theory of computing. ACM, pp 1–10

Bier E, Chow R, Golle P et al (2009) The rules of redaction: identify, protect, review (and repeat). IEEE Secur Priv 7(6):46–53

Blanco-Justicia A, Domingo-Ferrer J (2018) Efficient privacy-preserving implicit authentication. Comput Comms (Elsevier) 125:13–23

Blum M, Feldman P, Silvio M (1988) Non-interactive zero-knowledge and its applications. In: Proceedings of the twentieth annual ACM symposium on Theory of Computing. ACM, pp 103–112

Bolot J, Fawaz N, Muthukrishnan S et al (2013) Private decayed predicate sums on streams. In: Proceedings of the 16th international conference on database theory. ACM, pp 284–295

Boneh D, Franklin M (2001) Identity-based encryption from the Weil pairing. Annual international cryptology conference. Springer, pp 213–229

Burridge J (2003) Information preserving statistical obfuscation. Stats Comput (Springer) 13(4):321–327

Cao J, Carminati B, Ferrari E et al (2011a) Castle: continuously anonymizing data streams. IEEE Trans Dep Secur Comput (IEEE) 8(3):337–352

Cao J, Karras P, Kalnis P et al (2011b) SABRE: a sensitive attribute Bucketization and REdistribution framework for t-closeness. VLDB J 20(1):59–81. Springer, New York

Chakaravarthy VT, Gupta H, Roy P et al (2008) Efficient techniques for document sanitization. In: Proceedings of the 17th ACM conference on information and knowledge management. ACM, pp 843–852

Chaum D (1983) Blind signatures for untraceable payments. Adv Cryptol:199–203

Chaum D (1981) Untraceable electronic mail, return addresses, and digital pseudonyms. Commun ACM 24:84–90

Chaum, Van Heyst E (1991) Group signatures. Workshop on the theory and application of cryptographic techniques. Springer, pp 257–265

Chaum D, Claude C, Damgaard I (1988) Multi-party unconditionally secure protocols. In: Proceedings of the twentieth annual ACM symposium on Theory of computing ACM, pp 11–19

Chor B, Goldreich O, Kushilevitz E, Sudan M (1995) Private information retrieval. Foundations of computer science, 1995. In: Proceedings., 36th annual symposium on IEEE, pp 41–50

Cumby CM, Ghani R (2011) A machine learning based system for semi-automatically redacting documents. IAAI. Available at: https://www.aaai.org/ocs/index.php/IAAI/IAAI-11/paper/view/3528. Last access 7 July 2019

Department of Health and Human Services, USA (1996) The Health insurance Portability and Accountability Act of 1996. Public Law:104–191

Dingledine R, Mathewson N, Syverson P (2004) Tor: The second-generation onion router. Naval Research Lab Washington DC

Domingo-Ferrer J, Solanas A, Castellà-Roca J (2009) H(k)-private information retrieval from privacy-uncooperative queryable databases. Online Inf Rev (Emerald Group Publishing Limited) 33(4):720–744

Domingo-Ferrer J, Soria-Comas J (2017) Steered microaggregation: a unified primitive for anonymization of data sets and data streams. Data Mining Workshops (ICDMW), 2017 IEEE International Conference on IEEE:995–1002

Domingo-Ferrer J, Mateo-Sanz JM (2002) Practical data-oriented microaggregation for statistical disclosure control. IEEE Trans Knowl Data Eng 14(1):189–201

Domingo-Ferrer J, Muralidhar K (2016) New directions in anonymization: permutation paradigm, verifiability by subjects and intruders, transparency to users. Inf Sci (Elsevier) 337:11–24

Domingo-Ferrer J, Torra V (2005) Ordinal, continuous and heterogeneous k-anonymity through microaggregation. Data Min Knowl Disc (Springer) 1(2):195–212

Domingo-Ferrer J, Wu Q, Blanco-Justicia A (2015) Flexible and robust privacy-preserving implicit authentication. IFIP International Information Security Conference. Springer:18–34

Domingo-Ferrer J, Sara Ricci S, Domingo-Enrich C (2018) Outsourcing scalar products and matrix products on privacy-protected unencrypted data stored in untrusted clouds. Inf Sci (Elsevier) 436:320–342

Domingo-Ferrer J, González-Nicolás U (2010) Hybrid microdata using microaggregation. Inf Sci (Elsevier) 180(15):2834–2844

Douglass MM, Cliffford GD, Reisner A et al (2005) De-identification algorithm for free-text nursing notes. Comput Cardiol (IEEE):331–334

Du W, Yunghsiang SH, Chen S (2004) Privacy-preserving multivariate statistical analysis: linear regression and classification. In: Proceedings of the 2004 SIAM international conference on data mining. SIAM, pp 222–233

Dwork C (2006) Differential privacy. Automata, Languages and Programming. 33rd International Colloquium, ICALP 2006, Venice, Italy, July 10–14, 2006, Proceedings, Part II, pp 1–12

Dwork C, Naor M, Pitassi T, Rothblum GN (2010) Differential privacy under continual observation. Proceedings of the forty-second ACM symposium on Theory of computing. ACM:715–724

ElGamal T (1985) A public key cryptosystem and a signature scheme based on discrete logarithms. IEEE Trans Inf Theor (IEEE) 31:469–472

Finkel JR, Grenager T, Manning C (2005) Incorporating non-local information into information extraction systems by gibbs sampling. Proceedings of the 43rd annual meeting on association for computational linguistics. Assoc Comput Linguist:363–370

Gentry C (2009) Fully homomorphic encryption using ideal lattices. In: 41st ACM STOC, pp 169–178

Gentry C, Sahai A, Waters B (2013) Homomorphic encryption from learning with errors: conceptually-simpler, asymptotically-faster, attribute-based. In: Advances in cryptology – CRYPTO 2013. Springer, Berlin/Heidelberg, pp 75–92

Goldreich O, Micali S, Wigderson A (1987) How to play any mental game. In: Proceedings of the nineteenth annual ACM symposium on Theory of computing. ACM, pp 218–229

Goyal V, Pandey O, Sahai A et al (2006) Attribute-based encryption for fine-grained access control of encrypted data. In: Proceedings of the 13th ACM conference on computer and communications security. ACM, pp 89–98

Groth J, Sahai A (2008) Efficient non-interactive proof systems for bilinear groups. Annual international conference on the theory and applications of cryptographic techniques. Springer, pp 415–432

Hajian S, Domingo-Ferrer J (2013) A methodology for direct and indirect discrimination prevention in data mining. IEEE Trans Knowl Data Eng 25(7):1445–1459

Hajian S, Domingo-Ferrer J, Farràs O (2014) Generalization-based privacy preservation and discrimination prevention in data publishing and mining. Data Min Knowl Disc (Springer) 28(5–6):1158–1188

Hajian S, Domingo-Ferrer J, Monreale D et al (2015) Discrimination- and privacy-aware patterns. Data Min Knowl Disc (Springer) 29(6):1733–1782

Hoepman J-H (2014) Privacy design strategies. IFIP international information security conference. Springer, pp 446–459

Howe DC, Nissenbaum H (2009) TrackMeNot: resisting surveillance in web search. Lessons from the identity trail: anonymity, privacy, and identity in a networked society, vol 23. Oxford University Press, pp 417–437

Hundepool A, Domingo-Ferrer J, Franconi L et al (2012) Statistical disclosure control. Wiley, Chichester

Jagannathan G, Wright RN (2005) Privacy-preserving distributed k-means clustering over arbitrarily partitioned data. In: Proceedings of the eleventh ACM SIGKDD international conference on Knowledge discovery in data mining. ACM, pp 593–599

Jakobsson M, Shi E, Golle P et al (2009) Implicit authentication for mobile devices. In: Proceedings of the 4th USENIX conference on Hot topics in security, pp 9–9

Jiang W, Murugesan M, Clifton C et al (2009) T-plausibility: semantic preserving text sanitization. Comput Sci Eng, 2009. CSE'09. International conference on. IEEE, pp 68–75

Karr AF, Lin X et al (2009) Privacy-preserving analysis of vertically partitioned data using secure matrix products. J Off Stat 25(1):125

Kim S, Sung MK, Chung YD (2014) A framework to preserve the privacy of electronic health data streams. J Biomed Inf (Elsevier) 50:95–106

Li F, Sun J, Papadimitriou S, et al (2007b) Hiding in the crowd: privacy preservation on evolving streams through correlation tracking. ICDE 2007. IEEE 23rd international conference on data engineering. IEEE, pp 686–695

Li N, Li T, Venkatasubramanian S (2007a) t-closeness: privacy beyond k-anonymity and ℓ-diversity. Data engineering, ICDE 2007. IEEE 23rd international conference on, pp 106–115

Lindell Y, Pinkas B (2000) Privacy preserving data mining. Annual International Cryptology Conference. Springer, pp 36–54

Machanavajjhala A, Gehrke J, Kifer D et al (2006) ℓ-diversity: privacy beyond k-anonymity. ICDE 2006. IEEE 22nd International Conference on Data Engineering. IEEE, pp 24–36

Muralidhar K, Sarathy R, Domingo-Ferrer J (2014) Reverse mapping to preserve the marginal distributions of attributes in masked microdata. International conference on privacy in statistical databases. Springer, pp 105–116

National Security Agency (2005) Redacting with confidence: how to safely publish sanitized reports converted from word to pdf. Available at: http://www.ca7.uscourts.gov/forms/nsa-redact.pdf. Last access 7 July 2019

Paillier P (1999) Public-key cryptosystems based on composite degree residuosity classes. International conference on the theory and applications of cryptographic techniques, pp 223–238

Reiter MK, Rubin AD (1998) Crowds: anonymity for web transactions. ACM Trans Inf Syst Secur (TISSEC) (ACM) 1(1):66–92

Rubin DB (1993) Statistical disclosure limitation. J Off Stat 9(2):461–468

Safa NA, Safavi-Naini R, Shahandashti SF (2014) Privacy-preserving implicit authentication. IFIP international information security conference. Springer, pp 471–484

Samarati P, Sweeney L (1998) Protecting privacy when disclosing information: k-anonymity and its enforcement through generalization and suppression. Technical report, SRI International. Available at: http://www.csl.sri.com/papers/sritr-98-04/. Last access 7 July 2019

Sánchez D, Batet M, Viejo A (2012) Detecting sensitive information from textual documents: an information-theoretic approach. International conference on modeling decisions for Artificial Intelligence. Springer, pp 173–184

Sánchez D, Batet M, Viejo A (2013) Automatic general-purpose sanitization of textual documents. IEEE Trans Inf Forensic Secur 8(6):853–862

Shamir A (1984) Identity-based cryptosystems and signature schemes. Workshop on the theory and application of cryptographic techniques. Springer, pp 47–53

Shanqing G, Yingpei Z (2008) Attribute-based signature scheme. Information security and assurance, 2008. ISA 2008. International conference on. IEEE, pp 509–511

Sweeney L (1996) Replacing personally-identifying information in medical records, the scrub system. Proceedings of the AMIA annual fall symposium. Am Med Inform Assoc, p 333

Tveit A, Edsberg O, Rost TB et al (2004) Anonymization of general practitioner medical records. Second HelsIT Conference. Available at: https://pdfs.semanticscholar.org/c13b/fe9e6568c613f9e7a016a445bbc1372dd760.pdf. Last access 7 July 2019

Vaidya J, Clifton C (2003) Privacy-preserving k-means clustering over vertically partitioned data. In: Proceedings of the ninth ACM SIGKDD international conference on Knowledge discovery and data mining. ACM, pp 206–215

Verykios VS, Bertino E, Fovino IN et al (2004) State-of-the-art in privacy preserving data mining. ACM Sigmod Rec 33(1):50–57

Yao AC-C (1986) How to generate and exchange secrets. Found Comp Sci, 1986., 27th annual symposium on. IEEE, pp 162–167

# Chapter 15
# Best Practices and Recommendations for Cybersecurity Service Providers

**Alexey Kirichenko, Markus Christen, Florian Grunow, and Dominik Herrmann**

**Abstract** This chapter outlines some concrete best practices and recommendations for cybersecurity service providers, with a focus on data sharing, data protection and penetration testing. Based on a brief outline of dilemmas that cybersecurity service providers may experience in their daily operations, it discusses data handling policies and practices of cybersecurity vendors along the following five topics: customer data handling; information about breaches; threat intelligence; vulnerability-related information; and data involved when collaborating with peers, CERTs, cybersecurity research groups, etc. There is, furthermore, a discussion of specific issues of penetration testing such as customer recruitment and execution as well as the supervision and governance of penetration testing. The chapter closes with some general recommendations regarding improving the ethical decision-making procedures of private cybersecurity service providers.

**Keywords** Data handling · Data sharing · Penetration testing · Threat intelligence · Vulnerability disclosure

A. Kirichenko (✉)
F-Secure Corporation, Helsinki, Finland
e-mail: alexey.kirichenko@f-secure.com

M. Christen
UZH Digital Society Initiative, Zürich, Switzerland
e-mail: christen@ethik.uzh.ch

F. Grunow
ERNW. Enno Rey Netzwerke GmbH, Heidelberg, Germany
e-mail: fgrunow@ernw.de

D. Herrmann
Privacy and Security in Information Systems Group (PSI), University of Bamberg, Bamberg, Germany
e-mail: dominik.herrmann@uni-bamberg.de



M. Christen et al. (eds.), *The Ethics of Cybersecurity*, The International Library of Ethics, Law and Technology 21,
https://doi.org/10.1007/978-3-030-29053-5_15

## 15.1 Introduction: Dilemmas of Cybersecurity Service Providers

Security software and service providers—usually private companies—play a pivotal role in cybersecurity as they provide the competences and tools for defending the IT infrastructure, devices and data of their customers. Individuals, companies and state agencies put a considerable amount of trust in the tools and services of cybersecurity service providers. Furthermore, those specialised companies often obtain deep insights into the IT infrastructure and information processes of their customers and—more generally—a deep understanding of cyber threats, which provides them with a special responsibility on how to handle such knowledge and customer data. When cybersecurity service providers perform evaluations such as penetration testing, additional responsibilities come into play.

Complicating matters further, new dilemmas have emerged due to partially conflicting regulations, the possibility that some customers may break laws and the fact that state actors are increasingly involved in carrying out cyberattacks. We exemplify these challenges with a dilemma related to threat intelligence and malware detection capabilities of cybersecurity companies.

### *15.1.1 Example: Dealing with Governmental Malware*

The use of malware by governments and Law Enforcement Agencies (LEA) for surveillance and other purposes is a widely accepted fact. In 2014, F-Secure's CRO Mikko Hyppönen said: "If someone had come to me ten years ago and told me that by 2014 it will be commonplace for democratic Western governments to write viruses and actively deploy them against other governments, even friendly governments, I would have thought it was a movie plot. But that's exactly where we are today" (Thomson 2014).

The reasons for governmental use of malware and other details of such operations vary widely, including, for example, terrorist activities investigations, espionage or tracking opposition journalists. One early case is Magic Lantern (Martin 2003), a keystroke logging software developed by the United States' FBI. It could be installed remotely, via an e-mail attachment or by exploiting common operating system vulnerabilities. Already back then there were concerns expressed by antivirus vendors "that FBI software reportedly designed for covert keystroke monitoring could fall into the wrong hands" (Jackson 2001).

In 2011, a well-established group of German hackers accused the German government of releasing a backdoor Trojan into the wild. Security firm F-Secure confirmed that the program included a keylogger and code that could take screenshots and record audio (e.g. for room surveillance; Bott 2011). The group reverse-engineered and analysed the program, which it called "a lawful interception malware program used by German police forces". The malware also offered a remote control or backdoor functionality for uploading and executing arbitrary other programs. The program's behaviour went well beyond the ability to "observe and intercept Internet based telecommunication" (in other words, wiretapping Internet-based telephony), which is allowed by German courts. In addition, significant design and implementation flaws essentially made all of the functionality available to anyone on the Internet. Figures published recently (2017) revealed that the top five countries originating use of malware and other cyber-attacks were USA, China, Brazil, India and Russia (Ley 2018).

However, improving malware and attack detection capabilities of cybersecurity solutions clearly complicates the development and operation of malware by state agencies. Already in 2001, the public disclosure of the existence of Magic Lantern sparked a debate as to whether anti-virus companies should detect the FBI's keystroke logger or could agree to whitelist it. There were rumours that Network Associates (maker of McAfee anti-virus products at that time) had contacted the FBI following press reports about Magic Lantern to ensure their anti-virus software would not detect the program. Network Associates issued a denial, fuelling speculation as to which anti-virus products might or might not detect government Trojans.

It is likely that the news that North Korea's antivirus software whitelisted malware (Sharwood 2018) did not come as a surprise: "Just why North Korea's government wants software that won't spot some viruses is not hard to guess: a totalitarian dictatorship can only sustain itself with pervasive surveillance and leaving a backdoor that allows viruses in would facilitate just that." There is, however, little evidence on how malware used by Western governments is treated by Western cybersecurity companies. Responding to a transparency plea from leading privacy and security experts in 2013, a number of leading antivirus firms stated that they had strict policies against aiding law enforcement by whitelisting spyware or building backdoors into their software. For example, Symantec stated: "We have a strict policy against whitelisting malware for law enforcement and governments globally. We have never received such a request from law enforcement" (Westervelt 2013). We should note, however, that some of the approached companies failed to respond to the plea (Schwartz 2013). The summary published by Bruce Schneier at that time was: "Understanding that the companies could certainly lie, this is the response so far: no one has admitted to doing so" (Schneier 2013).

In fact, a need to comply with a law or a court order to whitelist governmental malware will clearly leave cybersecurity companies with no choice. Situations can easily be imagined, however, when a difficult choice does exist, because there are no appropriate laws, because a cybersecurity vendor is approached by a LEA from a different state, or due to other reasons. Should the vendor plainly say 'no' to the whitelisting request? Alternatively, should it weigh the consequences of preventing or hampering the LEA operations against privacy of its customers, dangers of a potential use of the backdoor by cybercriminals, and other relevant factors, which may also introduce serious uncertainties in the decision-making?

### 15.1.2 Dilemmas of Cybersecurity Service Providers

The example above is one of several dilemmas cybersecurity service providers may face in their daily operations, where often no clear legal guidance is provided. This is where ethical considerations come into play to find an optimal solution. In addition to the 'whitelist governmental malware?' question discussed above, the following list provides further examples of such dilemmas:

- *Should questionable customers be protected?* Not all customers of cybersecurity service providers may have good intentions; some may even be labelled 'criminals' with respect to certain legal systems. However, whether certain customers are considered 'questionable' may not in any case be clear, for example if they reside in authoritarian or totalitarian states and are surveyed for political reasons. Furthermore, cybersecurity service providers may also choose to collaborate with such states and thus may become instruments for questionable aims. Although the judicial system in which the cybersecurity vendor is operating (also with respect to export regulations or sanction regimes) may to a certain extent provide a framework for declining certain customers or allowing LEAs to monitor their devices, handling such cases sometimes remains an issue of the company's policy and attitude.
- *Should incidental findings be disclosed?* Cybersecurity service providers have considerable access to the information flows of their customers in order to detect, for example, hostile intrusions. However, what should a cybersecurity vendor do when they find traces of a crime committed by a customer company when monitoring its network? To a certain extent, the legal code of the customer's location may provide answers in such cases, e.g. when the crimes concern child pornography or crimes against humanity. It must also be considered that some legislation may forbid disclosing such information. In-between those legal boundaries, a space for ethical choices remains.
- *Should illegal breaches be profited from?* Some cybersecurity service providers (for example the Italian company 'Hacking Team') provide offensive technology to the worldwide law enforcement and intelligence communities; i.e. tools against which other cybersecurity vendors develop countermeasures. Sometimes, illegal breaches may reveal source-code of such offensive tools, which legally is considered a break of a trade secret. Should an antivirus company analyse the source code in order to improve their tools? Again, a clear legal regulation is not available for such cases and an ethical choice has to be made.
- *Should non-customers be informed about potential risks?* Private cybersecurity service providers operate under constraints to optimise revenue. How should such organisations deal with findings that do not directly lead to an increased revenue? For example, should they inform victims even if these are not their customers? Although most cybersecurity vendors work in a commercial environment, they rely on the work of many volunteers. It is therefore recommended that a commercial security organisation gives something back to the community, be

it information or tools. To what extent are cybersecurity service providers able to contribute to the community and how can such behaviour be incentivised?

In the following, we do not further discuss such dilemmas in detail. Rather, we provide an overview of domains, where cybersecurity service providers should implement policies in order to handle challenging situations in an optimal way.

## 15.2 Domains for Policy Implementations

### *15.2.1 Customer Data Handling*

Data handling is a fairly heavily regulated domain, especially if personal data is involved (see Chap. 5). Cybersecurity service providers operating under the regime of the General Data Protection Regulation (GDPR) of the EU have to fulfil the principles stated within, in particular transparency. Cybersecurity vendors need to inform their customers of what data they collect, how they process it, for what purposes, etc. To analyse this aspect, we distinguish between data emerging from consumers (e.g. individuals buying an antivirus tool) and companies that usually make use of a broader spectrum of services.

Taking the practices at F-Secure as an example, consumer-related data can be differentiated into the following categories:

- *Client relationship data.* This data is necessary to manage the relationship of the company with its clients, and to market and sell the company services to them or to the legal entity that they represent. Any company on the free market seeking customers will collect such data.
- *Service data.* This data is automatically processed in order to provide the clients with the services that they requested. This also includes the data that the clients actively submit to the vendors when subscribing to their services. Again, any entity on the free market that sells services to customers will collect such data.
- *Security data.* This usually concerns anonymous or pseudonymous data that the company needs to collect to keep the clients secure, for instance, execution details of certain programs on a client device or its networking activities.
- *Analytics data.* This concerns additional anonymous or pseudonymous data that the companies collect to learn when and how their services are found and used, for example, which protection features of a specific security product are enabled by a specific customer or how many infections were detected and blocked in a given customer device.

Whereas data from the first two categories are 'standard data' that any company will collect from their customers, the last two categories refer to specific data sets only available to cybersecurity service providers. It is therefore recommended to place these data sets in their own 'silos' to ensure that, in particular, security data is processed separately from data of the other types. To defend against a specific malware, a cybersecurity vendor does not need to know whether a particular user has been infected with that malware. Rather, the company only needs to know that this new form of malware emerged, analyse it, and then provide countermeasures to all of their customers. Analytics data should be processed in pseudonymised form by default, hence enabling the sharing of data among developers without privacy risks to an individual. Service data (i.e. name, email-address and other identifiers) and analytics data are combined only based on specific rules, for instance, to make it possible to send a reminder to a customer which purchased but did not activate certain security service. Via access control policies, cybersecurity service providers ensure that their marketing people do not have access to the analytics data, and all the other departments have no access to the service data.

Corporate customers often use the same products as consumers; hence, the same types of data and policies as described above are relevant. However, corporate customers may in addition use Advanced Threat Protection (ATP), vulnerability scanning and other products that go beyond the standard Endpoint Protection paradigm, as they enhance corporate networks security. Separating the device identity from the security analysis is no longer sufficient for ATP products. Since anti-malware activities have moved from detecting malicious code to detecting malicious behaviour, protecting corporate networks requires more context for analysing device and user behaviour.

The above observation means that anonymisation and data separation are no longer a viable approach. Hence, to safeguard privacy, more focus needs to be put into alternative protection means such as sufficiently granular access control mechanisms, security personnel activity logging or usage guidance. An increasingly typical occurrence is that security and service data of corporate security products are processed jointly, with a pseudonymisation that takes place between corporate customers and a cybersecurity provider, as opposed to pseudonymisation within the provider's systems. In particular, this means that the only way for a security provider to learn actual names of employees of a corporate customer under protection is to ask the customer's Information Security department or management (this may be necessary, e.g., in a security incident investigation). To avoid further complications, analytics data (for product improvement purposes) is usually not collected from corporate security products.

Many cybersecurity vendors publicly state their privacy and data handling principles and practices (one can find examples of such statements at https://www.f-secure.com/en/web/legal/home and https://www.f-secure.com/en/web/legal/privacy). To conclude this section, we would like to list the following—more technical—recommendations to keep in mind when working with different types of data:

- Steps should be taken to ensure that the *telemetry data* collected and stored about security incidents and system configurations *is always anonymous or pseudonymous*.
- *The STRIDE model should be used (*Swiderski and Snyder 2004*), which stands for six categories of security threats:* Spoofing of user identity, Tampering, Repudiation, Information disclosure (privacy breach or data leak), Denial of

Service (DoS), Elevation of privilege. Threat analysis sessions should be conducted when planning new data handling-related functionalities and reviewing their readiness.

- *The quality of pseudonymisation functionality and procedures should be ensured.* The small amount of (e.g. marketing related) telemetry data which contains identifiable data must be pseudonymised before it can be used for analytics purposes, and the ability to reverse the pseudonymisation must be very strictly limited and controlled. Every effort should be made to remove personal identifiers from file paths and file names before they are made available for analytics systems and the pseudonymisation code should be concentrated to a common library as far as possible. Its performance should be reviewed regularly.
- *Unnecessary data should not be collected.* Data collected should always be for a purpose. Review processes should be implemented to regularly check whether telemetry and other data is really needed and to stop collecting it if it is not.
- *Clear data management procedures should be implemented.* Cloud accounts should by default be read-only and extra privileges should be required to be able to make even small changes there. Cloud service account boundaries (e.g. for Amazon Web Services accounts) should be used as a means to isolate more general accounts from data accounts and maintain tight access control on who has access to which data. Encryption contexts should be used to limit the power to decrypt data.

It must be emphasised that such policies and principles would not resolve all problems that may arise in practice. For example, the highly desirable data integrity property may conflict with the rectification and erasure requirements defined by the GDPR. Such a problem can arise if a user asks their cybersecurity provider to remove certain parts of security data collected from her or his machine. Satisfying the user's request will effectively make the collected security data incomplete and possibly useless in incident investigations.

### 15.2.2 Information About Breaches

A sensitive issue for cybersecurity service providers is when they become a victim of a data breach themselves, as this may have a direct impact on their reputation. There are several incentives to 'hack' a cybersecurity vendor. For example, state actors may be interested in knowing malware detection mechanisms to be able to circumvent them for specific intelligence operations.

According to the GDPR, cybersecurity vendors that are active in the EU have a legal obligation to provide protection against "accidental or unlawful destruction, loss, alteration, unauthorised disclosure of, or access to personal data". Failure to fulfil the obligation may result in authority investigation or administrative fines.

It is therefore necessary that cybersecurity service providers have procedures for managing personal data breaches. This includes criteria for determining whether a security incident constitutes a personal data breach according to the GDPR and procedures for decision-making and evidence preservation that must be followed when handling such breaches. We list here a number of practical considerations for handling personal data breaches that are relevant for a typical cybersecurity service provider:

- All personal data breaches should be recorded, including suspected ones and confirmed false positives. Timestamped minutes detailing all the facts and assumptions should be included as well as the risk-based reasoning for whether to treat a specific incident as a personal data breach.
- In a team managing a suspected personal data breach case, members of the Chief Information Security Office, Legal Department and Executive Team should be included.
- When performing a risk assessment of a breach, the following factors should be considered: number of impacted individuals; data types; breach types (e.g. accidental, unlawful), data protection mechanisms used for the affected data (e.g. was the data encrypted).
- When making a decision to publish a Personal Data Breach Notification, the following factors should be considered: whether the identities of the affected parties and impact of the breach to them is known; whether the relevant aspects of the security incident and breach are known at a reasonable confidence level; whether taking extra investigation time would benefit the understanding of the breach or help limit its negative effects to the involved parties (data subjects, controller(s), and the cybersecurity service provider), or whether it would instead be likely to aggravate the situation; whether there are specific items that should be omitted when sharing information because disclosing those would aggravate the impact of a breach to the data subjects.
- Unless a personal data breach is unlikely to result in risks to the rights and freedoms of natural persons, the Supervisory Authority should be notified about the breach.

### *15.2.3 Threat Intelligence Activities*

Threat intelligence is information that helps understand threats targeting organisations and citizens, in the past, at present and in the future. Thus, the production of threat intelligence is a core activity of cybersecurity providers for preventing, detecting and responding to threats to their customers and general public. Threat intelligence is what cyber threat information becomes once it has been collected, evaluated in an appropriate context (in particular, considering information source and reliability), and analysed through structured techniques, identifying similarities and correlations in vast quantities of data. Threat intelligence production is not an end-to-end-process; rather, it is a circular process whereby requirements are stated; data collection is planned, implemented and evaluated, the results are analysed to produce intelligence, and the resulting intelligence is disseminated and re-evaluated in the context of new information and consumer feedback. The process is a cycle because it identifies intelligence gaps and unanswered questions, which prompt new collection requirements, thus restarting the intelligence cycle (Intel 2019).

In this circular process, regular access to—potentially sensitive—information is necessary for cybersecurity service providers, which obviously requires defined data management procedures. Ideally, cybersecurity vendors must ensure that they are open about what they collect, that only necessary data is collected, that they use it only for pre-defined and justified purposes and give it out only on a need-to-know basis for legally permissible and ethical use, that they keep it secure and destroy it when they no longer need it, and that sensitive pieces of data are removed or anonymised whenever possible. In reality, however, they often face threat intelligence-related trade-offs and choices with no clearly defined rules.

We focus here on the potential privacy impact of threat intelligence activities. It is typical for cybersecurity vendors to collect publicly accessible data on the Internet, extract metadata from selected files collected on the Internet or received from various feeds (e.g. exchange with other vendors and research groups, see also Sect. 15.2.5), and analyse it all to gather more information for further pivoting and putting context around threats. In the collected data and extracted metadata, important for incident investigations and research, Personally Identifiable Information (PII) may be found and, by connecting pieces of data from multiple online sources and samples, actual identities of persons targeted by the analysed threats may be discovered. For instance, public social media data and profiles, including names, locations, workplaces, etc., may be valuable when only very selected profiles are associated with possible attackers or attack targets. Alternatively, data extracted from decoy documents and malicious emails can be used for pivoting, threat attribution and the identification of attacked organisations, or URL strings and whois data related to threat campaigns may include names, physical and email addresses and organisation names.

It is crucial for cybersecurity service providers to ensure that such data are collected and processed only for specific use cases and the goals of the research or investigation. The collected sensitive data should be assessed for relevance for the use case in question and, if found irrelevant, deleted immediately. Data relevant for the use case should be stored only as long as the use case continues to be relevant and preferably locally in researcher machines. If such data is ultimately stored in external services, appropriate safeguards must be designed and applied. If other organisations are involved in data collection (e.g. business or research partners), the process must be made transparent for all the parties and its privacy impact must be analysed. If collected data or produced intelligence are shared with others (e.g. with law enforcement agencies or cybersecurity research groups), Sect. 15.2.5 discusses the relevant considerations and practices. An important aspect of data sharing to consider is whether data are moved across borders and—if so—to what states.

We conclude this section with a simple piece of advice: Always consider carefully if your threat intelligence goals can be reasonably achieved with less identifiable data.

### 15.2.4 Vulnerability-Related Information

Finding vulnerabilities in software or system configurations of their customers is among the key activities of cybersecurity service providers. However, if a vulnerability has been found, defined processes are necessary for a proper response. Policies are required regarding documentation, handling, and what kind of and when vulnerability information is shared with other parties or made public. These policies include Security Advisory publishing and communication to ensure the controlled disclosure of security vulnerability information and appropriate balance between (a) letting the customers and partners know enough to protect themselves, and (b) communicating in a way that does not help attackers who want to exploit vulnerabilities. The following considerations should be remembered when preparing a security advisory on a vulnerability:

- Appropriate sensitivity classification of the vulnerability-related information should be assigned and ensured before the public release.
- Providing deep technical details about the vulnerability is typically more useful for persons who want to exploit it than for those who want to protect their systems, so unnecessary details should be avoided.
- All affected products and versions should be listed even if no fix is provided for some of those. There should be openness about the fact that users of discontinued and unsupported versions are running vulnerable software and that the only way to secure their systems is to upgrade to a supported version.
- It is always good to explicitly mention the product groups and versions that are NOT affected by the vulnerability.
- If the vulnerability is found externally, how the reporter wants the credits to be stated should be checked. Some external parties may not want the credits to be stated publicly. Contact information should only be included if approved by the reporter.
- Appropriate national CERTs can be informed before the issue becomes public, in particular, to communicate it to other CERT organisations around the world.
- The correct preparation should be put in place for when the media calls!

One instrument to gain information about vulnerabilities in own software are bug bounty programs. Using such programs, individuals can receive recognition and compensation for reporting bugs in software, especially those pertaining to exploitable vulnerabilities. Such programs allow the developers to discover and resolve bugs before malicious actors become aware of them, preventing abuse. Many organisations and companies have implemented bug bounty programs—and cybersecurity vendors use such programs, too. Again, policies are necessary if cybersecurity vendors launch bug bounty programs to identify vulnerabilities in their own software.[1] In particular:

[1] An example of a bug bounty program of F-Secure can be found here: https://www.f-secure.com/en/web/labs_global/vulnerability-reward-program

- A group of experts has to be established for reviewing cases reported to a bug bounty program.
- Rules for setting amounts of money to be paid for reported vulnerabilities need to be defined.
- The up-to-date program conditions and details should be clearly presented on the vendor's public website.
- A procedure for communicating with the bug reporters has to be defined and followed.
- Metrics for measuring the effectiveness and efficiency of the program are important for its business viability.

At first sight, bug bounty programs are beneficial, because they are a means to decrease the number of vulnerabilities while ensuring that independent analysts are compensated for their effort. However, such programs come with their own set of problems. High-profile companies have to dedicate sufficient manpower to the program in order to triage the incoming reports. Moreover, bug bounty programs can be criticised because they create harsh working conditions due to high fluctuations in pay and a work model that is entirely driven by results.

### 15.2.5 Data Sharing with Peers

Threat intelligence and attack-related objects (so-called samples, which are primarily malicious or unwanted programs, documents and other files or URLs) that result from the activities of cybersecurity service providers can be shared with (usually only) a limited number of reputable and vetted partners in the cybersecurity domain to improve global cyberattack resilience. This enables faster and more accurate protection for customers of cybersecurity vendors and high-impact cybersecurity research. In this section, we present some simple principles and considerations in establishing exchange partnerships which are followed by many organisations and groups in the cybersecurity domain.

Very informal agreements often suffice between reputable partners in the cybersecurity industry and research, in particular if they meet the following criteria:

- They are members of well-established groups, such as the Anti-Malware Testing Standards Organization (https://www.amtso.org/) and the Association of Anti-Virus Asia Researchers (https://aavar.org/), or they are represented in the Computer Antivirus Research Organization (http://www.caro.org/index.html).
- They have no known misdemeanour in their track record, including activities that cast doubts over their ethics as an organisation.
- They are involved in activities within cybersecurity, such as antivirus, security research, data protection and suchlike.

Depending on the sensitivity and type of information being exchanged and the partners' background, a written signed agreement may also be concluded prior to any exchanges. In any case, the following points are usually stated explicitly to avoid any doubts:

- Samples and URLs must be handled in a safe manner.
- Samples and URLs that are exchanged must not be re-shared as such without a clear additional contribution.
- Samples and URLs must not be redistributed to untrusted parties.
- Shared samples and URLs are free from compensation.
- Each party is responsible for its own use of the exchanged material.
- Each party is responsible for having the necessary rights and authorisations for this activity.

If a potential partner does not meet the criteria mentioned above, an extensive background check is usually carried out and the community is contacted for feedback regarding that organisation. A written agreement is always required in such cases prior to any exchanges to confirm the partner's commitment to comply with the established terms and rules of sample and URL exchange.

On-demand sample and URL sharing is normally allowed with trusted individuals in the cybersecurity community without formal agreements in place as long as they comply with best practices in the safe handling of samples and URLs. In this scenario, PGP encryption is always the preferred option to avoid the risk of unintended recipients being able to open exchanged packages.

As a part of such best practices, exchanged samples and URLs are never decrypted nor packaged on production machines, only in special safe environments. Furthermore, files inside packages should not have their original file extensions and package names must clearly describe their contents to prevent accidental execution. Samples and URLs marked as confidential, marked as illegal or containing potentially private data (e.g. email addresses, usernames and passwords within a URL) are excluded from sharing by all responsible organisations and groups. Whenever feasible, the origin of exchanged objects and data is anonymised.

A good example of a formal intelligence sharing partnership is presented by Cyber Threat Alliance (CTA, https://www.cyberthreatalliance.org/), a not-for-profit organisation working to improve the global digital ecosystem cybersecurity by enabling near real-time, high-quality cyber threat information sharing among its members. Members are granted access to the CTA's automated platform for sharing timely, actionable, contextualised and campaign-based cyber threat intelligence which can be used to improve their products and services to protect their customers, and regularly share insights and best practices. All potential members undergo a thorough vetting process, and the CTA also considers their potential value to the Alliance along with any possible security risks.

CTA intelligence sharing is grounded in five guiding principles, as stated on their website (available at: https://www.cyberthreatalliance.org/who-we-are/; last access July 7, 2019):

1. "*For the greater good.* We protect customers, strengthen critical infrastructure, and defend the digital ecosystem. Our automated platform empowers members to share, validate and deploy actionable intelligence to customers in near-real time.

2. *Time is of the essence.* We prevent, identify and disrupt malicious activities by rapidly sharing timely, actionable intelligence and reducing the effectiveness of malicious actors' tools and infrastructure.
3. *Context rules.* We reward context sharing to identify indicators of compromise and provide useful information about those.
4. *Radical transparency.* We attribute intelligence to the member who submits it, but anonymise any and all victim and sensitive data.
5. *You must give to receive.* We require all members to share a minimum amount of intelligence with the alliance to prevent the free-rider problem."

It is noteworthy that one of the key CTA's rules states: "Affected entity's data in shared intelligence must be anonymised".

## 15.3 Special Considerations for Penetration Testing

Building systems that are absolutely secure from the beginning is virtually impossible due to high complexity and limited resources. Security-relevant mistakes can also be made during deployment and operations. A common approach to reduce the resulting risk is to perform regular security assessments (see Chap. 2). Penetration tests are one type of such assessment (Bishop 2007). In a penetration test, white-hat hackers (also called ethical hackers; see Chap. 9) target productively used systems under realistic conditions in a systematic fashion. Testers use similar or the same tools and techniques as malicious actors. Penetration tests are usually carried out by specialised cybersecurity service providers. The result of a penetration test is a report with a list of security-relevant findings and their severity, often including the steps to reproduce (exploit) them.

Conducting a penetration test involves numerous ethical dilemmas. In the following, we survey selected challenges. We also provide guidance for ethical decision-making based on experience obtained in various engagements.

### *15.3.1 Order Initiation*

Clients that request the services of a penetration testing provider may not be upfront with their intentions. For instance, a client might request a test of a particular version of a product which is not in use in their organisation at all. However, it could very well be the case that the client secretly knows that this version is in use at another organisation, for instance a competitor. The client could also be a nation state agency involved in law enforcement or political espionage. Many penetration testers aspire to 'improving security' by improving defence measures and closing vulnerabilities. They would not be willing to help clients gain technical expertise for offensive activities. However, it is quite difficult to identify such cases. For instance, clients could pretend that they do not use the to-be-tested product because they are in the middle of a buying decision and this particular product is one of the promising candidates.

Accepting such a job and delivering an in-depth report with details about found vulnerabilities could make the penetration testers complicit in conducting morally questionable activities. Depending on the financial situation at the penetration testing provider, rejecting such ambiguous assignments may not be an option. However, due to the information asymmetry between testers and clients, the testers can still influence the outcome and the potential harm resulting from their findings. For instance, they can refrain from creating and providing a working exploit and omit technical details to make it more difficult to write such an exploit based on their report. The ethical dilemma arises from the fact that it is now the testers who are not completely honest with their client, which is another facet of professional integrity.

Some penetration testers may research particular products independently (i.e. without a mandate by the vendor and without receiving payment) in their spare time. Such activities are often used to advertise the competencies of a penetration testing service provider. Typically, the testers will follow responsible disclosure procedures, i.e. notify the vendor about any security vulnerabilities (see Chap. 2), before a report with the results is published.

Several ethical dilemmas can be encountered during this process. Firstly, vendors of high-profile products know that many penetration testing providers will scrutinise their products immediately upon release because of the comparatively large advertisement value of finding vulnerabilities in them. Effectively, this means that these vendors get high-quality penetration testing without having to pay for it. Should penetration testers react to this form of financial exploitation and refrain from testing the products of vendors that implement this approach to create an incentive for vendors to perform security testing on their own? Alternatively, should it be considered that consciously refraining from independent tests of particular vendors introduces a systematic disadvantage for the (large numbers of) customers of these vendors?

Secondly, during the responsible disclosure process, vendors may try to prevent the penetration testers from publishing a report of their findings at the end, which might result in a loss of reputation for the vendor. This can either be done by threatening the penetration testers with legal means or by offering them a well-paid engagement, which—of course—comes with a non-disclosure agreement that prevents the testers from reporting the findings publicly. Again, it is necessary to establish a balance between professional integrity and generating a steady stream of revenue.

### *15.3.2 Execution*

During the execution of penetration tests, testers make many decisions with significant technical and ethical implications. One of the most straightforward questions is: How aggressively should the test be conducted? More aggressive tests may uncover more vulnerabilities but may also create more harm (e.g. downtime). It is also interesting to ask how thoroughly a discovered vulnerability should be demonstrated. Is it sufficient to state that a vulnerability gives full access to a database with sensitive information of all employees or should the tester actually 'go the extra mile' and retrieve records from this database and include them in the final report to make it 'juicier'? Although this may actually be required to stress the severity of a vulnerability, it can also be seen as an avoidable violation of privacy.

Many penetration tests involve 'social engineering' (Mitnick and Simon 2005). Here, employees of the penetration testing provider deceive employees of the client in order to assess their security awareness and compliance. Social engineering ranges from sending tailored spear-phishing mails or giving them calls, for instance "from the IT department that needs their password", to entering the premises under the pretext of gaining physical access.

These interactions are problematic for both parties, client and service provider, and the ethics of social engineering are quite involving (Hatfield 2019). In contrast to searching for bugs in software, social engineering uncovers unprofessional behaviour in humans. It is all too easy to jump to the conclusion that the 'problem' can be resolved by replacing a particular employee who made a mistake. It may be difficult for a client to accept the more inconvenient explanation: a successful attempt at social engineering means, firstly, that the organisation lacks training procedures, and, secondly, that it lacks technical means such as strict access control and segmentation that limit the power that attackers can gain via social engineering. Therefore, engagements involving social engineering should always be implemented in a way that ensures that the client's employees do not face personal consequences based on the results.

Social engineering is also challenging for testers. Not only does it involve lying to other humans, it means strategically deceiving and tricking them, with the explicit objective of making them fail. Testers might have to go to great lengths to build up sufficient trust with their 'victims' to be successful. Social engineering providers should establish clear boundaries of acceptable behaviour for such engagements and should offer dedicated training to their employees. Moreover, they should give employees the freedom to reject social engineering assignments.

The final stage of a penetration test is the creation of a report. Clients may have a political agenda, asking for a 'green' report that plays down the severity of the findings. Other clients may ask for the opposite: a 'red' report, for instance, as the basis to request more funding within their organisation or to discredit the work of colleagues or other units. Such negotiated and intentional modifications of the original assessment conflict with professional integrity and are seldomly justifiable. However, the original message may also be modified unintentionally, for instance, when clients ask for a management summary without too many technical details. Such a 'dumbed down' report can be easily misinterpreted.

### *15.3.3 Supervision and Governance*

In the previous sections, we discussed ethical dilemmas in the realm of penetration testing. How can service providers ensure that they act in a responsible fashion?

First, penetration testing providers and their employees are in a powerful position because of a significant information asymmetry. Only the testers know the full truth. Their employer and the client have to trust them that they report all findings accurately and completely. Although it may be possible to reproduce the actual findings, it is difficult to verify their severity judgement, and virtually impossible to determine whether anything has been omitted or forgotten.

There are two ways of mitigating this information asymmetry between clients and providers. Firstly, clients can choose to engage different penetration testing providers to correlate their findings. Secondly, before the penetration test, clients can intentionally introduce vulnerabilities into their systems to test the abilities of the testers. A historic example of this approach is reported by Karger and Schell (2002) for the Multics system, who inserted malicious code in the system that was not uncovered even after the testers had been informed of its existence.

Even in the absence of such incentives, penetration testing service providers should work towards establishing a sense of work ethics and procedures that ensure high-quality work. For instance, it may make sense to pair up highly skilled junior security analysts with more experienced personnel to channel the curiousness and drive of the young and to avoid them overshooting the mark when they are 'in the flow'. This is especially important because, as stated in Sect. 15.3.2, it may not be desirable to do everything that is technically possible during an attack, even though it may be very enticing.

Moreover, penetration testing providers should encourage their employees to reflect on the effects of their work on their clients and society at large as well as the way how they conduct it (i.e. whether the end result justifies the means). In addition, formal training, an open culture with informal meetings and discussions as well as opportunities for engaging with the community of security professionals may help penetration testers keep track of the right course.

Penetration testing providers should also consider institutionalising ethical decision making. One approach which seems to work well in practice consists of establishing an Ethics Board that is given authority to decide on the course of action in all morally questionable cases, ranging from whether or not to take an ambiguous engagement to operational questions during testing. Ideally, members of the Ethics Board should be elected by the workforce. Executive stakeholders may be members of the Ethics Board; however, they should be in the minority. Decisions of the Ethics Board should be binding for the company.

## 15.4 Conclusion: Improving Ethical Decision-Making

Policies, practices and recommendations explained in this chapter are an important instrument for cybersecurity service providers in order to ensure that the handling of sensitive data or operations is ethical and secure. However, not all dilemmas exemplified in the beginning of this chapter can be resolved by policies and guidelines. It remains important that cybersecurity vendors also develop some competences in ethics (e.g. by providing their personnel with training in ethics) and an 'ethical culture' that supports the handling of unexpected situations. In several domains such as health care and business ethics, decision heuristics have been developed for an ethical assessment of problems (for example in computer science, see Linderman and Grillo 2006). Those decision heuristics usually involve a step-wise procedure for analysing problems where no clear guidelines are available:

1. Ethical sensing: As a starting point, an attempt should be made to answer the following question: What provokes ethical debate? Feelings of outrage, shame, guilt or bad conscience could be indicators of an ethical challenge.
2. Gather the facts and legal framework of the case. This also includes identifying the relevant stakeholders and contextual information. It is desirable to include all perceptual perspectives of the participating experts to avoid bias.
3. Identify the moral question and own positions/values. The goal of this step is to identify the 'ethical core' of the problem. Disclosing the personal values of the involved experts should also be integrated here—again to avoid (normative) bias.
4. Analyse the arguments by using ethics frameworks. Examples for frameworks to be used are provided in Chap. 4 of this book.
5. Develop options and decide. Here, developing several courses of action that lead out of an 'either-or' can be helpful. When evaluating and weighing arguments, one-sidedness in the argumentation patterns should also be identified and discussed.
6. Implement the solution. This includes assessing the possibilities of implementing the decision and taking measures for successful implementation. Communicative aspects (how is the decision communicated to whom?) should be considered as well. Finally, possible criteria for reassessment should be identified and examined to learn from the decision.

In addition to such decision heuristics, cybersecurity service providers should also consider implementing procedures for whistleblowing. Company insiders should have ways to raise their concerns without risking losing their employment or becoming the object of other sanctions. We have many great examples of high ethical standards of technology-minded people and we strongly encourage cybersecurity vendors to support the ethical awareness and culture of their employees.

Finally, intensifying education and training about ethical decision-making is undoubtedly important for vendors of security products and services. However, it is equally important that ethics and security are much more deeply integrated into the education of software engineers, system designers and operators. After all, these roles make much more significant decisions with critical consequences for security and morality.

**Acknowledgments** The chapter was created with funding from the European Union's Horizon 2020 research and innovation programme under grant agreement No 700540 and the Swiss State Secretariat for Education, Research and Innovation (SERI) under contract number 16.0052-1. We would like to thank Karmina Aquino, Mikko Hyppönen and Hannes Saarinen for their comments and helpful discussions.

## References


Bishop M (2007) About penetration testing. IEEE Secur Priv 5(6):84–87

Bott E (2011) German government accused of spying on citizens with state-sponsored Trojan. ZDNet. https://www.zdnet.com/article/german-government-accused-of-spying-on-citizens-with-state-sponsored-trojan/. Last access 7 July 2019

Hatfield JM (2019) Virtuous human hacking: the ethics of social engineering in penetration-testing. Comput Secur 83:354–366

Intel & Analysis Working Group (2019) What is cyber threat intelligence? https://www.cisecurity.org/blog/what-is-cyber-threat-intelligence/. Last access 7 July 2019

Jackson W (2001) Antivirus vendors are wary of FBI's Magic Lantern. The Uppernet. https://archive.is/20120910214651/http://www.gcn.com/online/vol1_no1/17572-1.html. Last access 7 July 2019

Karger P, Schell R (2002) Thirty years later: lessons from the multics security evaluation proceedings of the annual computer security conference

Ley J (2018) State-sponsored hacking out of the shadows and into a business near you. Ivanti. https://www.ivanti.com.au/blog/state-sponsored-hacking-shadows-business-near. Last access 7 July 2019

Linderman J, Grillo J (2006) Ethical decision making and information technology: an introduction with cases, 2nd edn. McGraw-Hill Higher Education

Martin RS (2003) Watch what you type: as the FBI records your keystrokes, the fourth amendment develops carpal tunnel syndrome. Am Crim Law Rev 40:1271

Mitnick KD, Simon WL (2005) The art of intrusion: the real stories behind the exploits of hackers, intruders and deceivers. Wiley Publishing, Indianapolis

Schneier B (2013) How antivirus companies handle state-sponsored malware. Schneier on security blog. https://www.schneier.com/blog/archives/2013/12/how_antivirus_c.html. Last access 7 July 2019

Schwartz MJ (2013) Do antivirus companies whitelist NSA malware? Dark reading. https://www.darkreading.com/vulnerabilities-and-threats/do-antivirus-companies-whitelist-nsa-malware/a/d-id/1112911. Last access 7 July 2019

Sharwood S (2018) North Korea's antivirus software whitelisted mystery malware. The Register. https://www.theregister.co.uk/2018/05/02/north_korea_silivaccine_av_software_analysis/. Last access 7 July 2019

Swiderski F, Snyder W (2004) Thread modeling (Microsoft professional). Microsoft Press

Thomson I (2014) Government-built malware running out of control, F-Secure claims. The Register. https://www.theregister.co.uk/2014/02/28/governmentbuilt_malware_running_out_of_control_fsecure_tells_trustycon/. Last access 7 July 2019

Westervelt R (2013) Antivirus firms: whitelisting malware for law enforcement against policy. CRN. https://www.crn.com/news/security/240159502/antivirus-firms-whitelisting-malware-for-law-enforcement-against-policy.htm. Last access 7 July 2019

# Chapter 16
# A Framework for Ethical Cyber-Defence for Companies

**Salome Stevens**

**Abstract** Private sector companies are becoming increasingly frustrated over the lack of effective solutions to growing criminal threats in cyberspace, leading to calls by security experts for a more active cyber-defence including offensive actions in cyberspace taken with defensive purposes in mind. However, should private companies use active cyber-defence measures or would they by such an act implicate themselves in illegal actions? As long as there is no specific regulation defining the legal grounds for active cyber-defence, the conventional doctrine of a right to self-defence may be the closest analogy within the physical realm. This chapter examines cyber-defence along the lines of a right to self-defence and concludes that the categorisation of passive and active does not allow for a thorough analysis of the legal and ethical justification of a specific defensive measure. Instead, a categorisation based on the effects of a specific measure is suggested. Along the lines of this effect-based categorisation—and considering the capabilities as well as the limits of the application of a right to self-defence to cyberspace—this chapter proposes some concrete recommendations for companies on how to define ethical cyber-defence within their security strategy.

**Keywords** Attribution · Necessity · Proportionality · Self-defence · Subsidiarity

## 16.1 Introduction

The number of cyberattacks have grown exponentially in recent years. As a consequence, private companies have invested more resources into building a cybersecurity strategy that uses digital tools to protect computer systems and networks from malicious intrusions. One way of doing this is the use of more active cyber-defence strategies (see for example Schmidle 2018). However, how far can a company go before it crosses the line and implicates itself into committing illegal actions? In the

S. Stevens (✉)
Institute of Criminal Law, Criminal Procedural Law and International Criminal Law, University of Zurich, Zurich, Switzerland



M. Christen et al. (eds.), *The Ethics of Cybersecurity*, The International Library of Ethics, Law and Technology 21,
https://doi.org/10.1007/978-3-030-29053-5_16

absence of any legal regulation on the use of cyber-defence for private companies, this chapter examines cyber-defence along the lines of a right to self-defence within the physical realm. It begins with a straightforward question underlying this article: Should a company use active cyber-defence? It then examines cyber-defence from the perspective of a right to self-defence, which considers not only the final effects of a cyber-defence measure, but also the circumstances in which the measure is applied. The chapter concludes with some concrete recommendations for companies regarding what to consider when defining ethical cyber-defence within their security strategy.

## 16.2 Should a Company Use Active Cyber-Defence?

Whereas there have been a number of different attempts to classify cyber-defence, the distinction between 'active cyber-defence' and 'passive cyber-defence' is the most common one. There are differing definitions of what active and passive could mean in the context of cyber-defence. Denning and Strawser define active cyber-defence as any "direct defensive action taken to destroy, nullify, or reduce the effectiveness of cyber threats (…)" and passive cyber defence as "all measures, other than active cyber defence, taken to minimise the effectiveness of cyber threats" (Denning and Strawser 2017: 3). However, if we examine cyber-defence from a right to self-defence, then the distinction between active– and passive defence becomes less relevant, as they can in principle both be legitimised under the right to self-defence and there are few cases where one would be obliged to revert to passive– defensive measures. For the above reason, we choose to add another description to the usual categorisation of passive and active defence; one which considers the effects of a specific measure rather than its characteristics. Therefore, a specific cyber-defence measure could either have the effect of breaking the law or not.

Returning to the categorisation of active and passive cyber-defence, some defensive measures showing an active component are clearly against the law. Gaining unauthorised access to a computer system for example, or 'hacking' is illegal in most countries (on hacking see Chap. 8). Consequently, this is the case also for 'hacking back'. As a result, a company deciding to infiltrate another computer system or network without the permission of the user or network owner is breaking the law in the same way the initial attacker does. The same could be said for such active defensive measures that destruct external networks or data. For this reason, we here categorise such cyber-defence measures that regularly break the law as being problematic cyber-defence measures.

Passive cyber-defence measures on the other hand, such as a firewall, an antivirus or an encryption program, would regularly not break any law, because they would not create any negative effects. We call these measures unproblematic.

However, more interestingly, some cyber-defence measures with an active component could either be problematic or unproblematic depending on the manner in which they are used. Such defensive measures would fall within a grey zone, being

**Table 16.1** Application of a second layer of categorisation to cyber-defence

| | | | |
|---|---|---|---|
| Definition based on the **characteristics** of the cyber-defence measure | **Passive cyber-defence** | **Active cyber-defence** | |
| Definition based on the **effects** of the cyber-defence measure | **Unproblematic cyber-defence measures**<br>For example Firewalls, antivirus, encryption programs | **Grey zone**<br>For example IT blocking, traffic deflecting, honeypots, beacons | **Problematic cyber-defence measures**<br>For example hacking back, disruption or destruction of external networks or data |

neither clearly problematic nor unproblematic. An Internet Protocol (IP) blocking, traffic deflection or a honeypot, for example, could be within the law if it does not inflict any harm on third parties. The same could possibly count for beacons or white-hat ransomware depending on the manner in which they are being applied (Hoffman and Nyikos 2018: 17–25, 51; for a conceptualisation of different defence measures see Chap. 2).

Consequently, our categorisation results in the distinction of three different groups: Defensive measures that are regularly unproblematic (marked in white in Table 16.1), defensive measures that may be problematic depending on their concrete application (marked in light grey in Table 16.1) and defensive measures that regularly fall within the category of problematic defensive measures (marked in dark grey in Table 16.1).

From this new effect-based categorisation of cyber-defence measures, we conclude that the question of whether a company may use active defence in its security strategy is formulated too broadly, and the fact that a defensive measure shows an active component does not directly imply its unlawfulness. Even if some active cyber-defence measures could imply a higher risk for companies (problematic measures marked in red in Table 16.1), the question of whether a specific active defence measure could break the law should be analysed on a case-by case-basis and demand the careful consideration of the potential effects it may cause in the given circumstances vis-à-vis the laws that may apply to a given situation. Such evaluation requires the consideration of direct as well as secondary or unintended effects that result from the application of a specific measure.

## 16.3 Applying Self-Defence to Cyber-Defence

The right to self-defence as considered in this chapter is incorporated in criminal law and aims to regulate the conduct of private citizens. As such it is to be distinguished from the concept of self-defence in international public law, which regulates the right of states to apply force in response to armed attacks. Self-defence—as defined in criminal law—can allow for the use of force against an attacker and thus render an otherwise illegal act lawful, provided it was necessary to defend one's own interests. Self-defence is recognised by a majority if not all domestic legal systems and has found recognition as a legal principle in core disciplines of international law (on self-defence in international law see: Hessbruegge 2017). Common law jurisdictions distinguish between defence of oneself, defence of others, and defence of property, while most civil law systems include all three concepts under the notion of legitimate self-defence (Hessbruegge 2017: 4). Although this chapter attempts to provide a holistic understanding on the ethical implications of cyber-defence, some of the following considerations may be based on the notion of self-defence under the Swiss Criminal Code (SCC) (see Art. 15–18 SCC).

If we are to apply the principle of self-defence to the categorisation of cyber-defence measures into problematic and unproblematic measures (cf. Sect. 16.4), then the parameters could shift once again. Whereas the categorisation in Sect. 16.3 emphasises the final effect—the result—of an applied defensive measure, the paradigm of self-defence considers the circumstances that led to the application of the said measure. As a result, even such active cyber-defence measures that fall within the category of problematic cyber-defence measures could in principle be justified under law and thus rendered lawful, provided they fulfil the requirements of an act of self-defence. To illustrate, consider a person using force against a thief to safeguard his or her property. Most people would approve of the defender's act even if in principle it breaks the law. This is, of course, depending on how much force the defender applies. Whether the same could apply for a company's security team using force on an attacker's computer system or network to ward off a cyberattack is to be explored in the following sections.

## 16.4 Could Self-Defence Justify Cyber-Defence Otherwise Considered Unlawful?

Unsuprisingly, self-defence provisions were drafted for a physical realm, far before a scenario of active cyber-defence was foreseen, and up until today there has been no relevant case law on the application of self-defence to the realm of the cyber world. This is why it remains uncertain if and how the right to self-defence would apply to cyber-defence by a private company. It could be argued that the physical paradigm of self-defence is unsuited to draw the line between such cyber-defence measures that may be deemed acceptable under law and ones that should be forbidden by it. The argument fundamentally rests on the assumption that active cyber-defence is essentially different from any conventional case of self-defence, which is why the conventional self-defence doctrine cannot tackle the particularities of cyber-defence. We examine some of the most prominent claims against applying self-defence to cyberspace.

### 16.4.1 The Argument of Vigilantism

It has been argued that the particularities of active cyber-defence measures are such that they are never defensive but rather serve revenge goals or deter future attacks. This is why a majority of cybersecurity experts say that the right solution in response to a cyberattack is always be to leave the matter in the hands of law enforcement (see, for example, reader comments to Volokh 2007).

Self-defence is indeed to be distinguished from punishment. Whereas self-defence can only cover acts taken to prevent a harm, counteracting an attack may entail punishment. Actions of a punishing nature, except for a few exceptions regarding minor criminal offences, are generally not allowed by contemporary domestic criminal orders. This is so because they go against the state's monopoly of the use of force. As a result, acts that are in breach of the state's monopoly of the use of force are generally considered acts of vigilantism (see also Dittrich and Himma 2005: 673 ff.).

In the realm of cyber-defence, this would mean that a legitimate act of defence must be able to stop an imminent unjust attack. If an applied technique of active cyber-defence cannot stop an imminent unjust attack, then it cannot be defensive but may, rather, be considered offensive (see also Denning and Strawser 2017: 11). The problem lies when such counteract is executed in a second moment, meaning when it is too late for it to be considered self-defence (see for example Fletcher 1989: 201). To illustrate, let us consider active cyber-defence techniques used for attribution, namely the identification of the perpetrators of the hacking attack. In a number of cases, such techniques may be applied after an attack has occurred and may be used to report an attacker to the authorities or to send a strong message of deterrence to the attackers. Accordingly, such active cyber-defence techniques applied for the purpose of attributing the initial attack to the perpetrators may be said to have a primarily punishing or retaliatory nature rather than a defensive one (see also Himma 2004: 4). Thus, they would be unjustified under self-defence. This may, however, not be the case if the cyberattack is to be considered ongoing (on this point see Sect. 16.4.2) and if the attribution measure is applied with the aim of ending the attack. Furthermore, if we consider the blockage of traffic coming from a malicious IP address, then this active measure could in principle be defensive in nature.

Based on the above considerations, it would be premature to conclude that every measure of active cyber-defence would necessarily always have to be vigilant. In the end, it is precisely the aim of any self-defence provision to be outlined in such a way as to reliably draw the line between defensive and retaliatory measures. To define the defensive element of an act, it has to incorporate several indicative elements. An act can thus only be considered a case of self-defence if it satisfies the requirements of self-defence, namely if (1) It comes as a direct response to an imminent unlawful attack (2) It is necessary to ward off the attack, and (3) The preserved interest is not disproportionate to the harm inflicted on the attacker (based on Art. 15 SCC as commented in Niggli and Göhlich 2019a, b with further references).

### 16.4.2 The Argument of the Speed of Cyberattacks

If we take the example of the requirement of imminence of an attack, then we come across several situations where the term demands further clarification within a scenario of active cyber-defence. One peculiarity of cyberattacks is their speed, which often outpaces human-dependent cyber-defence. In the case of encryption, for example, most ransomware can complete encryption within less than 1 min after intrusion. In the case of cyber-defence, this would mean that any justifiable active defence measure would have to happen within these couple of seconds before successful encryption. It is unlikely that any human-dependent cyber-defence system could act timely in this case even if intrusion is detected before encryption is completed. The technical characteristics of the speed of such cyberattacks would thus render the proof of imminence of any cyber-defensive action close to impossible.

A similar line of argument could apply to preventive defensive measures, namely such measures that are applied in advance of an attack and aim to prevent an attack from happening. While the requirement of imminence does not oblige a defender to wait with the defensive action until it is too late to effectively defend oneself, the lawful application of a preventive defensive measure in cyberspace would essentially require a company to have known about the attack in its planning phase. Considering the limitations of the legal possibilities of private companies to gather intelligence outside of their own network, it is unlikely that a company would be aware of a planned attack on itself to such a degree that a preventive counterstrike could comply with the requirement of imminence for a situation of self-defence (Stevens 2019: 326 ff. with further references).

Consequently, the requirement of imminence significantly narrows the scope of situations of cyberattacks in which self-defence could apply. Essentially, self-defence in cyberspace would be limited to cyberattacks that imply the resilience of a cyber-attacker within a company's system or network for a prolonged period of time or to such attacks that entail some sort of persistent attacking behaviour, as for example in the case of a Distributed Denial of Service (DDoS) attack or possibly even the intrusion sequences of a cyber kill chain (for a consideration of this argument see Stevens 2019: 335 ff.; on the conceptualisation of a cyber kill chain see Chap. 2).

### 16.4.3 The Argument of the Harm to Innocent Third Parties

Because the right to self-defence relies essentially on the distinction between an attacker and innocent third parties, attribution is a central element of every case of self-defence. It answers the question of who is to be held responsible for an attack and consequently against whom a defensive measure may be justified. The nature of cyberspace, however, makes it particularly easy for attackers to hide their identity through third-party systems, which get hijacked for the purpose of initiating an attack. This is why in the realm of cyber-defence, an attack needs to be attributed on several levels: (1) It needs to be attributed to a specific computer or server; (2) The identified computer or server needs to be attributed to an owner or legitimate user(s);

and (3) The attack needs to be attributed to the specific person or organisation that is behind it.

The challenges connected to the attribution of cyberattacks thus puts active cyber-defence at particular risk of causing unintended damage to innocent third-party computer- or server users. In extreme situations, an active countermeasure against the source of a cyberattack could lead to the disruption or destruction of a hospital's computer system, thereby indirectly causing physical harm or even death to patients who rely on the functioning of the hijacked computer system. Considering the risks of false attribution in cyberspace, it is argued that the best way to avoid the uncertainties related to the attribution of cyberattacks would be to completely forbid any problematic defence measure in cyberspace.

Generally speaking, self-defence does not justify harm inflicted on an innocent third-party. Its parameters are limited to acts directed against the person to which the attack can be attributed. However, in some particular circumstances, criminal behaviour against an innocent third-party may still be justified defence, for example: (1) If the defender had no other way to ward of the attack and the preserved interest weights proportionally more than the harm caused to innocent third-parties (i.e. situation of necessity); (2) If the defender reasonably believed that the act was directed against the attacker and would not inflict harm on any innocent third-party (i.e. error of fact; putative self-defence).

Whereas situation 1 essentially relies on the parameters of subsidiarity and proportionality of the applied defensive measure (cf. Sect. 16.4.4), situation 2 acknowledges the uncertainty of a given situation and allows for a reasonable margin of error (cf. Sect. 16.4.5). The question would thus be whether the defensive act against a third party could fulfil the requirements of subsidiarity and proportionality or whether it was the result of a reasonable error of fact in a given situation; both points discussed hereafter. It remains to be said that even if a right to self-defence could exclude criminal liability for a defensive act applied against a third party, the company could still face financial liability for the damage caused to the third party under tort laws. (based on Art. 52 II Swiss Code of Obligations (SCO)).

### *16.4.4 Subsidiarity and Proportionality*

For an act to be considered defensive, it needs to be appropriate in view of the prevailing circumstances. The appropriateness of an act is measured using the notions of subsidiarity and proportionality (based on Art. 15 SCC as commented in Niggli and Göhlich 2019a, b, n 28 ff. with further references). It cannot be said with certainty how a court would apply the requirements of subsidiarity and proportionality to a case of cyber-defence as there is no relevant case law on this matter. However, subsidiarity would likely imply that the threat could not have been effectively averted or minimised using a less invasive measure or that the used measure could have been applied in a less invasive manner. Acts directed against third party-users would set stricter parameters to the requirement of subsidiarity; obliging a defender to revert to non-invasive defensive measures should they be appropriate to avoid the threat (based on Art. 17 SCC as commented in Niggli and Göhlich 2019a, b: n 16 with further references). In practice this could mean that if a court finds that an attack could have effectively been stopped without inflicting damage on the third party, then it would not justify the use of any more invasive cyber-defence measure.

The requirement of proportionality would require a balance to be carefully struck between the imminent harm avoided by a company against the damage done to an innocent third party, and possibly also the initial attacker. The infliction of physical harm to hospital patients that are kept on life support by the hospital computer system would, for example, be disproportionate to the financial interest of a company and could thus not be justified under self-defence. It would be more difficult to strike a balance between the financial interest of a company and the financial interest of a cyber attacker or a third party computer user. Here again it can be noted that the requirements to proportionality would be higher if the act was to cause damage to a third party rather than the attacker. It is therefore to be expected that the safeguard of a financial interest of a company is unlikely to justify the considerable financial damage on a third-party user. This situation could be altered if the attack on the company poses imminent danger to life or physical well-being. As has been shown, striking a balance between two interests is by no means an easy task; in practice it can prove quite challenging and because the equation of proportionality needs to consider all the prevailing circumstances, no general line can be drawn.

### *16.4.5 The Argument of Uncertainty*

Recognising that the paradigm of self-defence depends essentially on the parameters of subsidiarity and proportionality, another aspect of attribution that should be discussed when considering the application of self-defence in cyberspace is uncertainty. To calculate the parameters of a certain defensive action, foreseeing the consequences of our actions is an inevitable necessity, as well as foreseeing the harm averted at least to a degree of reasonable certainty. Even if in very specific circumstances self-defence could justify the act of a defender who mistakenly believes the requirements of self-defence to be satisfied—even if objectively these requirements are not met (i.e. error of facts; putative self-defence; cf. Sect. 16.4.3)—such a right can only apply to the one whom truly errs. A defender knowingly accepting the uncertainty over all relevant factors of a defensive act no longer errs and can thus no longer benefit from a right to err (confirmed by the Swiss federal court in BGE 135 IV 12, E. 2.3.1).

This could mean that if a defender cannot reliably attribute the source of the attack to a person or a server to a specific user, then consequently he or she cannot calculate the effects of an active cyber-defence action nor in some cases the harm it aims to avert. Consequently, because the defender cannot calculate the effects of his or her act, he or she lacks reason to think that the requirements of self-defence could be satisfied (see also Dittrich and Himma: 675). This is especially true given that many active cyber-defence tools operate automatically and do not give the opportunity to contextualise the circumstances of a particular situation (see also Denning and Strawser 2017: 12). To illustrate this, consider the case of data theft. Whereas the security team of a company could detect that someone had been in their system and had possibly stolen some internal data, it is likely that at the time at which they decide to get unauthorised access to the attacker's computer system, they would not know who the hackers were nor what they intended to do with the removed company information. If the security team does not know what harm the company or any third parties would face or whether the information has already been passed on at the moment of the hack, then how could they decide whether their counter-action is necessary or proportionate at that given moment?

Even if we argue that attribution can be done quite reliably on all levels if done by the right people with the relevant capabilities, the problematic factor of applying self-defence to cyber-defence lies in the fact that the reasonable certainty of attribution increases the more time is spent on such activities (see for example Lin 2016: 13; Rid and Buchanan 2015: 32). In fact, a reliable attribution of an attack asks for follow-up investigations that go beyond the initial attribution at the time of the detection of the intrusion (Lin 2016: 13). In the case of APT10 (Mandiant's naming of the Chinese Advanced Persistent Threats (APTs) group) for example, it took a group of anonymous researchers almost 2 years of investigation to identify what they thought was a hacking campaign masterminded by the Chinese government (Anonymous 2018). Considering the requirement of imminence of an attack discussed in Sect. 16.4.2, it becomes questionable if any attribution made to a degree of reasonable certainty could be concluded within the given time frame to make it possible for the defender to comply with the requirement of imminence (cf. Sect. 16.4.2). Furthermore, reliable attribution may require active cyber-defence techniques that would be considered within the realm of problematic defence measures and could thus be breaking the law. This would lead to the paradoxical situation of attribution being simultaneously the motive as well as the precondition of a justifiable defensive countermeasure. From the above, we conclude that the particular uncertainty connected to attacks in cyberspace could be the most convincing argument against the use of active cyber-defence in cyberspace.

### *16.4.6 Is Active Cyber-Defence Worth the Risk?*

In addition to considering the legal legitimation of any active cyber-defence measure, it makes sense to weigh up the potential gains from deploying a problematic cyber-defence measure against the potential risks and drawbacks of that measure (see also Dewar 2017: 16). If a cyberattack cannot reliably be attributed, then a company can consequently not know who is behind the attack. It could, for example, be a skilled teenage hacker, operating from his or her living room, a bunch of criminals seeking financial gains, an organised crime group, a competing company trying to gain insight into company operations and trade secrets, a group of activists hacking a private company for political or ideological reasons or an adversary country controlling strategic cyberattacks for political and economic reasons. In fact, even if a person operating a specific attack was identified, it is not certain that this person is also the mastermind behind the specific operation. Depending on who is on the other end, the tools at a cybersecurity team's hands may be very limited and counterattacks could provoke further and more harmful attacks on the company's system or even have the potential of escalating into hostilities between nations, with severe consequences.

### *16.4.7 The Cross-Border Element of Cyber-Defence*

There are a number of scholars who support the claim that it is best to specifically regulate active cyber-defence in separate new legislation (see for example Brunoni 2016: 3). The need to further regulate active cyber-defence by private companies has been especially vocal among United States scholars (see for example Rabkin and Rabkin 2016) and on 25 May 2017, U.S. Congress Member Thomas Graves introduced the 'Active Cyber Defence Certainty Act'. The bill would amend the Computer Fraud and Abuse Act (CFAA), the U.S. legislation that made it a federal crime to access a protected computer without proper authorisation, so as to authorise certain active cyber-defence measures by private sector organisations that go beyond their own network. The bill currently in congress has been heavily disputed by cybersecurity experts, who fear allowing private companies to use active cyber-defence could create a 'cyber wild west' and make vigilantism the norm (Swinhoe 2018). Despite the potential consequences of changing the CFAA, the act has one important limitation: The bill does not specifically tackle nor prohibit cross-border active countermeasures, and this is where the situation becomes more challenging.

In fact, examining the highly interconnected cyber-space, it could be argued that by allowing companies to use active cyber-defence techniques at home it is likely to result in such companies stepping across their home jurisdiction boundaries and perpetrating attacks in other countries. In such an event, the affected country, for example France, whose policy stance prohibits private companies from using any active cyber-defence, will find the ones in charge of the execution of the measure as criminals under French law, regardless of how they may be considered under any other domestic law (Smolanoff and Brill 2018: 6 ff.). From there it is easy to imagine how what would at first may seem like a legitimate defensive act by a private company could lead to a conflictual claim of states over criminal jurisdiction of the respective cyber-defence act. In fact, the international nature of data flows may be the biggest obstacle to any attempt to regulate active cyber-defence for private companies on a national level.

## 16.5 Recommendations

Recalling the categorisation of defensive measures in Chap. 4, we conclude that, although in principle it cannot entirely be excluded that very specific cases of cyber-defence could fall under a right to self-defence, the nature of cyber-defence, such as the implied uncertainty connected to the attribution of cyber attacks (cf. Sect. 16.4.5ff.) and the likelihood of third party damages (cf. Sect. 16.4.3), pose significant challenges to the reinterpretation of a physical concept of self-defence to the cyber world and thus make the use of problematic cyber-defence measures (marked in red in Table 8) particularly risky for a private company. It is best to entirely avoid their use. This counts in particular for such defensive measures that could result in physical harm to innocent third parties (such as in the case of the unintended take-down of a hospital server or a critical infrastructure for example) or considerable financial damage, no matter how small the risk of such an outcome may be (see also: Hoffman and Nyikos 2018: 53). A private company considering the application of a problematic cyber-defence measure should also keep in mind that such an act may result in financial liability for damages caused to third parties.

The decision to revert from using a problematic defensive measure does not always come lightly (see also Chap. 2), especially when it means accepting considerable damage to the company and allowing the criminal to get away with his or her malicious attack. To avoid facing such a conflictual decision of whether to use a problematic cyber-defence measure, there are a number of security measures a company can take that typically fall within the category of unproblematic measures and that aim to prevent the negative effects of a cyberattack. Encryption could be such a preventive measure. This ensures that the company's data is encrypted in such a way that it makes it more difficult for an attacker to read data and consequently use it in a malicious manner against the company. Other examples of preventive measures could be to run a firewall or other suitable security programs. There are several other security tools and techniques that can ensure the continued functionality of a system and limit the damaging effects in case of a hacker attack (see Dewar 2017). Securing an offline data backup could, for example, be an effective measure to avoid losing access to company data as a consequence to a hacking attack. At the same time, a power station could ensure the continued supply of electricity in the case of an attack (Dewar 2017: 12; for a conceptualisation of different cyber-defence measures see also Chap. 2).

If applied consciously, a range of active cyber-defence measures placed in the grey zone of Table 8 could be useful to complete a security strategy, provided they are applied in such a way as to avoid any negative effects or create tension with other countries. Their application would demand a careful consideration of all related effects (direct and secondary) and should include not only the location of the effects (within own network or outside own network) but also the thorough understanding of the scale of the effects (temporary or reversible impact, permanent or destructive impact) (Hoffman and Nyikos 2018: 57; on the benefits and problems connected to different active cyber-defence tools, see for example Jarko 2016). The considerations implied in choosing to consciously apply such defensive measures should not be the responsibility of a company's security person or team but should be a policy decision backed up by the management and taken in consultation with the right experts and in view of the relevant legislation. Finally, we should accept that no security technology is perfect, and as long as there are security measures there will be cyber criminals calculating ways to evade them.

## References

Anonymous (2018) APT10 was managed by the Tianjin bureau of the Chinese Ministry of State Security. Intrusion Truth. https://intrusiontruth.wordpress.com/2018/08/15/apt10-was-managed-by-the-tianjin-bureau-of-the-chinese-ministry-of-state-security/. Last access 7 July 2019

Brunoni L (2016) Private cyberwars and the right to hack back. Jusletter. https://jusletter.weblaw.ch/juslissues/2016/872/private-cyberwars-an_d13bbca261.html__ONCE. Last access 7 July 2019

Denning DE, Strawser BJ (2017) Active cyber defence: applying air defence to the cyber domain. Carnegie Endowment for International Peace https://carnegieendowment.org/2017/10/16/active-cyber-defence-applying-air-defence-to-cyber-domain-pub-73416. Last access 7 July 2019

Dewar R (2017) Active cyber defence. Research Gate. https://www.researchgate.net/profile/Robert_Dewar5/publication/321057804_Active_Cyber_Defence/links/5a0af4570f7e9b0cc024f3c2/Active-Cyber-defence.pdf?origin=publication_detail. Last access 7 July 2019

Dittrich D, Himma KE (2005) Active response to computer intrusions. In: Handbook of information security 3. Wiley, New Jersey, pp 664–681. https://staff.washington.edu/dittrich/misc/handbook-arc.pdf. Last access 7 July 2019

Fletcher GP (1989) Punishment and self-defence. Law Philos 8(2):201–215

Hessbruegge JA (2017) Human rights and personal self-defence in international law. Oxford University Press, New York

Himma KE (2004) The ethics of tracing hacker attacks through the machines of innocent persons. Int J Info Ethics 2(11):1–13

Hoffman W, Nyikos S (2018) Governing private sector self-help in cyberspace: analogies from the physical world. Carnegie Endowment for International Peace. https://carnegieendowment.org/2018/12/06/governing-private-sector-self-help-in-cyberspace-analogies-from-physical-world-pub-77832. Last access 7 July 2019

Jarko C (2016) Finding the fine line – taking an active defence posture in cyberspace without breaking the law or ruining an enterprise's reputation. SANS Institute. https://www.sans.org/reading-room/whitepapers/legal/finding-fine-line-%E2%80%93-active-defence-posture-cyberspace-breaking-law-36807. Last access: 7 July 2019

Lin P (2016) Ethics of hacking back. Ethics + Emerging Sciences Group. ethics.calpoly.edu/hackingback.pdf. Last access 7 July 2019

Niggli M, Göhlich C (2019a) Art. 15 – Rechtfertigende Notwehr. In: Basler Kommentar, Strafrecht I, 4. Helbling Lichtenhahn Verlag, Aufl., Basel, pp 249–260

Niggli M, Göhlich C (2019b) Art. 17 – Rechtfertigender Notstand. In: Basler Kommentar, Strafrecht I, 4. Helbling Lichtenhahn Verlag, Aufl., Basel, pp 265–271

Rabkin J, Rabkin A (2016) Hacking back without cracking up, A Hoover Institution essay. Aegis Paper Series 1606. https://www.hoover.org/sites/default/files/research/docs/rabkin_webreadypdf.pdf. Last access 7 July 2019

Rid T, Buchanan B (2015) Attributing cyber attacks. J Strategic Stud 38(1–2):4–37

Schmidle N (2018) The digital vigilantes who hack back. The New Yorker. https://www.newyorker.com/magazine/2018/05/07/the-digital-vigilantes-who-hack-back. Last access: 7 July 2019

Smolanoff JN, Brill A (2018) Hacking back against cyberterrorists – risks & benefits analysis for NATO's COE-DAT. Kroll. https://www.kroll.com/en/insights/publications/cyber/hacking-back-against-cyberterrorists. Last access: 7 July 2019

Stevens S (2019) Do we need a new paradigm of self-defence for cyberspace? In: Dal Molin-Känzlin A, Schneuwly AM, Stojanovic J Digitalisierung - Gesellschaft - Recht, Analysen und Perspektiven von Assistierenden des Rechtswissenschaftlichen Instituts der Universität Zürich, DIKE, Zürich/St.Gallen, pp 323–340

Swinhoe D (2018) US 'hacking back' law could create a cyber wild west of vigilantism. IDG Connect. https://www.idgconnect.com/abstract/29246/us-hacking-law-create-cyber-wild-west-vigilantism. Last access: 7 July 2019

Volokh E (2007) The rhetoric of opposition to self-help. Volokh Conspiracy. http://www.volokh.com/posts/1176319370.shtml. Last access: 7 July 2019

# Chapter 17
# Towards Guidelines for Medical Professionals to Ensure Cybersecurity in Digital Health Care

**David Koeppe**

**Abstract** There are no independent foundations and systems for general information security in medicine. For the special processing situations and in particular for the very high protection requirements of data and processes—ultimately health and life can depend on bits and bytes—a corresponding implementation of the essentially industry-independent procedure must take place. This topic is set to receive a special boost both among patients and among those responsible in the institutions because of the considerable increase in data protection awareness following the EU data protection basic regulation. This set of regulations addresses not only the lawfulness but also the security of the processing and threatens considerable sanctions in the event of gross negligence in this area. Regardless of whether this leads to the implementation of a proper information security management system in a larger institution—or whether the resources for such a large solution are not available in a small medical practice and it is instead sufficient for a successive long-term project to be processed—the topic must be addressed systematically.

**Keywords** Authorisation · Data protection · Information security management system · Patient safety

## 17.1 Introduction

### *17.1.1 Why Data Protection in Health Care?*

What is the core motivation to seriously address security issues in data processing? In addition to the abstract insight into the advantages of taking precautionary measures, it is, above all, the fear of the disadvantageous incidents occurring that

D. Koeppe (✉)
Vivantes – Netzwerk für Gesundheit GmbH, Berlin, Germany
e-mail: david.koeppe@vivantes.de



M. Christen et al. (eds.), *The Ethics of Cybersecurity*, The International Library of Ethics, Law and Technology 21,
https://doi.org/10.1007/978-3-030-29053-5_17

may even result in the termination of one's own (business) activity. This focus on the business processes of classical information security has been expanded with an additional type of disadvantage, namely the legal sanctions imposed in the event of a failure of data protection because of the General Data Protection Regulation (GDPR) in the European Union that applies from 2018 onwards (see also Chap. 5). The adoption of suitable and appropriate cybersecurity measures now no longer depends solely on a personal sense of responsibility and on liability risks. Rather, it is actively demanded by the legislator.

From the perspective of data protection law, the physician or medical institution involved in data processing poses a risk for the person concerned (here: the patient) and his or her 'rights and freedoms'. In this respect, this perspective differs from that of traditional information security. In accordance with this significant increase in motivation prompted by the sanction regime of data protection law and based on the professional view of the author, the problem of cybersecurity in health care is here primarily approached from a data protection perspective. The contribution discusses the technical-organisational measures—also legally required (GDPR, Art. 32)—for the security of data processing.

### *17.1.2 The Problem*

A (executive or freelance) physician, apart from his actual profession, hardly has a real chance of creating a state-of-the-art level of security in the processing of the patient data entrusted to him using his own specialist knowledge and his own resources. Either he works in a large organisation that guarantees cybersecurity for him, or he makes use of an appropriate service provider. However, this does not release him from his responsibility, especially since he has to make or confirm a number of specifications in a sophisticated information security management system.

The starting point of all considerations are the primarily medical and administrative requirements of opening one's own IT to 'the outside', in particular to other service providers, cost carriers and increasingly also to patients. This is a dynamic environment to which constant adjustments are necessary. In addition, the health ecosystem is currently undergoing rapid changes towards a patient-centred and technically increasingly ubiquitous landscape.

As a rule, information security cannot be designed from scratch, as health systems have their own history. The demand of dealing more intensively with cybersecurity usually arises during the day-to-day operations of an institution. It is based on amendments to the law (such as the GDPR), due to incidents or because of a general sensitisation towards the subject. Accordingly, at the beginning of all activities, an inventory of the existing processing methods and the system landscape is necessary. However, it does not make sense to stare at the cybersecurity dangers like a deer in the headlights. Without an overall view of processing security, only a patchwork would emerge. Thus, a checklist is not sufficient.

### 17.1.3 *Setting the Framework*

It should be emphasised at the beginning that, due to the proximity of the topics of cybersecurity and data protection, a joint processing of the respective requirements in a unified process and uniform documentation is urgently recommended. A separate consideration ultimately leads to considerable additional effort, since the same item is touched several times and potentially viewed and described in different ways. This involves the considerable risk of inconsistencies. Therefore, a combined approach to the data processing landscape, primarily from the broader perspective of data protection, is followed in this contribution.

A systematic and documented procedure is indispensable for assessing the completeness of the consideration as well as the appropriateness and effectiveness of the cybersecurity measures. Derived from the requirements of data protection law, there are essentially three elements:

- (Inventory and) Description of processing activities
- Risk analysis
- Design of measures

Essentially, these are the same elements required for a data protection impact assessment following the GDPR. This is a prescribed, formalised process to establish or ensure the legality and security of the processing of personal data. It is a generic process, whereas the peculiarities of the health care system usually require a very high level of protection for processes and data and that specific processing situations are considered.

## 17.2 Approach

From the perspective of classical information security, the focus is on processes, structures and technology. The view of data protection goes a little further and enriches the topic with legal and content-related aspects.

### 17.2.1 *The Data Protection Perspective*

From the perspective of data protection, the central subject to be described is 'processing activity'. This is a process or a chain of individual processing steps that represents the logical totality of the handling of personal data that is required to achieve a purpose or bundle of purposes. Such processing activities include, for example, a clinical study, payroll accounting, diagnostics using a medical device, video monitoring in a sleep laboratory, or debt collection for defaulting debtors in health insurance. From a European point of view, the compulsory 'Register of

Processing Activities' of the GDPR (Art. 30) provides guidance for structuring such activities. However, the minimum data specified there alone are not practicable; in addition, all available data that constitute the processing, e.g. with regard to the required transparency vis-à-vis the data subjects (Art. 12 ff. GDPR), should be collected centrally.

The mandatory information to be collected is as follows:

- Purpose(s) of processing (e.g. billing of services)
- Categories of data subjects and categories of personal data (e.g. patients and their master file data)
- Categories of recipients (e.g. internal: patient administration, external: insurance provider)
- Third country transfers and documentation of appropriate guarantees (e.g. Switzerland: adequacy decision of the EU Commission, India: use of EU standard contractual clauses)
- Deletion periods for the categories of data (e.g. billing data 10 years after the end of billing)
- General description of the technical and organisational measures taken to ensure the security of the processing (note: a reference to an existing security concept would be ideal here).

In addition, further information should be documented, in particular:

- Legal basis of the processing (e.g. for the implementation of the treatment contract pursuant to Art. 9 para. 2 lit. h GDPR)
- Origin of data (e.g. transmission from referring physician)
- If not obvious: description of the processing process with participants, interfaces, pseudonymisation levels, etc.
- Description of the measures to guarantee the principles of processing (according to Art. 5 GDPR)

The structuring of these activities for the purpose of description is the most demanding aspect to guarantee data protection and data security. It must be carried out in such a way that, on the one hand, all processing operations of the institution or the person responsible are actually recorded in their entirety and there are no 'blind spots' in the documentation. On the other hand, the handling of the individual processing activity should still be possible with a view to a meaningful description. The coarser while simultaneously more abstract the description, the lower the risk of overlooking something. At the same time, the associated complexity makes it difficult to create a comprehensible and functional description. Patient treatment as a single processing activity may make sense in a small medical practice, where all possible sub-processes (admission, diagnostics, findings, therapy, documentation, etc.) can still be potentially summarised in a single description. In a hospital, however, this would no longer be possible due to the complexity. Here, a modular decomposition into logical and self-contained sub-processes such as admission, medical diagnostics, medical and nursing documentation, discharge management, food supply, patient care service, archiving of treatment documentation etc. would be appropriate.

From a technical point of view, there is an obvious impulse to equate processing with the system (software, medical device) that is used for this purpose, to which manual activities are then added to complete the process description. This may be appropriate in individual cases, but in more complex processing environments, a specific software is often used for different purposes and thus for several processing operations and/or several applications, devices are required for one single processing. This requires adequate integration. For example, it makes sense to summarise similar processing operations in one description to avoid turning 100 blood glucose meters distributed over the hospital into 100 processing operations.

### *17.2.2 The Information Technology Perspective*

A modularisation of the descriptions is urgently advisable in a more complex environment. Components or technical sub-processes that are repeatedly used, e.g. the institution's e-mail solution, the use of multifunction devices or simply the—ideally standardised—terminal (PC, smartphone) should be described and correlated with the relevant parameters in each case (technically and organisationally) to ensure they can then be referred to in the legal and functional context from the higher-level processing description.

With regard to information technology, the institution should be modelled. At least in larger institutions, this will have to be realised with appropriate software support, in order to be able to assign the components (software, terminals, servers, networks, rooms, personal groups) available in the underlying layers to each processing or business process (as a bundle of processing). Such a hierarchical model is indispensable for an information security management system. Appropriate handling will be possible, however, only with appropriate personnel and technical resources and thus remain rather reserved for larger institutions. A meaningful differentiation and grouping of components (e.g. networked PC versus stand-alone PC) can also be done manually in the medical practice.

To move from the rather abstract basics for security considerations to the practical conditions, the components that make up a processing activity must be analysed. From a purely technical point of view, these are the classic IT components such as servers, networks, end devices, operating systems, software, etc. However, the latest patch status helps little if the access door to the doctor's practice is not locked at the end of the day. Therefore, in addition to the technical layers in the narrower sense, other organisational aspects must also be considered.

## 17.3 Risk Analysis and Assessment

As soon as the systematic description has provided an overview of which elements of the IT landscape exist and what they are used for, the actual problems can be identified in a differentiated risk analysis.

Both the basic principles of information security (see also Chap. 2) as well as the data protection requirements for processing security (see also Chaps. 5 and 10) call for a risk-oriented approach. This enables scarce resources to be managed in such a way that only relevant risks are adequately addressed. However, a systematic risk assessment primarily contributes to ensuring that no hazards are overlooked (completeness of the risk model). A conscientious assessment of the identified risks based on this also provides the appropriate prioritisation for the following measures.

It is important to mention that risk assessment does not exclusively concern the risks for the operational information processing and thus the legal and economic interests of the physician. It also concerns the possible regulatory sanctions for breaches of duty. Thus, the European GDPR can now be regarded as decisive—regardless of the possible consequences for the patients (or employees) themselves. Essentially, three dimensions play a role here: warranty targets, protection requirements and threats.

### *17.3.1 Warranty Targets*

The essential step before starting a risk inventory is the definition of warranty targets, i.e. the overarching aspects of data processing which should be protected against threats. The categorisations resulting from the different approaches are largely similar. There is not yet a European standard for the implementation of warranty targets from the GDPR. For the time being, reference is made here to the scheme of the 'standard data protection model' agreed upon within Germany by the data protection supervisory authorities (see https://www.datenschutzzentrum.de/sdm/ and Chap. 10 for details). The warranty targets provided for therein are:

- *Availability*
- *Integrity*
- *Confidentiality*
- Transparency
- Intervention capability
- Non-linkability
- Data minimisation

The objectives that are important for the security of processing in the narrower sense are availability, integrity and confidentiality (in italics), which are also the classic warranty objectives in information security. Thus, regardless of the different perspectives of operational information security and data protection, not only are the terms identical, but in the long run the measures to be taken are too. The four further objectives are primarily oriented towards the rights of the persons concerned and are initially ignored at this point, as they affect the risks for the persons concerned but less so cybersecurity, which is the focus here.

### 17.3.2 Protection Needs

The warranty targets relevant for cybersecurity are to be supported with measures depending on the risk. To achieve scalability here, a protection requirement is defined for each processing or for each data category to be processed, depending on the processing purpose and environmental conditions. It makes a considerable legal and practical difference whether an email (which per se contains personal references by sender and recipient) is used to order a catalogue of goods from a supplier or whether it is used to send a report of findings to another doctor. Usually, the level of protection required is normal, high and very high and can be defined as follows:

- 'Normal' stands for a personal reference that has hardly any potential for abuse or stigmatisation with regard to the individual concerned. Depending on the processing scenario, this can be simple contact data, a company telephone directory or the functional designation of a jobholder.
- 'High' would be a need for protection if the person concerned had an increased interest in the data not being disclosed, uncontrolled or misappropriated. This could concern the amount of salary, a bank account or a reference.
- A 'very high' need for protection must be provided for special categories of personal data and for data which are subject to a separate legal obligation to maintain secrecy—i.e., ultimately for all patient-related data arising in the context of health care or medical research.

This means that a very high need for protection for processing will usually have to be assumed in the health care system. Lower protection requirements will usually only arise in the handling of (most) employee data, information on relatives and in the B2B context (suppliers, service providers, colleagues from other institutions).

The category of data in connection with the category of data subject is not the only decisive factor for the classification. It also depends on the processing context. For example as soon as the absence of an employee is due to health reasons, the need for protection for confidentiality rises from normal to very high.

As is the case for the warranty targets, the protection requirements must also be presented from the perspective of those affected. The result is a matrix in which the need for protection is determined for the respective processing in relation to the warranty objectives. In simplified form, this could look as follows (Table 17.1):

**Table 17.1** Example of a protection needs matrix

| | Availability | Integrity | Confidentiality | ... |
|---|---|---|---|---|
| Salary statement | High | High | High | |
| Data exchange with collaborating physician | High | Very high | Very high | |
| Patient record | High | Very high | Very high | |

As far as possible, a qualitative or even quantitative assessment of the protection requirement categories is recommended in order to arrive at comprehensible definitions. For example, the integrity (e.g. in the case of manipulation/falsification of data) would have to be measured in the following cases: a) detection of the error is very likely, does not have major consequences and is easy to correct (= normal, e.g. wrong academic title in the salutation), b) detection of error has potentially temporary unpleasant consequences for the person concerned and a higher correction effort is needed (= high, e.g. incorrect payroll), c) danger to life or physical condition of the person concerned and errors possibly cannot be corrected (= very high, e.g. findings that serve as the basis for medication or surgery).

### *17.3.3 Hazards*

To arrive at measures from the warranty targets (What must not be impaired?) and the need for protection (How in need of protection is it?), it is necessary to operationalise the hazards (What must I protect myself against?) as concretely as possible. These hazards must be related to the individual components (categories). A workplace PC faces other dangers than a cloud platform or a sonography device.

Many relevant hazards can be identified with systematic thinking in a rather simple process. However, it makes sense to use existing schematisations to avoid the risk of overlooking relevant aspects. The international standard for information security management systems is ISO 27001, which includes a catalogue of 'controls' for both processes and systems. However, the basic IT protection documentation (IT-Grundschutz-Kompendium; available at: https://www.bsi.bund.de/DE/Themen/ITGrundschutz/ITGrundschutzKompendium/itgrundschutzKompendium_node.html; last access: July 72,019) of the German Federal Office for Information Security (BSI), which is similar in approach and freely available, is much more detailed and comprehensive. A complete implementation for the entire organisation would be a project of considerable scope. However, as long as there is no obligation to implement and no need for an audit, the relevant and/or interesting building blocks for one's own circumstances can be selected and successively worked through. The IT-Grundschutz-Kompendium currently contains 80 modules (e.g. 'Home Workstation', 'Web Browser', 'Clients under Windows 10', 'Remote Maintenance', 'Sensitization and Training'). For each module, there are hazard catalogues along with requirements (measures/guidelines/recommendations) graded according to protection requirement levels (basic, standard, increased). The 47 'elementary hazards' that are independent of the modules alone are a helpful catalogue for analysing an individual's situation.

As long as we move only between the three more technology-related warranty objectives of availability, integrity and confidentiality, there is usually no major difference in the result between the information security (facility-related) or data protection (affected-related) view. Ultimately, the data protection perspective in the basic protection system is an additional one which, by referring to the 'standard data protection model' of the German data protection supervisory authorities, will in future offer an operational implementation of the requirements of the basic data protection regulation, above all with regard to the additional warranty objectives.

## 17.4 Design of Measures and Possible Conflicts

### *17.4.1 Balancing Measures*

The risk analysis determines whether a measure should be taken in order to encounter a hazard that has been recognised and identified as relevant. The character and intensity of a measure depends on the requirement resulting from the risk in connection with the need for protection. It is not a question of maximising the protective effect but of appropriateness, which includes assessing the concrete circumstances of the processing, the state of the art and the implementation costs (see also Chap. 7). Excessive costs, however, do not speak in favour of foregoing processing security as such but rather in favour of foregoing this specific form of processing.

Data security measures do not only include obvious technical measures, such as installing a patch or activating an encryption feature. Organisational measures are also indispensable, especially when dealing with the human factor. Work instructions, restrictive allocation of authorisations, and the sensitisation and empowerment of employees are just as important and belong equally to an overall concept.

When designing measures, it is not only important to take the measure (e.g. data carrier encryption). Rather, a systemic perspective must be adopted to ensure that the measure is only taken if necessary. The mechanisms of an information security management system serve this purpose. In less complex environments, the proven PDCA cycle should be implemented at least: Plan-Do-Check-Act, i.e. a regular review with regard to the completeness of the risk inventory and assessment as well as the appropriateness and effectiveness of the measures with any necessary adjustments. In the case of significant changes in the processing or the environment at least, the continued legal conformity and thus the security of the processing should be checked.

It is advisable to consult a proven expert when designing measures in the technical environment. The correct configuration and administration of a firewall, a possibly mixed IT and medical technology network or a mail server should not take place at the amateur level—too much depends on it.

Finally, it is essential to document the measures to be taken and those actually taken based on the previous process steps. In addition, the justification for not taking a certain measure should be part of this documentation.

### 17.4.2 Data Security Vs. Patient Safety

IT disruptions can jeopardise the care of patients and, to a serious extent, their health. Carefully designed data security ensures that medical systems are protected against data loss and falsification or a considerable restriction of availability. However, it is possible that the measures to be implemented already affect the supply process and not the disruptions that are prevented by them. This creates a further level that must be included in the risk assessment. This view is most likely to be manageable if it follows the original design of the measures as a control loop.

An example of this would be a networked blood glucose meter that requires the entry of patient and employee IDs to ensure the traceability of the measurement and documentation process and to assign measured values to the correct patient. However, it must be technically possible at any time to carry out a measurement without an administrative lead-time, especially in medical emergencies. In such a case, an organisational determination would have to be made as to how the non-automatically assignable measurement values are to be addressed in the course of operations.

### 17.4.3 Authorisation Restrictions

In complex IT systems, a differentiated assignment of authorisations is necessary, not only from the point of view of confidentiality. Whereas in a small medical practice it is merely a matter of controlling certain functions in accordance with professional responsibilities and authorisations, in larger organisations particular attention must be paid to confidentiality. It is unacceptable that in a hospital, hundreds or even thousands of employees can access a patient record. Classical authorisation matrices have emerged, such as the authorisation of nursing staff for patients within their care units or the authorisation of physicians to the organisational units assigned to them, such as the specialist department and, at given times, also the emergency unit or specialist departments within the framework of night on-call services. In the course of increasingly variable treatment processes and increasing staff shortages, this simple basic principle of authorisation restriction is maintained increasingly infrequently.

The consequence of this is the urge to expand authorisations for being able to address any exceptional case in order to ensure the data are always available. Here, the argument of the ‘obstruction of work’ must not be given too much room at the expense of data protection; a relativisation of the articulated needs is often possible. Occasional requirements, e.g. on the part of administrative functions, can often be met by the division of labour processes, and in a great hurry, e.g. in the case of resuscitation, the physician also has better things to do than tackle an information system. A differentiated consideration is necessary, but in the end, a dampening of the safety effect by concessions to the work ability will have to be accepted.

A decisive element is how short-term adjustments of access can be made by the user administration, especially in the case of flexible personnel deployment. Automated approaches for the process-controlled and patient-centred assignment of authorisations exist in modern systems. However, this is still a dream of the future for most institutions whose static information systems are architecturally rooted in the 1990s.

## 17.5 Aspects Deserving Special Attention

Regardless of the requirement to carry out a systematic and area-wide examination of all aspects of cybersecurity, several 'classic' topics are often neglected in everyday data protection, although they can affect the security of processing. These aspects are often overlooked, especially in smaller institutions that lack the expertise and resources for a sound approach in the form of an information security or data protection management system. In the following, some of these aspects are outlined.

### *17.5.1 Data Transfer*

As soon as the (electronic) release of data is concerned, a distinction has to be made between whether the data are transferred to a service provider who only processes them on behalf of the recipient (order processing in accordance with the GDPR, Art. 28) or whether it is a transfer in which the recipient pursues his own purposes with the processing. This could be a co- or aftercare provider, a cost unit, the holder of a research or quality assurance register, a patient transport service or a service provider of the patient who operates an electronic health record on behalf of the patient. In such cases, the transfer of the data also represents the transfer of responsibility (also under civil law). This means that—after ensuring the legality and a secure design of the transfer—the further responsibility lies with the recipient. As a rule, this also means that no further efforts are required to influence the recipient's processing circumstances, e.g. through data protection clauses in a cooperation agreement.

### *17.5.2 Order Processing of Data*

If a service provider is commissioned with data processing that does not pursue its own content-related purposes, this falls into the domain of data protection order processing. An example could be a computer centre in which servers are hosted or applications are operated, a billing service provider, an envelope-inserting copy centre or a company that provides service and maintenance for IT, medical or office communication systems. Even if the data is not physically transmitted, order processing must be carried out regularly in the case of (remote) maintenance if the service provider's activities could impair the achievement of even one of the warranty targets. The legal distinction between order processing and transmission can be difficult to make in individual cases, and the competent data protection officer should be consulted for advice.

The existence of order processing not only entails the obligation to conclude a highly formalised contract pursuant to Article 28 of the GDPR, but it also has a decisive significance for the allocation of responsibility. The client remains responsible for the processing and its legality, and for guaranteeing the rights of the data subjects. Accordingly, no contractor may be commissioned who does not offer the guarantee that he fulfils the requirements of data protection law—including those on data security—during processing. This must be checked before the order is placed and if necessary also during the course of the contractual relationship. As it is not possible to carry out more than superficial plausibility checks on the basis of one's own expertise, meaningful certificates or attestations by independent bodies should be demanded regarding the suitability of the service provider (in particular with regard to the security of the processing, e.g. in accordance with ISO 27001). A small typing office will not be able to offer this, but such certifications can be expected from a provider of cloud solutions. Certifications specifically relating to data protection exist sporadically, but the market will certainly develop a wider range of meaningful certificates in the coming years.

### *17.5.3 Mobile IT*

A conventional, stationary IT environment is not easy to protect. However, as soon as mobile devices with possibly special mobile operating systems are added, additional and serious risks arise. Classic consumer devices are still hardly usable for operational use for processing health data. The presettings for synchronisation with the manufacturer's cloud, device location and the assumption that the device user would always be willing to transfer data to social media can hardly be mastered by an average user. Without the use of a restrictively set up mobile device management and an administration solution for restricting the possibilities while simultaneously processing risks of the end devices, the use of smartphones and tablets should be discouraged.

Another problem is the large and somewhat functionally tempting range of applications for communication and for medical use, and increasingly also for health professionals. In general, we can assume that the developers have maximised benefits and usability but were insufficiently effective in data protection and data security. In recent years, this has been confirmed by various studies on the security and data protection conformity of apps. Before using such applications (this also applies to web platforms and applications on stationary IT), the certification or at least the manufacturer's promise with regard to data protection and data security must always be checked. Otherwise, the following applies: Although the patients may use such devices on their own responsibility, such an unexamined solution is unsuitable for professional use.

### *17.5.4 Internal Networks and Applications*

The fact that IT components are operated in the premises of the institution does not mean that they are not exposed to any dangers and therefore do not have to be designed securely. Today, networking is omnipresent. Without a connection to the Internet, almost no information technology can be adequately operated. Whether for data exchange, for downloading patches and updates, or even for access by service providers, access to the Internet is nowadays technically and above all economically almost unavoidable.

However, it would be irresponsible to confine oneself to a single hurdle at the Internet access point (firewall, malware filter), since on the one hand hundred percent protection can never be guaranteed there and on the other hand dangers can also get into one's own network, e.g. by a data medium exchange. In recent years, there have been several examples where hospitals have had to do without core elements of their IT for days despite the usual protection mechanisms, due to malware.[1]

### *17.5.5 Communication with Patients*

From the perspective of data security, the manifold possibilities for electronic communication with patients represent an increasing problem. It is not enough that patients increasingly expect health care professionals to use the e-mails, messengers and social media they have become fond of in other areas of life. Medical institutions also offer corresponding channels—partly in response to patient needs, partly on their own initiative. The fact that very few are suitable for communication with confidential information is often ignored or sometimes even not recognised.

Regardless of the patient's ignorance, indifference or simple comfort, the strict requirements for the integrity and confidentiality of data processing also and especially apply to communication via public networks by medical institutions. In any case, state-of-the-art transport encryption is indispensable, ideally end-to-end. This means that standard e-mail communication is already ruled out as a medium, unless an obligatory encryption technique is set up. However, most recipients cannot handle such an encryption technique. In addition, solutions of the platform operators and telecommunications service providers must meet the warranty targets obligatory

[1] See https://rp-online.de/nrw/staedte/neuss/neuss-computer-virus-legt-das-lukaskrankenhaus-lahm_aid-9614119 (last access 25.09.2018) or https://www.england.nhs.uk/2017/05/cyber-attack-updated-statement-and-background-information/ (last access: July 7, 2019).

for the health professional. The obligation to transmit all contact data in one's own database is, for example, a knockout criterion under data protection law for the use of a widely used, albeit end-to-end encrypting messenger.

It is advisable to offer patients a confidential digital communication channel in addition to telephone, fax and letter. Even if hardly anyone uses the PGP public key provided for email communication, it is still a signal to the interested public that inspires confidence.

### *17.5.6 Obligation to Report Data Breaches*

If the efforts in data security have been insufficient and an incident occurs, there are regulatory consequences in addition to practical coping. Incidents in data or information security are frequently simultaneous violations of data protection. If personal data are disclosed unlawfully or unintentionally, destroyed, altered or lost, at least in the case of patient data, a reporting obligation to the data protection supervisory authority (Art. 33 of the GDPR) is necessary. In addition, the existence of an obligation to notify the persons concerned (Art. 34 of the GDPR) should also be assumed. Since failures to report or give notice in accordance with obligations are threatened with sanctions, the educational approach of the legislator to first understand these provisions as a deterrent should be appreciated by not underestimating efforts in data security from the outset.

### *17.5.7 Training, Awareness Raising and Instruction of Employees*

The majority of data security problems are likely caused by human actions or omissions. Whether the cause is insufficient sensitivity, lack of knowledge or simply convenience—or a mix of these factors—this can and must be counteracted. Whether it is clicking on links in ominous e-mails, forgetting to make regular backups or simply misusing devices and software: from the perspective of the person responsible, these aspects also need to be considered—not just technical expertise in patient treatment. Serious errors or omissions can endanger the existence of both the facility and those affected by the data breakdown. Work instructions, user training and regular sensitisations are indispensable. This applies even if no information security management system necessarily draws attention to it.

## 17.6 Conclusion

Although ensuring data security is laborious and systematic processing within the framework of an information security management system, or at least on the basis of it, requires considerable work, it is nowadays an indispensable duty, especially in the health sector. The integrated processing of data protection obligations—underpinned by sensitive sanction threats—and the requirements of conventional information security are urgently recommended. Although this increases the complexity of the task, both have to be accomplished anyway. This results in considerable synergy effects through uniform documentation and the avoidance of time-delayed double consideration of the relevant aspects. Professional support from experts should be a matter of course, both in the conception of the procedure (to the extent appropriate to the size and complexity of the institution), in the processing, and not least in the design of the measures.

Nevertheless, the worst solution is doing nothing and hoping for the best. In any case, it is better to venture into the subject with work aids published by an expert and with the support of relevant advisers in the literature, and to fill the obviously largest gaps successively. In the course of dealing with the subject and growing sensitivity towards it, the willingness to ask experts for advice from a certain point will also increase. Ultimately, it comes down to a simple statement: patients would like to visit their doctor and be able to entrust him with their health and intimate secrets.

# Chapter 18
# Norms of Responsible State Behaviour in Cyberspace

**Paul Meyer**

**Abstract** Cyberspace has witnessed a 'militarisation' as a growing number of states engage in a variety of cyber operations directed against foreign entities. The rate of this militarisation has outstripped the diplomatic efforts undertaken to provide this unique environment with some 'rules of the road'. The primary mechanism for discussing possible norms of responsible state behaviour has been a series of UN Groups of Governmental Experts, which have produced three consensus reports over the last decade. The 2015 report recommended a series of principles and confidence-building measures to prevent confllict, but prospects for its implementation have receded as differences amongst states persist over how security concepts should be applied to cyberspace. Renewed efforts to promote responsible state behaviour will require greater engagement on the part of the private sector and civil society, both of which have a huge stake in sustaining cyber peace.

**Keywords** Confidence-building measures · Cyber conflict · Norms of responsible state behaviour · OSCE · United Nations

## 18.1 Introduction

### *18.1.1 Cyberspace: A Realm of Peace or War?*

Cyberspace as a term was coined by William Gibson, a Vancouver-based writer of speculative fiction whose 1984 novel *Neuromancer* described it as "a consensual hallucination experienced daily by billions". Today, with over three billion users of the Internet, Gibson's projection has proven prescient, but few among current users would realise that this unique space has experienced, alongside exponential growth, a marked 'militarisation' in recent years. States, with their monopoly on organised

P. Meyer (✉)
Simon Fraser University, The Simons Foundation Canada, ICT4Peace, Vancouver, Canada
e-mail: pmeyer@sfu.ca



M. Christen et al. (eds.), *The Ethics of Cybersecurity*, The International Library of Ethics, Law and Technology 21,
https://doi.org/10.1007/978-3-030-29053-5_18

armed force, have energetically turned their attention to cyberspace, declaring this environment to be a domain for 'war-fighting' and investing heavily in the development of capabilities for offensive as well as defensive cyber capabilities. According to the US Director of National Intelligence, over 30 states currently possess cyber-attack capabilities, and such attacks now figure prominently in the intelligence community's ranking of global threats faced by the United States. (Coats 2018). In this chapter, the gradual efforts of the international community to define an order for cyberspace are examined, and in particular the ongoing effort to develop norms of responsible state behaviour in this new and unique environment. After surveying the contributions of the chief national and multilateral actors and inputs from other cyber stakeholders, the chapter concludes with some ideas for bringing this complex international discussion of norms to a practical outcome.

While states have long engaged in electronic intelligence-gathering, the emergence of cyberspace as a perceived domain for inter-state warfare with the attendant establishment of specialised units within militaries to conduct it is relatively recent (see also Chap. 12). It was only 2009 when the US created a dedicated Cyber Command, but as this element has enjoyed a rapidly increasing share of the defence budget ever since, America has set the global pace for military engagement in cyberspace. Many militaries now boast cybersecurity units and increasingly acknowledge that their capabilities extend beyond purely the defence of national systems to include offensive cyber action. This 'militarisation' process has proceeded with little political or public debate and is now frequently depicted as an inevitable development.

Significantly, however the US military, in acknowledging a 'diplomatic risk' of being seen as 'militarising' cyberspace, asserts that this environment represents "a domain already militarised by our adversaries". Given that the United States is widely perceived as the author of the 'Stuxnet' cyber weapon directed against Iran—the first cyber payload providing for actual physical destruction—the allegation that others were to blame for the 'weaponisation' of cyberspace rings rather hollow. This assertion from Cyber Command suggests, however, a certain sensitivity as to how its overt pursuit of military "superiority in cyberspace" will be perceived by other users, both governmental and non-governmental (Cyber Command 2018: 10).

States have struggled with incorporating the new, potent technology represented by cyberspace and its most salient embodiment, the Internet, into existing frameworks of international affairs. Part of the reason for this lies in the initial use of cyber capabilities by the intelligence community. As this covert activity was shrouded in secrecy and entailed accessing information from foreign targets without alerting them to this fact (the so-called Computer Network Exploitation) there was little incentive for states to acknowledge these actions, let alone discuss reciprocal limits on them. Espionage has eluded any effort at more than tacit agreement amongst states. In contrast, states have long cooperated in the field of international security and have negotiated agreements to regulate military activity and control armaments.

To the degree that intrusive cyber operations emerged from the shadows of the intelligence sphere into the somewhat more transparent field of military establishments and capabilities, it became more feasible to treat such activity as a potential realm for international agreement.

In the event, it was a Russian-led initiative at the UN in 1998 to adopt a resolution on "Developments in the field of information and telecommunications in the context of international security" (UNGA 1999) that first brought the issue of "information security" before a diplomatic forum. This resolution, introduced in the First Committee of the General Assembly (the committee responsible for issues of disarmament and international security), raised the threat that these new technologies could be employed in ways that could "adversely affect the security of states".

## *18.1.2 The GGE Process: Early Failure and Initial Success*

The Russian-initiated focus on this potential risk to international security was widely supported and led, 4 years later, to the authorisation of a UN Group of Governmental Experts (GGE) "to consider existing and potential threats in the sphere of information security and possible cooperative measures to address them…" (UNGA 2002).

This GGE met in the 2004–05 period but was unable to agree on a consensus report (as required by UN procedures for such GGEs). The chief issues that reportedly divided the group were how to characterise the threat represented by state exploitation of information and communication technology (ICT) for military purposes; and whether the concept of security should be limited to the ICT infrastructure itself or be extended to include the content of the information conveyed. In particular, there was a dispute over whether information that was the subject of trans-border transmission should be controlled as a matter of national security (UNIDIR 2016: 6).

This initial failure to agree did not impede efforts at the UN to pursue consideration of the issues contained in the information security- international security nexus. A second GGE was convened in the 2009–2010 timeframe and on this occasion, the 15 experts were successful in producing a consensus report. The report affirmed that "Existing and potential threats in the sphere of information security are among the most serious challenges of the twenty-first century". It went on to enumerate a series of malicious and disruptive ICT-enabled activity including the fact that "States are developing ICTs as instruments of warfare and intelligence, and for political purposes." In response to these developments, the report recommended that states pursue cooperative measures. Specifically, the GGE recommended that states should "discuss norms pertaining to state use of ICTs, to reduce collective risk and protect critical national and international infrastructure" and consider "Confidence-building, stability and risk reduction measures to address the implications of state use of ICTs" (UNGA 2011: 8).

## 18.2 National Strategies for Cyberspace

### *18.2.1 The US Strategy for Cyberspace*

The 2010 GGE report introduced the concept of norms for state conduct into the diplomatic discourse that hitherto had focused on state responses to malicious activity by non-state actors. The report also drew upon the past diplomatic tool box of arms control in advocating confidence-building and risk reduction measures. The United States was the first leading power to pick up on these suggestions in its *International Strategy for Cyberspace* issued by the Obama administration in May 2011. This policy document recognised the dangers that unchecked state cyber action could represent: "Cybersecurity threats can even endanger international peace and security more broadly, as traditional forms of conflict are extended into cyberspace" (White House 2011: 4). This application of traditional national power in cyberspace was occurring in the absence of "clearly agreed-upon norms for acceptable state behaviour in cyberspace" (White House 2011: 9). To rectify this situation, the *Strategy* affirmed: "We will engage the international community in frank and urgent dialogue, to build consensus around principles of responsible behaviour in cyberspace" (White House 2011: 11).

The initiation of this urgent dialogue, however, proved elusive and the Obama administration experienced difficulty in translating its clear interest in developing "norms of responsible behaviour" into an actual diplomatic process to achieve this end. Initial follow-up action seemed to have been delegated to the United Kingdom, where then Foreign Secretary William Hague hosted an international cyberspace conference in London in November 2011. Secretary Hague characterised the conference as an opportunity to discuss norms of acceptable behaviour in cyberspace and to explore mechanisms for giving such standards "real political and diplomatic weight" (Hague 2011). In his chairman's summation of the conference discussions, he indicated: "All delegates agreed that the immediate next steps must be to take practical measures to develop shared understanding and agree common approaches and confidence-building measures. There was no appetite at this stage to expend effort on new legally-binding international instruments" (Hague 2011).

While Secretary Hague's conclusions may have reflected British preferences to a degree, there did appear a broad consensus that the "common approaches" for governing state behaviour in cyberspace should take the form of politically as opposed to legally binding measures. Early in the UN's polling of national views, influential states such as the US and the UK argued that in the realm of cyber conflict, legally binding agreements were superfluous as the laws of armed conflict would apply (Tikk and Kerttunen 2017: 20). Whether it was the time-intensive character of negotiating international legal instruments, the absence of adequate verification means or the risk of such efforts being rendered obsolete by a rapidly developing technology, states in general seemed more comfortable with the idea of political versus legal arrangements in this new environment.

### 18.2.2 Sino-Russian Code of Conduct

This approach was reinforced when Russia and China (alongside Tajikistan and Uzbekistan) submitted to the UN General Assembly in September 2011 a proposal for an *International Code of Conduct for Information Security.* Although these states generally advocated legally binding agreements in the realm of international security, in this case the sponsors decided to utilise the less demanding and more palatable form of politically binding measures represented by the *Code of Conduct.* At the same time, the conflict prevention dimension of the proposal was stressed by the sponsors. In his introduction of the proposal, the Chinese Ambassador Wang Qun stated that "countries should work to keep information and cyberspace from becoming a new battlefield, prevent an arms race in information and cyberspace and settle disputes on this front peacefully through dialogue" (Qun 2011).

The co-sponsors of the *Code* characterised it, therefore, as a collection of voluntary measures designed to maintain international stability and security. The chief undertaking would be a commitment by states "not to use Information and Communication Technologies, including networks, to carry out hostile activities or acts of aggression, pose threats to international peace and security or proliferate information weapons or related technologies" (Code 2011). This external security aspect was associated with other measures with far more of an internal security focus. The *Code* affirmed the rights of states "to protect, in accordance with relevant laws and regulations, their information space and critical information infrastructure from threats, disturbance, attack and sabotage". How such hostile actions would be defined could prove problematic, as what one state might view as a "disturbance", another might consider a simple exercise of freedom of expression. From a classic arms control perspective, the definitional challenges inherent in determining what constituted an "information weapon" or an "act of aggression" in cyberspace were also significant obstacles. At the same time, the Sino-Russian *Code* represented the first major diplomatic effort to provide a set of "norms of responsible state behaviour" as called for in the 2010 GGE report and the US 2011 *Strategy*.

In the event, China and Russia chose to proceed cautiously with their initiative, engaging over the next few years in consultations on the margins of UN General Assembly sessions but not seeking to bring the *Code* forward for adoption by that body. A revised *Code* was circulated by the co-sponsors in January 2015 that essentially eliminated the previous "arms control" aspect but retained the bulk of the measures directed at prohibiting cyber interference "in the internal affairs of other States or with the aim of undermining their political, economic and social stability" (Code 2015). The internal control orientation of the *Code* was further evident in its affirmation of the sovereign rights of states to protect "their information space and critical information infrastructure against damage resulting from threats, interference, attack and sabotage". The Sino-Russian *Code of Conduct for Information Security* reflected, in its use of the term 'information security' over the prevalent terminology of 'cybersecurity', a fundamental conceptual difference with the West. Whereas 'cybersecurity' was seen as focusing on the integrity of the computer systems comprising cyberspace, "information security" implied that the content of information transmitted should also be viewed through a security prism. This conceptual distinction continues to colour the preferred approaches of leading cyber powers in pursuing common norms of responsible state behaviour.

## 18.3 International Developments

### *18.3.1 GGE 2013*

In parallel to these unilateral or plurilateral forays into suggesting norms to govern state conduct in cyberspace, the UN GGE process continued to act as a locus for multilateral cybersecurity diplomacy. A successful GGE report in 2013 contributed to the framing of the problem by flagging the increasingly sophisticated nature of malicious cyber activity and stressing "[T]the absence of common understandings on acceptable State behaviour with regard to the use of ICTs increases the risk to international peace and security" (GGE 2013: 7). The report established the principle that international law is applicable to cyberspace without attempting to delineate how it did so. In a counterbalancing finding, it also affirmed the applicability of the sovereignty principle to state cyber conduct and state jurisdiction over ICT infrastructure within its territory. The report stated that "States must not use proxies to commit internationally wrongful acts" (GGE 2013: 8) and indicated that states had the responsibility to ensure that non-state actors did not engage in such unlawful use of ICTs on their territory. The GGE reiterated the earlier call for states to consider "the development of practical confidence -building measures to help increase transparency, predictability and cooperation" and suggested a series of basic consultative and information-exchange measures towards this end (GGE 2013: 9).

### *18.3.2 GGE 2015*

The UN-centric GGE process reached a culmination of sorts with the successful conclusion of an enlarged (20 experts) GGE in the summer of 2015. This GGE, explicitly building on its two predecessors, stated that "Voluntary, non-binding norms of responsible state behaviour can reduce risks to international peace, security and stability" while observing that "norms do not seek to limit or prohibit action that is otherwise consistent with international law" (GGE 2015: 7). The report provided the fullest elaboration to date of the "norms, rules and principles for the responsible behaviour of states" and the "confidence building measures" that formed the chief headings of the GGE reports. Importantly on the normative side, the report recommended that "A state should not conduct or knowingly support ICT activity contrary to its obligations under international law that intentionally damages critical infrastructure or otherwise impairs the use and operation of critical infrastructure to provide services to the public" (GGE 2015: 8).

A further major restraint measure was set out to the effect that "States should not conduct or knowingly support activity to harm the information systems of the authorised emergency response teams (sometimes known as computer emergency response teams or cybersecurity incident response teams) of another state. A state should not use authorised emergency response teams to engage in malicious international activity" (GGE 2015: 8).

In these two restraint measures, there is a clear connection with pre-existing obligations under international humanitarian law not to target civilians or crucial infrastructure for the public. It also mirrors recognition of a certain "protective status" for the computer emergency response teams akin to that accorded to medical personnel and facilities under international humanitarian law.

In addition to these restraint measures, the 2015 GGE report also recommended proactive steps such as encouraging states to report "ICT vulnerabilities and share associated information on available remedies to such vulnerabilities" (GGE 2015: 8). Given that this reporting concerns the very vulnerabilities that states have secretly harboured to develop targeted exploits, it would seem doubtful that states will undertake such cooperation anytime soon. After its enumeration of proposed measures, the report acknowledged that "while such measures may be essential to promote an open, secure, stable, accessible and peaceful ICT environment, their implementation may not immediately be possible" (GGE 2015: 8). The 2015 GGE may have elaborated the most practical set of measures to date, but its experts were aware that their proposals remained only recommendations, the implementation of which would depend on state capacity or willingness to adopt them.

Some of the underlying problems of the GGE process in generating recommended measures that states would actually embrace were made manifest in the subsequent GGE (at 25 experts, the largest yet) which operated in the 2016–17 timeframe yet failed to achieve a consensus report. Whereas there was considerable speculation as to the reasons for the failure of the latest GGE, it seems likely that it reflected basic disagreement among leading cyber powers as to the relationship between inter-state cyber conflict and the laws of armed conflict. In brief, whereas states such as the US and UK wanted to elaborate on the rules around cyber operations in the context of the laws of armed conflict others, namely Russia and China, balked at this direction. As one observer remarked: "Russian and Chinese diplomats wanted to concentrate their efforts on preventing cyber-based conflict in the first place, instead of setting the rules for something that should not be allowed to happen" (Grigsby 2017: 114). This fundamental divergence over the appropriateness of state-conducted cyber operations helps explain why defining responsible state behaviour has proven so difficult. As another analyst of the GGE concluded, "Authoritative guidance for responsible state behaviour in cyberspace remains far-fetched, not just because of yawning technical capacity divides and the known difficulties of attribution of state behaviour in cyberspace, but also because the principal questions of the international cybersecurity discourse are far from settled politically" (Tikk and Kerttunen 2017: 5).

### *18.3.3 Regional Security Organisations and Cyber Confidence-Building Measures*

Although the UN and its GGE process has been the primary focus of discussion of norms of responsible state behaviour in cyberspace, it has not been the only inter-governmental forum to have taken up this issue. Notably, the 57-member Organization for Security and Cooperation in Europe (OSCE) has been engaged since 2012 in an effort to develop cybersecurity confidence-building measures to "enhance cooperation, transparency, predictability, and stability to reduce the risks of misperception, escalation and conflict that may stem from the use of ICTs" (OSCE 2012).

In 2013, the OSCE was able to adopt a set of 11 confidence-building measures relating to cybersecurity information sharing and in 2016 it was able to add five additional measures including the protection of critical infrastructure and the establishment of protected channels of communication. It has been noted that the measures adopted by the OSCE are cast in more prescriptive language than the comparable measures identified by the UN GGE. The OSCE has also established an on-going working group for discussion relating to the implementation of the agreed confidence-building measures (Hitchens and Gallagher 2018: 6). Other regional organisations such as the AU, OAS, and ASEAN Regional Forum have considered cybersecurity confidence building measures over the last decade, although none have progressed as far as the OSCE in agreeing on a substantial package of measures. It remains to be seen whether the relative success of the OSCE in addressing the issue of international cybersecurity cooperation will be sustained in a context of deteriorating East-West relations, notably between leading OSCE member states Russia and the US.

## 18.4 Other Stakeholders

While the inter-governmental discussion of norms of responsible state behaviour proceeds with various degrees of progress, there is increasing engagement in its subject matter by other stakeholders. The private sector, civil society, academia and mere Internet users have legitimate reasons to be concerned with how states will conduct themselves in cyberspace. Beyond the fact that this special, human-created environment is overwhelmingly owned and operated by non-governmental entities, disruptive or destructive state activity in cyberspace could have serious detrimental effects on the interests of 'netizens' and humanity in general.

In recent years, several of these stakeholders have begun to express their views on what would constitute responsible state behaviour in cyberspace in an effort to influence the inter-governmental debate.

### 18.4.1 International Committee of the Red Cross

Given its role as a custodian of international humanitarian law, it is not surprising that the International Committee of the Red Cross (ICRC) has been monitoring state action in cyberspace and has begun to air its concerns. In its statement to the 2017 session of the UN General Assembly's First Committee, the ICRC drew attention to the upswing in major cyber-attacks including those "affecting the functioning of electricity networks, medical facilities and a nuclear power plant". Such attacks, the statement noted, "are a stark reminder of the vulnerability of essential civilian infrastructure to cyber-attacks and of the significant humanitarian consequences that may ensure". The ICRC affirmed that international humanitarian law "applies to and restricts the use of cyber capabilities as means and methods of warfare during armed conflicts. Crucially, IHL prohibits cyber-attacks against civilian objects or networks, and prohibits indiscriminate and disproportionate cyber-attack" (ICRC 2017: 3).

The ICRC, however, also wanted to make it clear that "by asserting that IHL applies to cyber operations, the ICRC is in no way condoning cyber warfare, nor is it condoning the militarisation of cyberspace. Any resort to force by a State, whether physical or through cyberspace, remains constrained by the UN Charter (*jus ad bellum*)" (ICRC 2017: 3). The ICRC expressed its regret over the failure of the 2016–2017 GGE to adopt a consensus report and called upon all states "to renew discussions in appropriate forums on the critical issues raised by cyberwarfare, with a view to finding common ground on the protection afforded by IHL to civilian use of cyber space" (ICRC 2017: 3).

### 18.4.2 Civil Society

At the same session of the UN General Assembly's First Committee that heard the position of the ICRC on the threats posed by irresponsible state behaviour in cyberspace, there was also a statement delivered by the *Women's International League for Peace and Freedom* on behalf of several civil society organisations. This statement was especially noteworthy as it went beyond affirming the applicability of international humanitarian law to state cyber operations to challenge the militarisation of cyberspace itself. Expressing its regret over the failure of the latest GGE, the civil society statement suggested that it was "an opportune moment to put forward a few basic questions: how much more militarised are we going to allow cyberspace to become? When and under whose authority did it pass from a civilian domain to the so-called 'fifth domain' of conflict, and how was that allowed to happen?" (WILPF 2017: 1). According to the civil society statement there was still time to "turn back the clock" on militarisation: "States can choose to elaborate methods to preserve cyber peace, rather than resign themselves to formulating the norms of cyber war" (WILPF 2017: 1). This statement argued in effect for a new orientation for the future discussion of norms, one that would seek to reinforce the peace in cyberspace rather than merely set out the limits to warfare undertaken by states within it.

### *18.4.3 The Private Sector*

A relevant sector that might have been expected to be at the forefront of the discussion of state conduct in cyberspace given its implications for its business model is that of the ICT industry.

The industry has largely been silent on issues of international cybersecurity policy, however, and not particularly engaged with the nascent inter-governmental discussion of norms of responsible state behaviour. An important exception to this general trend of the industry has been the Microsoft Corporation, which has for several years been advocating cooperative approaches and restraint measures for international cybersecurity. Its president, Brad Smith, has been outspoken in voicing alarm about the implications of irresponsible state conduct in cyberspace and the threat posed to civil interests. He has stated: "A cyber arms race is underway with nations developing and unleashing a new generation of weapons aimed at governments and civilians alike, putting at risk the critical data and digital-powered infrastructure that we all depend on for our daily lives" (Smith November 2017).

Smith has not shied away from blaming governments for the damaging consequences for society flowing from their practice of hoarding software vulnerabilities in order to use them on their adversaries via targeted "exploits". In the aftermath of the 'WannaCry' ransomware attacks of early May 2017, Smith wrote "this attack provides yet another example of why the stockpiling of vulnerabilities by governments is such a problem …We have seen vulnerabilities stored by the CIA show up on WikiLeaks, and now this vulnerability stolen from the NSA has affected customers around the world. Repeatedly, exploits in the hands of governments have leaked into the public domain and caused widespread damage" (Smith May 2017).

These concerns have led Smith to propose a new international agreement that would set out standards for state cyber operations. In a keynote speech at a major industry conference, he explained "What we need now is a Digital Geneva Convention. We need a convention that will call on the world's governments to pledge that they will not engage in cyberattacks on the private sector, that they will not target civilian infrastructure, whether it's of the electrical or the economic or the political variety" (Smith February 2017). He went on to espouse the need for a neutral entity along the lines of the International Atomic Energy Agency or the ICRC to partner with governments in the development of such an accord. More broadly, he outlined prospects for the ICT industry as a whole to play a role as a "neutral Digital Switzerland on which everyone can depend and rely" (Smith February 2017).

Smith's advocacy on behalf of an international arrangement for responsible state behaviour and the engagement of the private sector in bringing such arrangements about seem to have yielded some further allies in the industry. In April 2018, 34 companies (including major actors such as Facebook, LinkedIn, Dell and Cisco) signed a 'Cybersecurity Tech Accord' which pledged to uphold four principles supportive of cybersecurity. The principles are to: (i) protect all of our users and customers everywhere; (ii) oppose cyberattacks on innocent citizens and enterprises from anywhere; (iii) empower users, customers and developers to strengthen cybersecurity protection and iv) partner with each other and with like-minded groups to enhance cybersecurity (Smith April 2018). Although these general principles are open to question and interpretation (e.g. who decides which citizens and enterprises are "innocent"?) they do represent some common ground on the part of leading firms in the ICT sector in espousing positions relevant to the future development of cyberspace and especially the trend towards its 'militarisation'.

## 18.5 Prospects and Proposals for Norms of Responsible State Behaviour

The failure of the 2016–2017 iteration of the GGE process has derailed to some degree the momentum that this process had developed in terms of agreed norms for state conduct in cyberspace. For some observers, the pursuit of agreed norms represents a "bridge too far" given the absence of shared ideological principles, and the more modest aim of accepting a few practical confidence-building measures is advocated instead (Grigsby 2017: 116–18). There has also been reference to the "cybersecurity dilemma" that generates fear amongst cyber powers and impedes cooperation, as intrusions into foreign networks are advantageous for both defensive and offensive purposes and thus promote "worse-case scenario" reactions by the intruded party (Buchanen 2016: 188). A general lack of transparency regarding policy and doctrine concerning offensive cyber operations in particular also constitutes an impediment to more cooperative approaches.

At the same time, the recommendations emerging from the GGE process, while falling short of the clear norms and rules of state conduct that some would have liked to see, still constitute an important step in that direction. As noted by one long-time observer: "In this reading, the 2015 GGE provides the international community with a very valuable roadmap to strengthening international cyber security". A roadmap that, for all of its utility in providing direction, leaves much of the distance to be completed as "There is hardly any state, even among those having participated in the OSCE and the GGE discussions, that to date fully implements all the GGE recommendations" (Tikk 2018 7–8).

The UN Secretary General sees a future role for himself in the prevention and peaceful settlement of cyber conflict as well as in "foster[ing] a culture of accountability and adherence to emerging norms, rules and principles on responsible behaviour in cyberspace" (ODA 2018: 56). How exactly these contributions are to be realised is unstated in the Secretary General's *An Agenda for Disarmament*, but the UN is likely to retain a vital convening role for the norms discussions, especially given the alignment between its universal membership and the universal nature of cyberspace. Member state action will remain crucial, however, in order to achieve progress in normative development, and unfortunately prospects for inter-state cooperation have become dimmer. The 2018 session of the General Assembly witnessed a bifurcation of future work on cyber security norms when two competing resolutions were adopted on divided votes. A Russian-led resolution established an Open-Ended Working Group (OEWG) to ensure "more democratic, inclusive and transparent" negotiations in developing "rules, norms and principles of responsible behaviour of states"; whereas a US-led resolution adhered to the traditional GGE format with limited membership (UNGA 2018). This splintering of the UN work on devising cyber security norms reflects the strained relations between the leading cyber powers and will further complicate the effort to identify and operationalise such norms at the universal level.

Even if states persist in disputes regarding the nature of the norms that should apply to state conduct in cyberspace, there are constructive proposals being generated by other stakeholders. The Swiss-based NGO ICT4Peace, for example, has suggested that the cooperative measures recommended by the UN GGE process (specifically the measures recommended in the 2015 GGE report) be taken up by states regardless of the future course of this UN mechanism. ICT4Peace has also engaged in cybersecurity capacity building and has promoted this as a crucial enabler for the developing world to participate effectively in international policy discussions.

Finally, we should expect to see a greater engagement by the private sector and civil society with the specialised forums where representatives of government debate these issues (see also Chap. 13). Heightened awareness of the damage to civil interests that offensive state cyber operations can cause, intentionally or inadvertently, is likely to foster greater lobbying efforts to press governments to support cooperative efforts and measures of restraint in cyberspace. The 'Digital Peace Now' campaign launched in September 2018 by Microsoft in cooperation with ICT4Peace and other NGOs is a manifestation of this reaction. Moves to accelerate an unregulated 'militarisation' of cyberspace are likely to call forth countervailing pressures to ensure that inter-state cyber conflict, if not precluded, is at least mitigated and subject to some form of reciprocal restraint. Diplomatic discussion and the negotiation of norms of responsible state behaviour are likely to continue to feature prominently in these efforts.

## References

Buchanen B (2016) The Cybersecurity dilemma: hacking, trust and fear between nations. Oxford University Press, Oxford

Coats DR (13 Feb 2018) Worldwide threat assessment of the US Intelligence Community. www.dni.gov. Last access: 7 July 2019

Gibson W (1984) Neuromancer. Ace Books, New York

Grigsby A (2017) The end of cyber norms. Survival 59(6):109–122
Hague W (2 Nov 2011) Closing remarks London conference on Cyberspace. www.fco.gov.uk/en/news/latest-news/?view=Speech&id=685672482. Last access: 7 July 2019
Hitchens T, Gallagher NW (Mar 2018) Building confidence in the Cybersphere: a path to multilateral progress. Center for International and Security Studies, University of Maryland. www.cissm.umd.edu. Last access: 7 July 2019
International Committee of the Red Cross (10 Oct 2017) Statement to UN General Assembly First Committee – General Debate on all disarmament and international security agenda items
GGE (2013) United Nations General Assembly Group of Governmental Experts on Developments in the field of information and telecommunications in the context of international security. A/68/98 (24 June). http://www.unidir.org/files/medias/pdfs/developments-in-the-field-of-information-and-telecommunications-in-the-context-of-international-security-2012-2013-a-68-98-eng-0-518.pdf. Last access 7 July 2019
GGE (2015) United Nations General Assembly Group of Governmental Experts on Developments in the field of information and telecommunications in the context of international security. A/70/174 (22 July). https://digitallibrary.un.org/record/799853/files/A_70_174-EN.pdf. Last access: 7 July 2019
ODA (2018) Securing our common future: an agenda for disarmament. www.un.org/disarmament. Last access: 7 July 2019
OSCE (26 Apr 2012) Permanent Council Decision 1039. www.osce.org/pc/90169. Last access: 7 July 2019
OSCE (3 Dec 2013) Permanent Council Decision 1106. www.osce.org/pc/109168. Last access: 7 July 2019
OSCE (10 Mar 2016) Permanent Council Decision 1202. www.osce.org/pc/227281. Last access: 7 July 2019
Qun W (19 Oct 2011) Work to build a peaceful, secure and equitable information and cyber space. Statement to UN General Assembly First Committee. www.fmprc.gov.cn/eng/wjdt/zyjh/t869580.htm. Last access: 7 July 2019
Smith B (14 Feb 2017) The need for a Digital Geneva Convention. https://blogs.microsoft.com/on-the-issues/2017/02/14/need-digital-geneva-convention. Last access: 7 July 2019
Smith B (14 May 2017) The need for urgent action to keep people safe online: Lessons learned from last week's cyberattack. https://blogs.microsoft.com/on-the-issues/2017/05/14/need-urgent-collective-action-keep-people-safe-online-lessons-last-weeks cyberattack/. Last access: 7 July 2019
Smith B (10 Nov 2017) We need to modernize international agreements to create a safer digital world. https://blogs.microsoft.com/on-the-issues/2017/11/10/need-to-modernize-international-agreements-to-create-a-safer-digital-world. Last access: 7 July 2019
Smith B (17 Apr 2018) 34 companies stand up for cybersecurity with a tech accord. https://blogs.microsoft.com/on-the-issues/2018/04/17/34-companies-stand-up-for-cybersecurity-with-a-tech-accord. Last access: 7 July 2019
Tikk E, Kerttunen M (Dec 2017) The alleged demise of the UN GGE: an autopsy and eulogy. Cyberpolicy Institute. www.cpi.ee. 22 Aug 2018
Tikk E (2018) "Introduction" Voluntary, non-binding norms for responsible state behaviour in the use of information and communications technology: a commentary. www.un.org/disarmament. Last access: 7 July 2019
UNIDIR (2016) Report of the International security cyber issues workshop series. www.unidir.org. Last access: 7 July 2019
UNGA (4 Jan 1999) Developments in the field of information and telecommunications in the context of international security A/RES/53/70
UNGA (30 Dec 2002) Developments in the field of information and telecommunications in the context of international security A/RES/57/53
UNGA (14 Sep 2011) International Code of Conduct for information security A/66/359

UNGA (13 Jan 2015) International Code of Conduct for information security A/69/723
UNGA (11 Dec 2018) Developments in the field of information and telecommunications in the context of international security A/RES/73/27 and 2 Jan 2019 Advancing responsible state behaviour in cyberspace in the context of international security A/RES/73/266
US Cyber Command (2018) Achieve and maintain cyberspace superiority: command vision for US Cyber Command www.cybercom.mil. Last access: 7 July 2019
White House (May 2011) International strategy for cyberspace: prosperity, security and openness in a networked world. whitehouse.gov/sites/default/files/rss_viewer/international_strategy_for_cyberspace.pdf. Last access: 7 July 2019
Women's International League for Peace and Freedom (10 Oct 2017) Civil society statement on cyber. UN General Assembly First Committee. www.reachingcriticalwill.org. Last access: 7 July 2019

# Appendix

## List of Cybersecurity Organisations

In the following, a non-exhaustive list of organisations (both public and private) that are active in the cybersecurity domain are presented with a focus on European Organizations. First, several groups of international organisations are listed including a short description and the respective URL. Then, a selection of national organisations is presented to the reader.

### International Organisations: Global

Electronic Frontier Foundation

The Electronic Frontier Foundation is the leading non-profit organization defending civil liberties in the digital world.
*https://www.eff.org/de*

International Telecommunication Union

ITU is the United Nations specialized agency for information and communication technologies. Founded on the principle of international cooperation between governments (Member States) and the private sector (Sector Members, Associates and Academia), ITU is the premier global forum through which parties work towards consensus on a wide range of issues affecting the future direction of the ICT industry.
*https://www.itu.int/*



M. Christen et al. (eds.), *The Ethics of Cybersecurity*, The International Library of Ethics, Law and Technology 21,
https://doi.org/10.1007/978-3-030-29053-5

NATO Cooperative Cyber Defense Centre of Excellence

The NATO Cooperative Cyber Defence Centre of Excellence is a multinational and interdisciplinary cyber defence hub. It does research, training and exercises in four core areas: technology, strategy, operations and law.

*https://ccdcoe.org/*

World Wide Web Consortium

The World Wide Web Consortium (W3C) is an international community where Member organizations, a full-time staff, and the public work together to develop Web standards. W3C's mission is to lead the Web to its full potential, especially by developing protocols and guidelines that ensure long-term growth for the Web.

*https://www.w3.org/*

## International Organisations: European Union Related

Art. 29 Data Protection Working Party

The Article 29 Working Party (Art. 29 WP) was the independent European working party that dealt with issues relating to the protection of privacy and personal data until 25 May 2018 (entry into application of the GDPR).

*https://ec.europa.eu/newsroom/article29/news-overview.cfm*

Computer Emergency Response Team EU

After a pilot phase of one year and a successful assessment by its constituency and its peers, the EU Institutions have decided to set up a permanent Computer Emergency Response Team (CERT-EU) for the EU institutions, agencies and bodies in 2012. It cooperates closely with other CERTs in the Member States and beyond as well as with specialised IT security companies.

*https://cert.europa.eu/*

DG Connect: Directorate General for Communications Networks, Content and Technology

The 'Directorate General for Communications Networks, Content and Technology' is the European Commission's department responsible to develop a digital single market to generate smart, sustainable and inclusive growth in Europe. It develops and carries out the Commission's policies on: Digital economy and society, Research and innovation, business and industry, as well as culture and media.

*https://ec.europa.eu/info/departments/communications-networks-content-and-technology_en*

Directorate E: Future Networks

The Directorate 'Future Networks' is responsible for strategic advancement of the policy, technological research and standardisation on all-encompassing Future Internet dimension, ensuring an innovative intertwining of all these aspects so that Europe can lead in the design, piloting and roll-out of the Internet of tomorrow.

Directorate H: Digital Society, Trust and Cybersecurity

The Directorate 'Digital Society, Trust and Cybersecurity' provides a strategic approach to the societal dimension of the DSM, focusing on applications that combine digital policy, digital Research and Innovation, and deployment and provide for leadership in cybersecurity and digital privacy and digital trust policy, legislation and innovation.

European Cybercrime Centre, Europol

Europol set up the European Cybercrime Centre (EC3) in 2013 to strengthen the law enforcement response to cybercrime in the EU and thus to help protect European citizens, businesses and governments from online crime. Since its establishment, EC3 has made a significant contribution to the fight against cybercrime.

*https://www.europol.europa.eu/about-europol/european-cybercrime-centre-ec3*

European Cybercrime Training and Education Group, Europol

The European Cybercrime Training and Education Group (ECTEG) is composed of European Union and European Economic Area Member States law enforcement agencies, international bodies, academia, private industry and experts. In close cooperation with Europol-EC3 and CEPOL it aims to support international activities to harmonise cybercrime training across international borders to build the capacity of countries to combat cybercrime.

*https://www.ecteg.eu/*

European Data Protection Supervisor

The European Data Protection Supervisor (EDPS) is the European Union's (EU) independent data protection authority. The objective of the EDPS is among other duties to monitor and ensure the protection of personal data and privacy when EU institutions and bodies process the personal information of individuals.

*https://edps.europa.eu/*

European Network and Information Security Agency

The European Union Agency for Cybersecurity, which was established in 2004, is actively contributing to European cybersecurity policy, in order to support member states and European Union stakeholders to support a response to large-scale cyber incidents that take place across borders in cases where two or more EU member states have been affected. This work also contributes to the proper functioning of the digital single market. The agency works closely together with member states and private sector to deliver advice and solutions as well as improving their capabilities.

*https://www.enisa.europa.eu/*

European Network for Cyber Security

The European Network for Cyber Security (ENCS) is a non-profit member organization that brings together critical infrastructure stake owners and security experts to deploy secure European critical energy grids and infrastructure.

*https://encs.eu/*

**International Organisations: Private**

Chaos Computer Club

The Chaos Computer Club e.V. (CCC) is Europe's largest association of hackers, providing information about technical and societal issues, such as surveillance, privacy, freedom of information, hacktivism and data security for more than 30 years. As the most influential hacker collective in Europe, the CCC organizes campaigns, events, lobbying and publications as well as anonymizing services and communication infrastructure.

*https://www.ccc.de/en/*

## ECO: Association of the Internet Industry

With more than 1100 members, eco is the largest Association of the Internet Industry in Europe. As a network of experts, ECO encourage communication between enterprises in the industry and support the marketing of their products and also lobbies on current issues such as Internet law, infrastructure, online services, and e-business, in political arenas and before international entities.

*https://international.eco.de/*

## European Cyber Security Organisation

The European Cyber Security Organisation represents the contractual counterpart to the European Commission for the implementation of the Cyber Security contractual Public-Private Partnership. ECSO members include a wide variety of stakeholders such as large companies, SMEs and Start-ups, research centres, universities, end-users, operators, clusters and association as well as European Member State's local, regional and national administrations, countries part of the European Economic Area (EEA) and the European Free Trade Association (EFTA) and H2020 associated countries.

*https://ecs-org.eu/*

## European Digital Rights

European Digital Rights (EDRi) is an international not-for-profit association of digital human rights organisations. The aim is to defend and promote rights and freedoms in the digital environment, such as the right to privacy, personal data protection, freedom of expression, and access to information.

*https://edri.org/*

## European Network of Forensic Science Institutes

The European Network of Forensic Science Institutes (ENFSI) was founded to improve the mutual exchange of information in the field of forensic science. This, as well as improving the quality of forensic science delivery in Europe have become the main issues of the network.

*http://enfsi.eu/*

ISF: Information Security Forum

The ISF is a non-profit organisation, dedicated to investigating, clarifying and resolving key issues in information security and risk management, by developing best practice methodologies, processes and solutions and therewith supplying authoritative opinion and guidance on all aspects of information security and delivering practical solutions to overcome the wide-ranging security challenges that impact business information.

*https://www.securityforum.org/*

Privacy International

PI is a independent charity that challenges the governments and companies that want to know everything about individuals, groups, and whole societies. PI conducts campaigns against companies and governments, driven by charitable aims: to promote the human right of privacy throughout the world.

*https://privacyinternational.org/*

SANS Institute

The SANS Institute was established in 1989 as a cooperative research and education organization. Its programs now reach more than 165,000 security professionals around the world. SANS is the largest source for information security training and security certification in the world. It also develops, maintains, and makes available at no cost, the largest collection of research documents about various aspects of information security.

*https://www.sans.org/*

**National Organisations: Computer Emergency Response Teams**

A Computer Emergency Response Team (CERT) is an expert group that handles computer security incidents. Alternative names for such groups include Computer Emergency Readiness Team and Computer Security Incident Response Team (CSIRT). The following list contains cyber security organizations on a national level in Europe and their online presences:

- *Austria*: Computer Emergency Response Team Austria; https://www.cert.at/
- *Belgium*: Centre for Cybersecurity Belgium; https://ccb.belgium.be/
- *Catalonia*: Centre of Information Security of Catalonia; https://ciberseguretat.gencat.cat/en/inici/

- *Croatia*: National CERT Croatia; https://www.cert.hr/en/home-page/
- *Czech Republic*: National Cyber Security Center; https://www.govcert.cz/en/
- *Denmark*: Danish Computer Security Incident Response Team; https://www.cert.dk/en
- *Estonia*: CERT Estonia; https://www.ria.ee/en/cyber-security/cert-ee.html
- *Finland*: Finnish CERT (Traficom); www.viestintavirasto.fi/en/cybersecurity.html
- *France*: Centre Expert contre la Cybercriminalité Français (CECyF); https://www.cecyf.fr/
- *Germany*: German Federal Office of Information Security (BSI); www.bsi.bund.de/
- *Greece*: National CERT; http://www.nis.gr/portal/page/portal/NIS/NCERT
- *Hungary*: National Cyber Security Center; https://nki.gov.hu/
- *Iceland*: CERT-IS; https://www.cert.is/en/node/2.html
- *Ireland*: National Cyber Security Centre; https://www.ncsc.gov.ie/
- *Italy*: Agenzia per l'Italia Digitale; https://www.agid.gov.it/
- *Latvia*: CERT.LV; https://cert.lv/en/about-us
- *Lithuania*: National Cyber Security Centre; https://www.nksc.lt/en/
- *Luxembourg*: Computer Incident Response Center Luxembourg; https://www.circl.lu/
- *Netherlands*: Cyber Security Council, Netherlands; https://www.cybersecurityraad.nl/
- *Norway*: NorCERT; https://www.nsm.stat.no/norcert/norcert-eng/
- *Poland*: CERT Polska; https://www.cert.pl/en/
- *Portugal*: National Cyber Security Centre Portugal; https://www.cncs.gov.pt/en/
- *Romania*: Romanian National Computer Security Incident Response Team; https://cert.ro/
- *Slovak Republic*: Slovak Computer Emergency Response Team; https://www.sk-cert.sk/en/about-us/index.html
- *Slovenia*: Information Commissioner, Republic of Slovenia; https://www.ip-rs.si/en/
- *Spain*: Instituto Nacional de Ciberseguridad; https://www.incibe.es/en/
- *Sweden*: National Defence Radio Establishment Sweden (FRA); https://www.fra.se/
- *Switzerland*: Swiss National CERT; https://www.govcert.admin.ch/
- *United Kingdom*: The National Cyber Security Centre; https://www.ncsc.gov.uk/

## National Organisations: Selection of Cybersecurity Expert Organisations

Below, a non-exhaustive selection of European academic, public and private organisations with a strong focus on cybersecurity is provided.

Austria: SBA Research

SBA Research is a research centre for Information Security funded partly by the national initiative for COMET Competence Centers for Excellent Technologies. Within a network of more than 70 companies, 15 Austrian and international universities and research institutions, and many additional international research partners we jointly work on research challenges ranging from organizational to technical security to strengthen Europe's Cybersecurity capabilities.

*https://www.sba-research.org/*

Austria: Vienna Centre for Societal Security

Vienna Centre for Societal Security (VICESSE) is a private non-profit research and consulting organisation, focussing on the analysis of a wide array of security issues in a broader societal context. Locating security problems and proposed solutions emerging at local, national and European levels in wider social and historical contexts VICESSE operates at the interface between science, technology, law and policy.

*https://www.vicesse.eu/*

Austria: TU Graz, Institute of Applied Information Processing and Communications

The Institute of Applied Information Processing and Communications (IAIK) focuses on information security. Fifty researchers at IAIK conduct research, teach, and consult private and as public organizations. The institute is part of the Faculty of Computer Science at Graz University of Technology.

*https://www.iaik.tugraz.at/*

Belgium: Brussels Privacy Hub

The Brussels Privacy Hub (BPH) is an academic privacy research centre with a global focus. As an entity of the Vrije Universiteit Brussel (Free University of Brussels or VUB), it uses its location in Brussels, the capital of Europe, to engage EU policymakers, data protection regulators, the private sector, and NGOs, and to produce innovative, cutting-edge research on important questions of data protection and privacy law and policy.

*https://brusselsprivacyhub.eu/index.html*

Belgium: KU Leuven, Computer Security and Industrial Cryptography (COSIC) Group

COSIC is part of the Department of Electrical Engineering at the KU Leuven. COSIC focuses on the protection of digital information. COSIC develops advanced cybersecurity solutions to protect data in the cloud and in the Internet of Things (IoT) and to protect the privacy of users.

*https://www.esat.kuleuven.be/cosic/*

Bulgaria: Institute of Information and Communication Technologies at the Bulgarian Academy of Sciences

The Information Technologies for Security Department of the Institute of Information & Communication Technologies studies the interrelation between the development of information technologies and the new security challenges of the twenty-first century. The interdisciplinary research team explores advances and applies methodologies and tools for IT governance and change management, design and analysis of architectures and capabilities, modelling and simulation for the security sector, and information security management.

*http://it4sec.org/*

Denmark: Technical University of Denmark, Department of Applied Mathematics and Computer Science

DTU Compute is an internationally unique academic environment spanning the scientific disciplines mathematics, statistics, computer science, and engineering. Our interdisciplinary research areas are big data and data science, artificial intelligence (AI), Internet of things (IoT), smart and secure societies, smart manufacturing and life sciences.

*https://www.compute.dtu.dk/english*

Finland: University of Helsinki, Department of Computer Science

The Department of Computer Science is a leading teaching and research unit in its area in Finland. The research groups address significant research challenges in their areas of expertise, such as data analytics, AI, and security and privacy.

*https://www.helsinki.fi/en/computer-science*

Finland: Aalto University, Department of Computer Science

The Department of Computer Science provides research and education in modern computer science to foster future science, engineering and society. The work combines fundamental research with innovative applications.

*https://www.aalto.fi/en/department-of-computer-science*

France: Ecole Normale Supérieure, CASCADE Team

The research activity of the project-team Construction and Analysis of Systems for Confidentiality and Authenticity of Data and Entities (CASCADE) at the ENS of Paris addresses the following topics, which cover most of the areas that are currently active in the international cryptographic community, with a focus on public-key algorithms: Implementation of cryptographic algorithms, and applied cryptography; Algorithm and protocol design, and provable security; Theoretical and practical attacks.

*https://crypto.di.ens.fr/web2py*

France: Eurecom

EURECOM is a Graduate school and Research Centre in digital sciences located in the Sophia Antipolis technology park (French Riviera), a major European place for telecommunications activities. It was founded in 1991 in a consortium form [GIE] that allowed EURECOM to build a large network of renowned academic and industrial partners. EURECOM research teams are made up of international experts.

*http://www.eurecom.fr/en*

Germany: Association of Data Protection Officers

The Association of Data Protection Officers (BvD) represents the interests of about 1500 company and official data protection officers and consultants in Germany. It was founded in 1989 and is the oldest association representing the interests of the sector. Headquartered in Berlin, we are promoting modern and feasible data protection.

*http://www.bvdnet.de*

Germany: Centre for Research in Security and Privacy

The National Research Center for Applied Cybersecurity CRISP is an institution of the Fraunhofer-Gesellschaft for its two Darmstadt-based institutes SIT and IGD, in cooperation with Technische Universität Darmstadt and Darmstadt University of

Applied Sciences. This unique and innovative collaboration model of university and non-university research combines the Fraunhofer competencies and strengths with the competencies and strengths of the universities.

*https://www.crisp-da.de/*

Germany: Cybersicherheitsrat Deutschland e.V.

The Cyber-Security Council Germany aims to advise businesses, government agencies and policymakers on issues relating to cyber security and to strengthen the fight against cybercrime. Objectives are to increase collaboration between politics, public administration, business and academia, to set up initiatives and projects, to develop a nationwide cyber-security network in a European and international context and to provide a knowledge platform, forum and network for members of the association.

*https://www.cybersicherheitsrat.de/english/*

Germany: Deutscher CERT Verbund

The German CERT Network is the alliance of German security and computer emergency teams that cooperate in collecting and processing Information. Furthermore, it aims to ensure the protection of the national information technology networks and the fast and common reaction on Internet security incidents.

*https://www.cert-verbund.de/*

Germany: Deutsche Vereinigung für Datenschutz

Founded in 1977 the German Privacy Association (DVD) represents interests of citizens as data subjects as a nonprofit association. The purpose of DVD is to give people advice concerning the risk in using electronic data processing and the possible restriction of their right to informational self-determination.

https://www.datenschutzverein.de/

Germany: German Association for Data Protection and Data Security

The German Association for Data Protection and Data Security (GDD) was founded in 1976 and stands as a non-profit organization for practicable and effective data protection. The GDD interacts with government officials, data protection authorities, associations and privacy experts world-wide. Main tasks are support for businesses, public authorities and data protection officers and promoting effective corporate self-regulation and self-monitoring.

*https://www.gdd.de/international/english*

Germany: Horst Görtz Institute for IT-Security

The Horst Görtz Institute for IT Security (HGI), Research Department of the Ruhr-Universität Bochum, was founded in 2002 to address shortcomings in IT security research in Europe as a whole. The HGI currently hosts 26 professors and their teams, who conduct research in electrical engineering and information technology, mathematics and computer science as well as the humanities and social sciences.

*https://hgi.rub.de/en/home/*

Germany: Technische Universität Berlin, Center for Technology and Society

The Zentrum Technik und Gesellschaft (ZTG; Center for Technology and Society) is an institution of the Technische Universität Berlin which was established to enable research beyond disciplinary boundaries. Since current and future challenges are complex, they carry out projects with a broad range of scientists and researchers from various fields, along with individuals, groups and institutions from civil society, business and government.

*https://www.tu-berlin.de/ztg/menue/startseite_ztg/parameter/en/*

Ireland: University College Dublin, Centre for Cybersecurity and Cybercrime Investigation

UCD Centre for Cybersecurity & Cybercrime Investigation (CCI) is a unique, world-class education and research centre with strong and well-established collaborative relationships with law enforcement and industry.

*http://www.ucd.ie/cci/*

Netherlands: Cyber Security Academy

Leiden University, Delft University of Technology and The Hague University of Applied Sciences have combined their knowledge and expertise in education for professionals in this field in the Cyber Security Academy (CSA) in The Hague. The CSA is an initiative of the municipality of The Hague. At the CSA scholars and lecturers together with experts from private and public sectors translate these issues into a varied range of multidisciplinary learning tracks for highly educated professionals.

*https://www.csacademy.nl/en/*

Netherlands: Maastricht University, European Centre on Privacy and Cybersecurity

Whilst a digital world brings enormous economic benefits, it also creates new vulnerabilities. Cyberspace is prone to malicious activities and the misuse of personal data. The delicate balance between privacy and security is an important issue within the scope on law enforcement in cyberspace. To tackle such challenges, the Faculty of Law at Maastricht University (UM) established the European Centre on Privacy and Cybersecurity (ECPC).

*https://www.maastrichtuniversity.nl/research/maastricht-european-centre-privacy-and-cybersecurity*

Netherlands: The Hague University of Applied Sciences – Centre of Expertise Cyber Security

Building and securing of developed expertise, insights and knowhow in the field of Cyber Security: is the mission of the Centre of Expertise Cyber Security of The Hague University of Applied Sciences. They provide state-of-the-art research and education.

*https://www.thehagueuniversity.com/research/centre-of-expertise/about-centre-of-expertise-for-cyber-security*

Norway: Sintef

SINTEF is one of Europe's largest independent research organisations. Every year we carry out several thousand projects for customers large and small. We apply our multidisciplinary approach in a wide range of projects, from small test and verification projects and expertise evaluations, to multinational research programmes with several partners. Our research on cyber security analyses technical, organisational and human aspects of cyber security and personal privacy.

*https://www.sintef.no/en/*

Norway: University of Bergen, Department of Informatics Selmer Center

The Selmer Center is a research centre for secure and reliable communication at the University of Bergen. The Selmer Center currently has 26 members with primary research fields including cryptology, coding theory and its application, cryptographic Boolean functions and discrete structures, quantum information theory and machine learning.

*https://www.uib.no/en/rg/selmer*

Switzerland: CERT for the Swiss University Network

SWITCH-CERT protects members of the Swiss academic community, holders of.ch and.li domains, Swiss banks and the entire Swiss Internet community against cyber-attacks.

*https://www.switch.ch/security/*

Switzerland, EPFL, Security, Privacy & Cryptography Group

EPFL has both a Swiss and international vocation and focuses on three missions: teaching, research and innovation. Research in the Security, Privacy & Cryptography Group covers the underlying mathematical principles and applications of cryptography; the foundations of secure and privacy-preserving machine learning; techniques to secure and verify large and complex software codebases; or the principles to design secure and privacy-preserving systems based on decentralized architectures (e.g., blockchains and cryptocurrencies).

*https://www.epfl.ch/schools/ic/research/security-privacy-cryptography/*

Switzerland: ETH Zürich, Institute of Information Security

The Institute of Information Security at ETH Zurich carries out research across the spectrum of information security, ranging from mathematical foundations of cryptography to building solutions to pressing problems in securing networks, cyber-physical systems, and applications. As security is highly interdisciplinary, work is collaborative, with strong links to industrial partners and other faculty areas.

*https://informationsecurity.ethz.ch*

Switzerland: Reporting and Analysis Centre for Information Assurance

MELANI is the Reporting and Analysis Centre for Information Assurance in Switzerland. MELANI is active in the area of security of computer systems and the Internet and protection of critical national infrastructures.

*https://www.melani.admin.ch/melani/en/home.html*

United Kingdom: Imperial College London, Institute for Security Science and Technology

Imperial College has a vibrant cyber security community tackling cutting edge research challenges, educating the next generation, and working with industry. Our community includes academics from the Department of Computing, Institute for Security Science and Technology (ISST), Department of Mathematics, and the Centre for Cryptocurrency Research and Engineering.

*https://www.imperial.ac.uk/security-institute/*

United Kingdom: Royal Holloway University of London, Information Security Group

The Information Security Group (ISG) at Royal Holloway University of London is a world-leading interdisciplinary research group dedicated to research and education in the area of information (cyber) security. The ISG comprises more than fifteen full-time academic faculty members, including a mix of computer scientists, mathematicians and social scientists.

*https://royalholloway.ac.uk/research-and-teaching/departments-and-schools/information-security/*

# Index




M. Christen et al. (eds.), *The Ethics of Cybersecurity*, The International Library of Ethics, Law and Technology 21,
https://doi.org/10.1007/978-3-030-29053-5

## D



## E



## F

The manufacturer's authorised representative in the EU is Springer
Nature Customer Service Centre GmbH, Europaplatz 3, 69115 Heidelberg,
Germany. If you have any concerns regarding our products, please
contact ProductSafety@springernature.com

Printed and bound by CPI Group (UK) Ltd, Croydon, CR0 4YY
30/09/2026
02225645-0018